Black Wealth/ White Wealth

TENTH-ANNIVERSARY EDITION

Black Wealth/ White Wealth

A New Perspective on Racial Inequality

MELVIN L. OLIVER

AND

THOMAS M. SHAPIRO

Routledge
Taylor & Francis Group
New York   London

Routledge is an imprint of the
Taylor & Francis Group, an informa business

Published in 2006 by
Routledge
Taylor & Francis Group
270 Madison Avenue
New York, NY 10016

Published in Great Britain by
Routledge
Taylor & Francis Group
2 Park Square
Milton Park, Abingdon
Oxon OX14 4RN

Printed in the United States of America on acid-free paper
10 9 8 7 6 5 4 3 2 1

International Standard Book Number-10: 0-415-95166-6 (Hardcover) 0-415-95167-4 (Softcover)
International Standard Book Number-13: 978-0-415-95166-1 (Hardcover) 978-0-415-95167-8 (Softcover)
Library of Congress Card Number 2005032020

Library of Congress Cataloging-in-Publication Data

Oliver, Melvin L.
  Black wealth, white wealth : a new perspective on racial inequality / by Melvin Oliver and Thomas Shapiro.-- 2nd ed.
      p. cm.
  Includes bibliographical references and index.
  ISBN-13: 978-0-415-95166-1 (hardback)
  ISBN-13: 978-0-415-95167-8 (pbk.)
  1. Wealth--Moral and ethical aspects. 2. Wealth--United States. 3. Equality--United States. 4. African Americans--Economic conditions. 5. United States--Race relations. I. Shapiro, Thomas M. II. Title.

HB835.O44 2006
339.2'20973--dc22   2005032020

Taylor & Francis Group
is the Academic Division of Informa plc.

Visit the Taylor & Francis Web site at
http://www.taylorandfrancis.com

and the Routledge Web site at
http://www.routledge-ny.com

For our mentors.
Harold M. Rose and Gerald Simmons—M.L.O.
Robert Boguslaw and Patricia Golden—T.M.S.
George P. Rawick—M.L.O and T.M.S

Contents

Preface to the Tenth-Anniversary Edition

This edition of *Black Wealth/White Wealth* represents an attempt to answer the question: What are the most important changes in the last ten years affecting racial inequality and the racial wealth gap? Since *Black Wealth/White Wealth* was published in 1995, we have had the great fortune of presenting our ideas nationally and internationally before interested citizens, students, social scientists, and policy makers. These conversations engaged our thinking, often pushing our ideas on many different levels. Often, too, interested readers have asked us if we had plans for a new edition. This is our attempt to engage old and new readers in the continuing conversation that *Black Wealth/White Wealth* tapped into.

The book touched a need for a new way of examining racial inequality and brought a fresh approach to these issues. The distinction between income and wealth, the racial wealth gap, the connection of the past and the present through examining wealth, the racialization of state policy, the role of the state, the centrality of institutional arenas in wealth accumulation, and the new policy directions we outlined have all stimulated scholarly discussion and debate and a new policy direction. An indication of the stimulating character of these ideas is that *Black Wealth/White Wealth* received two of the most prestigious awards in the social sciences—The C. Wright Mills Award from the Society for the Study of Social Problems and the American Sociological Association's Distinguished Scholarly Publication Award. While we are personally pleased with these awards, we understand that this recognition is, in part, because our work is part of an important paradigm shift.

The publication of *Black Wealth/White Wealth* also enabled us as citizens and scholars to help build and shape an emerging new policy direction around asset-based social policy. After the publication of *Black Wealth/White Wealth* we joined with other scholars, social entrepreneurs, advocates, policy analysts, and institutions who were involved in social policy efforts to address asset inequalities. Melvin Oliver was appointed by the incoming president of the Ford Foundation, Susan Berresford, as vice president and inaugurated The Asset Building and Community Development Program. Thomas Shapiro, meanwhile, continued research in the tradition of *Black Wealth/White Wealth*, publishing *The Hidden Cost of Being African American: How Wealth Perpetuates Inequality*, and being an active participant on research advisory committees and working with community-based organizations on asset building for poor and minority communities.

We decided to leave the original text untouched and offer new material updating the state of developments in an extended epilogue. Why this approach? Most important, we are convinced that the substantive and thematic contents are even more pertinent than when we first wrote the book. Making wealth the central focus has produced a fresh perspective on racial inequality in the United States. As we detail in the epilogue, work in this vein has exploded in the past decade. Furthermore, the patterns we established have persisted, even as the actual data points differ from year to year. Someone suggested updating the data, but we cannot simply plug new information in because, knowing what we know today, we would not choose to repeat the exact same analysis. Therefore, we decided the best approach is to leave the original analysis intact because it is as valid today as it was a decade ago. The new part of the project—the most important changes in the last ten years affecting racial wealth inequality—incorporates the analytic frame of the first edition with the changing context of the past ten years.

We can never acknowledge all the stimulating conversations, people, and ideas that pushed our thinking in the past decade. However, this project benefited specifically from several sets of contributions. In the spring of 2005, we called together a group of stellar scholars and activists to brainstorm about the most significant developments in race and wealth inequality. They provided a stimulating start to our thinking and an agenda that was far too large to accommodate in a mere epilogue. We know they (and perhaps others) will be disappointed that we did not engage all the big issues from our day's discussion, but we do expect future volumes on these topics from them: Dalton Conley, Frank DiGiovanni, Cheryl Harris, Lisa Keister, Manuel Pastor, john powell, Michael Sherraden, Bill Spriggs, and Howie Winant. We appreciate the support of the Ford Foundation, especially Frank DiGiovanni, that made this session possible.

We also want to thank friends, scholars, and colleagues who have been so supportive of this project and have offered ideas and suggestions along the way: Alison Bernstein, Larry Bobo, Michael Conroy, Jessica L. Kenty-Drane, Sy Spilerman, Heather Beth Johnson, Charles Gallagher, George Lipsitz, Pete Plastrik, Larry Brown, and the Institute on Assets and Social Policy at the Heller School for Social Policy and Management, Brandeis University.

While at the Ford Foundation, Melvin Oliver engaged with a staff of colleagues whose commitment to building assets for the poor was truly inspiring and enlightening. His senior staff, Betsy Campbell, Walt Coward, Pablo Farias, Frank DiGiovanni, Ginger Davis Floyd, and Mil Duncan, always pushed for clarity in both the conceptual and practical dimensions of asset building. Lisa Mensah is a tireless proponent of assets for people of color and continues to inspire our work in her current role at the Aspen Institute. In addition, a staff of domestic and international program officers provided continuous input on how an asset-building strategy was playing worldwide. The brilliant leadership of Susan Berresford and her commitment to develop the Asset Building and Community Building program helped moved this policy agenda forward. Finally, Kathy Lowery's support and attention to detail kept the office moving efficiently and, more importantly, kept Oliver grounded and enthusiastic.

The timing of our work was fortuitous because of the contributions of people and organizations that were ready to move on new policy ideas to reduce poverty and injustice. At the risk of leaving out many of our admired colleagues in this effort, we want to acknowledge the work of the following: Bob Friedman, the "godfather" of asset policy; Michael Sherraden (we stand on the shoulders of his seminal scholarship); Ray Boshar's policy expertise;

the brilliant Martin Eakes; and the indomitable Angela Glover Blackwell. Finally, we are inspired by the legions of "ground soldiers" who carry on this battle every day, like Eric Rodriguez, Javier Silva, Karen Edwards, and many, many more.

We wrote this epilogue at The Rockefeller Foundation's Bellagio Study and Conference Center, one of the world's great resources for reflection and writing. We are grateful for their splendid hospitality and magnificent living quarters and grounds. It allowed us the space to work out our ideas together and the stimulation of other resident scholars and artists whose presence provided just the right balance of intellectual and social interaction. We hope we have followed the suggestion of one of our colleagues to use the serenity and calmness of Bellagio to "focus" our anger about social injustice into sharper and more penetrating insights.

The past decade has been an amazing ride! Once again, Ruth Birnberg's love and support helped make this project possible. Izak is growing into a fine writer in his own right, and we only hope that our writing meets his standards. Suzanne Oliver's love has been a wellspring of sustenance during the past ten years. This support is lovingly appreciated!

Melvin Oliver and
Thomas Shapiro
Bellagio, Italy

Preface

Black Wealth/White Wealth represents an attempt to understand one of
America's most persistent dilemmas: racial inequality. We approach this topic
with much trepidation. However, we feel that the analysis presented here will
foster new approaches to this troubling conundrum. By making wealth the
focus of discussion, we approach racial inequality with a fresh perspective,
illuminating data and offering policy suggestions that do not simply repeat the
mantra of liberal or conservative analysts.

We first came to an intuitive understanding of the importance of private
wealth from the varying experiences rooted in our lives as black and white
Americans. As a first-generation college-educated African American, Melvin
Oliver experienced the continuing legacy of discrimination in housing access,
confronted racial residential segregation, and came to understand the inade-
quacy of income as the basis of black middle-class status. As a white American
who grew up in an affluent community, Thomas Shapiro observed the ways
in which historical decisions and the political structure benefit sectors of the
white population in their quest for wealth through housing, business development, and tax write-offs. Our diverse experiences in the real world moved us
to boldly argue that income, while crucial, is less important than the popular

discourse acknowledges. It is wealth that matters, and to paraphrase Cornel West, "race matters when the subject is wealth."

Our goal is not just to present an explanation of racial inequality, as if that were not enough, but also to develop ways of addressing the issue. While our work may at first appear to privilege race over other sources of financial disadvantage—and thus to join antagonistic and polarized camps already entrenched on this issue—our hope is to promote understanding and create new alliances for productive public policy. Social policy based on assets generates benefits for almost every group, except the most wealthy in society; it is this broad cross section of the American public that we hope to reach.

In writing *Black Wealth/White Wealth* we have tried to make our work accessible to a wide audience that will include as much of the interested reading public as possible. We have done so, however, with an eye toward maintaining the scholarly integrity and empirical complexity that the data and arguments presented demand. We have made our text as reader-friendly as possible, and moved our source material to the back of the book, eliminating subscript notes. To give room for our argument, many of our tables have been moved to the Appendix. We are confident not only that this book will appeal to scholars and students but that anyone seriously interested in issues of racial and economic inequality will find its arguments and evidence compelling.

Besides our varying backgrounds, we also came to this project with different sociological interests. Oliver's work has directly confronted racial and urban inequality, while Shapiro's has been more concerned with the politics of inequality surrounding medical and reproductive issues. Friends since graduate school, we became intellectually excited about this topic seven years ago by the availability of comprehensive wealth data, and our scholarly collaboration was launched. Not knowing where it would take us, how long it would take, or what form it would take—but certain we were onto something that had to run its course—we embarked on our project on "race and wealth." After presenting scholarly papers, publishing several articles, keynoting public policy-related conferences, and editing a research volume, we saw clearly that our work spoke to a number of different audiences and demanded a more appropriate outlet: thus this book.

In writing *Black Wealth/White Wealth* we acquired debts of all sorts along the way, and it is important for us to acknowledge the people who helped push this project forward and whose stimulating contributions make it a far better book. Without stellar research assistance in both Los Angeles and Boston this endeavor could neither have been attempted nor completed. Most especially, Julie Press deserves our heartfelt gratitude for her splendid intellectual judgment and superb computer skills. Michele Eayrs assisted in the earliest research phases and consulted on the final ones. Julie and Michele were our toughest critics, expecting of us precisely what we demanded of them. Lalita Pulvarti provided valuable research assistance on racial differences in home mortgage rates. Lanita Jacobs' research on housing discrimination was useful and necessary. Serena Cosgrove and Marlene Kenney did not simply transcribe interviews, they supplied important insights to them as well. Janelle Wong's careful transcription of interviews, critical readings of the manuscript, and help in the preparation of the final text were outstanding.

We owe much to the insights and suggestions of colleagues and reviewers. The book was "seasoned" through conversations with friends, colleagues, and critics; some read all or parts of the manuscript. It was George Lipsitz who first encouraged us to continue with our work and who always thought that it deserved as wide an audience as possible. Bart Landry's suggestions helped us fine-tune several lines of argument. Debra Kaufman's insistence on the value of interviewing families gave us the final nudge in that direction. Jim Johnson's unwavering support both as critic and as director of the UCLA Center for the Study of Urban Poverty helped us move forward. Larry Bobo's constant encouragement and implicit faith that we had something important to say buoyed our tired spirits at important times. John Sibley Butler supported and intervened on behalf of our work on several occasions. Richard Yarborough kept our goals high all through the project. In addition, a long list of people provided advice and solace throughout the writing and publication process: Herman Gray, Joe Feagin, Roderick Harrison, Jill Quadagno, Donna Cotton, David Grant, S. M. Miller, Michael Sherraden, Richard E. Ratcliff, Kimberlé Crenshaw, Ken Bailey, Jeffrey Prager, Roger Waldinger, Wini Breines, Ike Grusky, Angela James, Michael Blim, Alan Klein, Lee Maril, Ruth Klap, and Suzanne Loth. Finally, we would like to thank the anonymous reviewers whose words of praise and critical comments convinced us of the book's potential significance.

We also owe a debt of gratitude for the institutional support that we have received. Initial research was funded by a grant from the National Science Foundation to Melvin Oliver; we hope the people there accept the book as our final report. Through the Research and Scholarship Development Fund, appointment as Senior Research Fellow (1990), and sabbatical leave, Northeastern University's assistance at various phases of this project helped defray some of the research costs and provided blocks of time for Tom Shapiro. The funds used to support research assistance at UCLA came from the generous auspices of the College of Letters and Sciences, then headed by Provost Raymond Orbach and Acting Social Science Dean Richard Sisson. Finally, the Ford Foundation's Interdisciplinary Research and Training Program in Urban Poverty and Public Policy grant to the UCLA Center for the Study of Urban Poverty provided funds for the transportation that enabled us to carry out our Boston–Los Angeles collaboration.

We are most grateful to the families that gave us the privilege of interviewing them. Their hospitality, spirit, and generosity in sharing their life stories transformed our thinking in important ways.

Our partnership with Routledge has been a wonderful one. Marlie Wasserman was an early and enthusiastic supporter of this project and brought it to Routledge's attention. Jayne Fargnoli made the collaboration work beautifully. Anne Sanow and Adam Bohannon held our hands and walked us through the publication process. We owe a special note of gratitude to Joan Howard for her superb and incisive copyediting.

Most of our work was done in Los Angeles. We had the best hospitality, concierge and limousine service, ticket agency, restaurant guides, and friends in Joe and Adelle Shapiro. One regret in finishing this book is that we will not be spending as much time with them.

We benefited in a multitude of ways from all these associations. Collaborating with one another cemented a friendship through the hundreds of hours spent working together. In the process, however, we are well aware that our families paid a price. Without Ruth Birnberg's encouragement, understanding, and love writing this book simply would not have been possible. Izak Shapiro has known Uncle Melvin all his life: although he would rather know Uncle Melvin as a playmate and teacher of the finer points of hitting a baseball, Izak is remarkably understanding when his dad leaves town to work with Uncle Melvin. Betty Barnhill's patience in the face of many hours of absence provided the necessary space to get this work done. Having benefited from these many sacrifices, we know more than ever where the real wealth is in our lives!

Introduction

Each year two highly publicized news reports capture the attention and imagination of Americans. One lists the year's highest income earners. Predictably, they include glamorous and highly publicized entertainment, sport, and business personalities. For the past decade that list has included many African Americans: musical artists such as Michael Jackson, entertainers such as Bill Cosby and Oprah Winfrey, and sports figures such as Michael Jordan and Magic Johnson. During the recent past as many as half of the "top ten" in this highly exclusive rank have been African Americans.

Another highly publicized list, by contrast, documents the nation's wealthiest Americans. The famous *Forbes* magazine profile of the nation's wealthiest 400 focuses not on income, but on wealth.[1] This list includes those people whose assets—or command over monetary resources—place them at the top of the American economic hierarchy. Even though this group is often ten times larger than the top earners list, it contains few if any African Americans. An examination of these two lists creates two very different perceptions of the well-being of America's black community on the eve of the twenty-first century. The large number of blacks on the top income list generates an optimistic view of how black Americans have progressed economically in American society. The near absence of blacks in the *Forbes* listing, by contrast, presents a much more pessimistic outlook on blacks' economic progress.

This book develops a perspective on racial inequality that is based on the analysis of private wealth. Just as a change in focus from income to wealth in the discussion above provides a different perspective on racial inequality, our analysis reveals deep patterns of racial imbalance not visible when viewed only through the lens of income. This analysis provides a new perspective on racial inequality by exploring how material assets are created, expanded, and preserved.

The basis of our analysis is the analytical distinction between wealth and other traditional measures of economic status, of how people are "making it" in America (for example, income, occupation, and education). Wealth is a particularly important indicator of individual and family access to life chances. Income refers to a flow of money over time, like a rate per hour, week, or year; wealth is a stock of assets owned at a particular time. Wealth is what people own, while income is what people receive for work, retirement, or social welfare. Wealth signifies the command over financial resources that a family has accumulated over its lifetime along with those resources that have been inherited across generations. Such resources, when combined with income, can create the opportunity to secure the "good life" in whatever form is needed—education, business, training, justice, health, comfort, and so on. Wealth is a special form of money not used to purchase milk and shoes and other life necessities. More often it is used to create opportunities, secure a desired stature and standard of living, or pass class status along to one's children. In this sense the command over resources that wealth entails is more encompassing than is income or education, and closer in meaning and theoretical significance to our traditional notions of economic well-being and access to life chances.

More important, wealth taps not only contemporary resources but material assets that have historic origins. Private wealth thus captures inequality that is the product of the past, often passed down from generation to generation. Given this attribute, in attempting to understand the economic status of blacks, a focus on wealth helps us avoid the either-or view of a march toward progress or a trail of despair. Conceptualizing racial inequality through wealth revolutionizes our conception of its nature and magnitude, and of whether it is declining or increasing. While most recent analyses have concluded that contemporary class-based factors are most important in understanding the sources of continuing racial inequality, our focus on wealth sheds light on both the historical and the contemporary impacts not only of class but of race.

The empirical heart of our analysis resides in an examination of differentials in black and white wealth holdings. This focus paints a vastly different empirical picture of social inequality than commonly emerges from analyses based on traditional inequality indicators. The burden of our claim is to demonstrate not simply the taken-for-granted assumption that wealth reveals "more" inequality—income multiplied x times is not the correct equation. More importantly we show that wealth uncovers a qualitatively different pattern of inequality on crucial fronts. Thus the goal of this work is to provide an analysis of racial differences in wealth holding that reveals dynamics of racial inequality otherwise concealed by income, occupational attainment, or education. It is our argument that wealth reveals a particular network of social relations and a set of social circumstances that convey a unique constellation of meanings pertinent to race in America. This perspective significantly adds to our understanding of public policy issues related to racial inequality; at the same time it aids us in developing better policies for the future. In stating our case, we do not discount the important information that the traditional indicators provide, but we argue that by adding to the latter an analysis of wealth a more thorough, comprehensive, and powerful explanation of social inequality can be elaborated.

Our argument supporting the importance of wealth in understanding contemporary racial inequality develops and unfolds in three parts. Chapters 1 and 2 introduce the importance of wealth to racial inequality. Chapters 3 through 5 present a detailed analysis of wealth holding in America with an emphasis on how class and race have structured racial inequality. The final two chapters identify the main sources of the enormous racial wealth disparity and propose preliminary means of addressing that disparity. Through the development of a "sociology of wealth and racial inequality" we situate the study of wealth among contemporary concerns with race, class, and social inequality.

Economists argue that racial differences in wealth are a consequence of disparate class and human capital credentials (age, education, experience, skills), propensities to save, and consumption patterns. A sociology of wealth seeks to properly situate the social context in which wealth generation occurs. Thus the sociology of wealth accounts for racial differences in wealth holding by demonstrating the unique and diverse social circumstances that blacks and whites face. One result is that blacks and whites also face different structures of investment opportunity, which have been affected historically and contemporaneously by both race and class. We develop three concepts to provide a sociologically grounded approach to understanding racial differentials in wealth accumulation. These concepts highlight the ways in which this opportunity structure has disadvantaged blacks and helped contribute to massive wealth inequalities between the races.

Our first concept, "racialization of state policy," refers to how state policy has impaired the ability of many black Americans to accumulate wealth—and discouraged them from doing so—from the beginning of slavery throughout American history. From the first codified decision to enslave African Americans to the local ordinances that barred blacks from certain occupations to the welfare state policies of today that discourage wealth accumulation, the state has erected major barriers to black economic self-sufficiency. In particular, state policy has structured the context within which it has been possible to acquire land, build community, and generate wealth. Historically, policies and actions of the United States government have promoted homesteading, land acquisition, home ownership, retirement, pensions, education, and asset accumulation for some sectors of the population and not for others. Poor people—blacks in particular—generally have been excluded from participation in these state-sponsored opportunities. In this way, the distinctive relationship between whites and blacks has been woven into the fabric of state actions. The modern welfare state has racialized citizenship, social organization, and economic status while consigning blacks to a relentlessly impoverished and subordinate position within it.

Our second focus, on the "economic detour," helps us understand the relatively low level of entrepreneurship among and the small scale of the businesses owned by black Americans. While blacks have historically sought out opportunities for self-employment, they have traditionally faced an environment, especially from the postbellum period to the middle of the twentieth century, in which they were restricted by law from participation in business in the open market. Explicit state and local policies restricted the rights of blacks as free economic agents. These policies had a devastating impact on the ability of blacks to build and maintain successful enterprises. While blacks were limited to a restricted African American market to which others (for example, whites and other ethnics) also had easy access, they were unable to tap the more lucrative and expansive mainstream white markets. Blacks thus had fewer opportunities to develop successful businesses. When businesses were developed that competed in size and scope with white businesses, intimidation and ultimately, in some cases, violence were used to curtail their expansion or get rid of them altogether. The lack of important assets and indigenous community development has thus played a crucial role in limiting the wealth-accumulating ability of African Americans.

The third concept we develop is synthetic in nature. The notion embodied in the "sedimentation of racial inequality" is that in central ways the cumulative effects of the past have seemingly cemented blacks to the bottom of society's economic hierarchy. A history of low wages, poor schooling, and segregation affected not one or two generations of blacks but practically all African Americans well into the middle of the twentieth century. Our argument is that the best indicator of the sedimentation of racial inequality is wealth. Wealth is one indicator of material disparity that captures the historical legacy of low wages, personal and organizational discrimination, and institutionalized racism. The low levels of wealth accumulation evidenced by current generations of black Americans best represent the economic status of blacks in the American social structure.

To argue that blacks form the sediment of the American stratificational order is to recognize the extent to which they began at the bottom of the hierarchy during slavery, and the cumulative and reinforcing effects of Jim Crow and de facto segregation through the mid-twentieth century. Generation after generation of blacks remained anchored to the lowest economic status in American society. The effect of this inherited poverty and economic scarcity for the accumulation of wealth has been to "sediment" inequality into the social structure. The sedimentation of inequality occurred because the investment opportunity that blacks faced worked against their quest for material self-sufficiency. In contrast, whites in general, but well-off whites in particular, were able to amass assets and use their secure financial status to pass their wealth from generation to generation. What is often not acknowledged is that the same social system that fosters the accumulation of private wealth for many whites denies it to blacks, thus forging an intimate connection between white wealth accumulation and black poverty. Just as blacks have had "cumulative disadvantages," many whites have had "cumulative advantages." Since wealth builds over a lifetime and is then passed along to kin, it is, from our perspective, an essential indicator of black economic well-being. By focusing on wealth we discover how blacks' socioeconomic status results from a socially layered accumulation of disadvantages passed on from generation to generation. In this sense we uncover a racial wealth tax.

Our empirical analysis enables us to raise and answer several key questions about wealth: How has wealth been distributed in American society over the twentieth century? What changes in the distribution of wealth occurred during the 1980s? And finally, what are the implications of these changes for black-white inequality?

During the eighties the rich got much richer, and the poor and middle classes fell further behind. Why? We will show how the Reagan tax cuts provided greater discretionary income for middle- and upper-class taxpayers. One asset whose value grew dramatically during the eighties was real estate, an asset that is central to the wealth portfolio of the average American. Home ownership makes up the largest part of wealth held by the middle class, whereas the upper class more commonly hold a greater degree of their wealth in financial assets. Owning a house is the hallmark of the American Dream, but it is becoming harder and harder for average Americans to afford their own home and fewer are able to do so.

In part because of the dramatic rise in home values, the wealthiest generation of elderly people in America's history is in the process of passing along its wealth. Between 1987 and 2011 the baby boom generation stands to inherit approximately $7 trillion. Of course, all will not benefit equally, if at all. One-third of the worth of all estates will be divided by the richest 1 percent, each legatee receiving an average inheritance of $6 million. Much of this wealth will be in the form of property, which, as the philosopher Robert Nozick is quoted as saying in a 1990 *New York Times* piece, "sticks out as a special kind of unearned benefit that produces unequal opportunities,"[2] Kevin, a seventy-five-year-old retired homeowner interviewed for this study, captures the dilemma of unearned inheritance:

> You heard that saying about the guy with a rich father? The kid goes through life thinking that he hit a triple. But really he was born on third base. He

didn't hit no triple at all, but he'll go around telling everyone he banged the fucking ball and it was a triple. He was born there!

Inherited wealth is a very special kind of money imbued with the shadows of race. Racial difference in inheritance is a key feature of our story. For the most part, blacks will not partake in divvying up the baby boom bounty. America's racist legacy is shutting them out. The grandparents and parents of blacks under the age of forty toiled under segregation, where education and access to decent jobs and wages were severely restricted. Racialized state policy and the economic detour constrained their ability to enter the post–World War II housing market. Segregation created an extreme situation in which earlier generations were unable to build up much, if any, wealth. We will see how the average black family headed by a person over the age of sixty-five has no net financial assets to pass down to its children. Until the late 1960s there were few older African Americans with the ability to save much at all, much less invest. And no savings and no inheritance meant no wealth.

The most consistent and strongest common theme to emerge in interviews conducted with white and black families was that family assets expand choices, horizons, and opportunities for children while lack of assets limit opportunities. Because parents want to give their children whatever advantages they can, we wondered about the ability of the average American household to expend assets on their children. We found that the lack of private assets intrudes on the dreams that many Americans have for their children. Extreme resource deficiency characterizes several groups. It may surprise some to learn that 62 percent of households headed by single parents are without savings or other financial assets, or that two of every five households without a high school degree lack a financial nest egg. Nearly one-third of all households—and 61 percent of all black households—are without financial resources. These statistics lead to our focus on the most resource-deficient households in our study—African Americans.

We argue that, materially, whites and blacks constitute two nations. One of the analytic centerpieces of this work tells a tale of two middle classes, one white and one black. Most significant, the claim made by blacks to middle-class status depends on income and not assets. In contrast, a wealth pillar supports the white middle class in its drive for middle-class opportunities and a middle-class standard of living. Middle-class blacks, for example, earn seventy cents for every dollar earned by middle-class whites but they possess only fifteen cents for every dollar of wealth held by middle-class whites. For the most part, the economic foundation of the black middle class lacks one of the pillars that provide stability and security to middle-class whites—assets. The black middle-class position is precarious and fragile with insubstantial wealth resources. This analysis means it is entirely premature to celebrate the rise of the black middle class. The glass is both half empty and half full, because the wealth data reveal the paradoxical situation in which blacks' wealth has grown while at the same time falling further behind that of whites.

The social distribution of wealth discloses a fresh and formidable dimension of racial inequality. Blacks' achievement at any given level not only requires that greater effort be expended on fewer opportunities but also bestows substantially diminished rewards. Examining blacks and whites who share similar socioeconomic characteristics brings to light persistent and vast wealth discrepancies. Take education as one prime example: the most equality we found was among the college educated, but even here at the pinnacle of achievement whites control four times as much wealth as blacks with the same degrees. This predicament manifests a disturbing break in the link between achievement and results that is essential for democracy and social equality.

The central question of this study is, Why do the wealth portfolios of blacks and whites vary so drastically? The answer is not simply that blacks have inferior remunerable human capital endowments—substandard education, jobs, and skills, for example—or do not display the characteristics most associated with higher income and wealth. We are able to demonstrate that even when blacks and whites display similar characteristics—for example, are on a par educationally and occupationally—a potent difference of $43,143 in home equity and financial assets still remains. Likewise, giving the average black household the same attributes as the average white household leaves a $25,794 racial gap in financial assets alone.

The extent of discrimination in institutions and social policy provides a persuasive index of bias that undergirds the drastic differences between blacks and whites. We show that skewed access to mortgage and housing markets and the racial valuing of neighborhoods on the basis of segregated markets result in enormous racial wealth disparity. Banks turn down qualified blacks much more often for home loans than they do similarly qualified whites. Blacks who do qualify, moreover, pay higher interest rates on home mortgages than whites. Residential segregation persists into the 1990s, and we found that the great rise in housing values is color-coded.[3] Why should the mean value of the average white home appreciate at a dramatically higher rate than the average black home? Home ownership is without question the single most important means of accumulating assets. The lower values of black homes adversely affect the ability of blacks to utilize their residences as collateral for obtaining personal, business, or educational loans. We estimate that institutional biases in the residential arena have cost the current generation of blacks about $82 billion. Passing inequality along from one generation to the next casts another racially stratified shadow on the making of American inequality. Institutional discrimination in housing and lending markets extends into the future the effects of historical discrimination within other institutions.

Placing these findings in the larger context of public policy discussions about racial and social justice adds new dimensions to these discussions. A focus on wealth changes our thinking about racial inequality. The more one learns about wealth differences, the more mistaken current policies appear. To take these findings seriously, as we do, means not shirking the responsibility of seeking alternative policy ideas with which to address issues of inequality. We might even need to think about social justice in new ways. In some key respects our analysis of disparities in wealth between blacks and whites forms an agenda for the future, the key principle of which is to link opportunity structures to policies promoting asset formation that begin to close the racial wealth gap.

Closing the racial gap means that we have to target policies at two levels. First, we need policies that directly address the situation of African Americans. Such policies are necessary to speak to the historically generated disadvantages and the current racially based policies that have limited the ability of blacks, as a group, to accumulate wealth resources.

Second, we need policies that directly promote asset opportunities for those on the bottom of the social structure, both black and white, who are locked out of the wealth accumulation process. More generally, our analysis clearly suggests the need for massive redistributional policies in order to reforge the links between achievement, reward, social equality, and democracy. These policies must take aim at the gross inequality generated by those at the very top of the wealth distribution. Policies of this type are the most difficult ones on which to gain consensus but the most important in creating a more just society.

This book's underlying goal is to establish a way to view racial inequality that will serve as a guide in securing racial equality in the twenty-first century. Racial equality is not an absolute or idealized state of affairs, because it cannot be perfectly attained. Yet the fact that it can never be perfectly attained in the real world is a wholly insufficient excuse for dismissing it as utopian or impossible. What is important are the bearings by which a nation chooses to orient its character. We can choose to let racial inequality fester and risk heightened conflict and violence. Americans can also make a different choice, a commitment to equality and to closing the gap as much as possible. We must reexamine the values, preferences, interests, and ideals that define us. Fundamental change must be addressed before we can begin to affirmatively answer Rodney King's poignant plea: "Can we all just get along?" This book was written to help us understand how far we need to go and what we need to do to get there.

Race, Wealth, and Equality

1

Introduction

Over a hundred years after the end of slavery, more than thirty years after the passage of major civil rights legislation, and following a concerted but prematurely curtailed War on Poverty, we harvest today a mixed legacy of racial progress. We celebrate the advancement of many blacks to middle-class status. In sharp contrast to previous history, school desegregation has enhanced educational access for blacks since the late fifties. Educational attainment, particularly the earning of the baccalaureate, has enabled substantial numbers of people in the black community to take advantage of white-collar occupations in the private sector and government employment. An official end to "de jure" housing segregation has even opened the door to neighborhoods and suburban residences previously off-limits to black residents. Nonetheless, many blacks have fallen by the wayside in their march toward economic equality. A growing number have not been able to take advantage of the opportunities now open to some. They suffer from educational deficiencies that make finding a foothold in an emerging technological economy near to impossible. Unable to move from deteriorated inner-city and older suburban communities, they entrust their children to school systems that are rarely able to provide them with the educational foundation they need to take the first steps up a racially skewed economic ladder. Trapped in communities of despair, they face increasing economic and social isolation from both their middle-class counterparts and white Americans.

The stratified nature of racial inequality highlights the importance of social class background as a factor in the continuing divergence in the economic fortunes of blacks and whites. The argument for class, most eloquently and influentially stated by William Julius Wilson in his 1978 book *The Declining Significance of Race,* suggests that the racial barriers of the past are less important than present-day social class attributes in determining the economic life chances of black Americans. Education, in particular, is the key attribute in whether blacks will achieve economic success relative to white Americans. Discrimination and racism, while still actively practiced in many spheres, have marginally less effect on black Americans' economic attainment than whether or not blacks have the skills and education necessary to fit in a changing economy.[1] In this view, race assumes importance only as the lingering product of an oppressive past. As Wilson observes, this time in his *Truly Disadvantaged,* racism and its most harmful injuries occurred in the past, and they are today experienced mainly by those on the bottom of the economic ladder, as "the accumulation of disadvantages ... passed from generation to generation."[2]

We believe that a focus on wealth reveals a crucial dimension of the seeming paradox of continued racial inequality in American society. Looking at wealth helps solve the riddle of seeming black progress alongside economic deterioration. Black wealth has grown, for example, at the same time that it has fallen further behind that of whites. Wealth reveals an array of insights into black and white inequality that challenge our conception of racial and social justice in America. The continuation of persistent and vast wealth discrepancies among blacks and whites with similar achievements and credentials presents another daunting social policy dilemma. At stake here is a disturbing break in the link between achievement and rewards. If educational attainment is the panacea for racial inequality, then this break carries distressing implications for the future of democracy and social equality in America.

Disparities in wealth between blacks and whites are not the product of haphazard events, inborn traits, isolated incidents, or solely contemporary individual accomplishments. Rather, wealth inequality has been structured over many generations through the same systemic barriers that have hampered blacks throughout their history in American society: slavery, Jim Crow, so-called de jure discrimination, and institutionalized racism. How these factors have affected the ability of blacks to accumulate wealth, however, has often been ignored or incompletely sketched. By briefly recalling three scenarios in American history that produced structured inequalities, we illustrate the significance of these barriers and their role in creating the wealth gap between blacks and whites.

Reconstruction
From Slavery to Freedom without a Material Base

Reconstruction was a bargain between the North and South to this effect: "We've liberated them from the land—and delivered them to the bosses."

—James Baldwin, "A Talk to Teachers"

"De slaves spected a heap from freedom dey didn't get. ... Dey promised us a mule an' forty acres o' lan'."

—Eric Foner, *Reconstruction*

The tragedy of Reconstruction is the failure of the black masses to acquire land, since without the economic security provided by land ownership the freedmen were soon deprived of the political and civil rights which they had won.

—Claude Oubre, *Forty Acres and a Mule*

The close of the Civil War transformed four million former slaves from chattel to freedmen. Emerging from a legacy of two and a half centuries of legalized oppression, the new freedmen entered Southern society with little or no material assets. With the North's military victory over the South freshly on the minds of Republican legislators and white abolitionists, there were rumblings in the air of how the former plantations and the property of Confederate soldiers and sympathizers would be confiscated and divided among the new freedmen to form the basis of their new status in society. The slave's often-cited demand of "forty acres and a mule" fueled great anticipation of a new beginning based on land ownership and a transfer of skills developed under slavery into the new economy of the South. Whereas slave muscle and skills had cleared the wilderness and made the land productive and profitable for plantation owners, the new vision saw the freedmen's hard work and skill generating income and resources for the former slaves themselves. W. E. B. Du Bois, in his *Black Reconstruction in America,* called this prospect America's chance to be a modern democracy.

Initially it appeared that massive land redistribution from the Confederates to the freedmen would indeed become a reality. Optimism greeted Sherman's March through the South, and especially his Order 15, which confiscated plantations and redistributed them to black soldiers. Such wartime actions were eventually rescinded and some soldiers who had already started to cultivate the land and build new lives were forced to give up their claims. Real access to land for the freedman had to await the passage of the Southern Homestead Act in 1866, which provided a legal basis and mechanism to promote black landownership. In this legislation public land already designated in the 1862 Homestead Act, which applied only to non-Confederate whites but not blacks, was now opened up to settlement by former slaves in the tradition of homesteading that had helped settle the West. The amount of land involved was substantial, a total of forty-six million acres. Applicants in the first two years of the Homestead Act were limited to only 80 acres, but subsequently this amount increased to 160 acres. The Freedmen's Bureau administered the program, and there was every reason to believe that in reasonable time slaves would be transformed from farm laborers to yeomanry farmers.

This social and economic transformation never occurred. The Southern Homestead Act failed to make newly freed blacks into a landowning class or to provide what Gunnar Myrdal in *An American Dilemma* called "a basis of real democracy in the United States."[3] Indeed, features of the legislation worked against its use as a tool to empower blacks in their quest for land. First, instead of disqualifying former Confederate supporters as the previous act had done, the 1866 legislation allowed all persons who applied for land to swear that they had not taken up arms against the Union or given aid and comfort to the enemies. This opened the door to massive white applications for land. One estimate suggests that over three-quarters (77.1 percent) of the land applicants under the act were white.[4] In addition, much of the land was poor swampland and it was difficult for black or white applicants to meet the necessary homesteading requirements because they could not make a decent living off the land. What is more important, blacks had to face the extra burden of racial prejudice and discrimination along with the charging of illegal fees, expressly discriminatory court challenges and court decisions, and land speculators. While these barriers faced all poor and illiterate applicants, Michael Lanza has stated in his *Agrarianism and Reconstruction Politics* that "The freedmen's badge of color and previous servitude complicated matters to almost incomprehensible proportions."[5]

Gunnar Myrdal's *An American Dilemma* provides the most cogent explanation of the unfulfilled promise of land to the freedman in an anecdotal passage from a white Southerner. Asked, "Wouldn't it have been better for the white man and the Negro" if the land had been provided? The old man remarked emphatically:

> "No, for it would have made the Negro 'uppity,' ... and "the real reason ... why it wouldn't do, is that we are having a hard time now keeping the nigger in his place, and if he were a landowner, he'd think he was a bigger man than old Grant, and there would be no living with him in the Black District. ... Who'd work the land if the niggers had farms of their own?"[6]

Nevertheless, the extent of black landowning was remarkable given the economically deprived backgrounds from which the slaves emerged. Blacks had significant landholdings in the 1870s in South Carolina, Virginia, and Arkansas according to Du Bois's *Black Reconstruction in America*. Michael Lanza has suggested that while the 1866 act did not benefit as many blacks as it should have, it did provide part of the basis for the fact that by 1900 one-quarter of Southern black farmers owned their own farms. One could add that if the Freedmen's Bureau had succeeded, black landowners would have been much more prevalent in the South by 1900, and their wealth much more substantial.

John Rock, abolitionist, pre–Civil War orator, successful Boston dentist and lawyer, and the first African American attorney to plead before the U.S. Supreme Court, expressed great hope in 1858 that property and wealth could be the basis of racial justice:

> When the avenues of wealth are opened to us we will become educated and wealthy, and then the roughest-looking colored man that you ever saw ... will be pleasanter than the harmonies of Orpheus, and black will be a very pretty color. It will make our jargon, wit—our words, oracles; flattery will then take the place of slander, and you will find no prejudice in the Yankee whatsoever.[7]

The Suburbanization of America
The Making of the Ghetto

Because of racial discrimination, blacks were unable to enter the housing
market on the same terms as other groups before them. Thus, the most striking feature of black life was not slum conditions, but the barriers that middle-class blacks encountered trying to escape the ghetto.

—Kenneth T. Jackson, *Crabgrass Frontier*

A government offering such bounty to builders and lenders could have
required compliance with nondiscriminatory policy. ... Instead, FHA
adopted a racial policy that could well have been culled from the Nuremberg
laws. From its inception FHA set itself up as the protector of the all-white
neighborhood. It sent its agents into the field to keep Negroes and other
minorities from buying houses in white neighborhoods.

—Charles Abrams, *Forbidden Neighbors*

The suburbanization of America was principally financed and encouraged by
actions of the federal government, which supported suburban growth from the
1930s through the 1960s by way of taxation, transportation, and housing policy.[8]
Taxation policy, for example, provided greater tax savings for businesses relo-
cating to the suburbs than to those who stayed and made capital improvements
to plants in central city locations. As a consequence, employment opportunities
steadily rose in the suburban rings of the nation's major metropolitan areas. In
addition, transportation policy encouraged freeway construction and subsidized
cheap fuel and mass-produced automobiles. These factors made living on the
outer edges of cities both affordable and relatively convenient. However, the most
important government policies encouraging and subsidizing suburbanization
focused on housing. In particular, the incentives that government programs gave
for the acquisition of single-family detached housing spurred both the development and financing of the tract home, which became the hallmark of suburban
living. While these governmental policies collectively enabled over thirty-five
million families between 1933 and 1978 to participate in homeowner equity
accumulation, they also had the adverse effect of constraining black Americans'
residential opportunities to central-city ghettos of major U.S. metropolitan communities and denying them access to one of the most successful generators of
wealth in American history—the suburban tract home.[9]

This story begins with the government's initial entry into home financing.
Faced with mounting foreclosures, President Roosevelt urged passage of a bill

that authorized the Home Owners Loan Corporation (HOLC). According to Kenneth Jackson's *Crabgrass Frontier,* the HOLC "refinanced tens of thousands of mortgages in danger of default or foreclosure."[10] Of more importance to this story, however, it also introduced standardized appraisals of the fitness of particular properties and communities for both individual and group loans. In creating "a formal and uniform system of appraisal, reduced to writing, structured in defined procedures, and implemented by individuals only after intensive training, government appraisals institutionalized in a rational and bureaucratic framework a racially discriminatory practice that all but eliminated black access to the suburbs and to government mortgage money." Charged with the task of determining the "useful or productive life of housing" they considered to finance, government agents methodically included in their procedures the evaluation of the racial composition or potential racial composition of the community. Communities that were changing racially or were already black were deemed undesirable and placed in the lowest category. The categories, assigned various colors on a map ranging from green for the most desirable, which included new, all-white housing that was always in demand, to red, which included already racially mixed or all-black, old, and undesirable areas, subsequently were used by Federal Housing Authority (FHA) loan officers who made loans on the basis of these designations.

Established in 1934, the FHA aimed to bolster the economy and increase employment by aiding the ailing construction industry. The FHA ushered in the modern mortgage system that enabled people to buy homes on small down payments and at reasonable interest rates, with lengthy repayment periods and full loan amortization. The FHA's success was remarkable: housing starts jumped from 332,000 in 1936 to 619,000 in 1941. The incentive for home ownership increased to the point where it became, in some cases, cheaper to buy a home than to rent one. As one former resident of New York City who moved to suburban New Jersey pointed out, "We had been paying $50 per month rent, and here we come up and live for $29.00 a month."[11] This included taxes, principal, insurance, and interest.

This growth in access to housing was confined, however, for the most part to suburban areas. The administrative dictates outlined in the original act, while containing no antiurban bias, functioned in practice to the neglect of central cities. Three reasons can be cited: first, a bias toward the financing of single-family detached homes over multifamily projects favored open areas outside of the central city that had yet to be developed over congested central-city areas; second, a bias toward new purchases over repair of existing homes prompted people to move out of the city rather than upgrade or improve their existing residences; and third, the continued use of the "unbiased professional estimate" that made older homes and communities in which blacks or undesirables were located less likely to receive approval for loans encouraged purchases in communities where race was not an issue.

While the FHA used as its model the HOLC's appraisal system, it provided more precise guidance to its appraisers in its *Underwriting Manual*. The most basic sentiment underlying the FHA's concern was its fear that property values would decline if a rigid black and white segregation was not maintained. The *Underwriting Manual* openly stated that "if a neighborhood is to retain stability, it is necessary that properties shall continue to be occupied by the same social and racial classes" and further recommended that "subdivision regulations and suitable restrictive covenants" are the best way to ensure such neighborhood stability. The FHA's recommended use of restrictive covenants continued until 1949, when, responding to the Supreme Court's outlawing of such covenants in 1948 (*Shelly v. Kraemer*), it announced that "as of February 15, 1950, it would not insure mortgages on real estate subject to covenants."[12]

Even after this date, however, the FHA's discriminatory practices continued to have an impact on the continuing suburbanization of the white population and the deepening ghettoization of the black population. While exact figures regarding the FHA's discrimination against blacks are not available, data by county show a clear pattern of "redlining" in central-city counties and abundant loan activity in suburban counties.[13]

The FHA's actions have had a lasting impact on the wealth portfolios of black Americans. Locked out of the greatest mass-based opportunity for wealth accumulation in American history, African Americans who desired and were able to afford home ownership found themselves consigned to central-city communities where their investments were affected by the "self-fulfilling prophecies" of the FHA appraisers: cut off from sources of new investment their homes and communities deteriorated and lost value in comparison to those homes and communities that FHA appraisers deemed desirable. One infamous housing development of the period—Levittown—provides a classic illustration of the way blacks missed out on this asset-accumulating opportunity.[14] Levittown was built on a mass scale, and housing there was eminently affordable, thanks to the

FHA's and VHA's accessible financing, yet as late as 1960 "not a single one of the Long Island Levittown's 82,000 residents was black."

Contemporary Institutional Racism
Access to Mortgage Money and Redlining

It can now no longer be doubted that banks are discriminating against blacks who try to get home mortgages in city after city across the United States. ... In many cities, high-income blacks are denied mortgage loans more frequently than low-income whites. This is a persuasive index of bias, whether conscious or not. ... Construction of single-family housing is practically nonexistent, and much of the older housing is in disrepair. Some desperate homeowners, forced out of the conventional mortgage market, have fallen prey to unscrupulous lenders charging usurious rates of interest.

—*Boston Globe*, 22 October 1991

For years, racial discrimination in mortgage lending has been considered an issue of geographic "redlining" by banks reluctant to lend in minority neighborhoods. But new evidence raises the specter of an even more insidious form of discrimination, one that follows blacks wherever they live and no matter how much they earn.

—*Boston Globe*, 27 October 1991

In May of 1988 the issue of banking discrimination and redlining exploded onto the front pages of the *Atlanta Journal and Constitution*.[15] This Pulitzer Prize–winning series, "The Color of Money," described the wide disparity in mortgage-lending practices in black and white neighborhoods of Atlanta, finding black applicants rejected at a greater rate than whites, even when economic situations were comparable. The practice of geographic redlining of minority neighborhoods detailed in the articles had long been suspected, but one city's experience was not taken as conclusive evidence of a national pattern. Far more comprehensive evidence was soon forthcoming.

A 1991 Federal Reserve study of 6.4 million home mortgage applications by race and income confirmed suspicions of bias in lending by reporting a widespread and systemic pattern of institutional discrimination in the nation's banking system. This study disclosed that commercial banks rejected black applicants twice as often as whites nationwide. In some cities, like Boston, Philadelphia, Chicago, and Minneapolis, it reported a more pronounced pattern of minority loan rejections, with blacks being rejected three times more often than whites.

The argument that financial considerations—not discrimination—are the reason minorities get fewer loans appears to be totally refuted by the Federal Reserve study. The poorest white applicant, according to this report, was more likely to get a mortgage loan approved than a black in the highest income bracket. In Boston, for example, blacks in the highest income levels faced loan rejections three times more often than whites. These findings and reactions from bankers and community activists appeared in newspapers across the country. Bankers refuted the study's findings, labeling it unfair because "creditworthiness" was not considered. A later Federal Reserve study in 1992, taking creditworthiness into account, tempered the severity of bias but not the basic conclusion. We discuss this report more thoroughly in chapter 6.

The problem goes beyond redlining. Not only were banks reluctant to lend in minority communities, but the Federal Reserve study indicates that discrimination follows blacks no matter where they want to live and no matter how much they earn. A 1993 *Washington Post* series highlighted banks' reluctance to lend even in the wealthiest black neighborhoods.[16] One of the capital's most affluent black neighborhoods is the suburban community of Kettering in Prince George's County, Maryland. The average household income is $65,000 a year and the typical Kettering home has four or five bedrooms, a two-car garage, and a spacious lot. Local banks granted proportionately more loans in low-income white communities than they did in Kettering or any other high-income black neighborhoods. In Boston high-income blacks seeking homes outside the city's traditional black community confronted mortgage refusals far more often than whites who live on the same streets and who earn similar incomes. Previously banks responded to allegations of redlining by saying that it is only natural to have higher loan rejection rates in minority communities because a greater proportion of low income families live there. The lending patterns disclosed in the 1991 Federal Reserve study show, however, that disproportionate mortgage denial rates for blacks have little, if any, relation to neighborhood or income. The *Boston Globe* of 22 October 1991 cites Massachusetts congressman Joe Kennedy to the effect that the study's results "portray an America where credit is a privilege of race and wealth, not a function of ability to pay back a loan."

These findings gave credence to the allegations of housing and community activists that banks have been strip-mining minority neighborhoods of housing equity through unscrupulous backdoor loans for home repairs. Homes bought during the 1960s and 1970s in low-income areas had acquired some equity but were also in need of repair. Mainstream banks refused to approve such loans at "normal" rates, but finance companies made loans that, according to activists, preyed on minority communities by charging exorbitant, pawn-shop-style interest rates with unfavorable conditions. Rates of 34 percent and huge balloon payments were not uncommon. Mainstream banks repurchased many of these loans, and the subsequent foreclosure rates were very high. Civil rights activists noted, as reported in the 23 January 1989 *Los Angeles Times*, that this "rape" of minority communities was aided and abetted by the Reagan administration's weakening of the regulatory system built up in the 1960s and 1970s to combat redlining.

In Atlanta Christine Hill's story is typical. It started with a leaky roof and ended in personal bankruptcy, foreclosure, and eviction. Using Hill's home as collateral, the lender charged interest that, according to Rob Wells's piece in the 10 January 1993 *Chicago Tribune* "made double-digit pawnshop rates look like bargains." The Hills couldn't pay. The lender was a small and unregulated mortgage firm, similar to those often chosen by low-income borrowers because mainstream banks consider them too poor or financially unstable to qualify for a normal bank loan. Approximately twenty thousand other low-income Georgian homeowners found themselves in a similar predicament. The attorney representing some of them is quoted in Wells's *Tribune* article as saying: "This is a system of segregation, really. We don't have separate water fountains, but we have separate lending institutions." Senator Donald Riegle of Michigan in announcing a Senate Banking Committee hearing on abuse in home equity and second mortgage lending pointed to "reverse redlining."[17] This means providing credit in low-income neighborhoods on predatory terms and "taking advantage of unsophisticated borrowers."

In Boston more than one-half of the families who relied on these kinds of high-interest loans lost their homes through foreclosure.[18] One study charted every loan between 1984 and mid-1991 made by two high-interest lenders. Families lost their homes or were facing foreclosure in over three-quarters of the cases. Only 55 of the 406 families still possessed their homes and did not face foreclosure. The study also showed that the maps of redlined areas and high-interest loans overlapped.

Across the country a strikingly similar pattern emerged regarding home-repair loans. Banks redlined extensive sections of minority communities, denying people not only access to home mortgages but access to home-repair loans as well. States inexplicably failed to license or regulate home-repair contractors. Home-repair salespeople went door to door in the redlined areas "soliciting" business, and their subsequent billing routinely far exceeded their estimates. Finally, the high-interest mortgages needed to procure the home-repair work were secured through finance companies, often using existing home equity as collateral in a second mortgage. Mainstream banks then often bought these high-interest loans.

Even briefly recalled, the three historical moments evoked in the pages above illustrate the powerful dynamics generating structured inequality in America. Several common threads link the three scenarios. First, whether it be a question of homesteading, suburbanization, or redlining, we have seen how governmental, institutional, and private-sector discrimination enhances the ability of different segments of the population to accumulate and build on their wealth assets and resources, thereby raising their standard of living and securing a better future for themselves and their children. The use of land grants and mass low-priced sales of government lands created massive and unparalleled opportunities for Americans in the nineteenth century to secure title to land in the westward expansion. Likewise, government backing of millions of low-interest loans to returning soldiers and low-income families enabled American cities to suburbanize and their inhabitants to see tremendous home value growth after World War II. Quite clearly, black Americans for the most part were unable to secure the same degree of benefits from these government programs as whites were. Indeed, in many of these programs the government made explicit efforts to exclude blacks from participating in them, or to limit their participation in ways that deeply affected their ability to gain the maximum benefits. As our discussion indicates, moreover, contemporary patterns of institutional bias continue to directly inhibit the ability of blacks to buy homes in black communities, or elsewhere. As a result of this discrimination, blacks have been blocked from home ownership altogether or they have paid higher interest rates to secure residential loans.

Second, disparities in access to housing created differential opportunities for blacks and whites to take advantage of new and more lucrative opportunities to secure the good life. White families who were able to secure title to land in the nineteenth century were much more likely to finance education for their children, provide resources for their own or their children's self-employment,

or secure their political rights through pol
cess. Blocked from low-interest governm
financial institutions, or barred from hom(
lies have been denied the benefits of housin,
increase in home equity assets. Black Ameri
nomic base were much less likely to be able
their children, secure the necessary financi
or participate effectively in the political proc

in 1960. Further
tripled durin
in corpo

The relationship between how materia
and preserved and racial inequality provides ꞏ ꞏ‿‿ꞏꞏ of tnis book. From the
standpoint of the late twentieth century we offer an examination of black and
white wealth inequality that, we firmly believe, will substantially enhance our
understanding of racial inequality in the United States.

Before proceeding, however, it is necessary to set the larger context for an
investigation of racial differentials in this chapter. The critical importance of
the notion of equality needs a firm foundation. It is similarly crucial to present
the logic behind and the importance of examining wealth as an indicator of
life chances and inequality.

Racial Inequality in Context

At the most general level, "social inequality" means patterned differences in
people's living standards, life chances, and command over resources.[19] While
this broadly defined concern involves many complex layers, our analysis will
focus mainly on the fundamental material aspects of inequality. The specific
level of analysis will thus feature disparities in life chances and command over
economic resources between and among blacks and whites.

Taking into account the long history of black oppression in America, the
overall social status of African Americans improved dramatically from 1939
to the early 1970s as a result of the civil rights movement coupled with a period
of extraordinary economic growth.[20] Civil rights laws ended many forms of
segregation and paved the way for some improvement in blacks' position. The
evidence for this improvement includes a sizable increase in the number of
blacks in professional, technical, managerial, and administrative positions
since the early 1960s; a near doubling of blacks in colleges and universities
between 1970 and 1980; and a large increase in home ownership among blacks.
Twice as many black families were earning a middle-class income in 1982 as

ore, the number of blacks elected to public office more than
 the 1970s. Blacks hold prominent positions at major universities,
ations, government, sports, and television and films.

The most visible advances for blacks since the 1960s have taken place in
the political arena. As a result of the civil rights movement, the percentage of
Southern blacks registered to vote rose dramatically. The number of black elected
officials increased and the black vote became a crucial and courted electoral
block. Yet, in 1993, blacks still accounted for less than 2 percent of all elected
officials.[21] The political power of black officials is limited by their political isolation. Norman Yetman explains in his *Majority and Minority* that "given the
exodus of white middle-class residents and businesses to the suburbs, African
Americans often find they have gained political power without the financial
resources with which to provide the jobs and services (educational, medical,
police and fire protection) that their constituents most urgently need."[22]

Since the 1960s blacks have also made gains in education. By the late
1980s the proportion of blacks and whites graduating from high school was
about equal, reversing the late-1950s black disadvantage of two to one. The
percentage of blacks and whites attending college in 1977 was virtually identical, again reversing a tremendous black disadvantage. Since 1976, however,
black college enrollments and completion rates have declined, threatening to
wipe out the gains of the 1960s and 1970s. The trends in the political and education areas indicate qualified improvements for blacks.[23]

Full equality, however, is still far from being achieved. Alongside the
evidence of advancement in some areas and the concerted political mobilization for civil rights, the past two decades also saw an economic degeneration
for millions of blacks, and this constitutes the crux of a troubling dilemma.
Poor education, high joblessness, low incomes, and the subsequent hardships
of poverty, family and community instability, and welfare dependency plague
many African Americans.[24] Most evident is the continuing large economic gap
between blacks and whites. Median income figures show blacks earning only
about 55 percent of the amount made by whites. The greatest economic gains
for blacks occurred in the 1940s and 1960s. Since the early 1970s, the economic status of blacks compared to that of whites has, on average, stagnated or
deteriorated. Black unemployment rates are more than twice those of whites.
Black youths also have more than twice the jobless rate as white youths. Nearly
one out of three blacks lives in poverty, compared with fewer than one in ten

whites. Residential segregation remains a persistent problem today, with blacks being more likely than whites with similar incomes to live in overcrowded and substandard housing. Nearly one in four blacks remains outside private health insurance or Medicaid coverage. Infant mortality rates have dropped steadily since 1940 for all Americans, but the odds of dying shortly after birth are consistently twice as high for blacks as for whites. Close to half (43 percent) of all black children officially lived in poor households in 1986. A majority of black children live in families that include their mother but not their father. The word "paradoxical" thus aptly characterizes the contemporary situation of African Americans. A recent major accounting of race relations summarized it like this: "the status of black America today can be characterized as a glass that is half full—if measured by progress since 1939—or a glass that is half empty—if measured by the persisting disparities between black and white Americans."[25]

The distribution of wealth may reveal much about the dynamics and paradoxical character of racial inequality. Let's briefly look at a couple of examples. White and black incomes are nearing equality for married-couple families in which both husband and wife work: in 1984 such black households earned seventy-seven cents for every dollar taken home by their white counterparts. Yet in 1984 dual-income black households possessed only nineteen cents of mean financial assets for every dollar their white counterparts owned. A black-to-white income ratio of 77 percent represents advancement and is cause for celebration, while a 19 percent wealth ratio signals the persistence of massive inequality. The rapidly growing proportion of middle-income earners among blacks is often cited as evidence of the newly achieved middle-class status of blacks.[26] A focus on wealth, by contrast, alerts one to persistent dimensions of racial inequality. For every dollar of mean net financial assets owned by white middle-income households (yearly incomes of $25,000–50,000) in 1984, similar black households held only twenty cents.[27]

Dwindling Economic Growth and Rising Inequality

The standard of living of American households is in serious trouble. For two decades the United States has been evolving into an increasingly unequal society. After improving steadily since World War II, the real (adjusted-for-inflation) weekly wage of the average American worker peaked in 1973. During the twenty-seven-year postwar boom the average worker's wages outpaced inflation every year by 2.5 to 3 percent. The standard of living of most Americans improved greatly, as many people bought cars, homes, appliances, televisions, and other big-ticket consumer goods for the first time. The link between growth and mobility was readily apparent. Between the end of World War II and the early to mid-1970s, the economy created a steady stream of jobs that permitted workers and their families to escape poverty and become part of a growing and vibrant middle class. The economy could absorb millions of new workers and a growing part of the population found middle-class life within reach. Incomes grew faster than dreams. Dreams became grander. Working families could even afford a comfortable lifestyle with one breadwinner in the work force. Rising incomes also helped to fund a larger welfare state to assist people at the bottom of the distribution.

Since 1973, however, a far bleaker story has unfolded. Real wages have been falling or stagnating for most families. The 1986 average wage in the United States bought nearly 14 percent less than it had thirteen years earlier. Also beginning in the mid-1970s, after a long period of movement toward greater equality and stability, the distribution of annual wages and salaries became increasingly unequal. Bennett Harrison and Barry Bluestone in their 1988 book *The Great U-Turn* detail the reasons for this turnaround, led primarily by a growing polarization of wages. They make a strong case that the overall deterioration in the living standards of many Americans is traceable mainly to structural economic and corporate changes: "the increasingly vulnerable position of the United States in the volatile global economic system, the particular strategies adopted by corporate managers to reduce the cost of labor in an effort to cope with the profit squeeze engendered by this heightened competition, and the many ways in which the U.S. government has encouraged those corporate experiments in restructuring."[28] The link between slow wage growth and growing inequality is subtle, involving the way in which economic and political processes have divided a slowly growing pie.

These changes have profoundly affected blacks.[29] Plant closings and deindustrialization more often occur in industries employing large concentrations of blacks, such as the steel, rubber, and automobile sectors. Black men, especially young black men, are more likely than whites to lose their jobs as a result of economic restructuring. One study of deindustrialization in the Great Lakes region found that black male production workers were hardest hit by the industrial slump of the early 1980s. From 1979 to 1984 one-half of black males in durable-goods manufacturing in five Great Lakes cities lost their jobs.

The fading middle-class dream, shrinking incomes, and soaring costs have prompted an assortment of survival strategies affecting the quality of life.[30] Individuals marry later, families postpone having children, more families send additional members into the work force, young adults stay longer with the families that raised them, and leisure time is reduced as individuals work longer hours. The ability, perhaps shortsighted, of consumers, government, and businesses to maintain accustomed spending levels by accumulating more and more debt may have kept hidden the 1980s jobs and wage declines.

Besides these demographic adjustments and changes in basic social organization, keeping the middle-class dream alive also required financial modifications. Certainly there is no better symbol of the American Dream than home ownership. Overall home-ownership rates peaked in the mid- to late 1970s, with young families finding it most difficult to enter the overheated, inflationary housing market. Between 1974 and 1983, home-ownership rates for those under age twenty-five fell from 23.4 percent to 19.4 percent. For those between twenty-five and twenty-nine years of age the decline was from 43.6 percent to 40.7 percent. No wonder. Frank Levy and Richard Michel calculate that in 1959 the average thirty-year-old male afforded a median priced house on 16 percent of his monthly earnings; by 1973 it took 21 percent of the average wage of a thirty-year-old male to afford a median priced house;[31] and in 1983 it took 44 percent of his monthly paycheck.[32] As we have shown elsewhere, by 1990 the average home consumed nearly one-half (48 percent) of his paycheck. If the future was not bleak, minimally it was much more expensive than it had been to purchase a home and something else had to be sacrificed. It is no mystery, then, why home-ownership rates have been declining for young families. The decline in home-ownership rates would have been greater had it not been for two paycheck households, smaller families, financial help from parents (particularly for first-time home buyers), and the purchase of smaller homes.[33]

The underlying weakness of the economy in the 1990s is increasingly apparent.[34] Debt and global competition pose enormous challenges to stable economic growth and vitality. The larger economic context for the analysis of contemporary race relations is dominated by slow or stagnant growth, deindustrialization, a two-tiered job and earning structure, cuts in the social programs that assist those at the bottom, budget deficits, increasing economic inequality, a reconcentration of wealth, a growing gap in incomes between whites and blacks, and a much-diminished American Dream, however one wishes to define or gauge it.

Politicians find it fashionable, and rewarding, to discuss and court America's declining "middle class." Meanwhile, little political currency is given to how economic restructuring and political processes are also reshaping racial inequalities. Racial economic inequality significantly decreased during the postwar period until the early 1970s, as measured by average black-to-white income comparisons. The role played by economic growth in promoting equality was evident, at the same time that the political mobilization of blacks and whites, civil rights measures, social programs, and a raised public consciousness in the 1960s contributed as well to narrowing the gap between the races. Declining economic fortunes since 1973 coupled with a changed public attitude on civil rights and the easing of federal enforcement have stalled or reversed many of blacks' postwar advances. The median income of black families in 1990 was virtually the same as it had been in 1970. Providing an ominous bellwether, the postwar pattern of greater black-white income equality began to reverse in 1973, as the gap between black and white incomes started to grow wider again, in both absolute and relative terms.

Most social scientists and members of the knowledgeable public share this assessment of the facts, if they do not agree on its causes. Even the conservative analyst and political operative Kevin Phillips acknowledged, in his 1990 book *The Politics of Rich and Poor,* that during the early 1970s "caste and class restraints that had eased after World War II began to reemerge."[35]

One traditional line of explanation regarding observed inequalities in status or income among racially or ethnically differentiated groups involves the idea of natural inequalities in ability or chance occurrences like luck. In this view inequality is the result of "natural" causes found in all societies and is thus to be expected; structural inequality is viewed as minimal. Another tradition explains observed inequalities by focusing on barriers to equal opportunity. This view pays attention to policies designed to minimize structural or institutional barriers to equal opportunity, or to remedy historical injustices. Indeed, one premise of the modern welfare state in industrialized countries, now under serious challenge, is that it is the role of the state to secure equal opportunity for economically disadvantaged and politically disenfranchised groups. The presumption here is that welfare, tax, housing, child, and educational policies can act to bolster the opportunities of otherwise disadvantaged groups and individuals.

An investigation of wealth presents an important challenge to these perspectives. A brief descriptive glance at wealth inequality should demonstrate the ultimately ideological character of the first position. The second view, one closer to our hearts, may also wither when confronted with an analysis of wealth. What if, for example, inequalities in opportunity are narrowing for minorities but huge cleavages and disparities in wealth remain? Put another way, what if strides toward equality of opportunity do not result in a reduction of social inequality? We suggest that one theoretical and political implication of our unfolding argument involves a rethinking of equal opportunity, one that radically extends the concept to encompass asset formation as well as income enhancement and maintenance.

Income and Wealth Inequality

The accumulation of wealth is difficult for most Americans. Whatever we attain in the form of wages and salaries does not easily convert into wealth assets, because immediate necessities deplete our available resources. Income is distributed in a highly unequal manner in the United States, as in all societies. For example, the top 20 percent of earners receive 43 percent of all income while the poorest one-fifth of the population receives a scant 4 percent of the total income. The distribution of wealth is even more unequal, making the pattern of income distribution look like a comparative leveler's paradise.

Recognizing that wealth is distributed far more unequally than income, however, does not intuitively lead to a greater understanding of the different origins of income and wealth inequality. Great wealth is likely to be inherited in the United States today; thus the base of many high incomes is also inherited. Thomas Dye's 1979 *Who's Running America* updated C. Wright Mills's classic 1950 study of the social backgrounds of the nation's richest men, *The Power Elite*, to 1970. In asking whether great wealth was largely inherited or earned, Dye found that 39 percent of the wealthiest men in America came from the upper social class in 1900; by 1950, 68 percent of the richest men were born to wealth; and this figure climbed to 82 percent by 1970. C. Wright Mills estimates that 39 percent of the richest men in 1900 had struggled up from the bottom, whereas Dye finds that by 1970 only 4 percent of the richest men came from lower-class origins.[36] The important issue of the role of inherited wealth in financial success is a subject of considerable contention among economists, whose theoretically driven models of the significance of inherited wealth support a wide and quite contradictory range of findings. For example, one viewpoint concludes that the bulk of wealth accumulation, about 80 percent, is due to intergenerational transfers; another view argues that the contribution of inherited wealth is closer to 20 percent.[37] Chapter 4 examines the relationship between income and wealth in considerably more depth.

Why Study Wealth?

Income is the standard way to study and evaluate family well-being and progress in social justice and equality in the United States. Some of the best work in the emerging area of wealth studies is done by Edward Wolff, who points out in his 1995 article "The Rich Get Increasingly Richer" that families receiving similar income can experience different levels of economic well-being depending on assets such as housing and consumer durables. Wealth can create certain income flows like interest from bank accounts or dividends from stocks. Even wealth that produces no income, like owner-occupied housing or vehicles, can help secure a family's well-being and stability by using up only minimal housing and transportation expenditures out of income or by providing the resources to survive economic and personal crises.

Over thirty years ago Richard Titmuss cautioned in his 1962 book *Income Distribution and Social Change* that the study of material equality and inequality must look beyond income. He had in mind a broader notion of life chances than the standard of living commonly measured by income. Unfortunately, social scientists have not thought carefully about Titmuss's advice, nor have they been very careful in distinguishing between income and wealth. One result is that income remains the sole lens through which we view family well-being, economic inequality, and progress in social justice.

Although related, income and wealth have different meanings.[38] *Wealth* is the total extent, at a given moment, of an individual's accumulated assets and access to resources, and it refers to the net value of assets (e.g., ownership of stocks, money in the bank, real estate, business ownership, etc.) less debt held at one time. Wealth is anything of economic value bought, sold, stocked for future disposition, or invested to bring an economic return. *Income* refers to a flow of dollars (salaries, wages, and payments periodically received as returns from an occupation, investment, or government transfer, etc.) over a set period, typically one year.

There are many reasons why income has become a surrogate for wealth. Lack of access to systematic, reliable data on wealth accumulation explains the retreat from thoroughgoing and methodical analyses of wealth-holding patterns in American society.[39] One paradox is that data on wealth gets better the further back in time one goes. Federal censuses in the mid-1800s provided adequate representation of wealth holdings. No comprehensive census of wealth has appeared since the mid-nineteenth century.

Some explicitly argue that income can substitute for wealth. Many contend that the two present different sides of a single coin, since vast wealth generates extremely high income and extremely high income creates enormous wealth. Thus income inequality within the United Sates also indicates whether growth in wealth inequality has reached critical political or economic levels. As Denny Braun notes in *The Rich Get Richer*, because of the difficulty in finding wealth data as opposed to income data, it is easier to trace income inequities and their immediate consequences than to analyze disparities in wealth holding. Wealth disparities take on a more historical, ex post facto character. Income data would be the only means predicting whether a politically and economically disastrous acceleration of wealth concentration was about to occur.

Three important criticisms can be made of using income as a surrogate for wealth. The first concerns the alleged relationship between the distribution of income and that of wealth. We submit that this relationship is considerably more complicated than previously envisioned. The second pertains to the inequality between sectors of the population: in the absence of data on a group's (say, blacks') share of wealth, general distributions or concentrations are not very informative measures in assessing the inequality of life chances. The third challenges the assumption that reliable wealth data cannot be procured, an assumption that is no longer valid. The appropriate theoretical inclination is to examine wealth—instead, income gets used as the next best, nearly identical piece of evidence.

Others have taken a different tack by suggesting that in modern capitalist society wealth has become separated from power, thereby presuming that wealth has declined in meaning. Thomas Dye, for example, in *Who's Running America* says it is a mistake to equate personal wealth with economic power. He rightly points out that individuals with relatively little wealth may nonetheless exercise considerable economic power because of their institutional positions and thus criticizes calls for a radical redistribution of wealth. While distinguishing between power based on personal wealth and power based on institutional position is certainly valid in some respects, the larger impression Dye casts is spurious. His estimate of how little a confiscation of the financial resources of the richest would accomplish belittles the importance of disparities in personal wealth. Alternatively, if we were to examine the life chances and opportunities of various groups, then inequities in access to wealth might assume a more major role and hold a more consequential place in our assessment of structured inequalities for racial groups.

Social theorists from Karl Marx to Max Weber to Georg Simmel have stressed the bedrock theoretical significance of wealth. Harold Kerbo reminds us in his 1983 textbook *Social Stratification and Inequality* that "despite the importance of income inequality in the United States, in some ways wealth inequality is more significant."[40] Income and wealth resemble one another in some respects and differ in others. One undergoes continuous and extensive examination, while the other encounters only a rare surface scratching. Kerbo elaborates some of the ways in which wealth is significant, beyond providing income. Most people use income for day-to-day necessities. Substantial wealth, by contrast, often brings income, power, and independence. Significant wealth relieves individuals from dependence on others for an income, freeing them from the authority structures associated with occupational differentiation that constitute an important aspect of the stratification system in the United States. If money derived from wealth is used to purchase significant ownership of the means of production, it can bring authority to the holder of such wealth. Substantial wealth is important also because it is directly transferable from generation to generation, thus assuring that position and opportunity remain in the same families' hands.

Command over resources inevitably anchors a conception of life chances. While resources theoretically imply both income and wealth, the reality for most families is that income supplies the necessities of life, while wealth represents a kind of "surplus" resource available for improving life chances, providing further opportunities, securing prestige, passing status along to one's family, and influencing the political process.

In view of the limitations of relying on income as well as the significance of wealth, a consideration of racially marked wealth disparities should importantly complement existing income data. An investigation of wealth will also help us formulate a more detailed picture of racial differences in well-being. Most studies of economic well-being focus solely on income, but if wealth differences are even greater than those of income, then these studies will seriously underestimate racial inequality, and policies that seek to narrow differences will fail to close the gap.

A Sociology of Wealth and Racial Inequality

2

Understanding Racial Inequality

African Americans are vastly overrepresented among those Americans whose lives are the most economically and socially distressed.[1] As William Julius Wilson has argued in *The Truly Disadvantaged*, "the most disadvantaged segments of the black urban community" have come to make up the majority of "that heterogeneous grouping of families and individuals who are outside the mainstream of the American occupational system," and who are euphemistically called the underclass.[2] With little or no access to jobs, trapped in poor areas with bad schools and little social and economic opportunity, members of the underclass resort to crime, drugs, and other forms of aberrant behavior to make a living and eke some degree of meaning out of their materially impoverished existence. Douglas Massey and Nancy Denton's *American Apartheid* has reinforced in our minds the crucial significance of racial segregation, which Lawrence Bobo calls the veritable "structural linchpin" of American racial inequality.[3]

These facts should not be in dispute. What is in dispute is our understanding of the source of such resounding levels of racial inequality. What factors were responsible for their creation and what are the sources of their continuation? Sociologists and social scientists have focused on either race or class or on some combination or interaction of the two as the overriding factors responsible for racial inequality.

A focus on race suggests that race has had a unique cultural meaning in American society wherein blacks have been oppressed in such a way as to perpetuate their inferiority and second-class citizenship.[4] Race in this context has a socially constructed meaning that is acted on by whites to purposefully limit and constrain the black population. The foundation of this social construction is the ideology of racism. Racism is a belief in the inherent inferiority of one race in relation to another. Racism both justifies and dictates the actions and institutional decisions that adversely affect the target group.

Class explanations emphasize the relational positioning of blacks and whites in society and the differential access to power that accrues to the status of each group. Those classes with access to resources through the ownership or control of capital (in the Marxian variant) or through the occupational hierarchy (in the Weberian variant) are able to translate these resources into policies and structures through their access to power. In some cases this can be seen in the way in which those who control the economy also control the polity. In other cases it can be observed in the way in which institutional elites control institutions. In any case the class perspective emphasizes the relative positions of blacks and whites with respect to the ownership and control of the means of production and to access to valued occupational niches, both historically and contemporaneously. Because blacks have traditionally had access to few of these types of valued resources, they share an interest with the other have-nots. As Raymond Franklin notes in *Shadows of Race and Class*, "Ownership carries with it domination; its absence leads to subordination."[5] The subordinated and unequal status of African Americans, in the class perspective, grows out of the structured class divisions between blacks and a small minority of resource-rich and powerful whites.[6]

Each of these perspectives has been successfully applied to understanding racial inequality. However, each also has major failings. The emphasis on race creates problems of evidence. Especially in the contemporary period, as William Wilson notes in *The Declining Significance of Race*, it is difficult to trace the enduring existence of racial inequality to an articulated ideology of racism. The trail of historical evidence proudly left in previous periods is made less evident by heightened sensitivity to legal sanctions and racial civility in language. Thus those who still emphasize race in the modern era speak of covert racism and use as evidence racial disparities in income, jobs, and housing. In fact, however, impersonal structural forces whose racial motivation cannot be ascertained are often the cause of the black disadvantage that observers identify. Likewise, class perspectives usually wash away any reference to race. Moreover, the class-based analysis that blacks united with low-income white workers and other disadvantaged groups would be the most likely source of collective opposition to current social economic arrangements has given way to continued estrangement between these groups.[7] The materialist perspective that policy should address broad class groups as opposed to specific racial groups leaves the unique historical legacy of race untouched.

Despite these weaknesses it is imperative that race and class factors be taken into consideration in any attempt to understand contemporary racial inequality. It is clear, however, that a singular focus on one as opposed to another is counterproductive. Take, for example, earnings inequality. As economists assert, earnings are affected today more by class than by racial factors. Human capital attributes (such as education, experience, skills, etc.) that may result from historical disadvantages play an important role in the earnings gap between blacks and whites. But because of the unique position of black Americans, earnings must be viewed in relation to joblessness. If you do not have a job, you have no earnings. Here it is clear that race and class are important. As structural changes in the economy have occurred, blacks have been disproportionately disadvantaged. Such structural changes as the movement of entry-level jobs outside of the central city, the change in the economy from goods to service production, and the shift to higher skill levels have created a jobless black population.[8] Furthermore, increasing numbers of new entrants into the labor market find low-skill jobs below poverty wages that do not support a family. Nevertheless, race is important as well. Evidence from employers shows that negative racial attitudes about black workers are still motivating their hiring practices, particularly in reference to central-city blacks and in the service economy.[9] In service jobs nonblacks are preferred over blacks, particularly black men, a preference that contributes to the low wages blacks earn, to high rates of joblessness, and thus to earnings inequality.

Because of the way in which they reveal the effect of historical factors on contemporary processes, racial differences in wealth provide an important means of combining race and class arguments about racial inequality. We therefore turn to a theoretical discussion of wealth and race that develops aspects of traditional race and class arguments in an attempt to illuminate the processes that have led to wealth disparities between black and white Americans.

Toward a Sociology of Race and Wealth

A sociology of race and wealth must go beyond the traditional analysis of wealth that economists have elaborated. Economists begin with the assumption that wealth is a combination of inheritance, earnings, and savings and is enhanced by prudent consumption and investment patterns over a person's lifetime. Of course, individual variability in any of these factors depends on a whole set of other relationships that are sociologically relevant. Obviously one's inheritance depends on the family into which one is born. If one's family of origin is wealthy, one's chances of accumulating more wealth in a lifetime are greater. Earnings, the economists tell us, are a function of the productivity of our human capital: our education, experience, and skills. Since these are, at least in part, dependent on an investment in training activities, they can be acquired by means of inherited resources. Savings are a function of both our earning power and our consumption patterns. Spendthrifts will have little or no disposable income to save, while those who are frugal can find ways to put money aside. Those with high levels of human capital, who socially interact in the right circles, and who have knowledge of investment opportunities, will increase their wealth substantially more during their lifetime than will those who are only thrifty. And since money usually grows over time, the earlier one starts and the longer one's money is invested, the more wealth one will be able to amass. Economists therefore explain differences in wealth accumulation by pointing to the lack of resources that blacks inherit compared to whites, their low investment in human capital, and their extravagant patterns of consumption.

Sociologists do not so much disagree with the economists' emphasis on these three factors and their relationship to human capital in explaining black-white differences in wealth; rather they are concerned that economists have not properly appreciated the social context in which the processes in question take place. Quite likely, formal models would accurately predict wealth differences. However, in the real world, an emphasis on these factors isolated from the social context misses the underlying reasons for why whites and blacks have displayed such strong differences in their ability to generate wealth. The major reason that blacks and whites differ in their ability to accumulate wealth is not only that they come from different class backgrounds or that their consumption patterns are different or that they fail to save at the same rate but that the structure of investment opportunity that blacks and whites face has been dramatically different. Work and wages play a smaller role in the accumulation of wealth than the prevailing discourse admits.

Blacks and whites have faced an opportunity to create wealth that has been structured by the intersection of class and race. Economists rightly note that blacks' lack of desirable human capital attributes places them at a disadvantage in the wealth accumulation process. However, those human capital deficiencies can be traced, in part, to barriers that denied blacks access to quality education, job training opportunities, jobs, and other work-related factors. Below we develop three concepts—the racialization of the state, the economic detour, and the sedimentation of racial inequality—to help us situate the distinct structures of investment opportunity that blacks and whites have faced in their attempts to generate wealth.

Racialization of the State

The context of one's opportunity to acquire land, build community, and generate wealth has been structured particularly by state policy. Slavery itself, the most constricting of social systems, was a result of state policy that gave blacks severely limited economic rights. Slaves were by law not able to own property or accumulate assets. In contrast, no matter how poor whites were, they had the right—if they were males, that is—if not the ability, to buy land, enter into contracts, own businesses, and develop wealth assets that could build equity and economic self-sufficiency for themselves and their families. Some argue that it was the inability to participate in and develop a habit of savings during slavery that directly accounts for low wealth development among blacks today.[10] Using a cultural argument, they assert that slaves developed a habit of excessive consumerism and not one of savings and thrift. This distorts the historical reality, however. While slaves were legally not able to amass wealth they did, in large numbers, acquire assets through thrift, intelligence, industry, and their owners' liberal paternalism. These assets were used to buy their own and their loved ones' freedom, however, and thus did not form the core of a material legacy that could be passed from generation to generation. Whites could use their wealth for the future; black slaves' savings could only buy the freedom that whites took for granted.

Slavery was only one of the racialized state policies that have inhibited the acquisition of assets for African Americans. As we have seen in chapter 1, the homestead laws that opened up the East during colonial times and West during the nineteenth century created vastly different opportunities for black and white settlers. One commentator even suggests land grants "allowed three-fourths of America's colonial families to own their own farms."[11] Black settlers in California, the "Golden State," found that their claims for homestead status were not legally enforceable.[12] Thus African Americans were largely barred from taking advantage of the nineteenth-century federal land-grant program.

A centerpiece of New Deal social legislation and a cornerstone of the modern welfare state, the old-age insurance program of the Social Security Act of 1935 virtually excluded African Americans and Latinos, for it exempted agricultural and domestic workers from coverage and marginalized low-wage workers.[13] As Gwendolyn Mink shows in "The Lady and the Tramp," men's benefits were tied to wages, military service, and unionism rather than to need or any notion of equality. Thus blacks were disadvantaged in New Deal legislation because they were historically less well paid, less fully employed, disproportionately ineligible for military service, and less fully unionized than white men. Minority workers were covered by social security and New Deal labor policies if employed in eligible occupations and if they earned the minimum amount required. Because minority wages were so low, minority workers fell disproportionately below the threshold of coverage in comparison to whites. In 1935, for example, 42 percent of black workers in occupations covered by social insurance did not earn enough to qualify for benefits compared to 22 percent for whites.

Not only were blacks initially disadvantaged in their eligibility for social security, but they have disproportionately paid more into the system and received less. Because social security contributions are made on a flat rate and black workers earn less, as Jill Quadagno explains in *The Color of Welfare*, "black men were taxed on 100 percent of their income, on average, while white men earned a considerable amount of untaxed income."[14] Black workers also earn lower retirement benefits. And benefits do not extend as long as for whites because their life span is shorter. Furthermore, since more black women are single, divorced, or separated, they cannot look forward to sharing a spouse's benefit. As Quadagno notes, again, the tax contributions of black working women "subsidize the benefits of white housewives." In many ways social security is a model state program that allows families to preserve assets built over a lifetime. For African Americans, however, it is a different kind of model of state bias. Initially built on concessions made to white racial privilege in the South, the social security program today is a system in which blacks pay more to receive less. It is a prime example of how the political process and state policy build opportunities for asset accumulation sharply skewed along racial lines.

We now turn to three other instruments of state policy that we feel have been central to creating structured opportunities for whites to build assets while significantly curtailing access to those same opportunities among blacks. Sometimes the aim was blatantly racial; sometimes the racial intention was not clear. In both instances, however, the results have been explicitly racial. They are the Federal Housing Authority already discussed in chapter 1, the Supplementary Social Security Act, which laid the foundation for our present day Aid to Families with Dependent Children (AFDC); and the United States tax code. In each case state policies have created differential opportunities for blacks and whites to develop disposable income and to generate wealth.

FHA

As noted in chapter 1, the development of low-interest, long-term mortgages backed by the federal government marked the appearance of a crucial opportunity for the average American family to generate a wealth stake. The purchase of a home has now become the primary mechanism for generating wealth. However, the FHA's conscious decision to channel loans away from the central city and to the suburbs has had a powerful effect on the creation of segregated housing in post–World War II America. George Lipsitz reports in "The Possessive Investment in Whiteness" that in the Los Angeles area of Boyle Heights, FHA appraisers denied home loans to prospective buyers because the neighborhood was "a melting pot area literally honeycombed with diverse and subversive elements."[15] Official government policy supported the prejudiced attitudes of private finance companies, realtors, appraisers, and a white public resistant to sharing social space with blacks.

The FHA's official handbook even went so far as to provide a model "restrictive covenant" that would pass court scrutiny to prospective white homebuyers. Such policies gave support to white neighborhoods like those in East Detroit in 1940. Concerned that blacks would move in, the Eastern Detroit Realty Association sponsored a luncheon on "the benefits of an improvement association" where the speaker, a lawyer, lectured on how "to effect legal restrictions against the influx of colored residents into white communities."[16] He went on to present the elements needed to institute a legally enforceable restrictive covenant for "a district of two miles square." Such a task was too much for one man and would require an "organization" that could mobilize and gain the cooperation of "everyone in a subdivision." Imagine the hurdles that are placed in the path of blacks' attempts to move into white neighborhoods when communities, realtors, lawyers, and the federal government are all wholly united behind such restrictions!

Restrictive covenants and other "segregation makers" have been ruled unconstitutional in a number of important court cases. But the legacy of the FHA's contribution to racial residential segregation lives on in the inability of blacks to incorporate themselves into integrated neighborhoods in which the equity and demand for their homes is maintained. This is seen most clearly in the fact that black middle-class homeowners end up with less valuable homes even when their incomes are similar to those of whites. When black middle-class families pursue the American Dream in white neighborhoods adjacent to existing black communities, a familiar process occurs. As one study explains it:

> White households will begin to move out and those neighborhoods will tend to undergo complete racial transition or to "tip." Typically, when the percentage of blacks in a neighborhood increases to a relatively small amount, 10 to 20 percent, white demand for housing in the neighborhood will fall off and the neighborhood will tip toward segregation.[17]

Even though the neighborhood initially has high market value generated by the black demand for houses, as the segregation process kicks in, housing values rise at a slower rate. By the end of the racial transition housing prices have declined as white homeowners flee. Thus middle-class blacks encounter lower rates of home appreciation than do similar middle-class whites in all-white communities. As Raymond Franklin notes in *Shadows of Race and Class*, this is an example of how race and class considerations are involved in producing black-white wealth differentials. The "shadow" of class creates a situation of race. To quote Franklin:

In sum, because there is a white fear of being inundated with lower-class black "hordes" who lack market capacities, it becomes necessary to prevent the entry of middle-class black families who have market capacities. In this way, middle-class blacks are discriminated against for purely racial reasons.... Given the "uncertainty inherent in racial integration and racial transition," white families—unwilling to risk falling property values—leave the area. This, of course, leads to falling prices, enabling poorer blacks to enter the neighborhood "until segregation becomes complete."[18]

The impact of race and class are also channeled through institutional mechanisms that help to destabilize black communities. Insurance redlining begins to make it difficult and/or expensive for homes and businesses to secure coverage. City services begin to decline, contributing to blight. As the community declines, it becomes the center for antisocial activities: drug dealing, hanging out, and robbery and violence.[19] In this context the initial investment that the middle-class black family makes either stops growing or grows at a rate that is substantially lower than the rate at which a comparable investment made by a similarly well-off, middle-class white family in an all-white community would gain in value. Racialized state policy contributed to this pattern, and the pattern continues unabated today.

AFDC

Within the public mind and according to the current political debate, AFDC has become synonymous with "welfare," even though it represents less than 10 percent of all assistance for the poor. The small sums paid to women and their children are designed not to provide families a springboard for their future but to help them survive in a minimal way from day to day.[20] When the initial legislation for AFDC was passed, few of its supporters envisioned a program that would serve large numbers of African American women and their children; the ideal recipient, according to Michael Katz in *In the Shadow of the Poor House*, "was a white widow and her young children." Until the mid-1960s states enforced this perception through the establishment of eligibility requirements that disproportionately excluded black women and their children. Southern states routinely deemed black women and their children as "unsuitable" for welfare by way of demeaning home inspections and searches. Northern states likewise created barriers that were directly targeted at black-female-headed families. They participated in "midnight raids" to discover whether a "man was in the house" or recomputed budgets to find clients ineligible and keep

them off the rolls. Nonetheless, by the mid-1960s minorities were disproportionately beneficiaries of AFDC, despite intentions to the contrary. In 1988
while blacks and Hispanics made up only 44 percent of all women who headed
households, they constituted 55 percent of all AFDC recipients.[21]

In exchange for modest and sometimes niggardly levels of income support, women must go through an "assets test" before they are eligible. Michael
Sherraden describes it this way in his *Assets and the Poor*:

> The assets test requires that recipients have no more than minimal assets
> (usually $1,500, with home equity excluded) in order to become or remain
> eligible for the program. The asset test effectively prohibits recipients from
> accumulating savings.[22]

As a consequence, women enter welfare on the economic edge. They
deplete almost all of their savings in order to become eligible for a program
that will not provide more than a subsistence living. What little savings remain
are usually drawn down to meet routine shortfalls and emergencies. The result
is that AFDC has become for many women, especially African American
women, a state-sponsored policy to encourage and maintain asset poverty.

To underscore the impact of AFDC's strictures let us draw the distinction
between this program and Supplementary Security Income (SSI), a program
that provides benefits for women and children whose spouses have died or
become disabled after paying into social security. In contrast to AFDC benefits, SSI payments are generous. More important perhaps, eligibility for SSI
does not require drawing down a family's assets as part of a "means test."
The result, which is built into the structure of American welfare policy, is that
"means tested" programs like AFDC and "non-means tested" social insurance programs like social security and SSI, in Michael Katz's words, have
"preserved class distinctions" and "in no way redistribute income."[23] It is also
an example of how the racialization of the state preserves and broadens the
already deep wealth divisions between black and white.

The Internal Revenue Code

A substantial portion of state expenditures take the form of tax benefits, or
"fiscal welfare." These benefits are hidden in the tax code as taxes individuals
do not have to pay because the government has decided to encourage certain
types of activity and behavior and not others. In *America: Who Really Pays the
Taxes?* Donald Barlett and James Steele write that one of the most cherished

privileges of the very rich and powerful resides in their ability to influence the tax code for their own benefit by protecting capital assets. Tax advantages may come in the form of different rates on certain types of income, tax deferral, or deductions, exclusions, and credits. Many are asset-based: if you own certain assets, you receive a tax break. In turn, these tax breaks directly help people accumulate financial and real assets. They benefit not only the wealthy but the broad middle class of homeowners and pension holders as well. More important, since blacks have fewer assets to begin with, the effect of the tax code's "fiscal welfare" is to limit the flow of tax relief to blacks and to redirect it to those who already have assets. The seemingly race-neutral tax code thus generates a racial effect that deepens rather than equalizes the economic gulf between blacks and whites.

Two examples will illustrate how the current functioning of the tax code represents yet another form of the "racialization of state policy." The *lower tax rates on capital gains* and the *deduction for home mortgages and real estate taxes,* we argue, flow differentially to blacks and whites because of the fact that blacks generally have fewer and different types of assets than whites with similar incomes.

For most of our nation's tax history the Internal Revenue Code has encouraged private investment by offering lower tax rates for income gained through "capital assets." This policy exists to encourage investment and further asset accumulation, not to provide more spendable income. In 1994, earned income in the top bracket was taxed at 39.6 percent, for example, while capital gains were taxed at 24 percent, a figure that can go as low as 14 percent. One has to be networked with accountants, tax advisers, investors, partners, and friends knowledgeable about where to channel money to take advantage of these breaks. Capital gains may be derived from the sale of stocks, bonds, commodities, and other assets. In 1989 the IRS reported that $150.2 billion in capital gains income was reported by taxpayers.[24] While this sounds like a lot of capital gains for everyone to divvy up, the lion's share (72 percent) went to individuals and families earning more than $100,000 yearly. These families represented only 1 percent of all tax filers. The remaining $42 billion in capital gains income was reported by only 7.2 million people with incomes of under $100,000 per year. This group represented only 6 percent of tax filers. Thus for more than nine of every ten tax filers (93 percent) no capital gains income was reported. Clearly then, the tax-reduction benefits on capital gains income are highly concentrated among the nation's wealthiest individuals and families. Thus it would follow that blacks, given their lower incomes and fewer assets, would be much less likely than whites to gain the tax advantage associated with capital gains. The black disadvantage becomes most obvious when one compares middle-class and higher-income blacks to whites at a similar level of earnings. Despite comparable incomes, middle-class blacks have fewer of their wealth holdings in capital-producing assets than similarly situated whites. As we shall discuss in greater depth in chapter 5, our data show that among high-earning families ($50,000 a year or more) 17 percent of whites' assets are in stocks, bonds, and mortgages versus 5.4 percent for blacks. Thus while race-neutral in intent, the current tax policy on capital gains provides disproportionate benefits to high-income whites, while limiting a major tax benefit to practically all African Americans.

Accessible to a larger group of Americans are those tax deductions, exclusions, and deferrals that the IRS provides to homeowners. Four IRS-mandated benefits can flow from home ownership: (1) the home mortgage interest deduction; (2) the deduction for local real estate taxes; (3) the avoidance of taxes on the sale of a home when it is "rolled over" into another residence, and; (4) the one-time permanent exclusion of up to $125,000 of profit on the sale of a home after the age of fifty-five. Put quite simply, since blacks are less likely to own homes, they are less likely to be able to take advantage of these benefits.[25] Furthermore, since black homes are on average less expensive than white homes, blacks derive less benefit than whites when they do utilize these tax provisions. And finally, since most of the benefits in question here are available only when taxpayers itemize their deductions, there is a great deal of concern that many black taxpayers may not take advantage of the tax breaks they are eligible for because they file the short tax form. The stakes here are very high. The subsidy that goes to homeowners in the form of tax deductions for mortgage interest and property taxes alone comes to $54 billion, about $20 billion of which goes to the top 5 percent of taxpayers.

These examples illustrate how the U.S. tax code channels benefits and encourages property and capital asset accumulation differentially by race. They are but a few of several examples that could have been used. Tax provisions pertaining to inheritance, gift income, alimony payments, pensions and Keogh accounts, and property appreciation, along with the marriage tax and the child-care credit on their face are not color coded, yet they carry with them the potential to channel benefits away from most blacks and toward some whites. State policy has racialized the opportunities for the development of wealth, creating and sustaining the existing patterns of wealth inequality and extending them into the future.

Black Self-Employment: The Economic Detour

In American society one of the most celebrated paths to economic self-sufficiency, both in reality and in myth, has been self-employment. It is a risky undertaking that more often than not fails. But for many Americans the rewards of success associated with self-employment have been the key to economic success and wealth accumulation. Blacks have been portrayed in the sociological literature as the American ethnic group with the lowest rate and degree of success in using self-employment as a means of social mobility. The successful Japanese and Jewish experiences in self-employment, for example, have been used to demonstrate a range of supposed failings in the African American community.[26] This form of invidious comparison projects a whole range of "positive" characteristics onto those who have been successful in self-employment while casting African Americans as socially deficient and constitutionally impaired when it comes to creating flourishing businesses.[27] This same argument has been extended to newly arrived Cubans, Koreans, and Jamaicans. Ethnic comparisons that disadvantage blacks fail to adequately capture the harsh effects of the kind of hostility, unequaled in any other group, that African Americans have had to face in securing a foothold in self-employment. Racist state policy, Jim Crow segregation, discrimination, and violence have punctuated black entrepreneurial efforts of all kinds. Blacks have faced levels of hardship in their pursuit of self-employment that have never been experienced as fully by or applied as consistently to other ethnic groups, even other nonwhite ethnics.[28]

The deficit model of the so-called black failure to successfully create self-employment needs to be amended.[29] The stress placed by this model on the lack of a business tradition, the inexperience and lack of education that black business owners have often had, and the absence of racial solidarity among black consumers must be transcended. Instead we need to view the black experience in self-employment as one similar to that of other ethnic groups whose members have sometimes been encouraged by societal hostility to follow this path to economic independence. The distinction is that black Americans have taken this path under circumstances inimical to their success.

As Max Weber pointed out in *The Protestant Ethic and the Spirit of Capitalism*, when groups face national oppression, one form of reaction is entrepreneurship. Immigrant groups like the Japanese in California and the Chinese in Mississippi responded to the societal hostility (e.g., discrimination) against them by immersing themselves in small business enterprises. But unlike blacks, as John Butler states in his *Entrepreneurship and Self-Help Among Black Americans*, "they were able to enter the open market and compete."[30] They faced few restrictions to commerce. They could penetrate as much of a market as their economic capacity and tolerance for risk could accommodate. They thus carved comfortable economic niches and were able to succeed, albeit on a moderate scale.

Blacks, by contrast, faced a much grimmer opportunity picture. Here is where the concept of the "economic detour" has relevance. With predispositions like those of immigrants to the idea of self-employment, blacks faced an environment where they were by law restricted from participation in business on the open market, especially from the postbellum period to the middle of the twentieth century. Explicit state and local policies restricted the rights and freedoms of blacks as economic agents. Many types of businesses were off-limits to them, and more important, they were restricted to all-black segregated markets. While whites and other ethnic groups could do business with blacks, whites, and whomever else they pleased, black business was prohibited from entering into any but all-black markets. This restriction had a devastating impact on the ability of blacks to build and maintain successful businesses. As Edna Bonacich and John Modell point out in *The Economic Basis of Ethnic Solidarity* with regard to the Japanese, this group's greatest success occurred when they developed customer bases outside the Japanese community.[31] When they were restricted to their own group, their economic success was not nearly as great. The African American experience in entrepreneurship re-creates this duality. As John Butler observes, "it is true throughout history, when Afro-American business enterprises developed a clientele outside of their community, they were more likely to be successful."[32]

Barred from the most lucrative markets and attempting to provide high levels of goods and services under the constraints of segregation and discrimination, blacks remain the only group who have been required to take what Merah Stuart in 1940 first called an "economic detour."

> This [exclusion from the market] is not his preference. Yet it seems to be his only recourse. It is an economic detour which no other racial group in this country is required to travel. Any type of foreigner, Oriental or "what not," can usually attract to his business a surviving degree of patronage of the native American. No matter that he may be fresh from foreign shores with no contribution to the national welfare of his credit; no matter that he sends every dollar of his American-earned profit back to his foreign home ... yet he can find a welcome place on the economic broadway to America.[33]

The African American, by contrast, despite "centuries of unrequited toil" in service to building this country, "must turn to a detour that leads he knows not where."[34] What he does know is that he must seek his customers or clients "from within his own race," no matter the business. And in doing so, he must compete for those customers with others who simultaneously enjoy access to greater and more lucrative markets.

This policy created conditions in which blacks, again according to Stuart, "were forced into the role of consumer." Self-employment became an important symbol of community empowerment. As M. S. Stuart goes on to suggest:

> Seeking a way, therefore, to have a chance at the beneficial reaction of his spent dollars in the form of employment created; seeking a way to avoid buying insults and assure himself courtesy when he buys the necessities of life; seeking respect, the American Negro has been driven into an awkward, selfish corner, attempting to operate racial business to rear a stepchild economy.[35]

The inability of blacks to compete in an open market has ensured low levels of black business development and has kept black businesses relatively small. Despite the obstacles they have faced, however, blacks have produced impressive results at various times in American history, even under conditions associated with the "economic detour." Before slavery was abolished, free blacks, in both Southern and Northern cities, built successful enterprises that required substantial skill and ingenuity. The 1838 document entitled "A Register of Trades of Colored People in the City of Philadelphia and Districts" lists over five hundred persons in fifty-seven different occupations and a host of business owners in industries ranging from sailboat building to lumber, catering, and blacksmithing.[36] Free blacks during Reconstruction, as Abram Harris's classic *The Negro as Capitalist* points out, "had practically no competition" in spheres that whites avoided because of their "servile status."[37] Other cities also had considerable free black business activity. John Butler describes Cincinnati as the "center of enterprise for the free black population of the Middle West."[38] In 1840 half of Cincinnati's black population were freedmen who had begun acquiring property and building businesses. By 1852 they held a half million dollars worth of property.

Blacks also created their own opportunities for capital formation and business development. The first of these opportunities took the form of mutual aid societies. Initially organized to provide social insurance they soon started capturing capital for black business development.[39] But rather quickly free blacks also organized a "trade in money" that captured savings and formed the basis of an independent black banking system.

While these developments among free blacks before slavery ended looked promising, there were signs that the detour was about to occur. Investment opportunities were few and far between for blacks with money. In 1852, for example, Maryland passed a law designed explicitly to limit African American investments. In addition, during this period blacks were not allowed access to the stock market. After the Civil War, free blacks' fortunes began to dovetail with those of the freed slaves. As C. Van Woodward recounts in *The Strange Career of Jim Crow*, discriminatory laws prohibited free blacks and former slave artisans with skills from practicing their trade, and segregation became the law of the land.

Blacks nevertheless continued their pursuit of economic self-sufficiency through self-employment under these opprobrious conditions. As Butler reports, "Between 1867 and 1917 the number of Afro-American enterprises increased from four thousand to fifty thousand."[40] These businesses developed within the confines of the "economic detour:" they were segregated enterprises marketing goods and services to an entirely black clientele. Joseph A. Pierce, in his benchmark 1947 study of nearly five thousand black businesses in the North and South entitled *Negro Business and Business Education*, summarizes the effects of the economic detour that blacks faced.

> Restricted patronage does not permit the enterprises owned and operated by Negroes to capitalize on the recognized advantages of normal commercial expansion. It tends to stifle business ingenuity and imagination, because it limits the variety of needs and demands to those of one racial group—a race that is kept in a lower bracket of purchasing power largely because of this limitation. The practice of Negro business in catering almost exclusively to

Negroes has contributed to the development of an attitude that the Negro consumer is obligated, as a matter of racial loyalty, to trade with enterprises owned and operated by Negroes.[41]

The overwhelming odds that black business owners faced render all the more resounding the victories that they were able to achieve. In Durham, North Carolina, blacks were able to develop what we would describe today as an "ethnic enclave."[42] Anchored by a major African American corporation, North Carolina Mutual Insurance Company, by 1949 over three hundred African American firms dotted the business section of Durham dubbed "Hayti." Owing to a combination of factors, African Americans in Durham managed to establish thriving businesses that served both the black and white markets: restaurants, tailor shops, groceries, and a hosiery mill. Despite urban renewal in the 1960s, which destroyed over one hundred enterprises and six hundred homes, the enclave character of the "Hayti" district survives today. But this is a unique story. The other extreme is the experience of cities like Wilmington, North Carolina, and Tulsa, Oklahoma. Once home to flourishing black businesses that managed to provide decent livings for their proprietors and their families, these cities today retain no more than fleeting memories of a time long past, a time washed away from historical and contemporary memory by the deadliest obstacle of all to black business, organized violence.

What appear to have been vibrant middle-class business communities that served as the foundation of black life in both Wilmington and Tulsa were destroyed at the hands of white mobs. Black business success in these cities both threatened white business competitors and provoked the racial fears of poor whites. According to Leon Prather's *We Have Taken a City*, in Wilmington, "there was grumbling among the white professional classes" because ... "black entrepreneurs, located conspicuously downtown, deprived white businessmen of legitimate sources of income to which they thought they were entitled."[43] Marking the nadir of black oppression, the Wilmington Riot of 1898 created an "economic diaspora" in which black businessmen were forced to steal away in the night, seeking refuge in the woods and subsequently dispersing to Northern and Southeastern cities. Prather evaluates the impact of the riot by noting that, "immediately after the massacres, white businesses moved in and filled the economic gaps left by the flight of the blacks. When the turbulence receded the integrated neighborhoods had disappeared." Prather concludes that this racial coup d'état was largely forgotten in the annals of America but notes that blacks kept the story alive, combining it with similar incidents in a collective narrative.

A similar "economic diaspora" was promulgated in Tulsa in 1921. Blacks in Tulsa developed their own business district within the boundaries of the economic detour. John Butler recounts that the Greenwood district encompassed forty-one grocers and meat markets, thirty restaurants, fifteen physicians, five hotels, two theaters, and two newspapers.[44] The black community also included many wealthy blacks who had invested in and profited from oil leases. Some five hundred blacks who owned small parcels of oil land resisted all offers and threats made by whites to sell these lands. "Every increase in the price of oil made the strife more bitter."[45] In early 1921 prominent blacks had been warned to leave Oklahoma or suffer the consequences. Fearing that a local black delivery boy was about to be lynched for allegedly attacking a white woman, the black community took up arms to ensure that the judicial process would be followed. In response to a spiral of rumors, whites organized, looted stores of arms, and invaded the Greenwood District. Blacks fought back but the violence did not stop with individual assaults. Stores were burned. Churches, schools, and newspapers that had been built by blacks also met the torch. When the destruction was over, eighteen thousand homes and enterprises were left in cinder, over four thousand blacks were left homeless, and three hundred people died (both black and white). As Butler understatedly reports "what happened in Tulsa was more than a riot. It was also the destruction of the efforts of entrepreneurs and the end of the Greenwood business district."[46]

The Sedimentation of Racial Inequality

The disadvantaged status of contemporary African Americans cannot be divorced from the historical processes that undergird racial inequality. The past has a living effect on the present. We argue that the best indicator of this sedimentation of racial inequality is wealth. Wealth is one indicator of material disparity that captures the historical legacy of low wages, personal and organizational discrimination, and institutionalized racism. The low levels of wealth accumulation evidenced by current generations of black Americans best represent the position of blacks in the stratificational order of American society.

Each generation of blacks generally began life with few material assets and confronted a world that systematically thwarted any attempts to economically better their lives. In addition to the barriers that we have just described in connection with the racialization of state policy and the economic detour, blacks also faced other major obstacles in their quest for economic security. In the South, for example, as W.E.B. Du Bois notes in *Black Reconstruction in America*, blacks were tied to a system of peonage that kept them in debt virtually from cradle to grave. Schooling was segregated and unequally funded.[47] Blacks in the smokestack industries of the North and the South were paid less and assigned to unskilled and dirty jobs. The result was that generation after generation of blacks remained anchored to the lowest economic status in American society. The effect of this "generation after generation" of poverty and economic scarcity for the accumulation of wealth has been to "sediment" this kind of inequality into the social structure.

The sedimentation of inequality occurred because blacks had barriers thrown up against them in their quest for material self-sufficiency. Whites in general, but well-off whites in particular, were able to amass assets and use their secure economic status to pass their wealth from generation to generation. What is often not acknowledged is that the accumulation of wealth for some whites is intimately tied to the poverty of wealth for most blacks.[48] Just as blacks have had "cumulative disadvantages," whites have had "cumulative advantages." Practically every circumstance of bias and discrimination against blacks has produced a circumstance and opportunity of positive gain for whites. When black workers were paid less than white workers, white workers gained a benefit; when black businesses were confined to the segregated black market, white businesses received the benefit of diminished competition; when FHA policies denied loans to blacks, whites were the beneficiaries of the spectacular growth of good housing and housing equity in the suburbs. The cumulative effect of such a process has been to sediment blacks at the bottom of the social hierarchy and to artificially raise the relative position of some whites in society.

To understand the sedimentation of racial inequality, particularly with respect to wealth, is to acknowledge the way in which structural disadvantages have been layered one upon the other to produce black disadvantage and white privilege. Returning again to the Federal Housing Act of 1934, we may recall that the federal government placed its credit behind private loans to homebuyers, thus putting home ownership within the reach of millions of citizens for the first time. White homeowners who had taken advantage of FHA financing policies saw the value of their homes increase dramatically, especially during the 1970s when housing prices tripled.[49] As previously noted, the same FHA policies excluded blacks and segregated them into all-black areas that either were destroyed during urban renewal in the sixties or benefited only marginally from the inflation of the 1970s. Those who were locked out of the housing market by FHA policies and who later sought to become first-time homebuyers faced rising housing costs that curtailed their ability to purchase the kind of home they desired. The postwar generation of whites whose parents gained a foothold in the housing market through the FHA will harvest a bounteous inheritance in the years to come.[50] Thus the process of asset accumulation that began in the 1930s has become layered over and over by social and economic trends that magnify inequality over time and across generations.

Studying Wealth   3

Studying Wealth and Racial Inequality

As we argued in chapter 1, a thorough analysis of economic well-being and social and racial equality must include a wealth dimension. A lack of systematic, reliable data on wealth accumulation, however, partly explains the general absence of such an analysis until now. The data best suited to inform our study are of two different sorts: a large representative sample and in-depth interviews. In order to examine the importance of wealth to the average American family and to investigate racial wealth differences thoroughly we must have access to a large representative sample of households that mirrors the American population.

After exploring a large quantitative database, we concluded that while survey analysis is absolutely necessary to any attempt to answer the basic questions we were asking, it nevertheless fails to capture the experiential dimension of the social processes we sought to understand and clarify. A second and very different sort of evidence was needed to complement our statistical findings: specifically, targeted, purposeful, in-depth interviews with a range of black and white families. Interviews were conducted by the authors in Boston and Los Angeles focusing on how assets were generated, how families intend to use them, and what assets mean in terms of economic security. Our intention was not so much to obtain a random or geographic sampling of Americans as to gather authentic depictions of a distinctly American experience: a racially differentiated view of what it takes, looks like, feels like, and means for Americans to accumulate assets. Our interviews did not need to be random or representative, because they were intended to explore hypotheses, expand on social processes underlying findings in the national sample, and provide richer insight and meaning.

We set out to find and interview families that could illuminate the wealth issues uncovered in our quantitative analysis. We accomplished this by interviewing an assortment of families, most of them from the middle class and ranging in age from their thirties through their fifties, including a few seniors and single mothers, along with some affluent and working-class families. Melvin Oliver interviewed a set of black families in Los Angeles, and Tom Shapiro interviewed a set of white families in Boston. We employed snowball sampling to generate our prospects, looking for candidates from our personal and professional networks outside of academia, like neighborhoods, cooperatives, health clubs, spouses' acquaintances, and groups we had addressed. We told many people what the study was about and why we were looking for families to interview, asking if they were interested and encouraging them to suggest others who might fit our needs and be willing to talk with us for a few hours. We thought that a dozen or so actual interviews with each of the two racial groups that we wanted to sample would satisfy our needs.

The interviews lasted anywhere from forty-five minutes to two and a half hours. Given the way in which we contacted people, through friends and acquaintances, we gained a very high degree of cooperation and and were able to establish good rapport. Surprisingly to us, especially in reference to their personal finances, people were more than willing to open their homes and lives to us.

The geography of the interviews was purely a factor of the authors' locations. We recognize the urban and coastal bias that these interviews contain. They are drawn from communities that have experienced more economic growth and prosperity than have rural or other metropolitan areas. Furthermore, the unique housing markets in both cities may contribute to a greater emphasis on what it takes to purchase a house and the financial benefits of owning one. However, since the major purpose of collecting our interview data was to better understand the strategies used to acquire wealth and the meaning it holds for a family's sense of economic well-being, our respective settings made it easier for us to locate appropriate respondents.

The Quantitative Database

Federal censuses provided adequate information on wealth holdings up until the mid-1800s. Since then, less complete information for more recent periods comes from a variety of sources, such as the estate tax records of very wealthy deceased individuals, inheritances for the rich, reporting on the fortunes of the very rich, and sample surveys. Social scientists interested in wealth have made wealth estimates from these sources, which are often inconsistent with one another, based on differing methods, and dissimilar in their notions of wealth. Any assessment of the strengths and weaknesses of the various data to which we have access must thus occur within the context of the research questions being posed. For instance, a study attempting to determine the relative importance of inheritance versus individual, meritocratic achievement in the formation of great fortunes might want to look into the parental estate records of those currently holding great fortunes. Wealth is heavily concentrated among the very wealthy. Hence field surveys typically produce understated levels of wealth concentration, unless a study is designed to intentionally capture the very wealthy.

In order to study racial wealth differences in American society we clearly need large, random field surveys. Indeed, other types of wealth data, like estate data, do not contain information regarding average Americans, as they are more likely to pertain to the financial behavior of the very rich. Two household surveys incorporated materials on assets and liabilities during the 1980s. The Federal Reserve System and other federal agencies sponsored rounds of the Survey of Consumer Finances (SCF) in 1983 and 1989.[1] The overriding aim of this effort was to estimate the debt obligations and asset holdings of American families. In 1984 the Bureau of the Census began administering the Survey of Income and Program Participation (SIPP), an instrument used to track entry into and exit from participation in various government social programs. SIPP surveys have also included an extensive inventory of household assets and liabilities. In any effort to examine different sectors of the population, SIPP's larger sample facilitates more nuanced comparisons among demographic, racial, or ethnic groups without underestimating significantly larger society-wide levels of wealth inequality. The greater range and depth of the questions posed by SIPP, especially with regard to demographic detail and work experience, make a more expanded analysis of the patterning of black-white differences possible. The SIPP survey does, however, present both advantages and disadvantages, as we shall see in the next section.

The Survey of Income and Program Participation

The bulk of our analysis and discussion of wealth is drawn from the Survey of Income and Program Participation. SIPP is a sample of the U.S. population that interviews adults in households periodically over a two-and-a-half-year period.[2] A new panel is introduced every year. Data for this study come from the 1987 Panel. Household interviews began in June 1987, and the same households were reinterviewed every four months through 1989. The full data set of eight interviews was available for 11,257 households.

SIPP contains two main sections. The core interview covers basic demographic and social characteristics for each member of the household. Core questions, repeated at each interview, cover areas such as labor force activity and types and amounts of income. Topical modules, known as "waves," covering governmental program recipiency, employment history, work disabilities, and education and training histories as well as family occupational and educational background, and marital, migration, and fertility histories rotated among the seven waves of interviews. These extensive demographic, background, and employment-history sections constitute some of SIPP's major strengths. Information from the topical module on assets and liabilities included in Wave 4 of the 1987 panel, first gathered in mid-1988, is what qualifies SIPP as the best and most pertinent wealth data for our purposes. Its large random sample provides an exceptional opportunity to investigate the wealth resources of average American households and to examine asset inequality among significant social and demographic groups. The major types of resources covered by SIPP's assets module include savings accounts, stocks, business equity, mutual funds, bonds, Keogh and IRA accounts, and equity in homes and vehicles. Liabilities covered in the survey include loans, credit card bills, medical bills, home mortgages, and personal debts. (The study did not cover pension funds or the cash value of insurance policies, jewelry, and household durables.)[3] Thus SIPP provides an unusually comprehensive and rich source of information on assets and liabilities.

Other surveys, by contrast, offer little information on household asset holdings; they are also difficult to replicate. Most of the available wealth data, moreover, present other limitations. While all large-survey data contain errors, additional problems may arise with respect to the measurement of particular assets. Home equity determination, for instance, presumes knowledge of local housing markets. Furthermore, in reporting measures of wealth, some studies use the mean (arithmetic average) while others report median (the middle figure in a distribution, half above and half below) figures. There are advantages and disadvantages associated with each statistic, the mean being more sensitive to extreme values, for example. The median is a superior way to summarize observations when a distribution is strongly skewed one way or the other. Income generally produces such a skewed distribution, with a relatively small number of extremely high incomes. Since the distribution of wealth is even more highly skewed than that of income, we prefer to report medians as a way of summarizing wealth observations. Both statistics are reported, however, whenever it seems appropriate to present them, especially when we are comparing two populations on the axis of wealth where one of the population's median is zero.

Surveys of assets and wealth invariably underrepresent the upper levels, primarily because of the difficulty in obtaining the cooperation of enough very wealthy subjects.[4] Thus random field surveys conservatively understate the magnitude of wealth inequality. (It is for this reason that SCF reports, which oversample the very rich, may provide data better suited to the task of accurately charting distributional inequalities in America.) Random surveys also underestimate populations that are difficult to locate. Thus SIPP, like practically every other major social survey, tends to undersample such populations as unemployed young black males or other youthful populations.

But the SIPP survey does allow us to combine data in such a way as to capture the social and economic profile of an individual, family, or household over an extended period of time.[5] Our analysis focuses on households. Examining individuals is appropriate when one is interested in individual educational achievement, occupational attainment, or labor force experience. We maintain that it is preferable to look at households, however, when examining economic resources, because no matter how or by whom assets are accumulated, decisions regarding their expenditure affect the entire household network. We know, moreover, that families and households often pool resources to make ends meet and to implement strategies for social mobility.[6]

A household's resources can be determined in a straightforward way, but matters become more complicated when it comes to a household's demographic and social attributes. Typically, complications are avoided by assigning the household head's attributes to the entire unit. The traditional Census Bureau criterion limits "household head" to the "person in whose name the home is legally owned or rented." In a house owned jointly by a married couple, either the husband or wife may be listed, thereby becoming the "householder."[7] Census Bureau criteria contain an inherent gender bias against women. For traditional, economic, patriarchal, and sometimes legal reasons, men usually sign legal housing and mortgage documents. The male head of household's demographic and sociological characteristics along with his educational attainment, occupational profile, earnings, and work experience thus commonly come to identify the entire household. A household in which the woman has earned a college degree and the male partner has only completed grade school, for example, will be viewed according to traditional householder criteria as lowly educated.

We established alternative methods for indentifying the "head of household" in order to enhance the term's analytical usefulness with respect to our specific purposes. In our study "head of household" is defined (1) according to traditional Census Bureau criteria; (2) as the highest earner in a married household, or; (3) as the highest earner within an unmarried household.

Wealth Indicators

What is wealth? How does one define it? What indicators of wealth are the best ones to use? Definitional and conceptual questions about wealth have produced a diverse and sometimes confusing set of approaches to the topic.[8] Indeed, a major difficulty in analyzing wealth is that people define it in different ways with the result that wealth measures lack comparability. After working with the literature for several years, we decided to measure wealth by way of two concepts. The first, *net worth* (NW) conveys the straightforward value of all assets less any debts. The second, *net financial assets* (NFA), excludes equity accrued in a home or vehicle from the calculation of a household's available resources.

Net worth gives a comprehensive picture of all assets and debts, yet it may not be a reliable measure of *command over future resources* for one's self and family. Net worth includes equity in vehicles, for instance, and it is not likely that this equity will be converted into other resources, such as prep school for a family's children. Thus one's car is not a likely repository in which to store resources for future use. Likewise, viewing home equity as a reasonable and unambiguous source of future resources for the current generation raises many vexing problems.

Most people do not sell their homes to finance a college education for their children, start a business, make other investments, buy medical care, support political candidates, or pay lobbyists to protect their special interests.[9] Even if a family sells a home, the proceeds are typically used to lease or buy replacement housing. An exception to the general rule may involve the elderly. Mortgage payments, especially in times of high housing inflation, may be seen as a kind of "forced savings" to be cashed in at retirement or to pass along to one's children.

Notwithstanding these and other possible exceptions to the prevailing way in which families view home ownership and mortgage payments, home equity cannot be regarded as an unambiguous source of future capital. Home equity may be important for the next generation, because wealth built up in one's home is likely to be passed along to one's children. Our interviews captured the different perspectives people have on their homes. Kevin, seventy-five years old, and his wife have lived in their home for thirty-seven years, taking care of it like a "Swiss watch." What does home mean to him?

> The house is a place for me and my wife and my son to come *home* from whatever they do and go like that into a home ... I've got a real estate dealer who's haunting me. He desperately wants the house. By most standards the house is Mickey Mouse. But we like it, my wife likes it, and I've put a lot into it. And everything around me is personal. It's a personal thing. We love it.

At a later point in our interview Kevin is asked to tally all his assets.

> *Kevin*: Financial hands-on assets? It's between two hundred and three hundred thousand. Cash, like that.
>
> *Interviewer*: Not counting the house?
>
> *Kevin*: No, the house don't count.

Clearly, Kevin does not regard the house as a financial asset. Paid off twenty years ago and valued at around $175,000, it will go to Kevin's son upon his death.

Another perspective comes from Ed and Alicia, who with their two young daughters have lived in their house barely two years. They have about $8,000 equity in the house. Ed feels that "whatever *profit* we may make from it may buy us a better home in the future ... so, we don't really think of it as cash equity we can utilize at this stage, but something that might allow us to move into the next stage." Alicia figures that they "wanted something that would accommodate us now and would be easy to sell again so we were definitely thinking about it as an investment." Ed and Alicia plan to stay in their home another two years or so before moving on to the next stage.

People's age and experience, their feelings about what the future holds, and their stage in the life cycle all contribute to how they feel about their homes and any equity that may have built up over time. Older people, like Kevin, may have a great deal of equity in their houses but have no immediate plans to cash it out. Some elderly homeowners view equity as a hedge against medical crises, or they may intend to pass it along to their children. Younger people, like Alicia and Ed, may see their homes in more instrumental, calculated, and financial terms. In any case, the pertinent point is that one cannot presume that home equity is viewed as a financial resource.

Net financial assets, by contrast, are those financial assets normally available for present or future conversion into ready cash. The specific difference between net worth and net financial assets is that equity in vehicles and homes is excluded from the latter, although debts are subtracted from NFA. In contrast to net worth, net financial assets consist of more readily liquid sources of income and wealth that can be used for a family's immediate well-being. Because the distinction between net worth and net financial assets is somewhat controversial and still open to debate, we usually present both measures. Generally, in our view, however, net financial assets seem to be the best indicator of the current generation's command over future resources, while net worth provides a more accurate estimate of the wealth likely to be inherited by the next generation.

Let us now turn to the substantive questions at the heart of our study: How has wealth been distributed in American society over the twentieth century? What about the redistribution of wealth that took place in the decade of the eighties? And finally, what do the answers to these questions imply for black-white inequality?

The 1980s and Beyond
Bigger Shares for the Wealthy

Available information concerning wealth in the twentieth century, until very recently, comes mainly from national estate-tax records for the very wealthy collected between 1922 and 1981, and from sporadic cross-sectional household surveys starting in 1953. Drawing from these databases, we track trends in the distribution of wealth, paying particular attention to whether inequality is falling, remaining stable, or rising, into the late 1980s and early 1990s.

Estate-tax data show consistently high wealth concentrations throughout the early part of the twentieth century. According to Edward Wolff's "The Rich Get Increasingly Richer," the top 1 percent of American households possessed over 25 percent of total wealth between 1922 and 1972. Beginning in 1972, however, the data indicate a significant decline in wealth inequality. The share of the top percentile declined from 29 percent to 19 percent between 1972 and 1976. While this decline was unexpected, it was not permanent. In fact in the next five-year period, from 1976 to 1981, a sharp renewal of wealth inequality occurred. Between 1976 and 1981 the share of the richest 1 percent expanded from 19 to 24 percent.

The standard theory explaining wealth inequality associates the phenomenon with the process of industrialization.[10] Stable, low levels of inequality characterize preindustrial times; the onset of modern economic growth is characterized by rapid industrialization, which ushers in a sharp increase in inequality; and then advanced, mature industrial societies experience a gradual leveling of inequality and finally long-term stability. This explanation highlights industrialization as a universal, master trend in the evolution of market economies. The twentieth century in particular is said to represent a clear pattern, specifically from 1929 on, when, according to Jeffrey Williamson and Peter Lindert's *American Inequality,* wealth imbalance "seems to have undergone a permanent reduction."[11] One must question the persistence of this reduced inequality into the 1990s, especially in light of growing income inequalities.

Estimates of household wealth inequality from two relatively consistent sources of household survey data, the 1962 Survey of Financial Characteristics of Consumers and the Surveys of Consumer Finances conducted in the 1980s, furnish more recent information. Responses to these surveys indicate that wealth inequality remained relatively fixed between 1962 and 1983. The top 1 percent of wealth holders held 32 percent of the wealth in 1962 and 34 percent in 1983. The Gini coefficient, which measures equality over an entire distribution rather than as shares of the top percentile, rose slightly, from 0.73 in 1962 to 0.74 in 1983. The Gini ratio is a statistic that converts levels of inequality into a single number and allows easy comparisons of populations. Gini figures range from 0 to 1. A low ratio indicates low levels of inequality; a high ratio indicates high levels of inequality. Thus Ginis closer to 0 illustrate more distributional equality, while figures closer to 1 indicate more inequality. While the Gini coefficient is a very useful summary measure of inequality, it is probably most helpful and meaningful as a way of comparing distributions of wealth between time periods, given its sensitivity to small changes and its clear indication of the direction of change.

What happened during the 1980s? Quite simply, the very rich increased their share of the nation's wealth. One leading economist dubbed the resulting wealth imbalance an "unprecedented jump in inequality to Great Gatsby levels."[12] Notably, inequality had risen very sharply by 1989, with the wealthiest 1 percent of households owning 37.7 percent of net worth. An examination of net financial assets suggests even greater levels of inequality. In 1983 the top 1 percent held 42.8 percent of all financial assets, a figure that increased to 48.2 percent in 1989. The Gini coefficient reflects this increase in inequality, rising 0.04 during the period. Wealth inequality by the end of the 1980s closely approximated historically high levels not seen since 1922.

Our review of other wealth indicators and studies corroborates the finding that wealth is reconcentrating. It also goes a way toward revealing the relationship between trends toward wealth concentration and growing inequality and the lower standard of living noted earlier. The evidence presented by Edward Wolff in "The Rich Get Increasingly Richer" and by others using SFC data suggests that while the concentration of wealth decreased substantially during the mid-1970s, it increased sharply during the 1980s. In particular, the *mean* net worth of families grew by over 7 percent from 1983 to 1989. However, *median* net worth grew much more slowly than mean wealth, at a rate of 0.8 percent. According to Wolff, this discrepancy "implies that the upper-wealth classes enjoyed a disproportionate share [of wealth]" between 1983 and 1989.[13] Wolff's median net financial assets declined 3.7 percent during this period. Thus the typical family disposed of fewer liquid resources in 1989 than in 1983. In stark contrast, the wealth of the "superrich," defined as the top one-half of 1 percent of wealth-holders, increased 26 percent from 1983 to 1989. Over one-half (55 percent) of the wealth created between 1983 and 1989 accrued to the richest one-half of 1 percent of families, a fact that vividly illustrates the magnitude of the 1980s increase in their share of the country's wealth. Not surprisingly, the Gini coefficient increased sizably during this period, from

0.80 to 0.84. Indeed, U.S. wealth concentration in 1989 was more extreme than at any time since 1929.

SIPP as well as SCF data confirm that the wealth pie is being resliced, and that the wealthy are getting larger pieces of it. In a 1994 update on its ongoing SIPP study, the Census Bureau reports that the median net worth of the nation's households dropped 12 percent between 1988 and 1991.[14] The drop in median wealth is associated with a sharp decline in the middle classes' largest share of net worth: home equity. The median home equity declined by 14 percent between 1988 and 1991 as real estate values fell.

The trends of increasing income and wealth inequality have disrupted long-standing post–World War II patterns. The movement toward income equality and stability expired by the mid-1970s, while the trend toward wealth equality extended into the early 1980s. By 1983 wealth inequality began to rise. The time lag in these reversals is important. Along with declining incomes, a growth in debt burden, and fluctuations in housing values and stock prices, the actions of government—and the Reagan tax cuts of the early 1980s—can only be viewed as prime causes of the increase in wealth inequality.

How has this redistribution of wealth in favor of the rich affected the middle class? Examining wealth groups by ranking all families into wealth fifths provides one way to get at this question. The average holdings of the lower-middle and bottom wealth groups (fifths) declined in real terms by 30 percent. The wealth of the middle group remained unchanged, while that of the upper-middle group increased by slightly less than 1 percent a year. The average wealth of the top group increased by over 10 percent. Combining this with previous information showing a decline in median net financial assets strengthens the argument that the economic base of middle-class life is becoming increasingly fragile and tenuous.

During the 1980s the rich got much richer, and the poor and middle classes fell further behind. One obvious culprit was the Reagan tax cuts. These cuts provided greater discretionary income for middle- and upper-class taxpayers. However, most middle-class taxpayers used this discretionary income to bolster their declining standards of living or decrease their debt burden instead of saving or investing it. Although Reagan strategists had intended to stimulate investment, the upper classes embarked on a frenzy of consumer spending on luxury items.[15] Wolff's "The Rich Get Increasingly Richer" explains the redistribution of wealth in favor of the rich during the 1980s as resulting more from capital gains reaped on existing wealth than from increased savings and investment. He attributes 70 percent of the growth in wealth over the 1983–1989 period to the appreciation of existing financial assets and the remaining 30 percent to the creation of wealth from personal savings. Led by rapid gains in stocks, financial securities, and liquid assets, existing investments grew at an impressive rate at a time when it was difficult to convert earnings into personal savings.

One asset whose value grew dramatically during the eighties was real estate. Home ownership is central to the average American's wealth portfolio. Housing equity makes up the largest part of wealth held by the middle class, whereas the upper class and wealthy more commonly own a greater degree of their wealth in financial assets. The percentage of families owning homes peaked in the mid-1970s at 65 percent and has subsequently declined by a point or two. Forty-three percent of blacks own homes, a rate 65 percent lower than that of whites. Housing equity constitutes the most substantial portion of all wealth assets by far. SIPP results clearly demonstrate this assertion: housing equity represented 43 percent of median household assets in 1988. It is even more significant, however, in the wealth portfolios of blacks than of whites, accounting for 43.3 percent of white wealth and 62.5 percent of black assets. This initial glance at the role of housing in overall wealth carries ramifications for subsequent in-depth analysis. Thus, owning a house—a hallmark of the American Dream—is becoming harder and harder for average Americans to afford, and fewer are able to do so. The ensuing analysis of racial differences in wealth requires a thorough investigation of racial dynamics in access to housing, mortgage and housing markets, and housing values.

The eighties ushered in a new era of wealth inequality in which strong gains were made by those who already had substantial financial assets. Those who had a piece of the rock, especially those with financial assets, but also those with real estate, increased their wealth holdings and consolidated a sense of economic security for themselves and their families. Others, a disproportionate share of them black, saw their financial status improve only slightly or decline.

In *Warm Hearts and Cold Cash* Marcia Millman notes that for most of this century, the primary legacy of middle-class parents to children has been "cultural" capital, that is, the upbringing, education, and contacts that allowed children to get a good start in life and to become financially successful and independent. Now some parents have more to bestow than cultural capital. In particular, middle-class Americans who started rearing families after World War II have amassed a huge amount of money in the value of their homes and stocks that they are now in the process of dispatching to the baby boom generation through inheritances, loans, and gifts. Millman says this money is "enormously consequential in shaping the lives of their adult children."[16]

Much of this wealth was built by their parents between the late 1940s and the late 1960s when real wages and saving rates were higher and housing costs were considerably lower. For the elderly middle class, the escalation of real estate prices over the last twenty years has been a significant boon. We noted in the Introduction how unevenly this bounty will be dispersed.

One of the people we interviewed will bequeath over $400,000 and described the great lengths to which he has gone to ensure that it ends up exactly where he wants it.

> Here's how it goes. I have a drawer called "When I Go." It has in it twenty folders. The yellow folders, I call them. There's a folder for every single asset. All she has to know, you pick out the folder. All made out ahead of time. All she has to do is fill in the dates. Why do I do that? I signed it because all she has to do is date it and it doesn't go through probate. I've set up this whole goddamned file to avoid probate. Every asset is designed to avoid probate … I've worked too hard to have this get fucked up. It's a gold file. When I'm gone, gold. It's all there. The yellow folders. Follow the yellow road, that's me.

Wealth and Inequality in America **4**

What is the most important for democracy is not that great fortunes should
not exist, but that great fortunes should not remain in the same hands. In that
way there are rich men, but they do not form a class.

—Alexis de Tocqueville, *Democracy in America*

Introduction

In this chapter, we contend that the buried fault line of the American social
system is who owns financial wealth—and who does not. The existence of
such a wealthy class ensures that no matter the skills and talents, the work
ethic and character of its children, the latter will inherit wealth, property, position, and power.

In this chapter we provide evidence that what for Tocqueville and others
is "most important for democracy" is in peril. Instead of great fortunes being
built by each generation by dint of hard work and pluck, a small class of rich
men is perched atop America's social system. For some this is a polemical
claim, for others it is commonsense wisdom. We assemble evidence to support
this proposition by showing the distribution of financial resources in America,
that is, who controls what kinds of assets, the composition of wealth, and what
the typical American household owns. The clear implication for Tocqueville

and friends of democracy and justice is that wealth, position, and stature accrue to some by merit and to others by birth. The consummate genius of America—the chance for the individual to get ahead on his own merits and rise (or fall) according to his own talent—is thus seriously compromised by a wealthy and powerful upper class.

The SIPP data and our interviews allow us to present a distinctive portrait of the wealth holdings of the average American household. Social science and the popular media have been able to shed some light on the wealthiest Americans, their expansive holdings, and their personalities and lifestyles. Popular profiles of the wealthy would seem to tap a not-so-secret desire for wealth that is made all the more alluring by its absence among the great majority of Americans. For many, keeping tabs on the lifestyles of the rich and famous is a kind of national obsession. Ironically, we know more about this tiny group's wealth than we do about the resources of the average American family. A television show called "Lifestyles of the Average American Family," we suspect, would have a very brief run, and only a Hubble telescope would be able to find the ratings.

A relatively well-developed social science literature claims to understand what causes variation in income. The number of wage earners in a family, for example, is a factor in the level of a household's total income. When it comes to individual wage earners, education, occupation, and gender play a role, as do years in the labor force, one's work record, and even what industry one works in and where one lives. On these bases, social scientists explain why minorities have lower incomes than whites. The core understanding is that minorities generally measure lower on those attributes positively linked to higher incomes, such as education and occupation. We have stressed the differences between income and wealth. The time has now come to ask whether the same correlates and social processes used by analysts to predict incomes also are associated with unequal wealth holdings.

The Wealth of a Nation

Table 4.1 displays shares of aggregate income in 1988 along with comparable distributions for net worth and net financial assets. It demonstrates clearly how much greater is the maldistribution of wealth than that of income as well as the extent of wealth concentration. Whereas the top 20 percent of American households earn over 43 percent of all income, they hold over 68 percent of

TABLE 4.1 Shares of Income and Assets. 1988

Held by	% Share of Income	% Share of NW[a]	% Share of NFA[b]
Top 0.5 percent	2.2	7.8	13.9
Top 1 percent	4.1	11.6	20.1
Top 10 percent	26.0	47.3	67.4
20 percent	43.3	68.2	86.9
40 percent	68.7	89.8	100.6[c]
60 percent	85.6	98.6	102.8[c]
80 percent	95.8	100.5[c]	102.9[c]
Total sample median	$23,958	$34,720	$3,700

[a] Net worth
[b] Net financial assets
[c] Shares add up to more than 100 percent because of the inclusion of negative financial assets
Source: Unless otherwise indicated, data for all tables are from SIPP, 1987 Panel, Wave 4

net worth (NW) and almost 87 percent of net financial assets (NFA). Ten percent of America's families control two-thirds of the wealth.[1] The top 1 percent collected over 4 times their proportionate share of income, but hold over 11 times their share of net worth and over 11 times their share of net financial assets. Furthermore, to break into the lowest rung of the richest 1 percent takes $763,000 in net worth, an amount that is 22 times greater than the median of the remaining 99 percent. Net financial assets exhibit an even steeper concentration, as the holdings of the richest 1 percent start at $629,000, or 170 times the median of the net financial assets of the other 99 percent.

Besides demonstrating the lopsided distribution of American wealth, the survey results displayed in table 4.1 additionally suggest the precarious resource position of most Americans. Median household income in 1988 amounted to $23,958, and median net worth totaled $34,720.[2] If cash were needed tomorrow for any unforeseen event, the average American family could tap $3,700 in net financial assets. Thus without safety nets—relatives, friends, or government assistance—the average household's NFA nest egg would cushion only three months of financial hardship, provided the household lives at or below the poverty level.[3] Sudden unemployment or layoff, maternal or paternal leave, a medical emergency, the demise of the family car—or even the tax bill that comes dues on April 15—are only some of the factors likely to precipitate an immediate financial crisis for the average American household. Things are even more precarious still for the nearly one in three households that possess zero or negative financial assets.

Middle-Class America

When the nation was new, America was largely defined, as it still is today, by the reality, image, hope, and myth of its middle class. The middle class has been seen historically as a center between the extremes of wealth and poverty characteristic of societies with a feudal past. In *Habits of the Heart* Robert Bellah and his coauthors remind us that "our central, and largely unchallenged, image of American society" is that of an ever progressing and ever more encompassing middle class that eventually embraces everybody.[4] Nonetheless, the tremendous gap between the rich and the poor is a taken-for-granted fact of life. In light of the data that we have examined, one can only question the economic solidity—indeed, the modern meaning—of middle-class life in America.

SIPP gives us a means of examining the asset resources that middle-class households have at their disposal—provided, of course, one knows what one means by "middle class." Our essential sociological understanding is that the middle class is characterized by a variety of white-collar occupations ranging from sales clerks and teachers to executives, professionals, and the self-employed. However, we do not intend here to engage in a discourse about class in modern American life; the concept is important but not entirely germane to our purposes. Rather, as an exercise, we present several conceptions of the middle class, so that the subsequent analysis is not dependent on any one way of thinking about class.

Besides occupation, middle-class status is measured by two other indices: income and education. Those with incomes between $25,000 and $50,000 are designated middle class.[5] Also, for some observers a college degree is a necessary criterion for middle-class standing. Table 4.2 displays the resources that American middle-class households, as we have defined them, have at their command. This table shows that the income-determined middle class possesses $39,700 in net worth and $5,399 in net financial assets. It also surveys the capacity of net financial reserves to support (1) present middle-class living standards and (2) poverty living standards.[6] In the event of a financial nightmare in which incomes were suddenly shut off, families in the income-defined middle class could support their present living standards out of existing financial resources for only two months. They could endure at the poverty level for 5.6 months.

Table 4.2 "Making It" in the Middle Class

Middle-Class Definition:	Income	NW[a]	NFA[b]	Months at Middle-Class Standards[c]	Months at Poverty Standards[d]
Income	**$34,877**	**$39,700**	**$5,399**	**2.0**	**5.6**
($25,000-50,000)					
College degree	37,954	68,090	17,344	6.3	17.9
White-collar and self-employed	32,903	49,599	9,000	3.3	9.3

[a] Net worth
[b] Net financial assets
[c] Median monthly income for the middle class amounts to $2,750
[d] The poverty line equals $968 per month

The college-educated notion of the middle class produces the financially hardiest, and smallest, middle class. Table 4.2 shows that the educated middle class has a net worth of $68,090 and owns over $17,000 in financial assets. The educated middle class fares relatively well: deprived of income sources, their NFA reserves could support present living standards for half a year, and they could live at the poverty line for a year and a half.

In the occupationally-defined middle class, white-collar workers and the self-employed control $49,599 in net worth and $9,000 in financial assets. The white-collar middle class could thus sustain its standard of living for three and a third months, and its members could live three-quarters of a year at the poverty line. Fixing middle-class boundaries by occupation yields the largest and most inclusive middle class but also includes some jobholders with very large incomes. If one views the middle class only on the axis of income, occupation, or education status, then one sees a broad, strong, and solid social group. A resource focus, however, provides another perspective—one in which the middle class appears more precarious and fragile.

Albert and Robyn are middle-class by any standard. Both earned college degrees in the University of California system, with Albert going on to obtain a master's degree and Robyn earning a certificate in graphic design. They work in professional occupations, Albert as educational director for a large cultural institution and Robyn as a (part-time) designer. Coming from modest families (her mother is a bookkeeper; his father and mother worked respectively in inventory control for a large firm and as a cashier), they both worked, borrowed, and received scholarships to get through college. In a good year their family income is around $60,000, but it fluctuates because both have changed jobs, been laid off, or worked part-time in the last five years. When they were interviewed, Robyn was between part-time jobs. Albert is forty-five, she is thirty-five, and they have been married for five and one-half years. They bought a house a little over two years ago, just as their daughter, Rachael, was born.

> It felt like renting was throwing money away. It felt like a good thing to do. The interest is deductible. There are more tax advantages. There are more advantages in life in general in America to owning than renting. We were going to have our baby daughter. It was going to be difficult to find an apart-ment to rent that had been de-leaded. It would have taken all kinds of court proceedings, it would have been hard. So it was just the right time. We did not necessarily want to buy. Then we couldn't find anything that would take us because of Rachael. So there were no de-leaded places in this town? You make deals with landlords. But we were not lucky enough to find a situation like that. So then we were just up against the wall, not finding what we really wanted. The timing was right. Saved some money, not a whole lot. Prices were coming down, interest rates were coming down. There was talk of now is the time, there won't be a better time. The place we were living in was not the safest place for a child. It was really dirty and dark and horrible.

The down payment for the house wiped out their savings, and they could not have made the purchase without parental assistance.

Albert and Robyn have not been able to save any money since the pur-chase of their house and the birth of their daughter. Their savings account is empty. The only liquid financial assets they own are $14,000 worth of IRAs, which they want to save for their retirement. (Use of these restricted retirement accounts prior to age sixty-five carries an immediate 10 percent penalty and tax liability.) Albert also has some money vested in a retirement fund from a job several years ago, but he cannot touch it for another twenty years. Even though their family income may be the envy of many, their less-than-stable employment and the expenses of caring for a young child and owning a home make it very difficult for them to save anything and get ahead. "There has not been a month in a very long time when we haven't been in our reserve account," Robyn says. Basically, they borrow money at high interest for short periods to pay bills. They face some very difficult choices because they lack assets: Should they lower their current standard of living in order to save? Should they cash their IRAs (at a substantial loss) in order to procure needed resources now or let them build for retirement? Should they stay in less-than-satisfying jobs because the pay is good and the work stable or take a chance on more personally satisfying employment that may bring hardship? Should one parent stay at home with their child or go to work and pay for child care? Even as solid as their education and income appear, unexpected expenses or interruption of income precipitate a crisis. Last year they eyen borrowed against Albert's life insurance policy to pay their income taxes.

Albert and Robyn feel as if they have no financial assets. They are "tempted to use [their IRA funds] but scared to." How would their lives be different if they had adequate assets? They would like to be able to afford things like dance lessons for Rachael and to plan for her college education. In general they want to feel less anxious and more secure about their future because "it's going to hit us." When asked about changes in his professional or personal life he might make if they were economically secure, Albert's first reply is "I've stopped thinking about it." On a moment's reflection he said he would change his work to something more satisfying, like making documentary films or writing fiction or plays. Robyn wants her own business making crafts. "I'd like to stay home with Rachael more and have another child." Both movingly said that they want to have another child but will not consider it under the present financial circumstances. The story of this one, fairly typical middle-class American family provides a host of information about how family wealth is accumulated and distributed and about how it fits into a family's sense of its present and future security.

The Social Distribution of Wealth
Income and Wealth

Theories of wealth accumulation and inequality specify earning power as the best predictor of wealth. An examination of wealth holding by income class provides a clear picture of the strong relationship between income inequality and wealth inequality. Wealth accrues with increasing income because higher-earning groups accumulate wealth-producing assets at a faster pace. The savings rate rises with income, therefore those below the poverty line ($11,611 for a family of four) control virtually no financial reserves to ease them through a financial crisis or difficult periods of unexpected income curtailment.[7]

Bob and Kathy met in college in the late 1970s. He majored in speech communication and became a sales representative, now earning over $50,000 a year. She trained in nursing, later went back to school while working to obtain an MBA, and today works as a nurse manager, earning over $60,000 a year. Now in their late thirties, this prosperous couple have no children and bought a large suburban house a year and a half ago. Their "starter home" in a much less fashionable community was smaller, and they "stayed [there] a lot longer than financially necessary." Even with their high earning power and relatively modest living expenses they elected to wait to move until they were sure they would not be "house poor." They stayed seven years and amassed $50,000 in housing equity and savings to use as a down payment for their new home. Their home equity now is about the same, maybe a little higher. They have about $12,000 invested in mutual funds, another $10,000 in a savings account, and have contributed $16,000 to various IRA and Keogh accounts they control. Their net financial assets total approximately $38,000, and their net worth comes to about $90,000. In a sense Bob and Kathy are a classic couple who have the ability to put money aside for the future because their combined incomes exceed $110,000 and their expenses are modest. They are thrifty and have an engaging, if traditional, attitude about money. Their attitude is "if you have to borrow you cannot afford it," and they take great pride in not having to borrow money and being able to pay off credit card bills every month. Both say these values were instilled in them by their families. Luckily, because of their high combined incomes, they are able to put these values into practice. Others, perhaps instilled with the same values or inclination, but not as prosperous in their careers, are not so fortunate.

Figure 4.1 shows that the lowest income class possesses a median net worth of $5,700. For every dollar in capital assets the lowest income group owns, the average American family owns sixty. The median net worth of the next two lowest income groups registers three-fifths and four-fifths respectively of the country's median net worth. Those in the $35,000–$50,000 income bracket hold 1.63 times the national average. Bob and Kathy fit in the top income group, consisting of 14 percent of all households and possessing $118,661 in median net worth, or nearly three and one-half times the country's median.

The net financial assets figures illustrate the connection between income and wealth inequality even more powerfully. The lowest income group averages only $80 in median net financial assets, not quite enough to purchase a pair of designer jeans. Their median NFA amounts to only 2 percent of the country's average. The next two lowest income ranks check in at one-third and three-quarters of the national median. This ratio escalates rapidly for the

Figure 4.1 Wealth by Income, 1988

highest income bracket, which owns $30,914 in NFA or over eight times the average NFA.

The Age-Wealth Nexus[9]

Which age groups hold the predominant shares of household wealth? Asset accumulation requires years of steadily growing earning power (see table A4.1). Income increases with age, peaks for thirty-six- to forty-nine-year-olds, and then starts a swift descent, leaving those sixty-five and older with incomes only slightly above the official poverty line.[8] Age is a significant factor in amassing wealth assets. Most households headed by people thirty-five or under hold no net financial assets and relatively little net worth, and thereafter wealth accumulates at a spectacular pace until the retirement years. Wealth rises with age and peaks for fifty- to sixty-four-year-olds. However, median net worth drops off somewhat during the retirement years, probably because households downsize to smaller, less expensive homes for space or health care reasons. A poor household may need to liquidate the home to qualify for Medicaid. Once the members of a household have qualified for social security and Medicare, however, it would appear that these programs protect large portions of their wealth, despite the substantially reduced earnings characteristic of the elderly.

These findings generally fit the life-cycle model of wealth accumulation over the working years.[9] In *The Economic Future of American Families*

Frank Levy and Richard Michel explain, however, that the process of wealth acquisition is not uniform, because the well-being of families headed by persons under thirty-five has deteriorated in comparison to that of their 1970s counterparts. Furthermore, Levy and Michel found that members of the baby boom generation have experienced significantly lower growth in their net financial resources (wealth) than either their parents or older siblings. Those born between 1929 and 1938 outperformed other age cohorts at similar stages of their lives. Levy and Michel attribute the financial success of this group to their "being in the right place at the right time," as their early earning years occurred during decades of strong economic growth.[10]

Kevin's experience is illustrative of the relationship between age, career development, motivation, timing, and prosperity. After completing four years of vocational school, this son of Irish immigrants started work in 1939 at the naval shipyards in a civil service position. Kevin began working in the electronic trades for $13.89 a week. He retired early thirty-five years later and today pulls in a $50,000-a-year pension from the government

> I was a manager, a manager in charge of a major division that designed, implemented, and trained the users of a full-scale business management information system for naval shipyards. I was the man for the industrial area. Production is my trade experience … 'cause I worked my way through a dozen positions before I got into this business. This is the business after I got my degree [at night school]. With my degree, computers are [were] just starting to mushroom. Management was terrified. I was a junior manager at the time; I had worked my way up, as you know in the government you have to take exams for everything and I was a great exam taker. I love exams. I was hot from school. Hot. The other guys, managers, were terrified to go to school to learn about computers. They didn't want any part of it. How? They're not going to learn. I step forward and I say take me. They train me from ass over teakettle, from computer school to computer school. I put the time in. As a result, I just floated like crap to the top and here I am. OK? There I am—I got the job and I left a lot of dead bodies behind me. I passed a whole slew of people who rated the job better than I, had more time, more seniority, but no get up and go. And they were terrified and those died on the vine as the years came.

> I had a GS–15 in my hand when I quit, when I resigned. I resigned after thirty-five years at the age of 55 cause I was fed up with the rat race … [it] was killing all my friends. Six of them had heart attacks, died, across the country, died on the job. Too much pressure for them. I quit.

Kevin's parents "had no conception of acquiring assets when they came to this country." Assisted by a modest lifestyle and a healthy pension that is indexed to inflation, Kevin has amassed close to $300,000 in savings over the course of his working life, with another $150,000 worth of equity in his house.

Family, Gender, and Marriage

Many factors contribute both to the diversity of families and to the resources they possess. In this chapter and the next we introduce a varied group of families, looking at their resources and how their values, needs, and priorities translate into what they do with economic resources. Table 4.3 demonstrates the clear resource advantage that married couples command in comparison to single heads of households. They bring in more than twice the annual income and accrue almost $45,000 more in net worth than single persons. Their net financial assets add up to $8,334 versus only $700 for single householders. The age of people in a household, the number of members in the paid labor force, and other interacting factors exaggerate these gross disparities; we intend to disentangle a number of variables as the analysis evolves.

Earnings provide the conventional measure of the material well-being of women in comparison to men.[11] A resource perspective, by contrast, shifts the question away from the value of women in the labor market and toward control over assets. The resource focus entails both strengths and weaknesses

Table 4.3 Family, Gender, Marriage, and Wealth

	Income	NW[a]	NFA[b]
All married couples	$31,412	$56,686	$8,334
Married couples, kids	31,569	26,950	1,003
All single heads	14,931	12,075	700
Single heads, kids	13,140	1,113	0
Gender			
Male	19,922	10,000	1,000
Female	12,530	13,550	526
Marital status			
Never married	19,643	4,000	150
Separated	14,819	1,500	0
Divorced	17,632	11,089	265
Widowed	9,031	50,103	8,645

[a] Net worth
[b] Net financial assets

for understanding gender relations. Including assets provides a more comprehensive indication of the economic condition of women and men than does
income alone. But determining control of assets in the family is a difficult
matter. While we are convinced that households and families are the appropriate units to analyze when the focus is on wealth, because it is families who
accumulate and plan how to use their economic resources, we are less certain about the relative control that women have over nonincome resources. A
household perspective may assume more gender equality in economic matters
within families than exists.

For example, the category single-headed households, especially among
women, may conceal as many individual situations as it reveals, because conspicuous distinctions emerge within this group. Table 4.3 delineates clear differences in resources according to marital status among single householders.
While relatively impoverished, the category of single householders nonetheless
contains at least one well-off group. The average widow possesses healthy net
worth and financial assets, amounting to $50,103 and $8,645 respectively. By
contrast, and no doubt because of their age and their point in the life course,
widows have the smallest annual incomes. The wealth assets of divorced, separated, and never married women pale in comparison, as none of these kinds
of single householders possess even as much as $300 in net financial assets.

Children being raised by both parents benefit from a huge resource advantage over those raised by single parents. This is not a moral, psychological, or
developmental advantage. Rather, it involves a recognition that these families
generally can draw from a larger stockpile of resources, and that may translate
into expanded choices and opportunities. As shown in table 4.3, married couples with children have more than double the income of single-headed households and a net worth advantage on the order of $25,000. A child living with
both parents typically grows up in a household that commands a little over
$1,000 in net financial assets, which will not go very far. Even so, it is clearly
more useful than no financial assets at all.

Stacie is a twenty-five-year-old single mother with a five-year-old daughter. She was just finishing law school at the time of our interview. Carrie was
born just after college graduation and Stacie took a year and a half off to
devote to her daughter before starting law school. During this time she also
worked full-time nights, waitressing and bartending. A thousand dollars sits
in her savings account. "I remember first-year law school, for every [job or

internship] I put a percentage of my check in my savings account supposedly for Carrie's education ... but that little tradition ended real quickly. The only thing I own outright is my car ... It's rapidly falling apart.' Having chosen to have a child, stay single, and go to law school, she could not fully support her family, at least until law school was over and she found a job. It also meant debt, lots of debt. Carrie's father was supposed to help out. Typically, however, Stacie says, "I had a child support order but it's never been enforced. He owes me about ten thousand dollars actually. I'll get a few checks and then they stop coming. ... He'll quit his job and go somewhere else and then it'll take a year to find him again."

Stacie's loans for law school and living expenses total $80,000, which she must start repaying six months after the completion of law school. She thinks she will be paying these loans off "for the rest of my life and Carrie's natural life as well." In addition, she has credit-card debt amounting to $5,000, a hospital bill for $2,500, and overdue child care bills. When asked whether she had job prospects after graduation, she laughed, "No, no. I mean I'm working in a firm now where I've been since last summer. But they'll never take me on as an attorney. I'm sure they'll continue to pay me eight dollars an hour."

Loaded with some heavy debt baggage, Stacie is full of determination and self-assurance about her family's future as she prepares to embark on her professional career.

> I've always paid my bills, I will always pay my bills. I go to school and work two to three jobs, and I'm always going to do what I have to do, and I'm not going to have Carrie wanting for necessities ... because I'm single and I chose to get an advanced degree. I mean she's not going to suffer because of my choices. It takes a lot of budgeting. It takes self-sacrifice, but you know, I've always gone by what I was motivated by. It may not be the great lifestyle that perhaps I enjoyed.

The obvious reason that married households sustain a resource advantage is their ability to send more than one person into the labor force, but households with married couples also fare much better than single-headed households, even when only one partner works. Among all married couples, the highest earnings are found in those households in which both spouses work; when only one spouse works, male single-earners take home about $7,000 more than their female counterparts. Interestingly, results show only minimal asset variation between those households in which only the husband works and those households in which both spouses work. A second income apparently supplies much-needed income but generates little wealth. The highest wealth assets and lowest incomes occur in households where neither spouse works, which is to say, as analyses not reported here indicate, primarily in the case of retired couples.

Alternatives to the traditional male-female couple are becoming more common, though they may not be gaining more social acceptance. We limit our observations here to economic resources. In this context, our findings indicate that married couples possess more resources than single householders and hence their standard of living and life chances are presumably more economically secure.

Just as Albert and Robyn's story indicated, much of a family's resources and wealth is directed at providing a nourishing environment for its children. Albert and Robyn emptied their savings account for a down payment on a house when their daughter was born. Everyone we interviewed who had children told us of the way in which they expended assets at critical junctures in their children's lives to enhance their social and educational well-being. The arrival of a child can have a critical effect on the resources of households: income drops precipitously in households with four or more children. Most likely, a higher proportion of women become full-time homemakers while raising several children. Both net worth and net financial assets decline drastically with the presence of the first child, with net worth dropping by one third. Except for the second child, the wealth decline continues with each successive child.

On the Road to Wealth

Mary Ellen is a self-assured young businesswoman who at the age of thirty-two is well on her way to securing the good life. She attended private schools and graduated from a prestigious private urban university in California. Armed with a degree in business administration, she began her career as the marketing director of a small computer company. As she helped the firm to grow, Mary Ellen's salary quickly rose from $27,000 to $37,000. Recognizing her talents, she quickly realized that her skills could be used to help her own family. She went to work in her father's business, because "Well, my family has a business, I'm making this business [the small computer firm] grow, why can't I do [it] with my own company, and also reap the benefits of the inheritance ... the future of our family."

Using his training as a mechanic, her father had started his own auto repair and parts sales company. The profits from this venture furnished a comfortable upper-middle-class upbringing for Mary Ellen and her six siblings. As the marketing director of the family business, Mary Ellen earns $50,000 annually, a sum in part dependent on the firm's "commission based upon sales volume."

While still young, Mary Ellen is laying the foundation on which to build a substantial wealth portfolio. While she only has $300 in a savings account, $2,000 in an IRA, and $2,300 in a money market fund, she already has some profitable property investments. She lives in a condominium in which she estimates she has already built up $31,000 in equity. Mary Ellen and her fiancé have secured additional property that generated $9,000 worth of equity almost overnight. Thus, minus car and other debts, she has a net worth of $24,000, with net financial assets of about $9,000.

Mary Ellen illustrates several factors positively associated with wealth acquisition. Her social background positions her to take advantage of opportunities for the accumulation of wealth. Growing up in an upper-middle-class environment presented a number of educational and career opportunities not available to most Americans. Her educational attainment and occupational skill provided her with the knowledge and direction to build on her earning power. Building on the wealth created by her father in his business, she is consolidating not only her assets but her family's future as well.

Below we examine how factors related to social background, education, occupation, and work are associated with asset acquisition for Americans. Not all Americans can count on being born into, or acquiring the skills needed to attain, financial security.

Social Background Disparities in Wealth

Mary Ellen's story shows how much being born to the "right" parents matters. How much it matters is the topic of a great deal of debate. The only reliable survey data on this topic indicates the importance of inheritances for the population as a whole.[12] At most income levels bequeathed wealth concerns a small and roughly constant proportion of the population. In 1962 less than 5 percent of Americans received "substantial" parental endowments. Most crucially, over one-half with incomes above $100,000 reported inheriting a substantial amount of their assets. Comparing householders' wealth by parental occupation provides some insight into the intergenerational consequences of wealth (see table A4.2).

Simply put, families whose parents held high-status jobs most likely control greater net worth and net financial assets than those with lower-status parents. Those from upper-white-collar origins control $8,230 median NFA, while those from lower-white-collar and upper-blue-collar families follow close behind with $7,659 and $5,800 respectively. Those from lower-blue-collar origins trail far behind with $1,239 in median NFA. Chapter 6 discusses in more detail the inter-generational consequences of occupational mobility for wealth.

Education

It comes as no surprise that people like Mary Ellen who have a degree in business would be directed toward making money. How much more prosperous and successful in accumulating wealth are the better educated? High educational achievement leads typically to better-paying jobs, which in turn results in greater wealth accumulation (see table A4.3). Wealth permits differential access to educational opportunity. Both income and wealth data demonstrate similarly positive resource returns from educational opportunity and achievement. Wealth, by contrast, increases dramatically relative to income for household heads holding college or postgraduate degrees. The median net worth of college graduates is double that of those who did not earn degrees; net financial assets increase from $3,300 for those with some college to $16,000 for graduates.

Surprisingly, housing and vehicle equity represents practically all—98 percent—of the assets held by the poorly educated. College graduates, by contrast, position over one-quarter of their substantial assets in investments that produce further income and wealth. In a rather bleak forecast for the future Frank Levy and Richard Michel, concurring that the poorly educated are more dependent on housing equity to build wealth, warn in *The Economic Future of American Families* that recent changes in housing and financial markets present increasing barriers to home ownership for many young, less-educated families.

Occupation and Work History

Mary Ellen's capacity to sustain her investments depends in great part on a large and steady stream of income. Her ability to secure a job in a small corporation and her usefulness in the family business point to the importance of career and labor market experience for economic security. The careers in education and graphic design chosen by Albert and Robyn, by contrast, will likely mean a life-long low level of wealth accumulation. This section takes a first glance at the relationship between work-related variables and income/wealth. Three factors are examined: occupation, labor-market experience, and the number of household earners in the labor market. How do different occupational groups fare?[13] The evidence shows that income varies less by occupational category than does wealth (see table A4.4). Upper-white-collar workers earn the most on average, with a median income of $39,000, and enjoy a high average net worth of $60,000. But the self-employed enjoy the highest level of median net worth, which at $93,000 ranges from one and a half to ten times that of their salaried counterparts. A very large gap between upper-white-collar workers and other salaried workers also appears. Since education interacts with occupation, these findings represent another measure of the impact of education on one's ability to accumulate wealth, especially for the well educated.

The breakdown of wealth by occupation shows us which groups have large amounts of financial assets at their disposal. Home equity accounts for almost all wealth held by lower-blue-collar, upper-blue-collar, and lower-white-collar households. In sharp contrast, not only do professionals, executives, managers, and the self-employed control large wealth portfolios, but their significant assets generate additional income and capital. Indeed, only the self-employed and white-collar professionals possess ample net financial assets, $36,824 and $12,710 respectively. Mary Ellen's involvement in the family business, given a favorable economic climate, prefigures an even sweeter economic future. The lower-white-collar and upper-blue-collar occupations trail far behind with minimal NFA holdings of $1,500 and $985 respectively. Semiskilled and unskilled households control zero NFA.

How true is Benjamin Franklin's utilitarian belief that worldly success is attained by hard work and careful calculation? How true is it that the longer a person works, the more assets he or she acquires? Income increases the longer one works, although those with more than thirteen years experience show a slight decline (see table A4.5). Median NW and NFA escalate rapidly the longer one works: net worth ascends from $3,950 for those with little labor market experience to over $70,000 for those employed over thirteen years. The relationship between wealth and years in the labor force remains intact, although slightly less dramatic, when the data are inspected by householder's age. For example, among thirty-six- to forty-nine-year-old householders, those with nine to thirteen years' working experience earn 41 percent more than those working less than five years, but their net worth increases fourfold.

While Mary Ellen's job is a classic breadwinner position, many observers note that since the early 1970s it has often taken more than one paycheck to sustain a middle-class lifestyle. As we stated earlier, income data for well over a decade demonstrate that more family members are finding themselves in the paid work force. The second and third workers in a household increase income flow by 65 and 21 percent respectively.

The Importance of Stable Work

Kevin worked steadily in a government job for thirty-five years. He prided himself on never missing a day's work and was owed six months of earned vacation when he retired. In today's work world, however, it is becoming less and less typical for people to work for a single employer or company through-out their entire work lives. Many analysts believe that work stability is associated with structurally distinctive industrial sectors, sectors that provide differential careers and rewards to workers.[14] This perspective contrasts a *core* sector of the economy, composed of basic industries such as steel, chemicals, and automobiles, with a *periphery* sector composed of industries such as textiles, personal services, and retail sales. Each is characterized by a contrasting set of structural characteristics. The core is characterized by greater productivity, higher profits, and a higher level of unionized labor. Consequently job careers are more stable and secure and wages are higher in the core. The periphery, by contrast, tends to be smaller, more labor intensive, less productive, and more likely to use nonunion labor. Not surprisingly, jobs are more likely to be less secure and wages are lower in this sector. Simply put, the core is more likely to have the "good jobs," the jobs with better pay, larger benefit packages, health care, stability, and present career opportunities. On the periphery, by contrast, jobs pay poorly, provide few benefits, are more likely temporary and unstable, and do not readily lead to career mobility.

Some note the importance of a *government* sector, as distinct from the core and periphery. This sector includes all employees of local, state, and federal governments. These jobs are characterized by stability, good wage levels, and career ladders. Some groups of workers, notably minorities and women, occupy "bad jobs" in the periphery sector in disproportionate numbers, a fact that helps explain racial and gender earnings inequality.

Jobs that provide stability, like Kevin's civil service position in the naval shipyards, are another key institutional feature shaping earnings and wealth.

Studies of work stability chronicle periods of unemployment, the frequency and duration of job layoffs,[15] and a worker's ability to find replacement work. Our analysis shows a strong and direct relationship between low, moderate, and high degrees of work stability and resources. The most stable group earns considerably more income than the moderate group and possesses three times the latter's net worth; it also controls $4,500 more in financial assets than either the moderate- or the low-stability group. Those groups with the most unstable work histories (6 percent of the sample) earn one-half ($6,120) of poverty-level wages and they possess minimal NW and zero NFA.

Like other accounts, our analysis shows that earnings inequity is related to industrial sector.[16] Notably, the "bad jobs" in the periphery pay substantially less ($25,316) than those in either the core ($30,564) or the government sector ($32,008). This points to the importance of economic organization, as well as individual factors, in understanding processes of discrimination. The wealth data demonstrate even more conclusively the disadvantages of employment in the periphery sector. Those employed in the periphery own less than two-thirds the total net worth of core- or government-sector employees. Their net financial assets amount to less than $1,200 in comparison to $3,700 for those in the core sector and $4,300 for government workers.

Region

Many of the people we interviewed began acquiring wealth by means of buying and selling property, particularly in areas of rapid economic growth where the demand for housing is strong. Very active residential markets lead to increased housing and property inflation. There are therefore regional differences in the importance of investment in residential real estate. It is improbable that Mary Ellen would have been as lucky in her initial real estate investment in Los Angeles if she had lived in St. Louis, Missouri, where housing values have risen only moderately since the 1980s.

It is also well known that income varies by region of the country. Incomes are highest in the West and Northeast, with the Midwest trailing not far behind. Research shows a rather large gap between the South and other regions. SIPP data corroborate these results (see table A4.6). Only a few dollars separate Western and Northeastern incomes; Midwestern incomes lag by about $1,800. Southern incomes rank last, trailing the rest of the country by $3,500. Several factors are probably at work in the Southern income gap, such as lower wage scales, fewer professional jobs, a larger agrarian economy, less education, and a higher proportion of blacks.

Predictably, given the income-wealth nexus, Southerners' assets also lag behind those of other regions. A $10,000 breach separates Southerners' total net worth from that of non-Southerners. This gap in Southerners' and non-Southerners' wealth is not simply a reflection of lower-valued housing appreciation. The same pattern appears in the realm of net financial assets, with $1,758 accruing to Southerners versus $5,030 for other U.S. regions.

The Great Racial Wealth Divide

As chapter 1 indicates, African Americans have not shared equally in the nation's prosperity. They earn less than whites, and they possess far less wealth, whatever measure one may use. Table 4.4 presents data on income along with median wealth figures. The black-to-white median income ratio has hovered in the mid-50 to mid-60 percentage range for the past twenty years or so. Fluctuations have been relatively minor, measured in tenths of a percent, and in many ways American society became accustomed to this standard of inequality. In 1988 results from SIPP showed that for every dollar earned by white households black households earned sixty-two cents. The median wealth data expose even deeper inequalities. Whites possess nearly twelve times as much median net worth as blacks, or $43,800 versus $3,700. In an even starker contrast, perhaps, the average white household controls $6,999 in net financial assets while the average black household retains no NFA nest egg whatsoever.

Access to Assets

The potential for assets to expand or inhibit choices, horizons, and opportunities for children emerged as the most consistent and strongest common theme in our interviews. Since parents want to invest in their children, to give them whatever advantages they can, we wondered about the ability of the average American

Table 4.4 Wealth and Race

Race	Median Income	Median NW[a]	Mean NW[a]	Median NFA[b]	Mean NFA[b]
White	$25,384	$43,800	$95,667	$6,999	$47,347
Black	15,630	3,700	23,818	0	5,209
Ratio	0.62	0.08	0.25	0.0	0.11

[a] Net worth
[b] Net financial assets

Table 4.5 Who Is on the Edge?

	Households with 0 or Negative NFA[a]	Households without NFA[a] for 3 months[b]	Households without NFA[a] for 6 months[b]
Sample	31.0%	44.9%	49.9%
Race			
White	25.3	38.1	43.2
Black	60.9	78.9	83.1
Hispanic	54.0	72.5	77.2
Age of Householder			
15–35	48.0	67.0	72.8
36–49	31.7	45.2	50.7
50–64	22.1	32.0	36.2
65 or older	15.1	26.4	30.6
Education			
Less than high school	40.3	55.5	60.0
High school degree	32.2	48.0	63.2
Some college	29.9	45.3	61.4
College degree	18.9	26.8	31.2
Family Type[c]			
Single parent	61.9	79.2	83.2
Married couple	36.9	53.8	59.9

[a] Net financial worth
[b] NFA reserves to survive at the poverty line of $968 per month
[c] Includes only households with children

household to expend assets on their children. This section thus delves deeper into the assets households command by (1) considering the importance of home and vehicle equity in relation to other kinds of assets; (2) inspecting available financial assets for various groups of the population; and (3) looking at children growing up in resource-deficient households. We found a strong relationship between the amount of wealth and the composition of assets. Households with large amounts of total net worth control wealth portfolios composed mostly of financial assets. Financial investments make up about four-fifths of the assets of the richest households. Conversely, home and vehicle equity represents over 70 percent of the asset portfolio among the poorest one-fifth of American households, one in three of which possesses zero or negative financial assets.

Table 4.5 reports households with zero or negative net financial assets for various racial, age, education, and family groups. It shows that one-quarter of white households, 61 percent of black households, and 54 percent of Hispanic households are without financial resources. A similar absence of financial assets affects nearly one-half of young households; circumstances steadily improve with age, however, leaving only 15 percent of those households headed by seniors in a state of resource deficiency. The educational achievement of householders also connects directly with access to resources, as 40 percent of poorly educated household heads control no financial assets while over 80 percent of households headed by a college graduate control some NFA. Findings reported in this table also demonstrate deeply embedded disparities in resource command between single and married-couple parents. Resource deprivation characterizes 62 percent of single-parent households in comparison to 37 percent of married couples raising children.

Besides looking at resource deprivation, table 4.5 also sets criteria for "precarious-resource" circumstances. Households without enough NFA reserves to survive three months at the poverty line ($2,904) meet these criteria. Nearly 80 percent of single-parent households fit this description. Likewise 38 percent of white households and 79 percent of black households live in precarious-resource circumstances.

Among our interviewees, parents with ample assets planned to use them to create a better world for their children. Those without them strategized about acquiring some and talked about their "wish list." Parents talked about ballet lessons, camp, trips for cultural enrichment or even to Disney World, staying home more often with the children, affording full-time day care, allowing a parent to be home after day care. The parents discussed using assets to provide better educational opportunities for their children. Kevin takes great pride in paying for his son's college and being able to offer him advanced training. Stacie wants to be able to afford private school for Carrie. Ed and Alicia told us about the private school choices and dilemmas facing their children.

Figure 4.2 looks at the percentage of children in resource-poor households by race. It provides information both on households with no net financial assets and on those with just enough assets to survive above the poverty line for at least three months. Close to one-half of all children live in households with no financial assets and 63 percent live in households with precarious resources, scarcely enough NFA to cushion three months of interrupted income.

A further analysis of this already disturbing data discloses imposing and powerful racial and ethnic cleavages. For example, 40 percent of all white children grow up in households without financial resources in comparison to

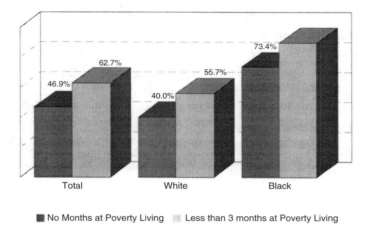

No Months at Poverty Living   Less than 3 months at Poverty Living

Degree of Resource Deficiency

Figure 4.2 Percent of Children in Resource-Deficient Households, by Race

73 percent of all black children. Most telling of all perhaps, only 11 percent of black children grow up in households with enough net financial assets to weather three months of no income at the poverty level. Three times as many white kids live in such households.

According to Richard Steckel and Jayanthi Krishnan, cross-sectional measures of wealth acquisition and inequality may disguise underlying changes in wealth status.[17] Analyzing surveys from 1966 and 1976, Steckel and Krishnan found that changes in marital status were associated with changes in wealth. The largest increase in wealth occurred for single women who later married. Other groups who experienced increases in wealth included households headed by the young, those with at least twelve years of schooling, and individuals who married. The greatest loss in wealth occurred among households headed by older individuals, single men, and those experiencing marital disruption.

Summary

Financial wealth is the buried fault line of the American social system. The wealth distribution portrait drawn in this chapter has disclosed the existence of highly concentrated wealth at the top; a pattern of steep resource inequality; the disproportionate asset reserves held by various demographic groups; the precarious economic foundation of middle-class life; and how few financial assets most American households can call upon. This chapter has also provided documentation concerning the relationship between income inequality and wealth inequality. At one level, income makes up the largest component of potential wealth. At the same time, however, distinctive patterns of income and wealth inequality exist. Put another way, substituting what is known about income inequality for what is not known about wealth inequality limits, and even biases, our understanding of inequality. A thorough understanding of inequality must therefore pay more attention to resources than has been paid in the past.

Perhaps no single piece of information conveys the sense of fragility common to those on the lowest rungs of the economic ladder as the proportion of children who grow up in households without assets. Reducing all life's chances for success to economic circumstances no doubt overlooks much, but resources nonetheless provide an accurate measure of differential access to educational, career, health, cultural, and social opportunities. In poignantly reciting the hopes they have for their children, parents recognize the importance of resources. Our interviews show how parents use assets to bring these hopes to life, or wish they had ample assets so they could bring them to life. Nearly three-quarters of all black children, 1.8 times the rate for whites, grow up in households possessing no financial assets. Nine in ten black children come of age in households that lack sufficient financial reserves to endure three months of no income at the poverty line, about four times the rate for whites.

A Story of Two Nations: Race and Wealth

5

To be a poor man is hard, but to be a poor race in a land of dollars is the very bottom of hardship.

—W.E.B. Du Bois, *The Souls of Black Folk*

Introduction

This chapter shifts our focus to concentrate more specifically on racial inequality in America. In stark, material terms we argue that whites and blacks constitute two nations. Our inquiry into the racial distribution of wealth looks at several areas of interest. The chapter opens by discussing and probing in considerable detail the black middle class, comparing its relative economic well-being to that of the white middle class. What will an examination of the black middle class reveal about its economic stability and material prospects? We next compare how much wealth whites and blacks possess and construct pertinent racial wealth portfolios for each group. These profiles allow us to answer some vital questions about this country's progress (or lack of it) toward racial equality, such as: Has the wealth of blacks grown? Is it catching up with that of whites, keeping pace, or falling further behind? A family's decision about what it does with resources reflects crucial information about both what kinds of assets are available and that family's sense of priorities and the future. Accordingly, examining the composition of assets for whites and blacks promises to yield meaningful insights. For example, how does the savings and investment behavior of whites and blacks differ? Our data is useful in exploring structural differences in the kinds and composition of assets held by whites and blacks.

Previous studies on black wealth were unable "to look at the wealth of blacks and whites with similar socioeconomic characteristics"[1] The SIPP data set allows us both to address the differential distribution of wealth among blacks and to compare black and white patterns of wealth holding more directly, extensively, and analytically than previous studies have done. Our focus will include such major factors in racial inequality as family structure, age, education, occupation, and income. Most important, we will tell a tale of two middle classes, one white and one black.

The Black Middle Class

One of the most heated scholarly controversies in the area of racial equality and social justice over the past two decades concerns the dispute over the nature, causes, and meaning of economic changes occurring within the black community. The way in which one views these changes has enormous inherent implications for social policy. In essence, commentators argue that the black community has become increasingly differentiated economically, dividing into a growing underclass trapped in urban misery and an improving middle class bent on escaping the ghetto. While die condition of the most disadvantaged African Americans deteriorated rapidly after 1970, the middle class grew, becoming substantially better off and less burdened by the effects of race.

The economic status of the black middle class is a vital factor in ongoing debates in the field of racial equity. A frequent question that arises concerns what one means by "the black middle class." Some demark the limits simply in terms of income; others include education or occupation in the definition.[2] Most scholars embrace a class conception based on the work of Karl Marx or Max Weber and make occupation their central focus. The evidence cited earlier showing an enlarged middle class touches all these bases—educational achievement, earnings, and occupation. As previously noted, middle class means working in a white-collar occupation or being self-employed. In using several different indicators of class status, we confirm that the economic foundation of the black middle class is not dependent upon any one way of thinking about class. The point of this exercise is to show that an accurate and realistic appraisal of the economic footing of the black middle class reveals its precariousness, marginality, and fragility. The case for this characterization rests not only on an inspection of the resources available to the black middle class but on the relative position of the latter with respect to the white middle class.

Carol illustrates the fragility of the black middle class. She and her husband seemed to have found financial security in the American middle class. Her husband was a sales manager, earning about $60,000 a year in salary and bonuses. He had acquired stock in the growing company he worked for, put money aside in a 401(k) retirement account, and invested in some treasury bills; he was also vested in the company's pension plan. Carol and her husband owned a home, as well as a rental property next door, and had invested some money in an apartment building. Carol raised the couple's three children, earned her college degree, and then began working full time after the children went off to college. Carol and her husband put their kids through private schools and college. Today they are divorced and Carol works as a receptionist for eight dollars an hour. In the divorce settlement she kept the home and the property next door as her share of the couple's joint assets.

Sometime after the divorce she went to work as the assistant director of a private elementary school run by her sister. The school became insolvent because her sister grew "sick and everybody else was tied up." Carol felt it was her familial responsibility to close the school for her sister. For seven months she continued as the school's unpaid assistant director while closing it down and settling accounts out of her personal funds. Carol's only income during this seven-month period consisted of unemployment compensation from the government. Her savings depleted, Carol had to sell the house next door in order to pay her own bills. Her total loss was on the order of $50,000.

As Carol's experience demonstrates, even the most seemingly secure financial status can be changed by unforeseen circumstances. For Carol the fall from middle-class grace is a story of divorce, family obligations, and low-paid work. She feels both lucky and vastly underpaid. Lucky, because unemployment had run out, she needed a job badly, and a friend she once worked for found her a job. Vastly underpaid, because she went "from making about $18 an hour down to $8," from $36,000 to $16,000 a year. "And that's where I am now." At fifty, she owns her home, with a handsome $85,000 worth of equity, as well as an insurance policy; but she has no liquid assets, not even a savings account. The limits of home equity as a source of ready cash became painfully clear to Carol when, during a recent drop in interest rates, she attempted to borrow some money by refinancing her home. Even though a new mortgage would have lowered her monthly payments, the bank refused to restructure her loan because she was unemployed at the time. It had taken years of hard work to gain entry into the middle class and a divorce and family financial crisis to jeopardize Carol's middle-class status. Even with ample "paper assets" in the home, Carol is no longer secure because a failure to meet her mortgage payments or some other financial crisis might force her to put her house up for sale.

Carol's story shows how a middle-class standard of living rests on the twin pillars of income and wealth. The two together create a solid economic foundation that simultaneously safeguards a secure standard of living and enhances future life chances. When either one is lacking, middle-class status is jeopardized. Without ample income families must draw on their available wealth reserves, which, as Carol learned, can be rapidly depleted. In the absence of wealth resources, especially liquid assets, middle-class living standards become dependent on an uninterrupted source of earnings, or rock-solid job security. Table 5.1 displays the resources that middle-class whites and blacks command. This table incorporates the three ways in which we have previously defined the middle class: first, those earning between $25,000 and $50,000; second, those with college degrees; and third, those working at white-collar jobs, including the self-employed.

The figures in table 5.1 vividly demonstrate our contention that the black middle class stands on very shaky footing, no matter how one determines

Table 5.1 Race, Wealth, and Various Conceptions of "The Middle Class"

	Income	Net Worth	Net Financial Assets
White			
	$25, 000–50,000	$44,069	$6,988
College-degree	38,700	74,922	19,823
White-collar	33,765	56,487	11,952
Black			
	$25,000–50,000	$15,250	$290
College-degree	29,440	17,437	175
White-collar	23,799	8,299	0

middle-class status. Most significant, we believe, is that blacks' claim to middle-class status is based on income and not assets. The net worth middle-class
blacks command, ranging from $8,000 for white-collar workers to $17,000
for college graduates, largely represents housing equity, because neither the
middle-income earners nor the well educated nor white-collar workers control
anything other than petty net financial assets. Without wealth reserves, especially liquid assets, the black middle class depends on income for its standard
of living. Without the asset pillar, in particular, income and job security shoulder a greater part of the burden.

Recalling the overall black-to-white income ratio of 0.62, we may note
that the gap for white-collar workers narrows to 0.7, and further tapers to 0.76
for college graduates. Turning to net worth, we see in table 5.1 that the least
amount of inequality occurs among middle-income earners, where the ratio
registers 0.35; but even among households with similar income flows the difference amounts to over $28,000. White-collar occupations disclose the most
inequality: the black middle class owns fifteen cents for every dollar owned
by the white middle class. We have already observed the trivial net financial
assets of the black middle class, comparing them to the net financial assets
available to the white middle class makes the plight of blacks even starker.
When one defines the middle class as those with college degrees, the most
numerically restrictive definition, one finds that the white middle class commands $19,000 more NFA; using the broadest definition, white-collar occupa-
tions, the white middle class controls nearly $12,000 more.

In *The New Black Middle Class* Bart Landry highlights the importance
of dual wage-earning couples in explaining how black families attain middle-
class living standards. The loss of breadwinner jobs that support a whole family has had a great impact on American life over the last two decades, pushing
more family members into the paid labor force. Following Landry's lead, first
using SIPP data from 1984, we inspected all middle-income earning households to see how many full-time wage earners were needed to attain middle-
class living standards.[3] One full-time breadwinner supported 57 percent of
white and 42 percent of black middle-income earning households. Most black
households attaining a middle-class standard of living managed to do so only
because both partners earned a wage (58 percent for black versus 43 percent
for white households).

Results from 1988 strengthen and extend Landry's argument. To sustain a middle-class living standard in 1988, two-thirds of white and close to three-quarters of all black households needed more than one worker. Among married couples enjoying a middle-class standard of living, both partners worked in 78 percent of black households versus 62 percent for whites. These figures represent those spending any time in the paid labor force, not necessarily in a full-time job. Looking only at full-time workers, one arrives at a fuller understanding of the work commitments and family sacrifice necessary for middle-class existence.[4] Among married couples it takes two full-time workers in 60 percent of black homes to earn between $25,000 and $50,000 yearly; the same is true for only 37 percent of white homes.

Gerald Jaynes and Robin Williams in *A Common Destiny* and Bart Landry in *The New Black Middle Class* noted that two-parent black and white families have relatively equal incomes. They have also observed that black families need more wage earners to approach the living standard of white families. We expect to find that black married couples fare better than other kinds of household units, both within the context of all types of black households and in comparison to their white counterparts. We also expect that households in which both partners work manage better still. Table 5.2 reviews the income and wealth resources that various kinds of black and white households govern. Fresh data are presented in this table concerning the resources of young couples, twenty-five to thirty-five years old, in which both husband and wife earn a living. Optimistic observers point to this group as typifying blacks' best chance for income equality. The typical young, two-earner black couple brings in four-fifths of the earnings of analogous white couples, leaving only a $5,000 income gap. This breach appears relatively small, but the net worth of these young black couples amounts to less than one-fifth that of their white counterparts, which puts them at a $19,000 disadvantage. Finally, young white couples have already accumulated $1,150 in net financial assets, of which blacks have none.

The lack of financial reserves among young two-earner couples heralds the fragility of black middle-class living standards more generally.[5] To gauge the precariousness of the black middle class, we calculated the number of months a household could survive without a steady stream of income, asking how far wealth reserves would stretch in a crisis or emergency. We discovered that the occupationally defined white middle class could support its present middle-class standard of living (the median middle-class income being

Table 5.2 Race, "Middle Class" Families, Work, and Wealth

	Income	Net Worth	Net Financial Assets
	Married		
White	$32,400	$65,024	$11,500
Black	25,848	17,437	0
Ratio	0.80	0.27	–
	Two-Earner Couple		
White	40,865	56,046	8,612
Black	34,700	17,375	0
Ratio	0.85	0.31	–
	Two-Earner Young Couple[a]		
White	36,435	23,165	1,150
Black	29,377	4,124	0
Ratio	0.81	0.18	–
	White-Collar[b]		
White	34,821	48,310	8,680
Black	34,320	7,697	0
Ratio	0.70	0.16	–

[a] Twenty-five- to thirty-five-year-olds
[b] Self-employed not included

$2,750 per month) for four and one-third months (see figure B5.1). The typical black middle-class household would not make it to the end of the first month. Whites' reserves allow them to survive at the poverty level ($968 per month) for over a year, while most blacks, yet again, would not make it through the first month. Put another way, just 65 percent of white middle-class households possess a large enough nest egg to maintain their present living standard for at least one month, and 55 percent could last at least three months. In unmistakable contrast, only 27 percent of the black middle class has enough NFA to keep up present living standards for one month, and less than one in five households could sustain their lifestyles for three months. At poverty living standards, 35 percent of the black middle class might last one month, and 27 percent might hold out for three.

A Wealth Comparison

Previous studies comparing the wealth of blacks and whites have found that blacks have anywhere from $8 to $19 of wealth for every $100 that whites possess.[6] Andrew Brimmer points out in his "Income, Wealth, and Investment

Behavior in the Black Community" that blacks owned only 3 percent of all accumulated wealth in the United States in 1984, even though they received 7.6 percent of the total money earned that year and made up 11 percent of all households.[7] Francine Blau and John Graham reported that young black families (twenty-four to thirty-four years of age) in 1976 held only about 18 percent of the wealth of young white families.[8] Looking at preliminary wealth data from the SIPP survey, Billy Tidwell characterizes the economic status of blacks as "very marginal" in his 1987 book *Beyond the Margin.* Table 4.4 in the previous chapter demonstrates the overall dimensions of this marginality: the 1988 ratio of black-to-white median household income reached 0.62, but the median net worth ratio stood at 0.08. Moreover, a comparison of net financial assets shows the enormity of blacks' wealth disadvantage—white households possess nearly ten times as much mean NFA as black households. Half of all white households have at least $6,999 in an NFA nest egg, whereas nearly two-thirds of all black households have zero or negative NFA. Of course these are averages; many whites as well as blacks command larger wealth portfolios than these figures suggest, just as many also control fewer resources. However, the asset deprivation to which blacks are subject, both absolutely and in relation to whites, reverberates throughout their economic circumstances and thus forms the focus of this analysis.

Eva and Clarence Dobbs and their three children live in a neat two-story craftsman home that architectural purists want to preserve. In this working-class area of South Central Los Angeles known as the Crenshaw District, historical preservation of homes takes a backseat to "struggling" and "surviving." The Dobbs family is a perfect example. Both adults are full-time workers who together bring in close to $50,000 annually but who are asset-poor and, in fact, live in the shadow of debt. Clarence works as an occupational therapist with stroke patients for a number of hospitals. The work is not steady, nor does it pay much. Eva is a personnel assistant in a Fortune 500 company. While she has been on a career ladder and done well, the corporation is in the midst of outsourcing their personnel functions, and her job may last for only a couple more years. The Dobbses' lives are organized around church and the children. The kids all go to a private Christian school to "protect them from the streets" and to give them the kind of education that will "teach their souls as well as their minds." For Eva the $3,000 cost is high but not excessive "if you think about clothes they need if they were in public school." Their rented home, which they have only moved into recently, is sparsely furnished. They have two cars, which they need to get around in a city whose public transportation is notoriously poor. Eva and Clarence are very proud of their oldest son, who has received a scholarship to go to a private university in the Midwest, but they are somewhat concerned about finding the money they will need to help him out. But this is a family that will survive.

In their everyday struggle to make ends meet there is little left over to save. Eva and Clarence have no savings account. They once had about $1,500 in savings, but "emergencies" and "nickel and dime" withdrawals for little things soon depleted these reserves. Their most fervent hope is to save enough money to be able to purchase a home. The housing market in Los Angeles, however, plays havoc with that desire. A median-priced home in Los Angeles costs $220,000, and the 20 percent down payment seems way beyond the Dobbses' reach. Furthermore, years of struggle have left a trail of bad credit that will hurt their chances of even qualifying for a home loan.

What few assets they have come from Eva's 401(k) account at the company for which she works. For the past couple of years Eva has been regularly making deposits that have earned a 50 percent company match. She now has about $4,000 in this fund. The high penalties for early withdrawal have prevented the Dobbses from drawing on these assets in their battle to survive.

The Dobbses have begun to attack their credit woes. A $2,500 loan from the credit union helped consolidate Eva's credit card debt. Unfortunately, however, Eva owes another $1,600 that she borrowed to help pay her auto insurance ("which is usually about $1,400 for the one car [the other car is not insured], because of the area I live in"), her state income taxes, and her son's college-related expenses. While both Eva and Clarence come from very poor backgrounds and have no family assets to draw on, Eva's mother bought her car for $6,000, a sum that Eva is determined to pay back. Thus, when the ledger is balanced, the Dobbses have no assets and are, in fact, in debt.

The Dobbses' asset poverty is well represented in the data from SIPP. SIPP provides a yardstick with which to measure absolute gains in wealth accumulation. As shown in figure 5.1, Henry Terrell reports in his "Wealth Accumulation of Black and White Families" that the average black family held $3,779 in mean net worth in 1967, a figure that by 1984 had risen to $19,736.[9] In 1988 the average black family's net worth had increased to $23,818. Yet this impressive progress among blacks pales somewhat when matched with wealth

Figure 5.1 Gains and Gaps in Racial Wealth Accumulation[a],
1967–1988
Sources: Terrell 1971; Oliver and Shapiro (1989); SIPP, 1987 Panel, Wave 4
[a] Mean net worth

gains among whites. The average white family's mean net worth in 1967 stood at $20,153 and rose to $76,297 in 1984. By 1988 it had increased to $95,667. Although there were impressive absolute gains for blacks between 1967 and 1984, the wealth divide widened by $40,000 during those years, and by 1988 it had reached a gaping $71,849.

Theories of wealth accumulation emphasize income as the preeminent factor in wealth differentials. Indeed, as we saw in chapter 4, there is a clear relationship between income inequality and wealth accumulation: wealth accrues with increasing income. Since black households earn less than two-thirds as much as the average white household, it only makes sense to ask, to what extent can the gross wealth disparities that we have noted be explained by the well-known income inequality between whites and blacks? Examining blacks' and whites' wealth at similar income levels provides a clear and direct way to respond to this question. Standardizing for income permits us to test whether the black-white disparity in wealth holding emanates from income differences. Henry Terrell reported in his 1971 study that black families owned less than one-fifth the accumulated (mean) wealth of white families; further-more, keeping income constant, he noted that black families held less than one-half the wealth of whites in similar income brackets. Thus, he concluded that racial differences in income alone are not sufficient to account for black-white wealth disparities. Francine Blau and John Graham conclude that while "income difference is the largest single factor explaining racial differences in wealth," even after one controls for income as much as three-quarters of the wealth gap remains.[10]

We standardized SIPP wealth data into four income brackets. *Poverty*-level households earn $11,611 or less. *Moderate*-level incomes range from $11,612 to $24,999. *Middle*-level household incomes fall between $25,000 and $50,000. *High*-income households bring in over $50,000. This data only represents households headed by those under age sixty-five, because we did not want the age effects noted in chapter 4 to cloud the relationship between income, wealth, and race. The well-being of white and black senior households will be considered separately later in this chapter.

The data are very convincing in one simple respect: differences in observed income levels are not nearly sufficient to explain the large racial wealth gap (see table A5.1). The black-to-white wealth ratio comes closest to equality among prosperous households earning $50,000 or more. Even here where the wealth gap is narrowest, however, blacks possess barely one-half (0.52) the median net worth of their high-earning white counterparts. For net financial assets, the mean ratio (not presented in table A5.1) ranges from 0.006 to 0.33. The highest-earning black households possess twenty-three cents of median net financial assets for every dollar held by high-income white households. One startling comparison reveals that poverty-level whites control nearly as many mean net financial assets as the highest-earning blacks, $26,683 to $28,310. For those surviving at or below the poverty level, this table indicates quite clearly that poverty means one thing for whites and another for blacks. The general conclusion to be drawn from these straightforward yet very revealing tabulations is that the long-term life prospects of black households are substantially poorer than those of whites in similar income brackets. This analysis of wealth leaves no doubt regarding the serious misrepresentation of economic disparity that occurs when one relies exclusively on income data. Blacks and whites with equal incomes possess very unequal shares of wealth. More so than income, wealth holding remains very sensitive to the historically sedimenting effects of race.

Figure 5.2 examines resource distribution within racial groups. Starting with income for whites, this figure shows that one in five households falls below the poverty line and over 15 percent earn more than $50,000. Almost twice as many black households (39 percent) survive on poverty-level incomes, and only

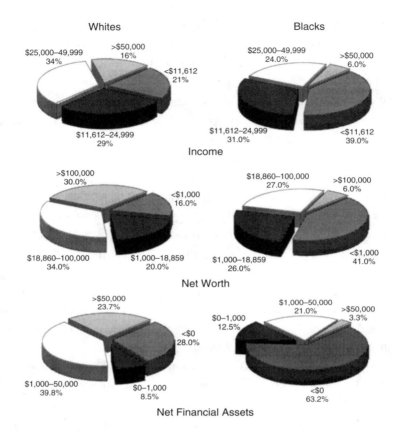

Figure 5.2 Shares of Income and Wealth Held by Whites and Blacks

6 percent make their way into the highest income bracket. In the second panel of figure 5.2, we find that 16 percent of white households possess less than $1,000 and nearly three in ten control over $100,000 in net worth. On the black side of the ledger, over four in ten households (41 percent) hold less than $1,000 in net worth and only about one in twenty (6 percent) controls over $100,000. The third panel of figure 5.2 reveals that over 28 percent of white households possess zero or negative net financial assets and almost one-quarter (24 percent) have amassed more than $50,000 in these valuable financial resources. Nearly two-thirds (63.2 percent) of all black households possess no net financial assets and only 3.3 percent make it into the $50,000-plus category.

The meager asset accumulation of black households clearly contributes to blacks' economic deprivation vis-à-vis whites in American society. While the contention that whites control the financial resources of American society is strongly supported when one examines their disproportionate control of all types of economic resources, their advantage is particularly obvious when it comes to accumulated assets. We examined the proportion of the nation's total income and wealth held by various racial groups. Using the percentage of blacks represented in the SIPP survey (9.2 percent) as an indicator of their relative numbers in the population, it is clear that blacks control a less than proportionate share of the nation's economic resources. The "black progress" narrative is most evident in blacks' share of total income, which amounts to 7.4 percent. This figure nonetheless reflects a 20 percent deficit between their slice of the income pie and their numbers in the population. The "no progress" narrative, moreover, is represented in blacks' meager portion of the nation's net worth, a portion amounting to a mere 2.9 percent and leaving blacks with 320 percent less net worth than their numbers would appear to entitle them to. Black net worth would have to increase more than threefold to reach parity with whites. However, it is their paltry share of the financial assets pie that is most distressing. Blacks control only 1.3 percent of the nation's financial assets. Whites, by contrast, who make up 82.5 percent of the population according to our SIPP data, and are in total command of the nation's NFA: 95 percent of the net financial assets pie rests on their plate.

These statistical portrayals of the distribution of economic resources at the command of black and white households help us to understand the dual economic fortunes of blacks and whites in American society. While income figures clearly show that progress was made in the post-civil rights era, the distribution of wealth paints a picture of two nations on diverging tracks labeled "black progress" and "no progress."

An examination of wealth concentration compares the wealth distribution within black and white communities. Henry Terrell presented evidence showing greater inequality in blacks' wealth distribution. He explains, however, that a substantial amount of the difference in relative wealth concentrations exists because "a large portion of the black population simply did not report any wealth accumulation at all."[11]

When the wealth pies are placed on the table, very few black households are served. Sixty-three percent of black households retain zero or negative net financial assets, in comparison to 28 percent of white households. Thus massive inequalities arise in wealth concentration: one in twenty households controls 46 percent of aggregated white net financial assets and 87 percent of those of blacks.[12] One-fifth of all households owns two-thirds of white net worth and three-quarters of the net worth of blacks.

Removing households with zero wealth assets from the mix, William Bradford reports similar wealth distributions in the white and black populations.[13] It would seem that the wealth stratification among blacks who have wealth is as egalitarian as it is because the few blacks who have wealth have so little of it.

Many authors, led by William J. Wilson in *The Truly Disadvantaged*, correctly point to increasing economic differentiation as the reason for growing economic inequality in the black community, but a comparison with white households provides a different perspective. In our analysis $43,000 in net worth situates a household smack in the middle of the white community's wealth distribution but a household with the same net worth in the black community ranks among the wealthiest one-fifth. Similarly, a small nest egg of $2,000 in net financial assets places a black household in the richest one-fifth of the black community, whereas the same amount puts a household only in the fortieth percentile among whites.

The Composition of Assets

Our interviews underscore the different ways in which blacks and whites accumulate assets. For most of the blacks we interviewed who had assets, real estate was the foremost investment made, and it provided the greatest returns. Indeed, many of our respondents who had capital to begin with used it wisely to invest in a booming Southern California real estate market. Some families took advantage of their gains to move up to better neighborhoods and homes. Others used residential equity to purchase income property that, in turn, generated further assets for them. Mary Ellen's first investment was in her own residence. But she quickly used the money she saved when she made the move from renting to owning to purchase an investment property that should garner her a healthy return. Carol has been involved in two real estate transactions, both of which created equity, and the sale of one property helped her to weather a difficult economic period. Another respondent, whom we will meet later in this chapter, has used her business, equity in her luxury home, and advice from a savvy real estate agent to purchase an income property. As is the case with these Southern Californians, real estate makes up the bulk of the wealth in the asset portfolios of African Americans.

Most of the whites we interviewed placed their assets in a more diversified range of investments. With the exception of Stacie, who is just starting her career as a lawyer, all the whites we interviewed owned homes or condominiums. Although both Boston and Los Angeles experienced similar real estate booms, none of our Boston respondents invested in income-producing properties. The only Boston respondent with income-producing property inherited it. Most of the Boston interviewees, as has been reported to be common among whites, had placed their assets in investment instruments such as certificates of deposit, high-interest bearing savings accounts, the stock market, mutual funds, bonds, IRAs, and Keoghs. Bob and Kathy's portfolio includes $12,000 in mutual funds, a $10,000 savings account, and $16,000 in IRA and Keogh accounts. Kevin concentrated his accumulated wealth in high-yield certificates of deposit. Another respondent's wealth was invested for him, through a family trust and financial advisers, in a highly diversified portfolio.

Only a handful of studies look at racial differences in asset composition. The general finding is that the assets owned by blacks differ markedly from those of whites. Several authors detail major structural differences in the asset holdings of blacks and whites.[14] Henry Terrell's analysis of 1967 data, for instance, entitled "Wealth Accumulation of Black and White Families," shows blacks investing a much higher proportion of their wealth, 64 percent, in functional assets (that is, homes and vehicles) than whites, for whom the corresponding figure is 37 percent. Conversely, whites invest a significantly greater share of their wealth, 63 percent, in income-producing and financial assets, in comparison to 36 percent for their African American counterparts. Blacks must commit a larger share of their wealth to functional assets and essential consumables largely because, as noted above, they start with substantially lower levels of wealth. Increasing the value of assets already owned is one basic way to generate wealth. Housing inflation creates "paper wealth" for those who already own homes, but at the same time inflated housing prices make it more difficult to buy a first home. If absolute wealth levels remain low for blacks and a comparatively small proportion of existing wealth is invested in productive or financial assets, the black-white wealth gap is likely to increase even more.

Table 5.3 Assets Owned by Blacks and Whites, 1988

Type of Asset	Percentage of Held Assets		Percentage of Households with Asset		Median Value, Households with This Asset	
	White	Black	White	Black	White	Black
Consumable Assets						
Home equity	43.3	62.5	65.6	41.6	$45,000	$31,000
Vehicle equity	5.7	10.1	86.5	62.2	4,700	2,750
Subtotal	49.0	72.5				
Financial Assets						
Real Estate	11.3	10.2	18.8	9.0	$29,000	$10,000
Businesses	7.6	4.3	10.9	2.4	25,239	10,000
Banks/Financial	16.0	7.5	75.6	42.8	5,000	1,000
Stocks	8.5	1.2	23.0	6.8	5,990	2,800
IRA/Keough	3.8	1.8	27.1	6.3	9,000	4,000
Bonds, Mortgages, etc.	3.8	2.5	60.2	32.3	700	500
Subtotal	51.0	27.5				

Note: Table 5.3 excludes households that do not report holding any wealth assets

Closely scrutinizing the composition of wealth may yield additional insights that help explain why the wealth gap between blacks and whites will increase. Table 5.3 portrays the composition and distribution of assets for black and white households who held some wealth in 1988. In findings consistent with previous studies, SIPP data show that consumable assets make up 73 percent of the value of all wealth held by blacks. Conversely, whites invest over one-half (51 percent) of their aggregate wealth in income-producing assets, in comparison to 28 percent for blacks. Refining asset categories further to include only liquid financial assets (stocks, mutual funds, bank deposits, IRAs, bonds, and income-mortgages), we find that blacks place only 13 percent of their wealth in direct income-producing assets. In sharp contrast, liquid financial assets account for almost one-third of the total white wealth package.

Table 5.3 also shows the percentage of black and white households holding a particular type of asset and reports the median value for each category of owned assets. Three noteworthy findings emerge here. First, the frequency of asset ownership for blacks trails that of whites by a considerable rate. For instance, 76 percent of whites maintain interest-bearing bank accounts versus 43 percent of blacks. Second, blacks fare especially poorly in the ownership of financial and income-producing assets. For example, four times as many white households invest in IRA or Keogh pension accounts as blacks. Similarly, 23 percent of white households control some stock or mutual fund assets versus 7 percent for blacks. Third, sizable differences remain in the dollar value of owned assets, even when we examine only asset holders. The median equity value of properties owned by blacks investing in real estate registered $10,000 in 1988 versus $29,000 for whites. The average dollar value of assets held by blacks thus substantially trails the white average in every asset category.

The figures we have noted represent the aggregate composition of assets for whites and blacks. Since a decision to invest in essential consumables or income-producing assets is partially a function of such factors as one's access to investment opportunities, the amount of one's available assets, attitudes about the future, and cultural inclination, an income breakdown may provide some important insights into the investment decision-making process. Results drawn on SIPP data not shown here generally show that as their income increases, blacks place larger shares of their resources in income-producing assets. Homes and vehicles make up over 90 percent of the assets held by poor black households. This hefty percentage goes down as incomes rise, with 62 percent of the assets held by high-income black households going into homes and vehicles. Poor white households invest their resources in income-producing assets at 5.8 times the rate of poor blacks. But at the highest income level whites' investment in income-producing assets exceeds blacks' by only 1.4 times. The racial difference in asset composition is most evident at the lowest income levels, with black portfolios beginning to resemble those of whites as income increases. These findings suggest that investment opportunity and asset availability play an important role in determining what kinds of assets one acquires, or to quote the inspired verse of Billie Holiday's "God Bless the Child," "Them that's got shall get."

Conspicuous consumption, usually interpreted as lavish spending on cars, clothes, and cultural entertainment, has often been seen as accounting for blacks' lack of financial assets.[15] A huge gap exists in the so-called comparative "income-to-savings rate" for whites and blacks (see figure B5.2), that is, the rate at which each group places funds in savings accounts.[16] Indeed, looking at savings as a proportion of annual income, the average white household saves much more than the average black household. However, this finding also contains some intriguing information regarding conspicuous consumption.

Savings generally increase with earnings. An examination of interest bear-ing bank accounts at different income levels reveals no discernible pattern for whites; that is, they do not save proportionally more as income grows. This is especially the case at the higher income levels, where it could be argued that more money is risked in higher-earning financial instruments than is placed in savings accounts. A clearer pattern emerges for blacks: as black house-hold income increases, the proportion of assets allocated to savings accounts increases. For example, savings accounts amount to only 2.4 percent of the assets of poor black households; this figure rises to 5.9 percent for moder-ate-income households, advances to 8.2 percent among middle-income house-holds, and reaches 10.4 percent for high-income households. Poverty-level white households allocate almost eight times as many of their assets to savings as poor blacks. This dramatic difference decreases substantially as income rises, with the two groups reaching virtual parity at the highest income level, where 11.3 percent of white assets versus 10.4 percent for blacks are devoted to savings. Alternative, and often more profitable, instruments for "saving" money other than passbook accounts and certificates of deposit exist (stocks, bonds, mutual funds, real property, etc.), and thus the traditional way of mea-suring savings may not be the last reliable word on this subject.

Studies find either that the savings rate of blacks exceeds that of whites or that black and white rates are identical.[17] Like our analysis, these findings are inconsistent with the conspicuous-consumption thesis, which has often been advanced to explain wealth differences between blacks and whites. Without making any definitive pronouncements concerning conspicuous consumption on the part of the black middle class at this juncture, we can safely assert that most data suggest the convergence of black and white savings behavior at high income levels, raising further issues that we will examine in the next chapter.

A Place of One's Own

Home ownership represents not only an integral part of the American Dream but also the largest component in most Americans' wealth portfolios. Therefore the topic merits special attention. Families with modest to average amounts of wealth hold most of that wealth in their home. The value of the average hous-ing unit tripled from 1970 to 1980, far outstripping inflation.[18] Thus households that owned homes before the late 1970s had an opportunity to accumulate wealth in the form of home equity, while those who did not missed an excellent opportunity.

The equity accumulated in homes constitutes the most important asset held by blacks.[19] Although specifics vary from one study to another, home ownership represents a much larger share of black assets than of white assets. Andrew Brimmer reported in "Income, Wealth, and Investment Behavior in the Black Community" that blacks held only 5.4 percent of the nation's combined home equity. The importance of home equity in the wealth portfolios of Americans is noted in table 5.3. In the 1987 SIPP data set, about two-thirds of white households enjoy the benefit of home equity, as do 42 percent of blacks. For whites and blacks alike home equity represents the largest share of accumulated wealth—63 percent of all black wealth and 43 percent of all white wealth. The median home value among black homeowners added up to an impressive $31,000, but the average white home was valued at $45,000, or one and half times as much. The black share of home equity amounted to only 3.9 percent of the total.

Table 5.4 compares home-ownership rates for blacks and whites at various income levels. Results show an overall 22-percentage point spread in home ownership, with blacks only about 65 percent as likely as whites to own a home. As table 5.4 shows, the probability of ownership increases with income. Bart Landry's *The New Black Middle Class* noted that most middle-class families, white or black, owned their homes. SIPP reaffirms that as incomes increase, more people tend to own homes. The white home-ownership rate starts at 47 percent for those living on poverty incomes and steadily climbs to 85 percent among the highest earners. The black home-ownership rate also climbs steadily, from 27 percent to 75 percent.[20] The white-to-black home-ownership gap closes at higher income brackets, so that home ownership differs by only 10 percent for high-earning whites and blacks. Clearly, much of the difference

Table 5.4 Home Ownership by Race

Household Income	Whites	Blacks	Difference
Total	63.8%	41.6%	22.2%
<$11,611	47.3	27.4	19.9
$11,611–24,999	54.9	40.8	14.1
$25,000–34,999	61.5	45.4	16.1
$35,000–49,999	76.5	66.8	9.7
>$50,000	85.4	75.0	10.4

in home-ownership rates is due to the poorer economic circumstances blacks face–they simply cannot afford to buy homes as readily as whites. We will find in chapter 6, however, that discrimination in the housing and mortgage markets cannot be ignored by anyone seeking to understand why blacks trail whites in home ownership and in equity accumulation.

Routes to Wealth and Poverty

As we have had occasion to observe, racial income differences are not nearly sufficient to explain the large racial wealth disparity that exists in America today. Perhaps, then, we would do well to turn to an examination of certain demographic and social factors often said to cause or exacerbate racial inequality, such as education, age, labor market experience, occupation, family status, gender, number of workers in a household, number of children, industrial sector of employment, and work stability.

A notable amount of research has documented the impact of remunerable human capital characteristics on earnings.[21] According to such research, equally trained, skilled, and experienced individuals receive roughly equal rewards for their human-capital investments. Chapter 4 demonstrated the powerful connection between resources and such major human-capital investments as education, age, and labor market experience. Let us now examine these factors for racial differences.

In chapter 4 we documented a relatively straightforward connection between educational attainment and income and wealth. The better educated work at higher-paying jobs, which yield not only higher incomes but larger wealth stockpiles. The issue in this chapter concerns the extent to which the impressive income and wealth gains associated with increased education can be said to obtain in the case of America's blacks. We have thus analyzed data on education and wealth for whites and blacks. Continuing to indicate methodical patterns of racial difference in resources, results show whites reaping enhanced incomes and considerably more wealth at every educational level (see table A5.2). Holding education constant, black-to-white income ratios range from 0.67 for those who completed high school to 0.99 for those with only elementary schooling. These income returns clearly indicate education's direct impact on observable levels of income inequality, but wealth adds another, more complicated dimension. Blacks who have earned the baccalaureate degree possess twenty-three cents for every dollar of wealth owned by similarly educated whites. In contrast, highly-educated blacks earn incomes that are nearly 80 percent of white incomes. Net worth ratios disclose depths of inequality, fluctuating as they do between 0.02 for those with some high school and 0.23 for college graduates.

These low wealth ratios need not deflect appreciation entirely from the positive impact of increased educational attainment. Table A5.2 also provides ample evidence of the abundant material reward education furnishes for whites and blacks alike. The difference between completing high school and obtaining a college degree for whites amounts to almost $18,000 in household income, $34,000 in net worth, and $14,000 in net financial assets. As blacks advance from a high school to a college degree, incomes increase by almost $17,000 and net worth grows by $14,000. Whites and blacks appear to share similarly hefty income gains, but blacks' inferior wealth return from education suggests that more complex dynamics are at work than we have yet been able to explain.

We need to gain a better sense of the monetary rewards that whites and blacks gain from increased investments in education. One way to do so is to examine the increase in income and wealth medians above the median for the prior educational level (see table A5.3). For example, whites who finish high school increase their household incomes by $5,774 over those who attend high school but do not graduate. For similarly educated blacks, household income increases by $2,810. Income returns for whites and blacks are nearly equal at high educational levels, but at lower levels whites gain more.

The net worth data contain an enticing double message. On the one hand, the otherwise impressive rewards blacks receive from education pale in contrast to the wealth gains for whites at progressively higher educational levels. The dividend for earning a high school diploma yields over $9,000 in net worth to whites but rewards a paltry $800 of net worth to blacks. Likewise, a college degree nets over $27,000 for whites but less than $10,000 for blacks. On the other hand, the percentage increase in wealth is quite impressive for blacks. Blacks with some college expand their net worth assets nearly four times in comparison to blacks with high school degrees. Blacks' net worth increases impressively because of their low wealth baseline, yet whites gain more in absolute terms and actually extend their already substantial relative advantage over similarly educated blacks. Only black college graduates manage—and just barely—to break into the positive financial asset column. In contrast, ample net financial assets accrue to white households at each successive educational level.

Three points merit emphasis here. First, white household income and wealth outdistance blacks' for similar educational accomplishments. White wealth accumulation at comparable educational levels is five to ten times greater than blacks. Second, increased education abundantly enhances resources for both whites and blacks. Third, even though increased education impressively rewards blacks, their returns dim in comparison to those of whites. To sum up, more formal schooling raises income and wealth for whites and blacks and narrows income inequality in the process, but improved education simultaneously enhances blacks' wealth and places them further behind similarly educated whites.

Senior Security?

The street where Etta and Henry Jones live often surprises visitors to the area. Off a major thoroughfare in South Central Los Angeles, the street is at odds with the run-down look of those around it. The Joneses' three-bedroom home is modest but brightened up by an add-on family room that looks out on a well-manicured lawn. This is their second home, purchased in 1962 with equity from their first home. Etta and Henry are retired today. Their combined eighty years of steady employment, employment that produced stable and growing incomes, pensions and retirement programs, and medical benefits, have left them with ample incomes and assets for their golden years. They both did well enough that they were able to retire early. Neither college educated nor professional, both Etta and Henry held working-class jobs; he was a custodian and she worked in clerical services. While the jobs were relatively low status, both were fortunate to work in large government organizations.

Having both reached the age of sixty-two, they now have a net worth approaching a half million dollars. This nest egg was built on years of steady work, real estate purchases, and job-sponsored savings and retirement programs. Making very modest contributions over the span of forty working years, they have seen their job-sponsored investments grow to a quarter of a million of dollars. Their first home, a duplex that brought in rental income, was purchased with a $1,500 gift from Etta's mother. Etta has since passed some of her good fortune on to her children. She has purchased a home for one son and his family, for which they pay a substantially reduced subsidized rent.

She gave the other son $4,500 for a down payment on a home. Etta sees her life as "blessed." She notes:

> I thank God every day that I'm retired and we are able to kind of do what we want, even though we don't do much. But, we're secure. I mean, we feel comfortable. I mean, anything can happen and come and wipe us all out, but I feel pretty secure.

The Joneses' good timing in the housing market has netted them handsome profits and equity. But if their homes and property were located in one of the predominantly white communities of Los Angeles, they would count their assets in the millions.

The story of the Joneses, along with that of Kevin, which we read in chapter 4, shows that one road to wealth is long-term steady employment in the kinds of work organizations that offer job-sponsored benefits and retirement packages. Rising standards of living and job and economic security in return for long-term productive work—this social contract with America applies less and less as we head toward the twenty-first century. Kevin's thirty-five years in a breadwinner federal job enabled him to save steadily and pay into a lucrative pension fund that gives him more money today than his last salary. With comfortable savings and outright ownership of his home, he was able to retire early. These accounts show how a stable job in a certain kind of work setting over a period of years can combine to generate opportunities to prosper.

In chapter 4 we saw that it generally takes years and years to accumulate substantial wealth assets, noting the powerful connection between wealth accumulation and the life cycle. Many seniors, we observed in particular, are relatively well-off, even at a point in their life cycles when incomes decline swiftly. In this chapter we will look at the extent to which the wealth and age nexus includes blacks as well as whites, and the extent to which blacks share the elderly's ostensible economic fortune and security.

The age and resource patterns for whites and blacks bring several stark differences to light (see table A5.4). Black wealth increases over the life cycle and then draws down after age 65. While this trend approximates the overall pattern, blacks' assets remain far behind whites' in every age grouping. A noteworthy observation concerns the initial disadvantage young blacks confront. On the one hand, blacks make remarkable progress in accumulating wealth assets. Median net worth expands from a paltry $500 for the average young black household to over $18,000 for the middle-aged; in like manner, mean net financial assets grow from $535 to $9,730. On the other hand, however, where income is concerned, young blacks trail whites by $12,000, a gap that closes to $10,000 for fifty- to sixty-four-year-olds. Less than $3,000 separates the incomes of white and black seniors. To conclude that income approaches parity in the latter stages of the life cycle, however, would wholly misinterpret the economic fortunes of blacks and whites. The data are misleading because white seniors possess so much more wealth than do blacks that fewer of them need to work to support themselves. The net worth gap opens at over $7,000, mostly because young blacks start out with nearly nothing, and stretches out at every successive age grouping, peaking at $70,000 for fifty- to sixty-four-year-olds. Because the average black household in each age group owns no net financial assets, one must also inspect *mean* NFA figures. Young blacks begin with an $11,000 shortfall that also expands with age, escalating to $64,000 for seniors. An apparent paradox arises: as the income gap narrows for the middle-aged and seniors, why does the wealth disadvantage expand tenfold for net worth and nearly sixfold for net financial assets? For one thing, wealth increases at a greater rate the more one starts with, so that financial assets such as stocks and bonds acquired in midlife grow over the remainder of one's life. In addition, Edward Wolff postulates on the base of evidence in "The Rich Get Increasingly Richer" that inheritances are typically received when an individual is in his or her forties and fifties, and that middle-aged blacks inherit very little compared to whites. Therefore, increasing racial inequality in the middle of the life course may have little to do with age or income.

Etta and Henry Jones are fortunate in their financial security, but unlike seniors generally, most older blacks simply do not fit the description of "economically secure," much less "well-off." The incomes of both white and black seniors fall below the poverty level, but, in contrast to many white seniors, blacks lack the wealth assets to compensate for their small income flow. Net financial assets illustrate the wealth discrepancy most vividly: even though senior black households have acquired assets throughout the life course, more than one-half are left without an NFA nest egg; and while mean NFA displays impressive growth, middle-aged and senior blacks trail behind even the youngest white households. Because social security coverage and benefits are lower for blacks, their children also face greater family obligations. The overall wealth-age connection, then, can clearly be said to obscure the black experience of a growing wealth disadvantage with age.

Certainly one aspect of the age-wealth relationship concerns an individual's work experience, how long that person has worked, at what kind of employment, and in what setting. Older workers have many years behind them, possibly benefiting from the good fortune of stable long-term employment, whereas the vagaries of unstable, low-paying jobs in the secondary sector are more likely to have affected younger workers. A very disconcerting tendency emerges when we examine the labor market experience and resources of blacks and whites. It might be called a kind of reverse treadmill effect: the longer blacks work, the further behind equally experienced white householders they fall (see table A5.5). It seems either that whites receive disproportionately greater rewards for longevity on the job or perhaps that they make their way up the career ladder more rapidly than blacks with similar experience, thus moving into higher-paying jobs. This tendency holds true for young, middle-aged, and older workers. Employment supplies income, but by itself it does not diminish inequality among those who work.

An examination of black and white years on the job reveals similar and even more pronounced differences in wealth resources. Looking at workers of all ages, one finds that the median net worth of white workers multiplies by two to four times depending on how long one has worked. Except for those who have more than thirteen years in the work force, blacks with comparable work experience accumulate almost no net worth. Blacks with the least work experience start out $4,000 behind, and this gap grows wider the longer they work, reaching $58,000 for the most seasoned workers. The assumption that inequality diminishes for blacks the longer their stint in the labor force can thus be added to the other conventional notions of racial disparity that this wealth examination seriously calls into question.

As we have noted in chapter 4, household wealth accrues as a function not only of the number of years its working members spend in the labor force but of the kinds of organizations they work for, the stability of their work, and how many people in the household have jobs. We shall thus now examine the connections between (1) the industrial sector in which a given worker is employed and resources; (2) work stability and resources; and (3) the number of people working and resources.

Etta and Henry Jones were fortunate enough to have government jobs. The Dobbses are just as hard-working as the Joneses and have also made costly sacrifices for their children, but their work experience has been uneven, with the result that, thus far, they have accumulated much less wealth. The financial condition of the Dobbses can be accounted for partly by the kind of work settings and industrial organizations in which they toil. Neither Clarence Dobbs nor Henry Jones can lay claim to a glamorous job; Clarence tends to the sick and injured as an occupational therapist, Henry cleaned buildings and offices. But Clarence does not enjoy the full-time employment that Henry did. In chapter 4 we noted the income and asset disadvantages of employment in the periphery industrial sector. Clarence Dobbs's experience is consistent with a leading theory's explanation of earnings differentials, namely, that periphery-sector jobs are less secure, more labor intensive, and lower paying. Essentially, according to one team of writers on this topic, economic segmentation divides employment into good jobs and bad jobs, and "various social institutions inhibit the free movement [of some] into good jobs."[22] Consequently, certain groups of workers, notably women and minorities, occupy bad jobs in disproportionate numbers. We will attend here particularly to (1) the disproportionate placement of blacks in the periphery sector; and (2) racial wealth differences within sectors.

Table 5.5 examines resources by industrial sector for whites and blacks. Those employed in the periphery industrial sector receive the lowest wages and possess far fewer assets, especially net financial assets, than those working in core or government sectors. Blacks' representation in "bad jobs" located in periphery industries is only slightly disproportionate to that of whites (42

Table 5.5 Good Jobs, Bad Jobs, Race, and Wealth

	Core	Periphery	Government
Income			
White	$31,974	$26,929	$33,913
Black	19,358	16,649	23,128
Net Worth			
White	41,875	31,920	52,364
Black	4,617	3,125	7,335
Net Financial Assets			
White	6,053	3,302	7,965
Black	0	0	0
Percent of Group Found in Each Sector			
White	49.2	39.0	11.8
Black	42.3	42.1	15.6

percent to 39 percent) while whites command "good jobs" in core industries more often than blacks (49 percent to 42 percent). Blacks' greatest advantage occurs in "steady" and "high-benefit" jobs in the government sector (15.6 percent to 11.8 percent).

Racial differences in both earnings and assets abound, however, within each industrial sector, as table 5.5 reveals. Inequality remains most tenacious in the core and periphery sectors and ameliorates a bit in the government sector, at least in relative terms. Blacks possess about one dollar of net worth for every ten dollars held by whites in both the core and periphery sectors. Blacks in public-sector jobs fare better both in comparison to other blacks and to government-sector whites in terms of net worth. The black-to-white net worth ratio rises to 14 percent, even though the asset gap between whites and blacks in government jobs adds up to over $45,000. Black median net financial assets, again, remain stuck at zero, no matter what the sector of employment. While the most rewarding jobs for blacks and whites are in the public sector, the NFA disadvantage for blacks in this sector still amounts to almost $8,000.

In the previous chapter we observed the strong and direct relationship between resources and work stability. Here we shall ask whether work stability differentially affects resources for whites and blacks. What we find is that black workers are prone to higher levels of work instability. The greater work instability of blacks cannot totally be accounted for by periphery jobs, nor is it a thing of the past. Blacks, for example, were the only racial group to suffer a net job loss during the 1990–91 economic recession.[23] Black employees were thus clearly let go at a disproportionate rate. They still tend to be the last hired, the first fired and laid off, and disproportionately relegated to seasonal and part-time employment. Consequently, work instability takes more of a toll on black earnings and assets, as table 5.6 demonstrates. Among those with moderate amounts of work stability (i.e., several weeks of not working over the course of a year), the income of whites averages $20,081 in comparison to $12,070 for blacks.

Table 5.6 Work Stability and Wealth

Degree of Work Stability	Income		Net Worth		Net Financial Assets	
	White	Black	White	Black	White	Black
High	$32,420	$23,545	$46,082	$6,675	$7,199	$0
Moderate	20,081	12,070	20,000	1,740	500	0
Low	6,553	5,129	1,000	0	0	0

Table 5.6 also allows us to examine the effects of varying levels of work stability on white and black financial resources with similar episodes of work stability. Race remains a significant factor even for those with high work stability, as whites control $40,000 more net worth than blacks and over $7,000 more in net financial assets. Among those with moderate levels of work stability, whites have a net worth of $20,000 and possess $500 in net financial assets versus $1,740 and zero for blacks. Among the most unstable workers, whites and blacks alike are left without resources.

In most of the married-couples families we interviewed both adults worked. We have already noted how increasingly important it is for families to send two wage earners into the work force if they desire to attain or maintain middle-class status, or even to survive. Etta and Henry Jones, a clerical worker and custodian respectively, are probably the best illustration of this social fact. Had only one of them worked, even in the fortunate employment situations they enjoyed, middle-class status would have been elusive. But by combining their incomes and benefits they were able to make it.

In the previous chapter we noted that the number of workers in the paid labor force was a major factor in determining a household's income and status. We explore this observation further now by looking at the connection between the number of earners and resource levels for whites and blacks (see table A5.6).[24] Black household incomes consistently trail those of white households with an equal number of earners by amounts ranging from $8,000 to $13,000. Turning to wealth, we find that the average household increases its wealth with additional workers. Adding a second member to the work force brings an extra $16,000 of net worth to white households but only about $5,000 to black ones. Ironically perhaps, blacks fall further behind their white counterparts as more household members work. Our data suggest that for blacks to procure white household income levels, one additional household member must enter the paid labor force; two extra members must do so to realize white net worth levels.

The information we have uncovered on wealth and work experience fortifies our conviction that traditional occupational status and class approaches obscure the institutional and historical structuring of racial inequality. We shall now turn our attention to these institutional and historical structures.

Occupation

Some sociologists think of the kinds of work people do as a sort of "master status" that confers upon its holders access to a broad range of human capital and material resources. Others employ the notion of class and often use broad occupational groupings to distinguish one class from another. One of our conjectures regarding racial differences in wealth concerns the pivotal role that work history and labor market experience play in structuring racial inequality within occupations and class formations. Table 5.7 contributes to our inquiry by inspecting occupation and resources for whites and blacks. Breakdowns in this table demonstrate persistent and growing present-day income inequalities even for householders with similar occupations. For example, white households headed by professionals, managers, and executives earn $9,000 more than analogous black households; a discrepancy that puts the black-to-white income ratio at 0.75. Figures like these supply some statistical validation to the notion advanced by Joe Feagin and Melvin Sikes in their *Living with Racism* that blacks have jobs and whites have careers in corporations. Most blacks do not find employment in upper-white-collar fields, rather they work in lower-blue-collar occupations, where the black-to-white income ratio (0.63) is lower still. The largest dollar gap arises among the self-employed, where whites outdistance their black counterparts by about $13,000 and relegate the latter to a

Table 5.7 Occupation, Income, and Wealth by Race

Occupation	Income	Ratio	Net Worth	Ratio	Net Financial Assets
		Whites			
Upper-white-collar	$39,994		$66,800		$15,150
Lower-white-collar	26,678		25,369		2,900
Upper-blue-collar	30,777		31,230		1,754
Lower-blue-collar	23,567		15,500		300
Self-Employed	29,271		100,134		43,450
		Blacks			
Upper-white-collar	$30,075	0.75	$12,303	0.18	$5
Lower-white-collar	20,011	0.75	3,178	0.13	0
Upper-blue-collar	22,984	0.74	7,125	0.23	0
Lower-blue-collar	14,894	0.63	1,401	0.09	0
Self-Employed	16,396	0.56	17,962	0.18	0

0.56 inequality ratio. While some of these figures certainly are an improve-ment on the overall 0.62 black-to-white income ratio, they also signal distress on the equality front in their patent indication of unequal rewards for similar skills and kinds of work, an inequality apparently stratified by race.[25]

Looking at wealth resources strengthens our contention, as one might anticipate at this point, because black-to-white median net worth ratios range between 0.09 and 0.24 for similarly employed householders. Households headed by semi- and unskilled whites possess $15,000 more net worth than blacks with comparable occupations. Black professional households fare well with a net worth of $12,303, but it nevertheless leaves them more than $50,000 behind white professionals. Median net financial assets, again, present the starkest comparisons. Only black households headed by professionals register positive net financial assets, and their average nest egg won't purchase a ticket at the movies. In contrast, white professionals control $15,000 worth of net financial assets, and self-employed whites command over $40,000 more than self-employed blacks. This last figure suggests that "self-employed" connotes one thing for whites and something quite different for blacks, perhaps point-ing to the difference between mom-and-pop operations in limited, segregated markets and heavily capitalized professional and retail outlets that serve large, diversified markets.

Evading the Economic Detour

With a home in an elite upper-middle-class black community, Camille and her two daughters enjoy an affluent lifestyle. A divorced former public school teacher, Camille has secured her family's level of economic comfort by way of well-paid self-employment and profitable real estate ventures. But her past prepared her for the present.

Camille grew up a pioneer. Her father, a doctor, and her mother, a dieti-tian, moved into an all-white neighborhood in the 1950s. Nevertheless, Camille was completely involved in black middle-class society, Greek fraternities, and Jack and Jill clubs (a black social club designed to provide enrichment activi-ties and imbue racial pride in youth). Earning a degree from the University of Southern California, she married an engineer and moved as far "west" in Los Angeles as blacks were allowed to "in those days." After helping her husband through law school, Camille found herself divorced with a house, two children in private school, and her teaching job as the only means of familial support.

Worried that her daughter "would not have all the things she might have had if I was not divorced," Camille seized on an opening. She "just decided she had had it up to here with the bureaucracy of LA Unified [School District]" and thought, "how could I make it happen?" Her little girl was in a specialized preschool. As Camille related:

> They needed a "feed-in" program that would prepare the kids for the spe-
> cialized curriculum. The director said we really need it, why don't you start
> one? And I said yes, but I need to eat. Gee, but after about a year I thought,
> you know, how bad could it be? It couldn't be horrible. I really needed to do
> something ... I borrowed $500 from my folks, rented a room from the church
> where the preschool was and started ...

So with these meager resources, but strong support, Camille started a one-room school operation.

> The first year went extremely well ... opening day, five students ... But by
> the end of October I had eighteen. That was enough to maintain that first
> year; then after two years, I began to get students' kids from the local col-
> lege. Because in those days, child care wasn't a big thing ... but it was begin-
> ning to become a concern. We developed a child care program. They would
> come over in the morning before they had class and come back after class.

Soon Camille had three centers and went back to school to obtain a Ph.D. in early childhood education. Today she lectures nationally on these issues, and her business is a resounding success. As she notes, "The rest is history."

Camille fits the tradition of what John Sibley Butler in his *Entrepreneurship and Self-Help Among Black Americans* calls the "truncated Afro-American middleman."[26] He describes this group as "grounded in the tradition of self-help and entrepreneurship within the Afro-American community." Camille's parents were clearly among that group who "created opportunities from despair at a time when Afro-Americans were legally excluded from the opportunity structure in America." Usually the descendants of this group do not pursue self-employment, opting instead for secure jobs in the professions. Camille had taken that road, until her circumstances changed and a different opportunity presented itself.

Family Structure

We are reminded from our interviews that family structure changes over time or over the life course. The static view that most social science is compelled to take, and that public debate emphasizes, mistakenly views one's family status today as an unchanging and unchangeable condition. The study of wealth needs to conceptualize how changing family structure over time contributes to the accumulation and the loss of assets, even though present data limit our ability to do so. Several of our interviews point to the ways in which divorce-related changes in family structure precipitate the liquidation or expenditure of assets and bring about other life changes. Carol's divorce left her with assets in the form of property, but she was forced to sell some of that property to meet family obligations and to supplement her unemployment income. Camille, as we have just seen, used resources borrowed from her parents to build a business after she was divorced. The point here is that if we looked at any of these women's lives at one point in time only, we would miss the dynamics of what changing family structure means, especially in terms of family, particularly women's economic well-being.

Let us return now to Eva and Clarence Dobbs, who illustrate a much more common set of family changes for black Americans. While struggling to survive with two jobs and three children, one about to enter college, the Dobbses remain in the shadow of debt. They are working very hard and succeeding at providing a decent home environment and the kind of upbringing they want for their children. Had Eva been part of a survey ten years ago, however, she would have been pegged then as "just another welfare mother." Living on the meager benefits of public assistance and constrained by a welfare system that not only discouraged mobility but kept families asset-poor, Eva and her children were in poverty and on the welfare rolls for ten years. This past still haunts Eva: "When I was on welfare I couldn't do anything for my family. I tried to go to college, but if I got a grant they took away my food stamps. They made me spend all my savings before I could get their little money, and they just kept me poor." Eventually, Eva did manage to take some junior college courses and enter the work force. Her marriage has helped her and her family achieve some of their goals, but the secure economic foundation she has striven to construct is still elusive. Without assets, any reduction in employment for either Eva, whose current position is being phased out, or Clarence, who already strings together several part-time jobs, will plunge them back into the depths of poverty.

Explanations of racial inequality often start, and too often end, with a discussion of changes in black family structure. In particular, more women head households, and black women head an increasing proportion of poor

ones.[27] The growing number of income-impoverished single-mother households relentlessly takes center stage in this discussion.[28] By the same token,
many authors and commentators point to the improving income status of black
married couples as evidence of positive economic changes in the black community. The previous chapter noted that married couples possess significantly
more resources than single household heads. Probing the resources held by
married-couple heads and single heads for whites and blacks, we can only
concur that there is reason for concern regarding households headed by single
women. Married couples possess significantly more resources than families
headed by single persons, regardless of race (see table A5.7). White couples
command twice as much income, three times as much net worth, and 5.8 times
as many net financial assets as single white heads. Among blacks, married
couples possess over twice as much income as single heads and over $16,000
more net worth; the net worth difference is most likely a factor of home equity,
however, because among blacks neither married couples nor single heads control any financial assets.

Considering only those households in which children are being raised, we
find several resource discrepancies between whites and blacks. Among married couples these differences are relatively modest. Whites outpace blacks
by $10,000 in income and $2,000 in net financial assets. White single-parent
heads bring in low incomes, command only about $4,000 in median net worth,
and have no net financial assets. Black single-parent households confront the
double resource jeopardy of surviving on below-poverty-level incomes and
commanding no asset resources whatsoever. Children growing up in economically deprived circumstances like these confront serious disadvantages.
They may never recover from such a formidable setback, no matter how smart,
lucky, talented, or hardworking they or their parents are.

The much-touted incomes of black married couples do indeed climb
closer to parity with those of their counterparts, adding up to eight-tenths of
white married couples' incomes versus the overall 0.62 black-to-white income
ratio. Clearly, married couples do command greater resources, and progress
toward racial parity is evident. The wealth-assets picture, however, casts this
economic success story in a different light, because black married couples
possess only about one-quarter as much net worth as white married couples.
More telling still, white married couples control $11,500 median net financial
assets, while the average black couple has no net financial assets at all. Earlier

in this chapter we observed that even among young couples blacks already shoulder a large resource disadvantage.

Never married, separated, divorced, and widowed whites all command substantially greater incomes and assets than similarly situated blacks. While the figures for single household heads as a group reveal plenty about resource allocations, the statistical breakdown of the members of the group according to their marital status divulges perhaps even more analytically important information. The wealth assets of white widows merit particular attention on several counts. First, these relatively well-off widows represent one-quarter of all the single heads in the SIPP sample. If their asset resources were removed from our calculations for all single heads, this group would be even more impoverished than our data indicate. Second, the healthy asset condition of widows is not merely a function of age or of what any given spouse may have left behind, because race powerfully stratifies the wealth circumstances of widows. This is one of several areas in which state policies efficiently protect the assets of some specified groups and not others. Those now receiving social security benefits had to have worked in occupations covered under the Social Security Act. Agricultural employees, laundry workers, and domestics, for example, became covered by social security only relatively recently. Proportionately more blacks and other minorities have traditionally labored in the kinds of jobs not covered by social security and therefore the state did not protect their assets by subsidizing their retirements. Financial assets, again, provide the starkest measure of racial imbalance: white widows command over $15,000, while black widows have none at their disposal. Indeed, even though both white and black widows have small incomes, whites are relatively well-off and blacks are impoverished. These asset findings pose a clear challenge to the contention that the predicament of female-headed households is primarily a factor of gender. In particular, our breakdown of wealth assets demonstrates the ways in which gender differences also interact with the dynamics of racial stratification.

Up to now we have assumed that the better-off economic status of married couples derives from combining incomes. It is vital to add employment to the analysis of family structure and resources under development here by looking at the labor force participation of white and black married and single households (see table A5.8). As we might expect, two-earner couples bring home the largest household incomes, over $40,000 for whites and nearly $35,000 for blacks. Table A5.8 confirms that these black and white couples draw near to income parity, with blacks attaining an impressive 0.85 income ratio. But, does a better income balance imply equality of wealth resources? Wealth holdings help to assess whether two-earner white and black couples also enjoy analogous life chances. An immediate, clear, and disheartening answer emerges: two-income black couples govern $39,000 less median net worth than whites, $17,000 in comparison to whites' $56,000. The black to white median net worth ratio stands at 0.31, which is certainly a significant improvement on the overall 0.08 ratio, but still quite meager. Median NFA figures tell what may be an even more revealing tale, as one-half of all two worker white couples command $8,612 or more, whereas more than half of similar black couples have no financial nest egg.

Our analysis of family status and resources and our portrait of Eva and Clarence suggest that the institution of marriage, per se, is not necessarily a permanent exit from poverty or a gateway to economic equality. Instead, we have found that significant racial resource stratification occurs regardless of family status, gender, or labor force participation.

Children

The black and white families we interviewed spoke in one voice about their desires and wishes for their children. While our group does not form a representative sample, it is striking that virtually every parent in it has sent or plans to send his or her children to private schools—an expensive proposition. Clearly, this is a powerful indictment of the state of public education and a telling indication of parental response in urban areas like Los Angeles and Boston. Even families with moderate incomes and few or no assets have made this sacrifice for their children. It seemed noteworthy to us that when we asked parents what they would do if they had ample resources, their first thought went to expanding their children's range of opportunities and choices. Parents wanted their children to have the chance to get a good education, to go to the right college, and to start their lives on the "right track." Assets were viewed as crucial to fulfilling these desires.

As we have already noted, however, the distressed situation of white single parents and the impoverished circumstances of black single parents make it very difficult to give children a good start in the world. But to what extent do compromised circumstances prevail for most families? Information reveals that most white families rearing children function on incomes well above the poverty line, while only those black families with one or two children operate with budgets above the poverty line, and even those small black families must make do with incomes amounting to only 60 percent of those of their white counterparts (see table A5.9). The average white family raising three children calls on $30,151 in income, a sum that contrasts sharply with the $12,286 that their black counterparts have at their disposal. Inspecting wealth, white households with one child possess over $31,000 in net worth in comparison to $3,610 for black households with one child. Black children grow up in households with inadequate resources, no matter how large or small the family. To reinforce a point made in the previous chapter, the average black youngster grows up in a household devoid of any financial assets, while white kids grow up in households with small amounts of net financial assets.

As we have just seen, the most important traditional sociological factors invoked in connection with issues of race and wealth explain only part of the racial inequality gap. Keeping these factors constant, appreciably large racial wealth differences remain unexplained, and in some cases the wealth gap even widens. In chapter 6 we seek to explain why the wealth gap that creates two nations, one black and one white, continues to be America's great racial divide.

The Structuring of Racial Inequality in American Life   6

The distribution of wealth depends, not wholly, indeed, but largely, on a [society's] institutions; and the character of [a society's] institutions is determined, not by immutable economic laws, but by the values, preferences, interests and ideals which rule at any moment in a given society.

—R.H. Tawney, *Equality*

Introduction

In this chapter we begin the process of identifying and explaining the factors, processes, and structures behind the vast wealth gap separating blacks and whites. We pose the central question of why the wealth portfolios for blacks and whites of equal stature and accomplishment vary so drastically, addressing this question in three stages. The first stage investigates the extent to which human capital and sociological and labor market factors explain the racial wealth disparity. In chapter 5, we investigated how racial wealth differences have been affected by individual factors one at a time, that is, how education alone or occupation alone affects wealth differently for whites and blacks. The task before us now is both more substantively significant and statistically complicated. Our analysis must address how much of the racial wealth difference can be explained by a multiple set of factors—education, income, occupation, and so on—working together. Furthermore, we want to identify which of these factors most influence changes in wealth while simultaneously controlling for the effects of all others. Finally, we want to determine how much of the existing wealth gap between blacks and whites is related to the fact that blacks do not share the same social and demographic characteristics as whites and how much can best be explained by race itself.

The second stage brings *institutional* and *policy* discrimination from the public and private spheres into the analysis. This section focuses on one institutional and policy arena—the mechanisms surrounding home ownership, most notably, housing and mortgage markets. Home ownership is a crucial social area for several reasons. In many ways owning a home represents the sine qua non of the American Dream. Yet racial segregation still characterizes neighborhoods and housing patterns in America. The effects of racial residential segregation go far beyond the mere restriction of blacks (and other minorities) to central-city ghettos and a few isolated communities elsewhere in the metropolitan areas. Racial segregation, as Ellis Cose notes in his *The Rage of a Privileged Class*, also denies African Americans and minorities access to jobs and high-quality schools, consigning these groups to socially and often spatially isolated inner-city ghettos. We have already discussed the importance of housing equity in both white and black wealth portfolios. For most Americans, excluding the very rich and the very poor, home equity represents the only major repository of accrued wealth, leaving aside the question of whether it is actually fungible. This section explores the ways in which the denial of access to mortgage and housing markets on equal terms severely constrains blacks' ability to accumulate assets. Using the racialization of the welfare state as a guide, this section also examines how the state fosters home ownership and asset accumulation among some groups and not others. In the process, public and private policies promote residential segregation.

The third stage adds a historical dimension to our analysis. By examining the *intergenerational transmission of inequality* we are able to empirically document how an oppressive racial legacy continues to shape American society through the reproduction of inequality generation after generation. This section brings a classic sociological question to bear on wealth resources: What are the respective contributions of inheritance (parental status) and personal achievement (individual accomplishment) to the wealth resources of a given generation? That is, to what extent are the wealth resources of American households affected by the presence or absence of intergenerational social mobility? Are equal wealth rewards gained by blacks and whites who inherit occupations similar in status to those of their parents? Or do blacks and whites reap similar wealth rewards for their achievement of upward occupational mobility from one generation to another?

Generating Contemporary Inequality

The previous chapter detailed the extraordinary magnitudes of wealth inequality between whites and blacks that remain even when the two groups were matched with regard to individual key characteristics such as salaries, schooling, jobs, family status, and age. This sort of analysis demonstrates that the racial wealth chasm cannot be attributed to a single or even a few sources but is, rather, more deeply grounded in contemporary American life. A more informed and comprehensive analysis therefore needs to (1) explore how much of the racial wealth differential can be explained by a combination of these key factors and (2) identify which factors are most important in creating the wealth gulf.

To our knowledge Francine Blau and John Graham's "Black-White Differences in Wealth and Asset Composition" is the only study that examines racial wealth differences and identifies a set of factors as the reasons for those differences. Blau and Graham found that income difference is the largest single factor explaining racial differences in wealth but that income and other demographic factors could only account for one-quarter of the wealth gap. Their results indicate that "even if society were successful in eliminating all the disadvantages of blacks in terms of their lower incomes and adverse locational and demographic characteristics, a large portion of the wealth gap—78 percent—would remain."[1] They conclude that over three-quarters of the racial wealth difference appears related to race. These findings are highly suggestive but limited for a couple of reasons. First, their data come from 1976 and 1978. Second, they only concern young families (twenty-four to thirty-four years of age).

In an effort to update these findings and extend the analysis previously presented in chapter 5, we now turn to a multivariate examination of the factors related to wealth accumulation. We have seen how individual factors affect racial wealth differences. A regression analysis allows a more complex understanding of the impact of a multiple set of variables, enabling us to isolate

Table 6.1 Regression of Income, Net Worth, and Net Financial Assets

	Income	Net Worth	Net Financial Assets
Intercept	-33,035.00***	32,243.00	44,888.00***
Race	-5,176.76***	-27,075.00***	-14,354.00***
South	-3,072.80***	-9,352.00***	-1,958.15
Highest Grade Completed	831.37***	666.18**	396.29
Age	1,390.49***	-3,620.57***	-3,442.74***
Age Squared	-12.91***	72.03***	54.31***
Work Experience	-40.42	-104.33	-6.29
Upper-White Collar	3,705.02***	28,635.00***	23,841.00***
No. of Workers	11,401.00***	-10,715.00***	-9,259.61***
Household Income	—	2.28***	1.31***
Male	2,811.54***	-9,389.11***	-6,703.24***
Children	300.23	-778.70	-2,783.85**
Widow	-6,173.47***	-6,898.71	-8,581.18
R^2	.386	.203	.107
N	7,625	7,625	7,625

$*\,p < 0.05$ $**\,p < 0.01$ $***\,p < 0.001$

which factors have the most influence on changes in wealth while simultaneously controlling for the effects of all others.[2] For example, regression can examine the effect of education on wealth while simultaneously holding all other important variables constant. The first step in regression analysis is to identify a set of variables that are theoretically expected or empirically proven to have an impact on the distribution of wealth.

Table 6.1 presents the results of the regression analysis that we performed.[3] Analyses were conducted on three material outcome variables: income, net worth, and net financial assets.[4] While our focus is on wealth, the inclusion of income provides an important benchmark from which to compare the varying patterns of determinants of wealth stockpiles and earned income. The variables identified explain differences in income better than differences in wealth. The adjusted R^2 indicates the percentage of the income or wealth variance explained by the set of independent variables. Thus these variables explain approximately 39 percent of the variation in income, 20 percent of the variation in net worth, and 11 percent of the variation in net financial assets. It is tempting to interpret these results as a clear demonstration that our knowledge of the factors responsible for the accumulation of wealth is less complete than that for income. While this may very well prove to be the case, these results may also indicate that contemporary variables better predict contemporary outcomes or that social science is not yet able to precisely quantify historical factors associated with social processes like inheritance. With no way to fully assess, in the context of regression analysis, the importance of historical legacy, we can only note here that we currently have more complete knowledge of the determinants of income than we do of those of wealth.

In order to allow for an intuitive understanding of the importance of each variable in accounting for differences in income, net worth, and net financial assets, we have presented unstandardized beta coefficients whose interpretation is relatively straightforward.[5] For example, one can observe from table 6.1 that residence in the South, holding all other variables constant, carries a $9,352 penalty in the accumulation of net worth. The most important variables that contribute to the accumulation of total net worth turn out to be the following (in order of importance): age, income, age squared, professional and self-employed status, number of workers in a household, race, male status, region, and education. As human-capital explanations have posited, age and income are the most important factors explaining variation in the accumulation of wealth. Age is modeled in our analysis as both a linear function (age) and a curvilinear function (age squared) of our income and wealth measures. We know that income and wealth change drastically in the retirement years, and the curvilinear function captures these changes. Where income is concerned, the onset of retirement usually means a sudden decrease; with regard to wealth, retirement can bring forth both sudden increases and drastic drawdowns. The negative and positive effects that we find for age capture both these dynamics. However, the positive age-squared function indicates that as households age, wealth increases not in a linear but in a curvilinear fashion. We will return shortly to the topic of age and its impact on wealth accumulation.

Income is the second most important variable determining net worth. Each additional dollar of annual income generates $2.28 in net worth. Thus the net worth difference between someone making an average income of $30,000 a year and someone who makes $60,000 a year is $68,400. Professional and self-employed status also brings significant net worth rewards ($28,635). Whereas high incomes are associated with having more than one earner in the household, multiple household earners are negatively related to the accumulation of net worth. The presence of multiple wage earners in the household carries with it a penalty of $10,715. While education is surprisingly not one of the most important variables, our analysis shows that for every year of additional schooling a household can lay claim to net worth increases of $666. Not surprisingly, regression analysis emphasizes the importance of race in the wealth accumulation process. Controlling for all the variables addressed here still leaves African Americans with a $27,075 disadvantage.[6]

Regression figures for net financial assets reveal a somewhat similar pattern. In this analysis age, age squared, income, professional and self-employed status, number of workers in a household, race, number of children in a household, and male status are the most important variables. Similar results emerged in the case of net worth for the importance of age and income. However, the same investments in education that positively influenced net worth do not produce significant additional net financial assets. Inversely, residing in the South has a considerably more detrimental effect on net worth ($9,352) than on net financial assets ($1,958). Southern residence is more detrimental to net worth because of substantially lower housing values in the South. Still, controlling for what social science believes to be the most important variables contributing to wealth, the black NFA disadvantage remains substantial at $14,354.

While our regression results point to the continuing importance of race in determining the accumulation of wealth, they do not capture the racial differences in the returns that blacks and whites receive for such factors as schooling, professional status, and living in certain regions of the country. In order to get at these differences we conducted separate analyses for blacks and whites. Table 6.2 presents our results. For whites the variables just mentioned explain approximately 36 percent of the variance in income, 19 percent of the net worth variance, and 10 percent of the variance in net financial assets. This level of explanation is roughly similar to that for the whole sample. In contrast, the same set of factors for blacks explain 51 percent of the variance in income, 22 percent of the net worth variance, and 12 percent of the variance in net financial assets. These variables are a substantially better set of income predictors for blacks than for whites, but they are only marginally better wealth predictors.

For each racial group different variables, to varying degrees, are significant in explaining increases in wealth. For whites the major determinants of net worth are, in order of importance: age, age squared, income, professional and self-employed status, number of household workers, gender of household heads by males, and years of education. Far fewer variables are significant in

Table 6.2 Regression of Income, Net Worth, and Net Financial Assets in Black and White Households

	Income		Net Worth		Net Financial Assets	
	White	**Black**	**White**	**Black**	**White**	**Black**
Intercept	-35,027.00***	-18,483.00***	26,410.00	946.22	44,053.00**	-1,443.89
South	-3,006.55***	-3,384.80***	-11,060***	-19.85	2,583.97	-255.10
Highest Grade Completed	855.13***	611.57***	729.35**	470.64	435.35	382.75
Age	1,448.19***	708.72***	-3,659.62***	-1,120.85	-3,591.00***	-578.36
Age Squared	-13.51***	-5.26	75.54***	19.41	57.46***	9.69
Work Experience	-37.36	-71.45	-218.29	513.03***	-38.08	63.48
Upper-White Collar	3,674.77***	3,915.52***	30,815.00***	665.64	25,438.00***	3,689.16
No. of workers	11,522.00***	10,531.00***	-9,864.10***	-7,462.70***	-8,892.22***	-5,397.28***
Household Income	—	—	2.32***	1.36***	1.34***	0.6225***
Male	2,806.09***	2,505.28***	-10,037.00***	-771.59	-7,265.26***	1,251.39
Children	399.18	-349.51	-1,190.94	-36.65	-3,503.5**	189.68
Widow	-6,775.93***	-3,109.16	-6,102.38	-4,586.95	-9,297.58	-1,783.33
R^2	.361	.512	.194	.222	.103	.118
N	6,851	774	6,851	774	6,851	774

* $p < 0.05$ ** $p < 0.01$ *** $p < 0.001$

explaining net worth variations among blacks. Income, the number of workers in a household, and work experience are the only variables that make large contributions to wealth accumulation, two of which are also factors in wealth accumulation among whites. Income translates into more wealth for whites than for blacks. Blacks accrue only $1.36 in wealth for each additional dollar they earn, in comparison to $2.32 for whites. For both blacks and whites a breadwinner job creates more wealth, but for whites such a job is more likely to entail professional status and the higher incomes that go along with it.

The regression figures for net financial assets reveal how little we can accurately predict variations in this category using cross-sectional data and ignoring historical materials. For both black s and whites only a few variables are significant. For whites age squared, age, income, professional and self-employed status, the number of workers in a household, children, and gender are significant wealth determinants. For blacks, by contrast, only income and the number of workers in a household make positive contributions. Again, the income returns vary, with whites generating $1.34 of net financial assets for each dollar earned, while blacks generate only 62¢ in net financial assets for the same dollar earned.

Not surprisingly, the otherwise consistent finding that life-cycle effects are the most important predictors of wealth breaks down when we consider blacks and whites separately. For whites, life-cycle effects are still important determinants of both net worth and net financial assets. These strong relationships are not significant for blacks. To better understand this finding we graphed the effect of age, controlling for all other variables in the regression, on net worth for the whole sample, whites only, and blacks only (see figure B6.1). The graph reveals distinct differences in the relationship between age and wealth for blacks and whites. For African Americans age has very little effect on the accumulation of wealth. The line for blacks is almost flat, with blacks showing a positive net worth, controlling for all other factors, at age fifty-eight. Wealth increases only slightly, however, beyond that age. For whites one notes a positive net worth at age forty-nine that increases sharply as householders age. The classical life-cycle hypothesis thus fits blacks marginally at best. The strong age effects noted earlier apply only to whites.

What these results vividly show is the continuing importance of race in the wealth accumulation process. To make our findings even more graphic we can "decompose" the results of our analysis; that is, we can take the regression results for whites and blacks and insert the characteristics of whites (e.g., mean income) into the black wealth equation. This procedure assures that blacks and whites have the same level of human capital and other factors. By recomputing the black results using white levels of income, education, occupation, and so forth, we can arrive at a hypothetical level of black wealth and compare it with the actual white one. Wealth differences will no longer relate to any disparities in the wealth-associated characteristics of whites and blacks but to the way these characteristics contribute to wealth differently for blacks and whites; in other words, they will reveal "the costs of being black."

Figure 6.1 illustrates the results of our decomposition for the entire sample.[7] As is clear, if blacks were more like whites with regard to the pertinent variables, then income parity would be close at hand. The average (mean) racial income difference would be reduced from $11,691 to $5,869. This robust reduction in income inequality is not repeated for wealth. A potent $43,143 difference in net worth remains, even when blacks and whites have had the same human capital and demographic characteristics. Nearly three-quarters

Income	Net Worth	Net Financial
Differential: $5,869	Differential: $43,143	Assets Differential
		$25,794

Percent Not Explained by Controlling for Differences between Similar White and Black Households

Figure 6.1 The Costs of Being Black

(71 percent) of the difference is left unexplained. A little over three quarters of the difference in net financial assets is also unaccounted for. Taking the average black household and endowing it with the same income, age, occupational, educational, and other attributes as the average white household still leaves a $25,794 racial gap. Clearly, something other than human capital and identifiably important social characteristics is at work here. We cannot help but conclude that factors related to race are central to the racial wealth gap and that something like a racial wealth tax is at work.

The sharp critic could easily respond to these results, however, by pointing out that we have not included in our analysis a central factor that may very well account for a great deal of the unexplained variance, namely marital status. The furor over marital status in relation to the economic condition of black America rages daily. The poor economic fortunes of black families are consistently, in both popular and scholarly discussions, linked to the disproportionate share of black female-headed households. If black households are poor, it is because they are headed by single women who have not made the necessary human capital investments and who have not been active earning members of the labor force. To demonstrate the relevance of these ideas for wealth we conducted similar decomposition analyses for black and white married and single households (see figure

B6.2). For married heads, differences in wealth-related characteristics between whites and blacks explain 25.8 percent and 23.1 percent of the net worth and net financial assets wealth differentials. Remarkably similar to the findings reported by Francine Blau and John Graham in 1990, our results indicate that even if the barriers and disadvantages blacks face were leveled tomorrow, about three-quarters of the net worth and net financial assets racial wealth differences would remain. In other words, if married blacks shared income, educational, family, occupational, regional, and work experience characteristics with whites, they would still confront a deficit of $46,294 in net worth and $27,160 in net financial assets.

If white and black single heads of households were to share the same characteristics, blacks would find themselves at a $32,265 net worth disadvantage and their NFA shortfall would amount to about $20,681 (see figure B6.3). In this scenario 78.5 percent and 83.6 percent of the net worth and NFA differentials would remain. Thus, even when we examine racial differences as a function of marital status, huge wealth gaps persist. More important, while it is true that the wealth gap for married blacks is greater, the gap for black single-headed households still ranges from 70 to 76 percent of that of their married counterparts.

These large unexplained differences in wealth apparently do not result from savings behavior, rates of return, or conspicuous consumption. Any assertion that these factors could conceivably account for such huge racial discrepancies goes against all existing evidence. Our previous analysis of savings and consumption behavior provides ample confirmation of this point. Findings showed (1) that savings behavior of blacks and whites converges as blacks earn more and (2) that consumption behavior as measured by vehicles and homes does not vary significantly. Blau and Graham concur, discounting similar explanations because "past studies appear to rule out major differences in the propensity to save as an explanation."[8]

Since contemporary social, locational, demographic, and economic factors fail to explain the vast disparities in wealth between blacks and whites, the search for additional explanations must continue. Two key ingredients therefore need to be layered into our analysis: first, racial differences in housing and mortgage markets and, second, racial differences in inheritance and other intergenerational transfers.

Institutional and Policy Factors Generating Wealth Inequality
Housing

The first chapter of this book noted how federal housing, tax, and transportation policies once effectively reinforced residential segregation. These flagrant official policies ceased in the late 1960s, yet an extremely high degree of segregation persists in America's residential communities today. In *American Apartheid* Douglas Massey and Nancy Denton report just how segregated American neighborhoods are: to desegregate housing entirely, 78 percent of blacks in Northern cities and 67 percent of blacks in Southern cities would have to move to new neighborhoods. Although there are more blacks in suburbia, no significant desegregation of the suburbs has taken place. By 1993, 86 percent of suburban whites still lived in places in which blacks represented less than 1 percent of householders. Joe Feagin and Melvin Sikes remind us in *Living with Racism* that continuing segregation is not a choice blacks freely make; rather, it is a social condition that results from racial steering, redlining, hostile white attitudes, and lender discrimination. How does this enduring residential seclusion affect the buildup of housing wealth among blacks? Our discussion will emphasize three key points at which institutional and policy discrimination often intervenes to restrict blacks' access to housing and to inhibit the accumulation of housing wealth. First, access to credit is important, because whom banks deem to be credit worthy and whom they reject may delineate a crucial moment of institutional racial bias occurring in access to home mortgages. In the past several years the Federal Reserve Bank has released thorough and detailed reports in this area that provide conspicuous answers to many questions pertaining to residential segregation. Chapters 1 and 2 suggested the significance of discriminatory regulations in the mortgage-lending process; we need to link the results of this discriminatory process to how racial wealth differences are generated. The second area of potential discrimination concerns the interest rates attached to loans for those approved for buying homes. SIPP supplies an excellent database containing specific information on home mortgage interest rates. Any significant institutional bias in mortgage-lending practices and rates carries serious implications regarding who has access to the American Dream and the cost of that dream. Third, as is well known, housing values ascended steeply during the 1970s and early '80s, far outstripping inflation and creating a large pool of assets for those already owning homes. Did all homeowners share equally in appreciating housing values, or is housing inflation color-coded? Again, the SIPP database furnishes a full and detailed answer to this important question.

Mortgage Loan Rejection Rates

In 1990 and 1991, according to Federal Reserve Bank studies, black and Hispanic applicants were denied mortgage loans two to three times more often than whites. Banks turned down high-income minorities in some cities more often than low-income whites. The publication of this information helped trigger a renewed and spirited debate on whether discrimination takes place in the home mortgage market. Community activists pointed to these discrepant denial rates as prima facie evidence of discrimination by banks and urged immediate redress. Bankers insisted that none of their lending practices could be considered discriminatory, claiming that the studies did not take into account information on creditworthiness, credit histories, loan-to-value ratios, and other financial factors.

Lenders' appeals to the shibboleth of creditworthiness, however, were starting to wear thin in the face of other evidence of banking bias. Banks were under pressure in many states for withdrawing services from low-income and minority neighborhoods. As Vivienne Walt reported in *Newsday*, 3 July 1989, one New York State legislator had his office conduct a survey of how blacks were treated in Manhattan. Blacks posing as customers were denied the right to open checking accounts three times more often than whites. Why? Because they did not live in the neighborhood.

Homeowners and spurned mortgage applicants were filing lawsuits against banks, accusing them of redlining. One such lawsuit was filed in San Diego County. A black couple alleged that a bank denied them standard loan terms because the property they wanted was in a minority neighborhood. They had already qualified to borrow 80 percent of the home's purchase price. Then, the couple alleged, a vice president and loan officer of the bank conducted a "drive-by appraisal" of the property. The couple were subsequently offered a 70 percent loan, meaning they would now have to come up with a 30 percent down payment rather than the 20 percent they had expected to invest. Bank officials told them that they had to recommend a stricter loan because of the "neighborhood's problems with crime, drugs, deteriorating properties and lack of pride in home ownership."[9] This "pride in home ownership" theme is often cited as a reason for rejecting loans on houses in minority neighborhoods, as some lenders credit white neighborhoods with higher levels of such pride. Many prospective homeowners apparently must meet the house- and lawn-care standards of their lenders.

According to housing economists interviewed by the *Washington Post*, discrimination has become more subtle. It is "hidden within the decisions bankers make about who is creditworthy ... It is hidden within their relationships with black real estate brokers."[10] It is also hidden within bankers' decisions to grant only certain types of loans. Some bankers are just plain oblivious to the treatment of minorities. A Boston reporter asked a senior vice president of a large bank about its minority lending record in 1992.[11] The banker replied that she was "delighted with our progress." When the reporter informed the official that the bank had written only one black mortgage application in the previous year, the executive conceded that "we need to do much better marketing."

The Federal Reserve Bank of Boston augmented previous Federal Reserve reports by gathering information on thirty-eight additional factors possibly accounting for the racial gap in mortgage denial rates. Taking bankers' objections seriously, the study specifically inspected the previously unexamined area of creditworthiness. The report showed that minority applicants, on average, did indeed have "greater debt burdens, higher loan-to-value ratios, and weaker credit histories," and that they were less likely to buy single-family homes than white applicants.[12] These negatives accounted for a large portion of the difference in denial rates, reducing the disparity between minority and white rejections from the originally reported 2.7-to-1 ratio to roughly 1.6-to-1. After controlling for financial, employment, and neighborhood characteristics, the report found that "black and Hispanic mortgage applicants in the Boston metropolitan area are roughly 60 percent more likely to be turned down than whites." The actual denial rate for minorities was 28 percent, but the Federal Reserve analysis indicates that the denial rate for minority applicants would have been 20 percent if the race of the applicant had not been a factor.[13]

The Boston study offered some keen insights into how and why the large difference in mortgage rejections had come about. Loan officers were far more likely to overlook flaws in the credit records of white applicants or to arrange creative financing for them than they were in the case of black applicants. Everything else being equal, the report said, "whites seem to enjoy a general presumption of creditworthiness that black and Hispanic applicants do not, and that lenders seem to be more willing to overlook flaws for white applicants than for minority applicants."[14] Lenders use applicants' credit reports to measure their commitment to repaying a loan. The stability of an applicant's income stream is also an important determinant of the risk of default. Mortgage application forms devote considerable space to questions regarding the potential borrower's labor force status. Along with earnings, the lender collects information on the applicant's profession, seniority, years in his or her current job, age, and education as well as on the industry the applicant works in. Lenders incur risk related to the applicant's labor market history and experience, since spells of unemployment affect the applicant's ability to meet monthly payment schedules. Instability of income therefore increases the probability of mortgage denial. Our data corroborate, once again, the widely-held view that minorities experience more unemployment than whites. Bankers, as well as social scientists, are aware of this fact and use their knowledge of unemployment rates to lower their risk of loan default. In some respects this behavior may seem harmless, motivated by a calculated assessment of risk, except to minorities who find the inequality caused by past labor market discriminations reproduced in the form of higher loan rejection rates.

In *The Rage of a Privileged Class* Ellis Cose recounts a relevant and revealing anecdote related to him by a black bank director. Evidence was presented at a board meeting that the bank was extending significantly fewer loans to blacks with earning and credit histories equivalent to those of whites. The directors discussed the problem and resolved to make a better effort at "affirmative action." The black director tells how another board member "bluntly disagreed, pointing out that the problem had nothing to do with affirmative action, that the bank was simply not acting in its own best interest in rejecting loans that should be approved."[15] Blacks did not need special initiatives to benefit them; what they needed was simply for the bank to comply with normal banking standards.

We saw in chapter 5 that much of the 22 percent difference in white and black home-ownership rates is explained by income levels. The Boston Federal Reserve Bank study reveals that, in addition, banks unjustly deny home loans to blacks. In the absence of racial bias 8 percent of the minorities who were denied loans every year would be homeowners today. The impact of neglect on the part of banking institutions is clearly seen in minority communities in other ways. Fewer qualified families own homes, which deprives communities of stability. Construction of single-family housing is practically nonexistent, and much of the older housing is in disrepair. Some desperate homeowners, forced out of the conventional lending market, have fallen prey to unscrupulous lenders charging usurious interest rates.

Addressing a Federal Reserve conference entitled "Credit and the Economically Disadvantaged" when the Boston Federal Reserve Bank released its report in October of 1992, John P. LaWare of the Board of Governors of the Federal Reserve System pointedly told bankers that it was too late to be arguing over bias in mortgage denial rates. Instead, the time had come to remedy the situation or pay the price.

Governor LaWare told the assembled bankers in 1992 that if they did not address institutional lending discrimination, then Congress would step in and mandate corrective practices and standards. Senator Donald Riegle, chairman of the Senate Banking Committee, told the *Washington Post* that banks should be judged on the loans they make, adding that "until the regulators change the rules of the game, we're not going to see any more progress."[16] Some congressional leaders are pushing for new, objective standards that could require banks to make a specific number of loans in the minority and low-income areas they serve. This prospect angers many bankers, as one told the *Washington Post*: "We don't need more rules and regulations. If anything is going to change, bankers have to want to make it change. You can't regulate that."

A little over one year after Governor LaWare's warning to bankers, the Federal Reserve Board stunned the banking world by rejecting a bid by Shawmut National Corporation, parent of one of Boston's largest banks, to acquire a New Hampshire bank.[17] The acquisition request was denied on the grounds that Shawmut had failed to comply with fair lending laws. The action is believed to be the first taken under the Equal Credit Opportunity Act. The Fed also cited the Home Mortgage Disclosure Act, which requires disclosure of loan application rejections by race. One banking analyst said, "The Fed is sending a strong signal to the banking industry that they're going to be looking at banks' lending practices."[18]

Private community organizations have been the major force for compliance with the nation's fair lending and community reinvestment laws. The key statute is the Community Reinvestment Act (CRA) of 1977, which requires lenders to be responsive to the credit needs of their entire service area. Beginning in 1990 the federal Home Mortgage Disclosure Act required the disclosure of mortgage loan application and rejection rates by race, gender, and income. According to *Capital and Communities in Black and White* by Gregory Squires, this information coupled with CRA requirements has altered the terms of the redlining debate and handed private community organizations, especially housing activists, the smoking gun on lending discrimination. No doubt this is what led the *Wall Street Journal* to campaign against these laws; on 26 September 1994 that paper referred to CRA data collection as "racial paperwork" and called its public disclosure a "political sledgehammer."

Interest Rate Differentials

Studies clearly demonstrate banks' discriminatory practices in approving home loans, and the Federal Reserve system is now sending pointed messages to member banks encouraging them to implement remedial programs. To this emerging picture we can now add information that suggests the existence of racial barriers to wealth accumulation even for those able to obtain home mortgages. Using information from SIPP, we investigated the mortgage interest rates banks charge their white and black customers. We surveyed all mortgages and all mortgages backed by the Federal Housing Administration (FHA) or Veterans Administration (VA). This procedure separates home loans into two types: (1) those wholly within the purview of the private banking sector and (2) those bank loans reviewed or regulated by governmental agencies. This provides a look at home mortgage bias in both the presence and the absence of government review and regulations. We assumed that, of their own accord, commercial banks perform in a more discriminatory fashion, as they have been shown to do at the mortgage approval stage.

Table 6.3 displays tangible racial differences in mortgage rates uncovered by our survey. Overall, blacks pay a 0.54 percent higher rate on home mortgages than whites. A half-point discrepancy may not seem like much, but consider its long-term effects: a half-point difference on the median black home mortgage of $35,000 adds up to $3,951 over the course of a twenty-five-year loan. Every black homeowner thus is deprived of nearly $4,000, money that potentially

Table 6.3 Racial Differences in Mortgage Rates

	Whites	Blacks	Difference
% homeowners	62%	40%	22%
Mortgage rate	9.07	9.614	0.54
Non-FHA/VA rate	9.19	10.11	0.92

could have been invested in financial instruments earning interest and accruing further capital. On home loans made without FHA or VA participation blacks pay nearly a full percentage point more, 10.11 versus 9.19 percent.

The black-white interest rate differential could reasonably be explained by several factors, most notably, income levels, the year in which a home was bought, the age of the mortgage holder, and "creditworthiness." We examined all home loans for these factors with the exception of creditworthiness (see table A6.5). Our findings supply clear evidence that racial differences persist regardless of income level, when the home was purchased, or the age of its purchaser. Interestingly, minimal rate differentials (0.1) were found among low-income homeowners. Blacks who bought homes between 1979 and 1988 paid 0.4 percent higher loan rates than whites. Rate differentials before 1978 were larger. Blacks under thirty years of age paid a full percentage point more than similar young whites. Findings based on the date of a loan suggest an alleviation of discrimination in recent years, but the age data indicate that young, presumably better-off blacks will still spend twenty-five to thirty years paying commercial banks 1 percent higher interest rates than whites.

We performed a regression analysis to determine if the racial differences in interest rates we discovered were actually dependent on other, non-race-related factors that might cause rates to vary. Our results are shown in table A6.6, which analyzes other important components of interest rate differences among all those with first mortgages.[19] Results confirm that even when one controls for other variables, race proves to be a powerful determinant of interest rates; coming in third after the year in which the home was purchased and FHA or VA financing.

As a narrowly defined legitimate concern, creditworthiness, the banking industry's way of perceiving risk, remains as the only institutionally logical nonracial justification for systematic discrimination in home interest rates. Banks insist that their standards help them make sound business decisions, decisions that enable them to keep their institutions financially viable. Creditworthiness represents a legitimate partial explanation of the interest rate differences between blacks and whites, but even in its absence significant discrimination would remain.

One way to approach the question of the racial gap in interest rates is to ask whether people in minority communities are indeed higher-risk borrowers than people in the white community. Because of the difficulties minorities face in securing mortgage loans from conventional banks, minorities finance homes more often from finance companies that charge higher interest rates than do whites. The Federal Reserve Bank looked into this matter in 1983 and again in 1986 by examining the financial condition of those who borrow from conventional banks and those who borrow from finance companies, both white and black. According to the *Boston Globe*, 28 May 1991, their study showed that borrowers from conventional, lower-interest lenders have financial resources equivalent to those of borrowers from finance companies charging higher interest.

Why, then, are minority borrowers doing business with finance companies, which charge much higher interest than banks? One reason is location. Banking industry experts and housing activists agree that to a large extent finance companies are more likely to operate in minority neighborhoods than full-service banks. Many conventional banks have deserted minority inner-city communities, leaving a large unserved need that finance corporations have stepped in to serve. This is in part a classic case of biased perceptions on the part of the banking community producing results that confirm their initial expectations. Minority customers are perceived as being higher-risk borrowers and are rejected more frequently for conventional loans. So they take their business to finance companies and pay higher rates than they would have paid on a conventional mortgage. In the process they actually become the higher-risk borrowers that banks originally perceived them to be. Ironically, minority customers would be lower-risk borrowers if their monthly payments were not inflated by high rates of finance-company interest.

The interest-rate numbers for blacks tell a story, but not the whole story. We are not alleging that blacks or other minorities pay higher interest rates because of intentional, sweeping discrimination. Loan rates are announced, posted, and even advertised, and loan officers do not raise rates when a minority borrower fills out a home loan application. When we approach bankers with the disconcerting information on interest rates uncovered by our analyses, they suggest several explanations for differential rates. Bankers speculate that variations in mortgage rates occur because customers purchase different loan "products," fixed- and variable-interest-rate loans, for example. Certainly not all customers go into a bank knowing the entire array of available loan products, and not all customers leave with the same information. Also, whites may be purchasing variable-rate loans, refinancing, or making larger down payments more often than blacks. Moreover, whites are more often than blacks in a position to use their assets to secure loans at lower interest rates by paying higher "points" on their mortgages.

The discretionary payment of a higher down payment or points is one thing, unwitting payment thereof is another. The *Real Estate News Service*, a newspaper of the industry, reported that buyers of modestly priced homes often pay excessive fees or discount points to obtain small mortgages. "It's purely a matter of economics," explains a senior staff vice president of the Mortgage Bankers Association of America, cited in a 1990 piece in the *Chicago Tribune*, because small mortgages are hard to sell on the secondary mortgage market and it costs banks just as much to complete a small loan as a large one.[20] Profit margins on small loans are frequently viewed as inadequate to justify the expense. Many lenders thus avoid the low end of the market; others charge more for low-end loans.[21] While such policies may well be predicated on no racial considerations, they clearly have racial effects. The practice of not writing low-end loans freezes a disproportionately larger number of minority applicants out of home-ownership, and the practice of charging higher interest rates or service fees for smaller loans costs minorities disproportionately more for the same banking service whites enjoy at more reasonable prices.

Some lenders tier interest rates for mortgages under a certain amount, increasing their rate, 0.5 percent for example, for every $5,000 below the floor amount.[22] This policy has a disparate impact on minority and female applicants and in minority, integrated, and ethnic neighborhoods. Because of tiered interest rates, minorities and low-income applicants pay more to borrow less. Furthermore, the interest rate increase can sometimes disqualify otherwise qualified applicants because of its negative effect on their income-to-debt ratio, a figure that banks use to determine mortgage loan eligibility.

Many bankers suggested that young white couples are more likely than blacks to receive parental help in buying a first house. Given the superior financial position of middle-aged and older whites, it is not surprising that the parents of young white couples are more apt to be in a position to help. Conversely, SIPP informs us that the likelihood of similar parental assistance for young blacks is minimal. This finding is substantiated by our interviews. Parental assistance often comes in the form of gifts, interest-free loans, or loans that are never paid back to help with down payments and closing costs or to reduce the interest rate a bank charges by enabling young buyers to pay higher points on their loans.

Preliminary findings from the Los Angeles Survey of Urban Inequality indicate that white home buyers are twice as likely to receive family assistance in purchasing a home as blacks. Judging by our interviews, it is rare for a young white couple to buy a home without some parental financial assistance.

This form of intergenerational wealth transfer, we believe, is crucial to any explanation of racial mortgage rate differences. Families with few amassed assets who cannot call on parental assistance probably pay higher interest rates. While the role of white parents in their children's purchase of a home somewhat moderates the notion of intentional institutional discrimination on the part of bankers, black mortgage holders still end up paying more.

Nonetheless, if creditworthiness is indeed a factor in banking decisions and these decisions consistently result in discrimination against minorities, then the criteria determining creditworthiness must be examined very carefully. In *Shadows of Race and Class*, Raymond Franklin reminds us that banks, insurance companies, and other financial institutions calculate risk factors in such a way as to "induce impersonal decisions that reinforce segregated patterns."[23] The discriminatory process may have come full circle. Because assets are a component of creditworthiness, banks regularly refuse loans to blacks with financial profiles similar to those of whites or else write higher interest rate mortgages for blacks. As a result, blacks tend to accumulate assets at a lower rate than whites. Home equity is more important in black wealth portfolios than it is for whites. It constitutes 63 percent of all assets held by blacks, thus biases in mortgage markets clearly and severely depress the total assets in the black community.

Some personal experience helped us to understand the banking perspective. In giving the keynote address at the 1992 Federal Reserve Board conference entitled "Credit and the Economically Disadvantaged," we focused on the role of wealth, race, and housing in structuring inequality in American society. The reaction of several bankers was disarming, because they liked the talk for the wrong reasons, at least to us. Some interpreted our data showing vast racial asset differentials between similarly achieving whites and blacks as vindicating banking practices that deny blacks home mortgages 60 percent more often than whites!

Institutional practices, it appears from our research, exact a very heavy toll on the asset accumulation process in the black community. Figure 6.2 projects the penalty blacks will pay for mortgage rate discrimination through the

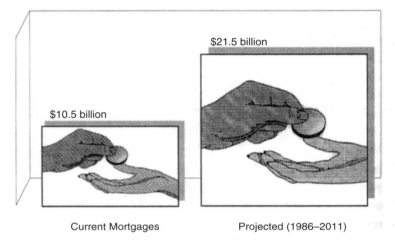

Current Mortgages   Projected (1986–2011)

Figure 6.2 Cost of Mortgage Rate Difference to Blacks

year 2011.[24] In stark terms, the half-point penalty that blacks regularly pay currently adds up to $10.5 billion in extra payments banks receive from black borrowers. Using the costs paid by current black homeowners, we project that the "price of being black" will be about $21.5 billion for the next generation of black homeowners.[25]

Racial Inequity in Rising Housing Values

Racial differences in housing values have not come under the same scrutiny as home-ownership rates or home mortgage practices. One report found that homes owned by black couples were valued substantially lower than those of similar white couples in 1980 and that the housing value differential had not shrunk significantly during the 1970s.[26] The homes of blacks in Atlanta were estimated in one study to be 28 percent less valuable than comparable houses owned by whites. Using national data for married couples, this study found that black-owned houses were $11,352 less valuable in real terms than white-owned houses in 1980 after making adjustments for racial differences in their regression analysis. Raymond Franklin reports in *Shadows of Race and Class* that blacks making middle and high incomes "live in lower-quality housing relative to their white counterparts because of the shortage of better housing in black neighborhoods."[27]

Chapter 1 recounted how federal government actions principally financed and encouraged suburbanization and residential segregation after World War II. Taxation, transportation, and housing policies promoted suburban growth. Discriminatory policies locked blacks out of the greatest mass-based opportunity for home ownership and wealth accumulation in American history. In *American Apartheid* Douglas Massey and Nancy Denton demonstrate the persistence of residential segregation. How does it affect the value and appreciation of homes? In general, homes of similar design, size, and appearance cost more in white communities than in black or integrated communities. Their value also rises more quickly and steeply in white communities. In theory, then, whites pay a premium to live in homogeneous neighborhoods, but their property appreciates at an enhanced rate. While this may mean that blacks find relative housing "bargains" in segregated communities, their property does not appreciate as much. We have already seen that blacks do not have the same access to mortgages as whites and that those approved for home mortgages pay higher interest rates. We shall now consider how these disadvantages are compounded by racial differences in housing appreciation.

A home's current market value minus its purchase price provides a rough estimate of the degree to which its value has risen or fallen.[28] We use the amount of a house's first mortgage as a proxy for its purchase price. Among those with mortgages, as shown in figure 6.3, the mean value of the average white home increased $53,000 in comparison to $31,100 for black homes from 1967 through 1988.[29] This $21,900 difference is a compelling index of bias in housing markets that costs blacks dearly. It accounts for one-third of the racial net worth difference among all homeowners with mortgages.[30] To refine our understanding of the housing-appreciation gap, we need to take into account the major factors that influence a home's increased valuation, namely, purchase price and date of purchase. A reliable comparison of black and white housing-appreciation rates therefore must include several checks to ensure comparability with regard to these factors. We have thus examined homes purchased during two broad time periods, those bought between 1967 and 1977 and those bought between 1978 and 1988. These periods were chosen to highlight the importance of housing inflation, which took off in the late 1970s and kept rising through the 1980s. Within these two periods we used median mortgage figures to distinguish more expensive homes (above the median) from less expensive (below the median) ones.

1967–1988

1967–1977

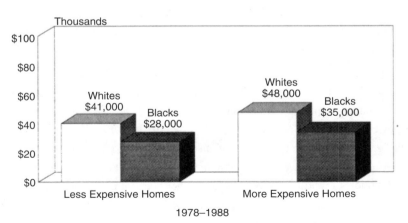

1978–1988

Figure 6.3 Housing Appreciation, 1967–1988

The two lower panels in figure 6.3 compare housing-appreciation means for whites and blacks who bought homes during two ten-year periods prior to the SIPP surveys. Examining the period of high inflation first, the median first mortgage amount between 1978 and 1988 was $52,000. Among blacks and whites who bought less expensive homes, the typical white homeowner's equity increased by $40,700 with an average black increase of $27,500. Among those buying less expensive homes, white home values grew 122 percent in comparison to 79 percent for blacks. Among those buying more expensive homes, the typical white home appreciated $47,800, or 56 percent, while the value of an average black one went up $34,900, or 44 percent.

The middle panel of figure 6.3 displays housing appreciation for those who bought homes between 1967 and 1977. These homeowners have enjoyed a longer period of equity accumulation, one including the recent era of high inflation. Whites who bought less expensive homes, with median home mortgages of less than $28,000, benefited from a $60,000 gain in home equity versus $28,700 for blacks in the same purchase bracket. And whites enjoyed a 325 percent increase in housing appreciation, while the increase for blacks amounted to 175 percent. Among those buying more expensive homes, the characteristic white home went up almost $78,000 in value and the typical black home value increased by $38,700; blacks experienced an impressive 88 percent growth in equity, but whites' home equity rose 148 percent.

A regression analysis confirms the importance of race in housing appreciation, even when non-race-related factors affecting home values are taken into account.[31] It thus reinforces the finding that similar housing investments made by whites and blacks yield vastly divergent returns—to the distinct disadvantage of blacks (see table A6.7).

Inflation and speculation in housing markets benefited all homeowners, but not all of them equally. Whether or not discrimination is intended, the racial housing-appreciation gap represents part of the price of being black in America. When housing prices tripled in the 1970s, white homeowners who had been able to take advantage of discriminatory FHA financing policies received vastly increased equity in their homes, while those excluded by those policies found themselves facing higher costs of entry into the market. Gregory Squires points out, moreover, in *Capital and Communities in Black and White* that the depressed value of their homes also adversely affects the ability of blacks to obtain home equity loans or loans for business start-ups or education. Many argue that the harm of residential segregation goes far beyond financial punishment. Ellis Cose reasons in *The Rage of a Privileged Class* that restricting blacks to inner-city ghettoes and a few isolated metropolitan pockets also denies them information about and access to jobs and better-quality school systems. Indeed, several studies demonstrate that when businesses, plants, and factories relocate or expand, they move away from metropolitan centers and locate in suburban growth zones.[32] This tendency creates a spatial mismatch between where the jobs are and where most minorities live. In *American Apartheid* Douglas Massey and Nancy Denton go so far as to attribute residential segregation to an intention to bar blacks from jobs and schools, thus linking persistent residential segregation to the conditions that create a black underclass.

This section on institutional and policy discrimination in housing supplies a rough method of tabulating the projected costs of being black in the housing market, as shown in figure 6.4. Among the current generation of black homeowners, to the $10.5 billion paid to banks in extra interest, one must add another $58 billion in lost home equity.[33] Finally, if black home mortgage approval rates were the same as those of similarly qualified whites, 8 percent of the blacks who are annually denied mortgages would be homeowners today. Hence, approximately 14,200 more blacks per year would own

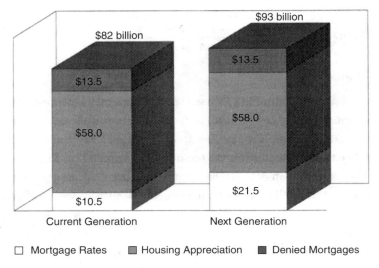

Figure 6.4 The Price of Being Black in Housing and Mortgage Markets

homes (8 percent of 177,501 applications in 1992).[34] Thus projecting current institutional bias in residential lending over a twenty-five-year period denies 355,000 qualified blacks home ownership and the opportunity of equity accumulation. Those 355,000 black homeowners would then receive $38,000 in increased home value, a figure that represents the median white housing-appreciation rate, thus acquiring another $13.5 billion.

As we see in figure 6.4, discrimination in housing markets costs the current generation of blacks about $82 billion. If these biases continue unabated, it will cost the next generation of black homeowners $93 billion. On the basis of our logic, one could take the $93 billion figure as the minimal target of public and private initiatives to help create housing assets in the black community, thus avoiding the controversial subject of making reparation for past injustices. We pursue this suggestion in our concluding chapter.

The Historical Transmission of Inequality

In chapter 2 we argued that a plethora of state policies from slavery through the mid-twentieth century crippled the ability of blacks to gain a foothold in American society. Owing to their severely restricted ability to accumulate wealth combined with massive discrimination in the private sector and general white hostility, black parents over several generations were unable to pass any appreciable assets on to their kin. We now turn to a closer examination of this process and its legacy for current racial inequality.

Inheritance and Race

Thus far our presentation has focused on contemporary aspects of inequality. To the explanation of racial wealth differences already elaborated we can now contribute tangible evidence suggesting the degree to which inequality is transmitted from one generation to another. Chapter 2 outlined our argument. We noted in the Introduction that the baby boom generation will inherit close to $7 trillion over the next twenty-five years, more than has ever been received by earlier generations. In the early 1960s less than 5 percent of the population said they had inherited substantial amounts of money, but most people with very high incomes reported having received sizable bequests. In 1970, four out of every five of the richest Americans were born to wealth.

However important they are in the lives of white Americans, and however much money they involve, inheritances are not likely to concern many African Americans. The historical reasons for this state of affairs are crystal clear. Segregation blocked access to education, decent jobs, and livable wages among the grandparents and parents of blacks born before the late 1960s, effectively preventing them from building up much wealth. Until the late 1960s few older black Americans had accrued any savings to speak of, as they likely had working-class jobs. Without savings no wealth could be built up.

Inheritance takes many shapes and forms. In our interviews people mentioned three kinds of material inheritance that had been or would be very important in determining their financial well-being. The first plays its role during a child's formative years, and consists of his or her education, experiences, friendships, and contacts. Wealth used thus to enhance a child's "cultural capital" helps provide a good start in life and can lay a good deal of the groundwork for financial success and independence later on. People often told us about the schooling, weeks at camp, after-school classes and sports, trips, and other experiences that they had enjoyed as kids and wanted to provide for their children. All parents pass along cultural capital to their offspring. Of the common enrichment that parents can provide, education is the most expensive, and it is where we found the most differences.

Alicia and Ed, who are white, come from affluent families. Ed's mother's family owned a chain of grocery stores and a small chain of dress shops. His father had inherited a substantial amount of money from his family's manufacturing concern. Alicia's mother taught school and her father was a self-employed attorney, then a state judge. Alicia went to a private school where her mother taught Latin and English, and Ed spent many years at a boarding school. Their families hoped these private institutions would furnish a better education than their public counterparts. For the same reason as well as others, Ed and Alicia will probably send their two children to private school too. Some of the parents we interviewed talked about moving to suburbs with "good schools." Other white parents, like Albert and Robyn and Stacie, lamented that they would not be able to afford an alternative to fiscally strapped and educationally unsuitable urban school systems.

Black parents also used their financial resources to provide broader educational experiences for their children than those available in public schools. Camille, the owner and director of several preschools, had taught in public schools and knew the value of being able to offer a private school education to her children. She realized that the advantage provided by private schooling is not only academic but social. Her child had interacted with students whose parents were in the movie industry and thus had earned a small but steady role in a hit situation comedy. While Carol has now fallen from middle-class status, she and her husband together had managed to put all three of her children through Catholic school. And even the Dobbses, whose financial condition corresponds most closely to the average in our quantitative data, sacrifice to send their children to a private religious-affiliated school that reflects their beliefs. Their sacrifice has paid off, for their oldest son will be attending college as a result.

The second kind of inheritance is most often bestowed on young adults and involves milestone life events like going to college, getting married, buying a first house, and beginning to raise a family. Many of the college graduates we interviewed did not pay their own expenses, especially among the white respondents. Both Alicia and Ed come from families that could afford to send them to expensive private colleges. The parents of Kathy and Bob and Stacie also paid their college tuition. Kevin proudly spoke of paying his son's private university bill. Among other things, parents who pay their children's college bills allow them to start life without huge educational loans. Albert and Robyn took out some loans to finance their education at a public university. Stacie starts her law career $80,000 in the red. Among the blacks interviewed, only Mary Ellen, whose parents were quite wealthy and who has now moved into the family business, had her college education paid for. But she is well aware of how fortunate she was: "Unlike other black students, I was able to go to college without any financial concerns." While a free college education is not often thought of as part of one's inheritance, the difference between having it paid for and borrowing for it is the difference between starting a career with a clean slate or doing so with a financial burden on one's shoulders.

Marriage and buying a first home are other milestones that often lead to wealth transfer. Our interviewees often mentioned getting cash as a wedding present, usually in the $1,000 to $5,000 range, a sum meant to help the young couple get a start in life. More important, though, is the wealth that is transferred when a couple buys a home. Other than death, a first home purchase is the event that triggers the largest asset transfer between generations. Albert and Robyn come from humble families and had to have help to buy the house they needed after the birth of their daughter. To afford this home they had to come up with a down payment of approximately $25,000. Their savings account could only provide half that sum. So they called Albert's mother. explained the situation, and asked her to advance the other half. She agreed, loaning them $12,000 with the arrangement that they would only pay her back the amount that she otherwise would have received in interest. The loan itself was not to be paid back, rather it was an "advance inheritance." When Albert's mother passes away, the sum he has already received will represent about one-half of Albert's share of her wealth.

The down payment money for Alicia and Ed's home came from her divorce settlement and his mother's estate. Both had been married before and divorced, and both had owned homes previously. Ed and his former wife could afford a small house that was bought with a $5,000 loan from Ed's former father-in-law, who "died before we could pay it back." Other interviewees told us about how their parents had paid the closing costs on mortgages, helped them to refinance a high-interest loan, or lowered the interest rate on a mortgage by paying points for them.

All of the black families we interviewed had obtained their homes with help from their parents. That help was often quite meager. Camille's parents' gift of $5,000 helped Camille and her husband buy into the most upscale neighborhood open to blacks at the time they bought their home. Carol's parents loaned her and her spouse $3,000 and helped them arrange financing through a "white lawyer." As Carol notes:

> Daddy went to a man by the name of Sherman Adelson [a pseudonym] ... It was his uncle or father that loaned us the money. Adelson was a very influential attorney in the city at one time ... He was Daddy's attorney when Daddy first went into business ... Daddy loaned us the money to get in the house and we had a second [loan] through Adelson's family.

The hard- and steady-working Joneses purchased their first home with funds from Etta's mother.

Wealth is also passed along when well-off families pay for their grandchildren's child care. Other families are able to offer in-kind assistance, in the form of income-saving services rather than cash. When family members live close by, as in Stacie's case, parents can provide child care services. Stacie's parents' assistance eases the cost of caring for Stacie's daughter Carrie while Stacie works or attends law classes. In other families, especially those without resources, in-kind parental assistance can provide valuable material, developmental, and psychological resources at once.

Assets bequeathed at death are, of course, the third and most direct form of inheritance. Among the whites we interviewed Alicia and Ed had inherited the largest sum. Ed's parents had died within the three years preceding our interview and his share of the inheritance came to more than $500,000. Albert and Robyn, by contrast, come from families without many financial assets. Robyn suggests that her mother will leave a debt. Nonetheless, they have already received an "advance inheritance" to buy their home. They also have reason to believe that Albert's mother will leave them another $12,000 when she dies. In point of fact, they are not sure about this amount: it may be the sum of her assets, or it may be Albert's share of those assets after they are split with a sibling. American society has not devised a way to comfortably address the question of financial inheritance; many of our interviewees said it is a touchy area families avoided discussing. Interestingly, one couple laughed when contrasting their parents' silence regarding financial affairs and what to do with property with the intense discussions they had with those same parents on the subject of heroic medical care and life support systems.

Among our white interviewees with living parents, most had an idea of what they would inherit. Bob and Kathy expect to receive about $50,000. Stacie is in line for about $100,000. Perhaps this sum contributes to her optimistic, self-assured, and independent attitude with regard to the debts and challenges she faces. Kevin's son will inherit about $450,000. Among the white families we interviewed everybody has inherited or will inherit hard assets.

Among the black respondents we interviewed only Camille and Mary Ellen were expecting large inheritances. Camille's parents will leave about $100,000 worth of assets for her and her children. Camille views that bequest not as money for her but as assets she expects to pass on to her children. Mary Ellen will inherit substantially more: the family business, which is valued at half a million dollars, and real estate investments approaching two million dollars to be divided among Mary Ellen and her five siblings. Since she works for the family business, it is not something she thinks about often.

We learned a great deal from our interviews about the life stages and milestones at which assets are transferred from one generation to another. They also helped inform us regarding the intent behind inheritances that are passed along before death. More systematic data are needed, however, if we are to examine other significant aspects of transmitting inequality from generation to generation.

Occupational Mobility and Race

SIPP data confirm and partially document that wealth is transmitted from one generation to another in two additional ways. First, they reveal the existence of distinctions between white and black patterns of occupational mobility. This part of the story is important, because it speaks to the comparative ability of white and black parents to pass along status to them and to help their children move up the social and occupational ladders. Second, and more directly bearing on wealth, SIPP data in conjunction with our interviews highlight the vastly different wealth rewards that social mobility confers on whites and blacks. One classic aspect of the American Dream is that children achieve a higher status than their parents. We ask if upward mobility carries with it similar levels of wealth for blacks and whites.

We examine mobility differences first by asking how much intergenerational occupational mobility was in evidence in American households in 1988. Table 6.4 displays a mobility matrix showing the degree to which the occupation of a current household head corresponds to that of his or her parent when the current household head was sixteen years old.[35]

Our results indicate a strikingly high degree of occupational inheritance for those at the top of the status hierarchy.[36] For respondents with upper-white-collar parents, occupational status is maintained nearly 60 percent of the time. By the same token, only one in eight of those with upper-white-collar backgrounds find themselves in the lowest ranking group. At the other end of the occupational range nearly one-third, like their parents, are in low-skilled occupations. Thus two-thirds of those from lower-blue-collar backgrounds achieved mobility. Those from lower-white-collar backgrounds experience a noteworthy amount of upward mobility; over half secure upper-white-collar professional and technical positions.

Things look very different, however, when we break down our findings by race. Results reveal a tale of "two mobilities." For whites the mobility figures for the general population are reproduced with a sharper emphasis on achievement and upward mobility. For blacks the achievement pattern changes significantly. The white population in 1988 evidences high levels of occupational inheritance at the top, with slightly over 60 percent of those from upper-white-

Table 6.4 Matrix of Occupational Mobility

	Parent's Background			
	Upper-White-Collar (UWC)	Lower-White-Collar (LWC)	Upper-Blue-Collar (UBC)	Lower-Blue-Collar (LBC)
Current Occupation				
All				
UWC	0.597	0.509	0.390	0.337
LWC	0.181	0.221	0.158	0.170
UBC	0.097	0.102	0.197	0.171
LBC	0.125	0.168	0.255	0.322
Whites				
UWC	0.608	0.526	0.422	0.364
LWC	0.179	0.218	0.159	0.166
UBC	0.097	0.106	0.202	0.177
LBC	0.116	0.150	0.218	0.293
Blacks				
UWC	0.362	0.294	0.201	0.280
LWC	0.298	0.265	0.178	0.208
UBC	0.106	0.059	0.154	0.118
LBC	0.234	0.382	0.468	0.395

collar backgrounds maintaining their lofty status. Over 70 percent of those from lower-blue-collar origins achieve higher-ranking occupations.

The black intergenerational mobility trend differs substantially from both the overall and white patterns. The differences are particularly salient in a number of areas. First, blacks from favorable social origins cannot pass this advantage on to their children as readily as whites, most likely because they lack the wealth assets necessary to optimize their children's life chances. Otis Dudley Duncan, back in 1968 in his "Inheritance of Poverty or Inheritance of Race," noted this pattern and it is striking, given the considerable amount of discussion and attention paid to "equal opportunity" since then, that the circumstances he observed remain essentially unchanged. Thus only a little over one-third of the black parents from upper-white-collar backgrounds successfully transmit their status to their children. Second, blacks are more likely to experience a steeper "fall from grace": twice as many blacks (0.234) as whites (0.116) from upper-white-collar backgrounds fall all the way to lower-blue-collar positions. Third, status inheritance for blacks is much more likely to produce negative results; nearly two out of five blacks from lower-blue-collar backgrounds remain stuck in unskilled and, for the most part, poorly paid jobs. Finally, rates of "long distance" upward mobility for this group are substantially lower (0.280) than for whites (0.364).

Another telling difference in mobility occurs for those with upper-blue-collar backgrounds, those from skilled blue-collar occupations. Nearly 60 percent of the whites from these backgrounds move up; among blacks, however, only slightly more than one-third do so. An astonishing one-half of all blacks who come from upper-blue-collar families fall to the bottom rung of the occupational hierarchy. The comparable figure for whites is 0.218, giving them less than half the downward mobility experienced by comparable blacks. A final indication of the difference between black and white mobility patterns resides in the tendency for blacks from lower-white-collar occupations not to make the short but important stride into professional occupations that typifies the white mobility trend. Less than three in ten blacks from lower-white-collar families prove able to advance to upper-white-collar occupations, as more than five out of ten of their white counterparts do.

Remember Kevin, who rose from electronics mechanic to production manager in the naval shipyards? The story he told about dropping his toolbox and getting all dressed up to work in the office is worth a thousand mobility tables.

> I got into that office by accident. They didn't want me. I went up to the boss, as I work on the waterfront. I'm an electronics mechanic. That's what I was. I don't want to work with tools the rest of my life. He's all dressed up and works over there. Never forget him. He says, "what do you do with your spare time?" This is how I get the job.

Kevin goes on to describe how he and his boss started talking about handball, which Kevin played. Noting that the "guy is a sports nut," Kevin recites a story told by his boss.

> "I had a father who had one leg, but what an athlete he was before he lost that leg. One day he was limping down by the high school and these students are all jumping over the crossbar. It was set at 5'7"." So here's this guy telling me this story, and I'm just a kid listening to him. "And, yes, he put his crutches down and jumped over that cross bar at 5'7" with one leg."

Kevin responded by saying his father was obviously "a phenomenal man." His boss replied with a genuine "Do you really think so?" and Kevin then spoke these words of loyalty: "If you tell me that your father with one leg or no legs jumped over a 5'7" bar, I have no reason to disbelieve you." Right on the spot Kevin was hired. As he points out:

> This was the early times of civil service. There's no exams. He says report to so and so. I get in the door. I drop my toolbox. I was up there the next Monday with a clean shirt and a shining face. Sat down in the middle of all these plutocrats who got their jobs for political appointment and every god-damned thing. And that's how I started.

To get an idea of the privileges associated with whiteness, compare Kevin's story of breaking into management with his account of how discrimination worked at the shipyards.

> There was one black at the supervisory, white-collar level [in 1962]. And one of the jobs that was given to me by the shipyard commander ... He calls me in and says, I want you to develop for me a system to tell me the extent of discrimination at the management level in this shipyard. That was the job he gave me. We produced a study by examining everyone of color. It proved conclusively there was a discrimination pattern in the shipyard over a ten-year period. I turned the study in, top secret, no one knew I did it. This mathematician did all the fancy work and I did all the exploratory work and the recommendations. I turned it in.
>   Promotion's very simple. You get in the door, but going somewhere is something else. The man that runs the department is going to have a new helper. A first-line supervisor. He appoints a panel of three people of his own department to pick someone to work in that department. In recent years they bring in a member of civil service to see if it was cricket, what they were doing. Now after they study all the records, then you write the standards for the promotion. Did you notice that the guy we like had a green eye and a blue eye? Did he? I must say I have one green eye and one blue eye and that's how it works. It worked backwards. Black, green, yellow, it never came up. It didn't have to. You wrote the man out. That's how you did it.

SIPP findings suggest that occupational achievement opens the door to higher status for many members of the general population. They also show, however, that upward mobility is heavily stratified by race. For whites we find a substantial inheritance of status at the top and, in general, at least some upward movement. For blacks we find a gnawing persistence of decades-old patterns: a comparative inability to transmit high occupational status inter-generationally coupled with a relative incapacity to move up, especially from lower-blue-collar and lower-white-collar origins. Discrimination in the work-place, a lack of access to quality education, and the exclusion from certain social networks are all implicated in this complicated process. However, for

some black Americans, particularly high-status blacks, the absence of sufficient wealth assets may be the crucial factor standing in the way of more
permanent class mobility. With this hypothesis in mind, we now look into the
relative contributions that occupational achievement and status transmission
make to wealth accumulation.

Mobility, Wealth, and Race: The Color of Horatio Alger's Skin

The SIPP data on assets, occupational attainment, and parental occupational
background provide a unique opportunity to examine a classic sociological
question: What are the relative contributions of inheritance and achievement
to wealth acquisition? Before turning to the data, however, we must outline the
logic and procedures that guide our inquiry.

The *case for achievement* is based on the notion that status and resources
reflect primarily from current, individual achievement and reflect near equal
earnings and wealth holdings within broad occupational groupings, irrespec-
tive of parental background. It is assumed from this perspective that wealth
stockpiles transmitted from one generation to the next are not the basis of
enduring economic privilege. Thus the command over resources that an occupational group has at its disposal is primarily the result of its own achievement
and not of inheritance. The key piece of evidence for the achievement hypothesis would find incomes and wealth to be roughly equal within each white- and
blue-collar grouping, regardless of parental status.

The *case for transmission* is founded on the thesis that the transfer of
parental wealth and status plays a crucial role in shaping the economic fortunes of the next generation. If substantial differences in wealth accumulation are found within similar occupational groups, and if these differences
are stratified by parental status, then the transmission thesis helps to explain
observed wealth differences.

Testing for income involves straightforward procedures: for example,
the income of upper-white-collar achievers should be relatively unaffected by
parental background. (Relatively, because of the hidden effects on income of
annual earnings on assets, meaning that some slight variation is expected.)
The test for wealth is somewhat more complicated. It is worth remembering
that only those with upper-white-collar occupations own substantial wealth
nest eggs, at a median level of $12,700. The lower-white-collar and upper-
blue-collar groups both possess very modest net financial assets, amount-

ing to $1,500 and $985 respectively. The lower-blue-collar group controls no such assets (zero median NFA). Thus there is a direct and strong relationship between occupational status and wealth accumulation.

Unfortunately, we do not know how much wealth the parents of SIPP householders owned, how much wealth householders inherited, or what parental gift-giving behavior was like. That is, SIPP (like all other surveys, to our knowledge) does not convey information on parental wealth holdings or their disposition. Our interviews were very informative on inheritance and parental financial assistance and lend much credence to the transmission argument. The case does not need to rest on a handful of stories, however. One can extrapolate social processes back a generation and assume that the powerful and direct relationship between occupational status and wealth accumulation was as valid then as it is today. We must stipulate an important qualification: because the total wealth pie was appreciably smaller a generation ago, the potentially transferable asset pool would also have been smaller. A logical test of the transmission thesis, then, compares the assets of those from the most divergent economic backgrounds who achieve similar occupational status. For example, in inspecting the wealth of current upper-white-collar households, we compare the assets of those from lower-blue-collar and upper-white-collar families. On the one hand, if neither substantial nor patterned differences emerge, then the empirical evidence supports the achievement position. On the other hand, if substantial and patterned differences appear, then the evidence lends support to the transmission argument. (Alternative explanations, such as class-centered conspicuous consumption, can be raised; unfortunately, most cannot be accurately tested with the SIPP data set.)

Chapter 4 demonstrated the powerful connection between wealth and parental status. Race deeply permeates this relationship. The effects of race surface clearly in table 6.5, which looks at household wealth and parental standing separately for whites and blacks. We can point out several conse-

Table 6.5 Parent's Occupation, Wealth, and Race

Parents' Occupation	Net Worth		Net Financial Assets	
	Whites	Blacks	Whites	Blacks
Upper-white-collar	$47,854	$21,430	$9,000	$230
Lower-white-collar	51,864	2,483	9,500	0
Upper-blue-collar	54,172	7,179	8.774	0
Lower-blue-collar	38,850	4,650	3,890	0

quential findings, even before taking current occupations into consideration. The wealth potentially transferable between generations is dramatically marked by race, with whites holding significantly more of it than blacks from similar backgrounds. This social discrepancy is confirmed and illustrated by our interviews. Of greatest consequence, the effect of parental occupation on household wealth is much stronger among blacks than whites. Whites from all backgrounds possess assets and their median net worth figures are relatively closely bunched together, ranging from $38,850 to $54,172. Blacks, by contrast, with the exception of those from professional families, control very few assets and their median net worth figures are more disparate, extending from $2,483 to $21,430. The results displayed in table 6.5 forge a strong link between a parent's occupation and household wealth for those from the highest and lowest status backgrounds. For whites and blacks from middle-status groups a cloudier pattern emerges. Those with upper-white-collar parents enjoy an unmistakably higher net worth than those with lower-blue-collar parents: $47,854 versus $38,850 for whites and $21,430 versus $4,650 for blacks.

Perhaps the most eloquent finding displayed in table 6.5 is the absence of net financial assets among black households, with the trifling exception of $230 for those from professional families. Among whites the situation differs considerably. Modest net financial assets are held in households from upper-white-collar, lower-white-collar, and upper-blue-collar origins amounting to $9,000, $9,500, and $8,774 respectively. Only whites from lower-blue-collar backgrounds trail far behind with median net financial assets of $3,890.

This information highlights two themes related to wealth, race, and family background. First, a severe average asset disadvantage characterizes those from semi- and unskilled working-class families. Second, the importance of parental occupational status appears racially stratified. Achievement endures for whites, while it apparently counts little for blacks, except for those few from upper-white-collar families. The overall wealth disadvantage of coming from a lower-blue-collar family is large, but it is less so for whites. For a lot of blacks, however, parental status does not signify much. Blacks from professional and self-employed origins possess much less wealth than whites from the lowest status families. Whites from families with unskilled occupations maintain $3,890 in net financial assets in comparison to $230 for blacks from professional families. Duncan's classic finding from the late 1960s, that' whites possess a greater ability to pass along occupational status to their children than blacks, is also reconfirmed in this study. To Duncan's lamentably still-current observations, despite public discussions and policy initiatives that supposedly addressed the problems uncovered by Duncan, we can now add that whites also possess a far greater ability to pass along wealth. This finding may be of even greater lasting importance. Blacks are less able than whites to pass on to the next generation any advantage that may accrue from occupational achievement in the present generation. The link between status and wealth thus starts to come into clearer focus. To pass status along, ample wealth may be vital; status by itself appears to be more easily transmitted to one's children when there is wealth to back it up.

The next step in our historical argument plugs occupational achievement into the wealth and parental status relationship. Table 6.6 displays information on income and wealth for mobility groups. Although the dollar figures exhibit some variation, a clearer pattern emerges when one compares earnings among equal occupational achievers who come from the highest and lowest status families (last column on the right). The ratio in question here represents the income of those from a lower-blue-collar background compared to those from an upper-white-collar background within current occupations. The ratio reveals relatively high equality levels and a narrow range, from 0.88 to 0.94. There would thus appear to be a high degree of income equality across occupational groups. These findings suggest that background matters little and that

Table 6.6 Intergenerational Occupational Mobility, Income, and Net Financial Assets

Current	Upper-White-Collar (UWC)	Lower-White-Collar (LWC)	Upper-Blue-Collar (UBC)	Lower-Blue-Collar (LBC)	Ratio: LBC to UWC
		Background			
	Mobility and Income				
UWC	$41,015	$39,700	$35,200	$37,382	0.91
LWC	30,934	30,330	27,049	27,170	0.88
UBC	22,256	33,727	30,555	31,244	0.94
LBC	24,893	27,608	23,082	23,370	0.94
	Mobility and Net Financial Assets				
UWC	$16,410	$22,288	$26,800	$11,029	0.67
LWC	2,550	2,624	5,008	1,312	0.51
UBC	900	2,707	3,790	390	0.43
LBC	916	346	200	5	0.005

achievement is the most important factor in determining income. The relatively minor variation in earnings, we suspect, results partly from differences in income-producing assets.

Wealth differentials reveal a far more complex story. Our interest is in determining whether the intergenerational transmission of status and wealth becomes the foundation for significant and enduring differences in command over resources. This stage of our analysis is focused more closely on net financial assets than net worth for one important reason. Unlike net worth, financial assets represent an unambiguous and unrestricted source of funds for improving the living standards and life chances of oneself and one's family. These resources are the kinds of liquid assets, unlike equity built up in one's home, that a family can readily tap to implement strategies of social mobility.

Two particularly pertinent observations can be made regarding the data on mobility and financial assets in table 6.6. First, if those from lower-blue-collar backgrounds are excluded, then wealth differences within occupational groups appear moderate and somewhat random. These data put the accent on achievement in the wealth accumulation process—provided one does not come from a low-status family.

The second observation, contradictory to the first, concerns those from lower-blue-collar origins. Here the more cogent interpretation strongly supports the transmission thesis. Those from lower-blue-collar origins remain far behind in wealth accumulation, no matter how extensive their own occupational achievement and mobility. For example, professionals and the self-employed from high-status backgrounds control over $16,000 worth of net financial assets, while professional achievers from low-status families possess $5,000 less. Similarly, among lower-white-collar households, those with high-status backgrounds hold median net financial assets amounting to $2,550, while those with low-status parents possess only slightly more than half that much. The lower-blue-collar obstacle is pronounced and systematic across all current occupation classes.

While the dollar figures provide one approach to the question of the wealth disparities that hinge on parental occupational status, wealth ratios for the various current occupational groupings afford us another, perhaps more incisive way of looking at this issue. The ratio in question here represents the amount of wealth that respondents from the lowest-status (lower-blue-collar) backgrounds currently own expressed as a percentage of the wealth held by those from the highest-status (upper-white-collar) backgrounds. We propose that of all the data we have at our command the wealth ratio represents the single most appropriate and crucial piece of evidence that we can use to resolve the achievement and transmission debate. A hypothetical example will illustrate this claim. If wealth is mainly a consequence of current achievement, then those who are born into low-status families but achieve the highest-status occupations should have levels of wealth similar to those of their counterparts from high-status backgrounds. Current achievement should override family background. If those from high-status backgrounds possess greater wealth, however, then the class background of one's family can be said to exert an effect. We are most likely to witness an intergenerational transmission of wealth resources.

Wealth ratios are displayed in the lower right-hand corner of table 6.6. Among upper-white-collar achievers, for instance, those from low-status families enjoy only two-thirds as many net financial assets on average as those from professional families. Similarly, lower-white-collar achievers from low-status families possess only fifty-one cents for every dollar those from high-status families own. Median wealth ratios range from 0.005 to 0.67, showing both persistent inequality and widespread variation. The income ratios we looked at, by contrast, differ only slightly, ranging between 0.88 and 0.94. These figures indicate the importance of achievement for earnings and that of transmission for wealth. Equality reigns where income is concerned, regardless of family background, and inequality permeates the process of asset accumulation, regardless of achievement.

Let us now examine the wealth and mobility data separately for whites and blacks. Net worth data must be used here, because blacks possess zero net financial assets on average; thus looking at their NFA data would yield nothing new. Examining wealth and mobility for whites, we find that table 6.7 uncovers a precipitous and dramatic change in the overall pattern, with findings that run counter to those we have previously encountered. Among similarly achieving whites, asset differences diminish to such an extent that significant variations in wealth ratios disappear. Indeed, the wealth advantage of having high-status parents and the disadvantage of a low-status background, both prominent features of table 6.6, apparently vanish for whites. For example, those attaining upper-white-collar status from lowest-status families have a median net worth outstripping that of those from the highest-status families by nearly $3,500, while possessing only nominally less in median net financial assets ($15,526 versus $16,420). The wealth accumulation of high-occupational achievers is not directly affected by

Table 6.7 Intergenerational Occupational Mobility, Wealth, and Race

	Background			
Current	Upper-White-Collar (UWC)	Lower-White-Collar (LWC)	Upper-Blue-Collar (UBC)	Lower-Blue-Collar (LBC)
	Net Worth			
Upper-white-collar				
White	$70,850	$77,825	$89,898	$74,333
Black	17,499	7,258	11,162	19,405
Lower-white-collar				
White	30,126	31,480	38,702	27,745
Black	19,225	10,055	6,001	3,012
Upper-blue-collar				
White	32,034	32,050	45,829	35,800
Black	15,812	12,315	31,410	8,604
Lower-blue-collar				
White	14,056	26,414	25,000	20,474
Black	40,933	500	7,100	1,680
	Net Financial Assets			
Upper-white-collar				
White	$16,420	$24,370	$29,199	$15,526
Black	5	3[a]	0	280
Lower-white-collar				
White	3,400	3,940	6,380	3,000
Black	-150	0[a]	730	0
Upper-blue-collar				
White	1,100	3,190	5,215	1,850
Black	-998[a]	-849	25	0
Lower-blue-collar				
White	878	550	724	385
Black	3,070[a]	0[a]	0	0

[a] Fewer than 15 cases

family background, an observation that pertains to the other achievement groups as well. Furthermore, within each occupational attainment grouping, no overall pattern surfaces. Mobility becomes a dominant factor in the wealth accumulation process of whites, even in the case of those from lower-blue-collar origins.

Unfortunately, the small number of cases in certain mobility groups, particularly white-collar backgrounds, inhibits our ability to interpret the data for blacks. Nonetheless, the relative asset impoverishment of blacks at every mobility level severely and conspicuously depresses the overall achievement scenario seen in table 6.6. By examining the reliable and sufficient data we do have, and basing certain deductions upon it, we can confidently offer this interpretation. Blacks constitute 16 percent of the lower-blue-collar group, and 53.6 percent of blacks come from lower-blue-collar families. Removing blacks from the analysis (leaving the mobility matrix and wealth table for whites) reverses the lower-blue-collar pattern of wealth disadvantage. *The wealth disadvantage among equal achievers, then, appears to be one of race and not class.* Table 6.7 suggests that the wealth mobility matrix for blacks parallels the overall pattern, which showed the enduring resource advantage of upper-white-collar families and the large handicap faced by those from lower-blue-collar families. For example, among lower-white-collar achievers, those from lower-blue-collar families possess a little over $3,000 in net worth in comparison to the $19,000 held by those from upper-white-collar families. The pattern does not hold true throughout, however, as professionals from the lowliest economic backgrounds possess slightly more net worth than those from professional households.

The final set of data we will use to complete this section compares wealth outcomes for mobility groups of blacks and whites. Long-distance mobility is movement from lower-blue-collar backgrounds to professional status. For whites who travel this distance, the wealth rewards are substantial: $74,333 in net worth and $15,526 in net financial assets. For blacks successfully accomplishing the same feat, however, the rewards diminish considerably, to $19,405 in net worth and $280 in net financial assets. Among the most successful upwardly mobile occupational achievers, then, blacks possess 26 percent of the net worth of whites and a minuscule fraction of their NFA. There may be no better evidence of the transmission of racial inequality than these drastically disparate rewards for similar achievements in social mobility.

Figure 6.5 vividly displays the magnitude of this racial disparity by exposing the mean net worth gap between whites and blacks at selected mobility stations. Among status inheritors at the top of the mobility ladder—their parents were professionals and they are professionals—both whites and blacks are relatively prosperous. But whites are dearly better off than blacks. Whites have a $105,010 edge over blacks with the same mobility credentials. In the same way, achieving long-distance mobility—from lower-blue-collar families to professional status—reaps $66,915 more for whites than blacks. The

Mean net worth gap between blacks and whites for selected types of mobility

Figure 6.5 The White Wealth Advantage for Different Types of Mobility

medium-distance mobility from lower-blue-collar parents to lower-white-collar status also pays off more handsomely for whites, by $40,053. Finally, figure 6.5 also illustrates that climbing up the mobility ladder to professional status from skilled working-class origins rewards blacks who accomplish this important upward step with $109,998 less than whites who travel the same distance.

Several answers to the classic sociological question regarding background, wealth, and status may now be proposed. The process is not uniform; rather, the dynamics of achievement and the transmission of wealth operate unevenly and differentially. Those from upper-white-collar families start off with, maintain, and perhaps extend to their children a considerable wealth advantage. Those from lower-blue-collar families best illustrate the mobility process. Generally, the higher up the occupational ladder they climb, the more their assets increase. But their low origins also present barriers that severely restrict their ability to accumulate assets, no matter how many rungs up the mobility ladder they climb. Because blacks bring virtually no assets forward from the previous generation, the wealth they amass pales in comparison to that of their white counterparts. No matter how high up the mobility ladder blacks climb, their asset accumulation remains capped at inconsequential levels, especially when compared to that of equally mobile whites.

Our analysis of mobility and asset accumulation indicates that occupational achievement apparently benefits most clearly and effectively those from lower-white-collar and upper-blue-collar origins. It enhances the financial positions of whites from all backgrounds. Intergenerational transmission seems most clearly relevant to wealth accumulation for those from high-status families, who maintain an advantage, and those from low-status families, who are unable to overcome their asset handicap. Among blacks, the transmission of wealth inequality from one generation to another would seem to explain huge disparities in wealth assets, no matter what the extent of occupational attainment or mobility. In telling the mobility story, it is important to know the skin color of Horatio Alger's heroes.

Summary

The analysis elaborated in this and previous chapters supports a comprehensive explanation of racial wealth differences that focuses on three layers of inequality. First, inequality is generated by the contemporary American social structure through severe distinctions in human capital, sociological, and labor market factors. We have seen that racially stratified experiences in schooling, jobs and family life result in resource circumstances unmitigatedly marked by race. We estimated in the regression equations that if whites and blacks were completely equal with regard to a range of human capital, sociological, and demographic factors, then about 29 percent of the existing wealth (net worth) inequality would be explained. Remarkably, however, more than 70 percent would still remain unaccounted for.

The second layer of inequality we have addressed concerns institutional and policy factors, both public and private. In examining the practices surrounding homeownership we found that differential access to mortgage and housing markets and the racial valuation of neighborhoods result in enormous asset discrepancies. We estimate that these institutional biases deprive the current generation of blacks of about $82 billion worth of assets. Home ownership is without question the single most important institutionally sanctioned means by which assets are accumulated. At the same time, however, it is worth remembering that housing represents only one arena, albeit the most important one, of institutional discrimination.

The third layer of racial inequality in America is transmitted from generation to generation. We saw who inherited money both during the lifetime and after the death of a parent. Disparities emerged at three levels of inheritance: cultural capital, milestone events, and traditional bequests. We also saw two distinct patterns of social mobility: whites evidence a substantial ability to pass on status at the top and, in general, show some upward movement; blacks, by contrast, display a comparative incapacity to transmit high occupational status to their offspring coupled with a relative stasis on the mobility ladder. We further observed dramatic variations in the financial payoff for mobility. No matter how high up the ladder blacks climb, they accumulate very few assets, especially in comparison to equally mobile whites. Asset poverty is passed on from one generation to the next, no matter how much occupational attainment or mobility blacks achieve.

Getting Along: Renewing America's Commitment to Racial Justice

7

In America, though, life seems to move faster than anywhere else on the globe and each generation is promised more than it will get; which creates, in each generation, a furious, bewildered rage, the rage of people who cannot find solid ground beneath their feet.

—James Baldwin, "The Harlem Ghetto"

Can we all just get along?

—Rodney King, Los Angeles, 1992

Introduction: The Meaning of Money

Wealth is money that is not typically used to purchase milk, shoes, or other necessities. Sometimes it bails families out of financial and personal crises, but more often it is used to create opportunities, secure a desired stature and standard of living, or pass along a class status already obtained to a new generation. We have seen how funds transferred by parents to their children both before and after death are often treated as very special money. Such funds are used for down payments on houses, closing costs on a mortgage, start-up money for a business, maternal and early childhood expenses, private education, and college costs. Parental endowments, for those fortunate enough to receive them, are enormously consequential in shaping their recipients' opportunities, life chances, and outlooks on life.

A common literary theme shows how money debases character, love, and relationships. In *A Room of One's Own* Virginia Woolf reminds us that the absence of money also deeply corrupts. As a woman, Virginia Woolf thought that her financial inheritance would be more important in her life than even gaining the right to vote. Suppose a black person inherited a good deal of money (let's not inquire about the source) at about the time the slaves were emancipated in 1863. Of the two events—the acquisition of wealth and the attainment of freedom—which would be more important in shaping the life of this person and his or her family? John Rock, the abolitionist, pre-Civil War orator, and first African American attorney to argue before the Supreme Court, lectured that "you will find no prejudice in the Yankee whatsoever," when the avenues of wealth are opened to the formerly enslaved.[1]

Over a century and a third later Ellis Cose disagrees with this assessment in *The Rage of a Privileged Class.* His book illustrates the daily discriminations, presumptions, and reproaches to which even very successful upper-middle-class blacks are subject. Cose reminds us that the color of the hand holding the money matters. The former mayor of New York, David Dinkins, stated pointedly: "a white man with a million dollars is a millionaire, and a black man with a million dollars is a nigger with a million dollars."[2] Even highly accomplished and prosperous black professionals bitterly lament that their personal success does not translate into status, at least not outside the black community.

This notion is further elaborated in *Living with Racism* by Joe Feagin and Melvin Sikes, a book based on the life experiences of two hundred black middle-class individuals. Feagin and Sikes found that no amount of hard work and achievement, or money and resources, provides immunity for black people from the persistent, commonplace injury of white racism. Modern racism must be understood as lived experience, as middle-class blacks "tell of mistreatment encountered as they traverse traditionally white places."[3] Occasions of serious discrimination are immediately painful and stressful, and they have a cumulative impact on individuals, their psyches, families, and communities. The repeated experience of racism affects a person's understanding of and outlook on life. It is from the well of institutionalized racism that daily incidents of racial hostility are drawn.

One's sense of autonomy and security about the future is not merely or necessarily characterological; it is also a reflection of one's personal position and status. "The secret point of money and power in America is neither the things that money can buy nor power for power's sake ... but absolute personal freedom, mobility, privacy," according to the writer Joan Didion. Money allows one "to be a free agent, live by one's own rules."[4]

Mary Ellen comes from an upper-middle-class business- and property-owning black family and is well on the road to building her own wealth portfolio. She talks about how her background helped shape her attitudes toward economic security and risk-taking.

> I think that growing up as I did, I think my mindset is a little different because I don't feel like I'm going to fall back. I don't feel that. A lot of people I talk to feel that. They don't see options that I see. They don't take as many risks. You know, I could always run home to my parents if something drastic happened. A lot of people don't have those alternatives.

As the twentieth century draws to a close the mixed legacy of racial progress and persistent racial disadvantage continues to confront America and shape our political landscape. Our focus in this book on assets has yielded a fuller comprehension of the extent and the sources of continued racial inequality. But how can we use this understanding to begin to close the racial gap?

This chapter steps back from the detailed examination of wealth to place our major substantive findings into the larger picture. Our exploration of racial wealth differences began with theoretical speculations about how wealth differences might force us to revise previous thinking about racial inequality. The unreflective use of income as the standard way to measure inequality has contributed to a serious underestimation of the magnitude and scope of the racial disadvantage, revealing only one of its causes. If income disparities are not the crux of the problem, then policies that seek to redress inequality by creating equal opportunities and narrowing racial differences are doomed to fail, even when such programs succeed in putting blacks in good jobs. The more one learns about pattern of racial wealth differences, the more misguided current policies appear. One of our greatest hopes is that this book brings to widespread attention the urgent need for new thinking on the part of those in the world of policymaking. Given the role played by racial wealth differences in reproducing inequality anew, we are more convinced than ever that well-intended current policies fail not simply because they are inadequately funded and prematurely curtailed but, perhaps more important, because they are exclusively focused on income. In some key respects our analysis of racial wealth differences forms an agenda for the future.

Why Racial Wealth Inequality Persists

The contemporary effects of race are vividly depicted in the racial pattern of wealth accumulation that our analysis has exposed. We have compiled a careful, factual account of how contemporary discrimination along demographic, social, and economic lines results in unequal wealth reservoirs for whites and blacks. Our examination has proven insightful in two respects. It shows that unequal background and social conditions result in unequal resources. Whether it be a matter of education, occupation, family status, or other characteristics positively correlated with income and wealth, blacks are most likely to come out on the short end of the stick. This is no surprise.

Our examination of contemporary conditions also found, more surprisingly, that equally positioned whites and blacks have highly unequal amounts of wealth. Matching whites and blacks on key individual factors, correlated with asset acquisition, demonstrated the gnawing persistence of large magnitudes of wealth difference. Because it allows us to look at several factors at once, regression analysis was then called into play. Even when whites and blacks were matched on all the identifiably important factors, we could still not account for about three-quarters of the racial wealth difference. If white and black households shared all the wealth-associated characteristics we examined, blacks would still confront a $43,000 net worth handicap!

We argue, furthermore, that the racialization of the welfare state and institutional discrimination are fundamental reasons for the persistent wealth disparities we observed. Government policies that have paved the way for whites to amass wealth have simultaneously discriminated against blacks in their quest for economic security. From the era of slavery on through the failure of the freedman to gain land and the Jim Crow laws that restricted black entrepreneurs, opportunity structures for asset accumulation rewarded whites and penalized blacks. FHA policies then thwarted black attempts to get in on the ground floor of home ownership, and segregation limited their ability to take advantage of the massive equity build-up that whites have benefited from in the housing market. As we have also seen, the formal rules of government programs like social security and AFDC have had discriminatory impacts on black Americans. And finally, the U.S. tax code has systematically privileged whites and those with assets over and against asset-poor black Americans.

These policies are not the result of the workings of the free market or the demands of modern industrial society; they are, rather, a function of the political power of elites. The powerful protect and extend their interests by way of discriminatory laws and social policies, while minorities unite to contest them. Black political mobilization has removed barriers to black economic security, but the process is uneven. As blacks take one step forward, new and more intransigent legislative or judicial decisions push them back two steps. Nowhere has this trend been more evident than in the quest for housing. While the Supreme Court barred state courts from enforcing restrictive covenants, they did not prevent property owners from adhering to these covenants voluntarily, thereby denying black homeowners any legal recourse against racist whites.[5] Similarly, while the Fair Housing Act banned discrimination by race in the housing market, it provided compensation only for "individual victims of discrimination," a fact that blunts the act's effectiveness as an antidiscrimination tool. These pyrrhic victories have in no way put an end to residential segregation, and black fortunes continue to stagnate.

Our empirical investigation of housing and mortgage markets demonstrates the way in which racialized state policies interact with other forms of institutional discrimination to prevent blacks from accumulating wealth in the form of residential equity. At each stage of the process blacks are thwarted. It is harder for blacks to get approved for a mortgage—and thus to buy a home—than for whites, even when applicants are equally qualified. More insidious still, African Americans who do get mortgages pay higher interest rates than whites. Finally, given the persistence of residential segregation, houses located in black communities do not rise in value nearly as much as those in white neighborhoods. The average racial difference in home equity amounts to over $20,000 among those who currently hold mortgages.

The inheritance of accumulated disadvantages over generations has, in many ways, shortchanged African Americans of the rather dramatic mobility gains they have achieved. While blacks have made stunning educational strides, entered middle-class occupations at an impressive rate, and moved into political positions in numbers unheard of a quarter of a century ago, they have been unable to surmount the historical obstacles that inhibit their accumulation of wealth. Still today, they bear the brunt of the sedimentation of racial inequality.

The Substantive Implications of Our Findings

What are the implications of our findings? First, our research underscores the need to include in any analysis of economic well-being not only income but private wealth. In American society, a stable economic foundation must include a command over assets as well as an adequate income flow. Nowhere is this observation better illustrated than by the case of black Americans. Too much of the current celebration of black success is related to the emergence of a professional and middle-class black population that has access to a steady income. Even the most visibly successful members of the black community—movie and TV stars, athletes, and other performers—are on salary. But, income streams do not necessarily translate into wealth pools. Furthermore, when one is black, one's current status is not easily passed on to the next generation. The presence of assets can pave the way for an extension and consolidation of status for a family over several generations.

This is not, however, an analysis that emphasizes large levels of wealth. The wealth that can make a difference in the lives of families and children need not be in the million-dollar or six-figure range. Nonetheless, it is increasingly clear that a significant amount of assets will be needed in order to provide the requisites for success in our increasingly technologically minded society. Technological change and the new organization of jobs have challenged our traditional conception of how to prepare for a career and what to expect from it. Education in the future will be lifelong, as technological jobs change at a rapid pace. Assets will play an important role in allowing people to take advantage of training and retraining opportunities. In the economy of the twenty-first century children will require a solid educational foundation, and parents will most likely need to develop new skills on a regular basis. The presence or absence of assets will have much to say about the mobility patterns of the future.

Second, our investigation of wealth has revealed deeper, historically rooted economic cleavages between the races than were previously believed to exist. The interaction of race and class in the wealth accumulation process is clear. Historical practices, racist in their essence, have produced class hierarchies that, on the contemporary scene, reproduce wealth inequality. As important, contemporary racial disadvantages deprive those in the black middle class from building on their wealth assets at the same pace as similarly situated white Americans. The shadow of race falls most darkly, however, on the black underclass, whose members find themselves at the bottom of the economic hierarchy. Their inability to accumulate assets is thus grounded primarily in their low-class backgrounds. The wealth deficit of the black middle class, by contrast, is affected more by the racial character of certain policies deriving in part from the fears and anxieties that whites harbor regarding lower-class blacks than by the actual class background of middle-class blacks. As Raymond Franklin suggests in his *Shadows of Race and Class*:

> The overcrowding of blacks in the lower class … casts a shadow on middle-class members of the black population that have credentials but are excluded and discriminated against on racial grounds.

Given the mutually reinforcing and historically accumulated race and class barriers that blacks encounter in attempting to achieve a measure of economic security, we argue that a focus on job opportunity is not sufficient to the task of eradicating racial disadvantage in America. Equal opportunity, even in the best of circumstances, does not lead to equality. This is a double-edged statement. First, we believe that equal opportunity policies and programs, when given a chance, do succeed in lowering some of the more blatant barriers to black advancement. But given the historically sedimented nature of racial wealth disparities, a focus on equal opportunity will only yield partial results. Blacks will make some gains, but so will whites, with initial inequalities persisting at another level. As blacks get better jobs and higher incomes, whites also advance. Thus, as Edwin Dorn points out in *Rules and Racial Equality*:

> To say that current inequality is the result of discrimination against blacks is to state only half the problem. The other half—is discrimination in favor of whites. It follows that merely eliminating discrimination is insufficient. The very direction of bias must be reversed, at least temporarily. If we wish to eliminate substantive inequality we waste effort when we debate whether some form of special treatment for the disadvantaged group is necessary. What we must debate is how it can be accomplished.

How do we link the opportunity structure to policies that promote asset formation and begin to close the wealth gap? In our view we must take a three-pronged approach. First, we must directly address the historically generated as well as current institutional disadvantages that limit the ability of blacks, as a group, to accumulate wealth resources. Second, we must resolutely promote asset acquisition among those at the bottom of the social structure who have been locked out of the wealth accumulation process, be they black or white.

Third, we must take aim at the massive concentration of wealth that is held by the richest Americans. Without redistributing America's wealth, we will not succeed at creating a more just society. Even as we advance this agenda, policies that safeguard equal opportunity must be defended. In short, we must make racial justice a national priority.

Toward a More Equal Equality

Our recommendations are designed to move the discourse on race in America beyond "equality of opportunity" and toward the more controversial notion of "equality of achievement." The traditional debate in this area is between fair shakes and fair shares. The thrust of our examination allows us to break into this debate with a different perspective. We have demonstrated that equal achievement does not return equal wealth rewards—indeed, our results have shown vast inequality. Of course, this may simply be another way of saying that wealth is not only a function of achievement; rather, it can rise or fall in accordance with racially differential state policies and in the presence or absence of an intergenerational bequest.

We are not left, however, with a pessimistic, nothing-can-be-done message. Instead, the evidence we have presented clearly suggests the need for new approaches to the goal of equality. We have many ideas related to this topic and several concrete suggestions for change than can lead to increased wealth for black and poor families. On the individual and family level, proposals are already on the table concerning the development of asset-based policies for welfare, housing, education, business, and retirement.[6] On the institutional level we have a whole series of recommendations on how to tighten up the enforcement of existing laws that supposedly prohibit racial discrimination on the part of banks and saving and loans. After presenting those recommendations we shall broach the sensitive, yet wholly defensible strategy of racial reparations. Then we will reflect on the leadership role that the black community must play in closing the wealth gap.

Promoting Asset Foundation for Individuals and Families

In the United States, as in advanced welfare states the world over, social policies for the poor primarily focus on ways to maintain an essential supply of consumptive services like housing, food, heat, clothing, health care, and education. Welfare is premised on the notion that families from time to time or on a more permanent basis lack adequate income sources to furnish these goods and services, in which case the government steps in to fill the breach. Questions about how well, adequately, or even if government should perform this function fuel public policy concerns.

In *Assets and the Poor* Michael Sherraden challenges conventional wisdom regarding the efficacy of welfare measures designed to reduce poverty and offers a fresh and imaginative approach to a persistent problem. He argues that the welfare state in its current and historical guise has not fundamentally reduced poverty or class or racial divisions and that it has not stimulated economic growth. He identifies a focus on income as the theoretically unquestioned and deficient basis of an imperfect welfare policy. Welfare as we know it provides income maintenance for the poor; welfare policies for the nonpoor, by contrast, emphasize tax and fiscal measures that facilitate the acquisition of wealth. Sherraden suggests that "asset accumulation and investment, rather than income and consumption, are the keys to leaving poverty," concluding that "welfare policy should promote asset accumulation—stakeholding—by the poor."[7] Welfare for the poor should be designed to provide the same capacity for asset accumulation that tax expenditures now offer the nonpoor. By giving individuals a "stake" in their society, Sherraden believes that this type of policy will channel them along more stable and productive paths. Sherraden's asset-based welfare policy combines maintenance of the consumptive goods and services with economic development. While the claim that stakeholding would provide a wide range of psychological and behavioral benefits is probably overly optimistic, and too deterministic in our view, Sherraden is clearly onto something.

Our analysis of assets and Sherraden's bold challenge to existing welfare policies spring from similar concerns, namely, that a family's life chances and opportunities emanate from the resources, or lack thereof, at its command. Sherraden's critique of the income-maintaining and consumptive welfare state leads him to advocate asset-based welfare policies. Our work points to how the welfare state has developed along racial lines, grafting new layers of accumulated disadvantage onto inequalities inherited from the past. It corroborates Sherraden's findings on the subject of asset accumulation among members of the middle class and the exclusion of the poor from the asset game. But it also shows how a racialized welfare state, both historically and in modern times, has either systematically excluded African Americans or made it very difficult for them to accumulate assets. Furthermore, our examination of assets reveals that assets, or the lack thereof, are a paramount issue: one in three American families possesses no assets whatsoever, and only 45 percent possess enough to live above the poverty line for three months in times of no income.

A number of policy implications follow from our focus on resources, economic well-being, and the racialization of the welfare state. Existing programs such as AFDC must be reexamined. In particular, the amount of assets an AFDC recipient may hold and remain eligible for benefits must be increased. Poor people should not be forced to draw down existing assets in order to meet draconian eligibility requirements any more than seniors should have to pass an asset-means test to receive social security. Personal and business assets should be separated so that recipients can engage in self-employment activities. The work-search requirement should be redefined to make it possible for the part-time self-employed individual to qualify for benefits as well.

Mechanisms to Promote Asset Formation

Welfare does not help young people prepare for the future, nor is it designed to. At best it allows young people and their families to survive at the subsistence level. Sherraden's *Assets and the Poor* is the most fruitful work in this area, and since its analysis of asset poverty and its effects is similar to ours, we believe that some of Sherraden's key policy ideas merit serious consideration. Sherraden suggests that maintenance income and services should be supplemented by broad-based asset accounts. In many situations, where accumulation is desirable and feasible, asset-based policies are preferable to those based on income. Some of the most promising areas include education, home ownership, start-up capital for businesses, self-employment, and funds for retirement. Each year a given sum of money could be invested in an asset account restricted to a specific purpose, and the accounts would have monetary limits. These accounts could be established at different points over the life course. Standard initial deposits could be matched by federal grants on the basis of a sliding scale for poor individuals who also meet asset criteria.

Education and Youth Asset Accounts

The global economy stresses job flexibility, training in multiple areas, and technological and computer literacy. Education, training, continual skill enhancement, lifelong learning, and the ability to shift fields are the new hallmarks of modern employability. Formal schooling is a minimum require-ment, with college education best preparing people for opportunities in the global marketplace. Blacks and the poor, we fear, are falling further behind in their quest to secure credentials necessary to qualify for the kinds of jobs and careers that lead to economic well-being. In the first chapter of this book we noted that since 1976 black college enrollment and completion rates have declined sharply, threatening to wipe out the gains of the civil rights era. The growing racial discrepancy in higher education is caused by blacks' increasing inability to afford the ever-soaring cost of college tuition, government's flag-ging fiscal commitment to higher education, and poverty rates that are more than twice as high for blacks as for whites. Without assets to fall back on, the average black family simply has no way to finance college.

Instead of asking students to assume heavy debts to foot the bill for college, Sherraden suggests establishing universal nontaxable educational asset accounts. Deposits would be linked to benchmark events: say, a one-thousand-dollar deposit at birth, a five-hundred-dollar deposit for complet-ing each grade, and twenty-five-hundred dollars for high school graduation. Student fund-raising projects and businesses could underwrite other con-tributions to these accounts. A year of military or civilian national service might earn a five-thousand-dollar deposit. While anyone could establish such an account, the government would subsidize these accounts for poor people on a sliding scale. For example, a poor child's family might deposit $250 with the government matching that amount. With the interest that they earn and their nontaxed status, educational asset accounts would be a wise investment in any child's future. The primary purpose of the accounts would be to provide resources upon high school graduation, after which funds would be available only for postsecondary education and training of the recipient's choosing. Such accounts would not only allow children from poor families to obtain a college education or other, equivalent training but also go a considerable distance toward closing the quality-of-education gap. After a certain age individuals could transfer the funds in their account to their children or grandchildren. Or they could cash out their account with-drawing only their original deposits and earnings, not the government's matched share, less a 10 percent penalty. They would pay income taxes on the full amount withdrawn.

Housing Asset Accounts

We have continually stressed how essential homeownership is to the American Dream: owning a home is not only a source of residential security, stability, and pride, but also a potential means of increasing one's wealth. We suggest here several ways to close the racial home owning and housing-appreciation gap. Homeownership rates declined significantly during the late 1980s and early 1990s. First-time buyers are edged out of the market when the rise in housing prices exceeds the rise in wages for most Americans. Down payments and closing costs are the most critical barriers to home ownership, and thus housing asset accounts should focus on accumulating funds for these purposes. We have taken Michael Sherraden's suggestions as a model of how a housing asset program might work.

Beginning at age eighteen individuals who are first-time homebuyers or who have not owned a home for longer than three years may open a housing asset account. These nontaxable interest-earning accounts would be open to everyone on the sole basis of housing status. There would be an annual deposit limit of two thousand dollars per individual account, with an overall family limit not exceeding 20 or 25 percent of the price of a region's median home. Individuals who fall below specified income and asset levels would be eligible for matching grants from the federal government, for up to 90 percent of their annual deposit. The government would thus match or supplement the deposits made by poor individuals, on a sliding scale, but would not match the deposits of those not in need. Funds accumulated in housing asset accounts would be available only for down payments and other costs associated with buying or owning a home. After ten years unused funds could be transferred to educational or housing accounts for children or grandchildren or else cashed in on the same terms we outlined in the case of educational asset accounts.

Self-Employment and Business Accounts

Self-employment is one of the most celebrated paths to economic self-sufficiency in American society. Even though self-employment is enshrouded in Horatio Alger–like cultural myths, and even though most small ventures fail within the first five years, the rewards of success, financial independence, and autonomy have been many. Severe economic restrictions have historically prevented many African Americans from establishing successful businesses. These include segregation, legal prohibition, acts of violence, discrimination, and general access only to so-called black markets. We want to emphasize the very risky nature and often low returns of self-employment. Yet, given a progressively less-favorable labor market, high unemployment rates in the black community, and the often entrepreneurial essence of the American Dream, we believe that for certain individuals self-employment represents an important path to economic well-being. Successful black businesses also contribute to community development. The absence of start-up capital is, among the asset-poor, one of the most formidable barriers to self-employment. Credit is needed to seed most businesses, and the banking record on this score leaves much to be desired. Self-employment accounts would provide another option.

We have already discussed proposals to restructure AFDC criteria and payments that would remove some of the disincentives to self-employment or the establishment of small business by poor people. Michael Sherraden's work proposes a more expansive program to encourage self-employment and business ventures. Self-employment asset trusts would be open to anyone eighteen or older to be used only for start-up money for business ventures. Annual deposits of $500 would be permitted, with an overall limit of $15,000. These accounts would be nontaxable as long they were used for starting a new business or for family expenses associated with running the business, such as child care. Income-poor individuals who meet certain asset criteria would be eligible for 50 percent matching contributions from the federal government. These funds could be used without penalty, according to Sherraden, "only after a business plan is developed and approved by a voluntary local review board made up of businesspeople."[8] Individuals could pool their accounts with others in order to launch a joint venture. Funds not used as seed capital after ten years could be disbursed, the fundholder receiving only his or her original contributions and earnings, less a 10 percent penalty; income tax would be paid on the full amount.

Removing Institutional Barriers to Asset Formation
The Homeowner Deduction

Our explication of the racialization of the welfare state draws attention to the ways in which a host of government programs and policies have historically assisted the white middle class to acquire, secure, and expand assets. One case in point is the nation's largest annual housing subsidy, a subsidy that goes not to the poor or to stimulate low-cost housing but to often well-heeled homeowners in the form of $54 billion in tax deductions for mortgage interest and property taxes. While the homeowner deduction primarily benefits the affluent, fewer than one in five low-income Americans receive federal housing assistance. Those with the highest incomes and the most expensive homes get the lion's share of federal subsidies. The Congressional Joint Taxation Committee analysis of taxation data shows that more than one-third (38.5 percent) of the $54 billion government subsidy goes to the 5 percent of taxpayers who have incomes above $100,000.[9]

The homeowner deduction has come under increasing scrutiny, however, and several reforms have been suggested. Recognizing that through the tax code the state has assisted home ownership and asset formation among certain groups, notably the middle class, that this aid has increasingly benefited the affluent, and that whites are far more likely than blacks to profit from current tax policy, many have suggested that a corrective is clearly in order. The goal of helping families purchase homes could be maintained and expanded in order to apply to more moderate income families, and thereby proportionately more minorities. Simultaneously, tax reform could place benefits to affluent Americans within a progressive context. Current home mortgage interest and property tax deductions should be scrapped and replaced by a simple homeowner tax credit available to all taxpayers, not just those who itemize deductions. The credit would apply to one's primary residence and could be capped at a specific amount or tied progressively to income, thus limiting subsidies for the wealthy while preserving them for the middle class and extending the goal of homeownership to moderate-income Americans. A homeowner tax credit could make the difference between renting and owning for millions of working families now shut out of the American Dream. Such a policy would enable more blacks to buy homes than can do so under the current tax law and thereby represents a step in the direction of greater racial equity.

Capital Gains Tax

All sources of earnings are not treated equally under America's tax laws. Most notably, net proceeds from financial assets are privileged over paycheck earnings. In 1993 the top tax bracket for wages, tips, and salaries was fixed at 39.6 percent on earnings over $250,000. Capital gains, by contrast—the profits from selling something for an amount more than it cost, whether it be stocks, bonds, homes, property, or works of art—are taxed at the more favorable top rate of 28 percent, a rate that can go down as low as 14 percent in some situations. Barlett and Steele in *America: Who Really Pays the Taxes?* refer to "different dollar bills; different rates."[10] They report that one twenty-fifth of one percent of Americans filing taxes collects one-third of all capital gains incomes. Conversely, 93 percent of all persons filing tax returns have no need to fill out a Schedule D form because they have no capital gains. We doubt if more than a relative handful of blacks are among the small affluent group advantaged by this favored child of free marketers and conservatives.

Reform of the capital gains tax would help simplify the tax forms and end an unfair subsidy designed for the rich. Income from playing the stock market should be treated just like income from work, and capital gains should be taxed at the same rates as earnings. Changes would affect only those in the highest income brackets, leaving people with modest investment unaffected.

Inheritance Tax

Donald Barlett and James Steele write in *America: Who Really Pays the Taxes?* that one of the most cherished tax privileges of the very rich resides in the ability of that group to pass along its accumulated wealth in stocks, bonds, and other financial instruments to heirs free of capital gains tax. Taxpayers who sell financial assets to fund a child's education, make a down payment on a house, or weather a financial crisis pay a capital gains tax on the increased value of their investment. But under current tax law, stocks, bonds, and other capital assets can be passed along at death and escape all capital gains. "Better still," according to Barlett and Steele, "when you inherit the stock it gets a new 'original' value—the price at which it was selling on the day you received it."[11] Thus, one can sell the stock immediately and pocket the entire proceeds without paying any capital gains tax. In large part, Barlett and Steele go on to say, "this is how the rich stay rich—by passing on from generation to generation assets that have appreciated greatly in value but on which they never pay capital gains taxes."

The wealth of many families has thus escaped taxes since the establishment of the income tax in 1924. The time has come to seriously challenge this capital gains tax exemption. Just how large is the inheritance tax break for the very rich? *America: Who Really Pays the Taxes?* cites a Treasury Department and Office of Management and Budget calculation that the very rich escaped paying $24 billion in 1991 alone because of this exemption. While Americans do not begrudge their fellow citizens the opportunity of becoming rich, they might not be so willing to accept the extent to which the very wealthy and powerful rig the rules to hold onto their wealth at everybody else's expense.

Antidiscrimination Laws

In the 1960s and 1970s Congress passed important legislation and strengthened the banking regulatory structure so that all groups would have access to credit and communities would not be written off by unscrupulous financial institutions. The Reagan administration weakened this regulatory system, and some banks read its change as an opportunity to revert to past practices and ignore or prey upon minority and low-income neighborhoods. We estimate that discriminatory mortgage practices, higher interest-rate charges, and biased housing inflation cost the black community approximately $83 billion. Both the private and public sectors have a lot of work ahead of them if they are to redress this history of institutional discrimination.

Bankers do not sit down with a map and census tract data and draw red lines around low-income and minority neighborhoods.[12] As we have seen, however, some have policies and practices that effectively do the same thing. Banks that set minimum loan amounts effectively exclude whole neighborhoods from the conventional mortgage market. Lenders must discontinue this practice.

We have also seen that the tiering of interest rates for mortgages has a disparate impact on minority and female applicants, and on minority, integrated, and ethnic neighborhoods. Because of tiered interest rates, minorities and low-income home buyers pay more to borrow less. This policy, too, must be changed.

Every good business designs a marketing strategy to capture the market it wants to serve. Lenders need to review the media they use to reach minority and low-income consumers as well as the messages they send. A bank becomes known, or fails to do so, not only by its advertising efforts but also by the services it offers to a community. A bank must be conveniently located and accessible to the consumers it wants to attract. The services it offers should be tailored to meet the needs and interests of its customers. To respond to their needs, some banks offer investment seminars free of charge to their high-income customers. They should also be offering free seminars on how to buy a home or start a small business to their low-income depositors. These ideas are not new, and they have had a public hearing. Their implementation is long overdue.

Closing The Gap is the name of a brochure put together in 1993 by the Federal Reserve Bank of Boston for lending institutions. It starts, "Fair lending is good business. Access to credit, free from considerations of race or national origin, is essential to the economic health of both lenders and borrowers."[13] The brochure proposes a series of practices and standards designed to constitute "good banking" and to close the mortgage loan gap. Its recommendations include reviewing minimum loan amounts because they negatively affect low-income applicants and giving special consideration to applicants who have demonstrated an ability to cover high housing expenses (relative to income) in the past. Lenders should allow down payment and closing costs to be paid by gifts, grants, and loans from relatives or agencies. Credit history criteria should be reviewed and made more sensitive to the needs of those with no credit history, problem histories, or low incomes. *Closing the Gap* also points out that subjective aspects of property and neighborhood appraisal using terms like "desirable area," "pride of ownership," "homogeneous neighborhood," and "remaining economic life" allow room for racial bias and bias against urban areas. It advocates the elimination of such concepts from the process of property appraisal. The brochure further advises lenders to distinguish between length of employment and employment stability in reviewing an applicant's work history, pointing out that many low-income people work in sectors of the economy where job changes are frequent. Lenders should focus on an applicant's ability to maintain or increase income levels, not on the number of jobs he or she has held.

"Good-Neighbor Mortgages" and Banking Restitution

"Good-Neighbor Mortgages" are new mortgage products featuring little or no down payment and minimal or no closing costs, often below-market interest rates, expanded debt-to-income ratios, no costly private mortgage insurance, and an open option to refinance at 100 percent of a home's appraised value. These mortgages can be used for purchase and rehabilitation, so homes in distressed communities can be revitalized. Credit for small business, on comparable terms, can also be obtained as part of a comprehensive community revitalization effort. The key to the success of Good-Neighbor programs is not only their generous terms but commitment on the part of the bank. Such programs should not be viewed as a penalty paid by a bank to redress past discriminatory practices; instead, they must be seen as establishing a new partnership designed to meet the needs of a once prejudicially underserviced community.

In 1994 Fleet Financial Group, a corporation that has drawn a lot of fire because of its biased community-lending policies, announced a stunning settlement with one of its most severe critics. The bank had been in trouble with community activists in Boston and Atlanta and with the Federal Reserve Bank because of its practice of redlining large sections of central cities and then quietly backing small second-mortgage companies that loaned money at pawnbroker rates. It set aside an $8 billion loan pool aimed at inner-city, low-income, and small-business borrowers. One Fleet insider ominously told the *Wall Street Journal* that "Fleet did nothing that wasn't common practice in the consumer-finance business. But we took the heat."[14]

An alternative and supplement to private-sector banks could come in the form of community development banks. These federally sponsored banks would give creative people in inner-city areas the tools with which to rebuild strong supportive communities and help poor people to develop assets for the future. They would hark back to the strong financial institutions that once helped American communities save their own money, invest, borrow, and grow. Modeled after Chicago's famous South Shorebank, enabling legislation sponsored by Senator Bill Bradley of New Jersey envisions developing a range of community-based financial institutions, all of which will respond to the capital and savings needs in their service areas.

The Racial Reparations Movement

A growing social movement within the black community for racial reparations attempts to address the historical origins of what House Resolution 40 in 1993 called the "lingering negative effects of the institution of slavery and discrimination" in the United States.[15] With a host of community-based organizations agitating and educating with respect to the issue, this movement has taken off since the passage of the legislation approving reparations for Japanese Americans interned during World War II. For the torment and humiliation suffered at that time each family was awarded $20,000. Since 1989 black Representative John Conyers of Michigan has introduced into the House Judiciary Committee each year a bill to set up a commission to study whether "any form of compensation to the descendants of African slaves is warranted." While the bill has yet to reach the floor of Congress, it has opened up this issue to public debate and discussion.

Given the historical nature of wealth, monetary reparations are, in our view, an appropriate way of addressing the issue of racial inequity. The fruits of their labor and the ability to accumulate wealth was denied African Americans by law and social custom during two hundred fifty years of slavery. This initial inequality has been aggravated during each new generation, as the artificial head start accorded to practically all whites has been reinforced by racialized state policy and economic disadvantages to which only blacks have been subject. We can trace the sedimented material inequality that now confronts us directly to this opprobrious past. Reparations would represent both a practical and a moral approach to the issue of racial injustice. As the philosopher Bernard Boxill argues:

> One of the reasons for which blacks claim the right to compensation for slavery is that since the property rights of slaves to "keep what they produce" were violated by the system of slavery to the general advantage of the white population, and, since the slaves would presumably have exercised their libertarian-right to bequeath their property to their descendants, their descendants, the present black population, have rights to that part of the wealth of the present white population derived from violating black property rights during slavery ... [Whites] also wronged [the slaves] by depriving them of their inheritance—of what Kunta Kinte would have provided them with, and passed on to them, had *he* been compensated—a stable home, education, income, and traditions.

While reparations based on similar logic have occurred in both the United States and other societies, it may be a testament to the persistence of antiblack racial attitudes in America that the prospects for such compensation are minimal. The objections are many: Are present-day whites to blame for the past? Who among blacks should receive such reparations? Would reparations of this sort really improve the economic situation of blacks today? We are not sure that racial reparations are the choice—political or economic—that America should make at this historical juncture. They may inflame more racial antagonism than they extinguish. But the reparations debate does open up the issue of how the past affects the present; it can focus attention on the historical structuring of racial inequality and, in particular, wealth. What we fear most is the prospect of reparations becoming a settlement, a payoff for silence, the terms of which go something like this: "Okay. You have been wronged. My family didn't do it, but some amends are in order. Let's pay it. But in return, we will hear no more about racial inequality and racism. Everything is now color-blind and fair. The social programs that were supposed to help you because you were disadvantaged are now over. No more!" Instead, racial reparations should be the first step in a collective journey to racial equality.

Any set of policy recommendations that requires new revenues and implies a redistribution of benefits toward the disadvantaged faces formidable political and ideological obstacles. In an era of stagnant incomes for the working and middle classes, race has become even more of an ideological hot button in the arena of national politics. The conservative cast of American political discourse in the 1990s is in large measure rooted in white opposition to the liberal policies of the sixties. According to Thomas and Mary Edsall's *Chain Reaction*, a pernicious ideology that joins opposition to opportunities for blacks and a distrust of government has "functioned to force the attention of the public on the costs of federal policies and programs."[16]

We believe that the program we have outlined could be put into place within the fiscal confines of present budget realities. For example, the tax structure reforms we discussed would help defray the expenses associated with asset development accounts and other increased social welfare benefits. But when it comes to race and social policy, ideology tends to reign. Despite the cost effectiveness of our program it is likely that it would be opposed mostly on ideological grounds. As Martin Carnoy in *Faded Dreams* resignedly notes:

> The negative intertwining of race with "tax and spend," "welfare state" economic policy remains a potentially highly successful conservative political card ... There is absolutely no doubt that the card will be played and played repeatedly.[17]

To move beyond the present impasse we must embark on a national conversation that realistically interprets our present dilemmas as a legacy of the past that if not addressed will forever distort the American Dream.

The African American Community's Role in Wealth Creation

Our interviews with African Americans revealed the importance of barriers to wealth creation that our policy proposals are designed to address. However, many interviewees also placed significant responsibility for the lack of assets in the black community on blacks themselves. Implicit in these criticisms was a feeling that blacks can do much to help themselves in creating greater wealth and using it more productively. The desire to increase wealth in the black community is seen in many ways as the civil rights theme of the twenty-first century. "The black community will not be free until we control the wealth in it," said one respondent. Three ideas continued to come up in our interviews regarding what the black community could do to increase wealth: entrepreneurship and business development, better education and information on the subject of financial planning, and networking to develop capital and economic opportunity.

The lack of business development was one of the key factors cited by one respondent as a barrier to black wealth accumulation: "I do believe that we really need to get into our own businesses." A lack of capital was cited as the most important barrier to business creation. As Mary Ellen, who left the corporate world to join her father's family business, noted, problems "in the banking system" stopped many people that she knew from being able to make their dream of self-employment a reality. Many of those who did start businesses had the age-old problem of being "undercapitalized." As Mary Ellen summarized, "You know you just can't succeed in a business without having capital. And we just don't have it."

While the lack of material resources was seen as important, our respondents were just as concerned about the dearth of social capital, particularly information and ways to communicate it, in the black community. Many worry that the kind of education that prepares one to take advantage of investment and business opportunities is not as available in the black community as it is elsewhere. Some of the information blacks are less apt to have access to is formal in nature: "People are not taught about entrepreneurship ... in the universities ... to go into business for themselves. ...In school we learn how to add and subtract and divide and all that, but you really aren't taught ... about finances." Much crucial information is transmitted informally, however. Interviewees often spoke of a separate "dialogue that goes on in the white community," generating investment information that is inaccessible to those in the black community. African Americans as a group are seen as "isolated" from basic knowledge pertaining to investment instruments, business opportunities, and financial markets. On a subtler level one respondent suggested that the real rules of the game are unknown to African Americans. As a consequence

> the playing field is not level—we do everything as we're supposed to do—we go through all the right channels. We don't know the back doors.

Our interviewees looked to the self-organization and self-activity of the black community for solutions to these problems. While supporting policies to force mainstream financial institutions to be more responsive to blacks, these respondents were quite pessimistic that any other aid would come from the wider society. They looked instead to actions that could be taken within, for, and by the black community. Pointing out significant increases in assets and financial knowledge in certain sectors of the black community (e.g., successful African American entrepreneurs), they argued that these resources had to be socially shared in order to help the less fortunate lay claim to a wealth stake. Over and over again respondents spoke of the way in which the well-off had to give back to the community. Our most affluent black respondent, the owner of several businesses, spoke of how she is

> attempting to help as many young people as I can now. I have a program now
> that is doing exactly that with a female organization. Business Opportunities
> Unlimited [a pseudonym] is helping young minorities open businesses. And
> I mentor young people that want to do that. The funding is there. The grants
> are there. It's knowing how to go in there and fill them out. Instead of training
> our children as my parents trained us, you know, work for the County, City, or
> State. Those are good stable jobs [laughter]. You gotta tell them, look, you're
> gonna take some risks. You know, you're young. What do you have to lose?
> You got the education. If you fall down, you pick yourself up again.

Another person in business talked about creating "rotating credit associations" that would help generate capital for new businesses and other financial opportunities.

> If banks are not going to give us money, we're going to get an investment
> pool together to help each other ... Basically what they [immigrants] do is
> everybody puts in ten thousand dollars into a pot, and let's say there are
> ten people in the pool. So there's a hundred thousand dollars. We give this
> hundred thousand to Johnny. He starts a business and gets it growing. Then
> it goes to the next person and they can start a business. Or they can borrow
> against this pool, so they have their own internal banking system.

Blacks need to "network" with each other in order to socialize people in the culture of business and finances, as well as to circulate the crucial information one needs to be successful. As an example Camille spoke of how her success is owed in part to the advice and business counsel that she has received from a successful black real estate entrepreneur. He informs her of "easy-ins without huge sums of money. Someone's losing something. Dell will say,

Camille, I have five thousand dollars. Do you have five thousand dollars? Let's pick this up. You know, that kind of thing."

Despite the concerns of our respondents, more and more blacks are taking advantage of financial self-employment opportunities—both formal and informal. Entrepreneurship programs are erupting everywhere. Schools and community-based organizations are teaching youth about the essentials of self-employment. In Los Angeles, the African American community's dominant response to the civil disorders that rocked the city in 1992 has been to "promote entrepreneurship among community residents as a primary job creation and wealth accumulation strategy."[18] Traditional black self-help organizations like the First African Methodist Episcopal Church (FAME) have launched entrepreneurial development programs that help fund and provide counseling and business services to budding businesspeople. Likewise, a recent spate of self-help books have begun to celebrate the power of networking for blacks.[19] One of the most successful black magazines is *Black Enterprise*, which, under the leadership of its editor, Earl Graves, has served as a clearing-house for information about black business and investment opportunities. National organizations like the NAACP and the Nation of Islam have also joined this effort.

We applaud these initiatives. They will help energize African Americans to seek ownership and control of their community. They will in time increase by some as yet unknown factor the wealth of some members of that community. The limits of unilateral community-based self-help measures also need to be recognized, however. Two interrelated concerns are paramount. First, the emphasis on owning and controlling business in the black community re-creates many of the negative features of the segregated market that characterized the economic detour described earlier. The purchase of small retail and service establishments within the black community places black entrepreneurs in unnecessarily restrictive economic markets. The key to growth is to break out of segregated markets and into the wider economic mainstream. Second, a primary focus on traditional retail and service outlets may very well leave blacks out of the most dynamic parts of the economy. Each period of economic growth in America has been ushered in by new industrial and technological breakthroughs. The winners have increasingly been those who have been able to master these technologies and to market them rapidly and economically. In order to succeed African American business in the twenty-first century needs to set its sights on the next great frontier of economic growth: information processing. An emphasis on retail and service will divert the energies of able black businesspeople away from the most fertile area of economic growth.

Any viable strategy for enhancing black wealth must include both the development of local community-based entrepreneurs and their penetration into the newest and most profitable sectors of the wider economy. Neither goal can be accomplished without the kinds of redistributive and wealth accumulation policies that we have outlined.

Conclusion

Racial inequality is still the unsolved American dilemma. The nation's character has been forged on the contradiction of the promise of equality and its systematic denial. For most of our nation's history we have allowed racial inequality to fester. But there are other choices. These choices represent a commitment to equality and to closing the gap as much as possible, and in so doing redefine the values, preferences, interests, and ideals that define us. Fundamental change must be addressed before we can begin to affirmatively answer Rodney King's poignant plea: "Can we all just get along?"

To address these fundamental issues, to rejuvenate America's commitment to racial justice, we must first acknowledge the real nature of racial inequality in this country. We must turn away from explanations of black disadvantage that focus exclusively on the supposed moral failings of the black community and attempt to create the kinds of structural supports that will allow blacks to live full and socially productive lives. The effort will require an avowedly egalitarian antiracist stance that transcends our racist past and brings blacks from the margin to the mainstream.

In her novel *Beloved* Toni Morrison tells the tale of forty-seven men on a chain gang in Alfred, Georgia. They all want to be free, but because they are chained together, no individual escape is possible. If "one lost, all lost," Morrison says, "the chain that held them would save all or none."[20] The men learn to work together, to converse, because they have to. When the opportunity presents itself, they converse quietly with one another and slip out of prison together. Like the convicts in Morrison's story, we need to realize a future undivided by race because we have to. No individual solution is possible. The chain that holds us all will save all or none.

Epilogue

Changing Context of Black Wealth/ White Wealth: 1995 to 2005

When we first wrote *Black Wealth/White Wealth* we optimistically and perhaps naively hoped to influence a new understanding about an effort to address racial inequality. We have been more successful than we could have imagined. In the intervening decade, however, much has changed. When our editor asked us to put out a Tenth Anniversary Edition, we consulted with colleagues who stressed how important it was to update the work, sometimes placing way too much hope in our ability to match the original impact of *Black Wealth/ White Wealth*. Our sense is that the trends, new developments, and challenges over the past decade deserve to be addressed to new and old readers of *Black Wealth/White Wealth*.[1] Being part of the events surrounding efforts to address racial wealth inequality makes it difficult to be dispassionate analysts of the situation. We have tried to provide as honest an assessment as possible of the most significant trends, developments, and challenges affecting the racial wealth gap, racial inequality, and ways to address these new realities.

This essay is organized in two parts. Chapter 8 analyzes the most important changes over the last ten years in wealth inequality trends and the racial wealth gap, highlights new dynamics in markets and institutions, and discusses how the most important developments and challenges of the decade affect racial wealth inequality.

Chapter 9 poses the question of the meaning and implications of these changes. We incorporate new understandings from the first section and then synthesize them with our assessment of asset-based policy for the poor. We conclude by suggesting ways to challenge deeply embedded structures that support racism and racial inequality, and how policies that help families and communities build resources for human development and change can be integrated into this strategy. Examining wealth inequality trends since 1995 is a good starting point.

Notes

1. As with the original book, we have chosen to continue the focus on the black–white racial dynamic. This is not to exclude the vital importance of other groups in the racial and wealth dynamics of the United States. Other scholars have taken up this agenda, and they are doing a more comprehensive analysis than we could conduct in this venue. For examples of new work in this vein, see Kochhar; the work of the First Nations Development Institute on Native American assets; Hao; and the forthcoming seminal collection edited by Nembhard and Chiteji.

Wealth Inequality Trends   **8**

The wealth story in the decade since we wrote *Black Wealth/White Wealth* involves two fundamental narratives. The growth and dispersion of wealth continues a trend anchored in the economic prosperity of post–World War II America. Between 1995 and 2001, the median net worth of all American families increased 39 percent, and median net financial assets grew by 60 percent. The growth of pension accounts (IRAs, Keogh plans, 401(k) plans, the accumulated value of defined contribution pension plans, and other retirement accounts) and stock holdings seems to account for much of this wealth accumulation.

While wealth grew and spread to many American families, there was little action at the bottom of the wealth spectrum as the percent of families with zero or negative net worth only dropped from 18.5 to 17.6, and those with no financial assets fell from 28.7 to 25.5.

Wealth remains highly concentrated, especially financial wealth, which excludes home equity. In 2001, the richest 5 percent of American households controlled over 67 percent of the country's financial wealth; the bottom 60 percent had 8.8 percent; and the bottom 40 percent just 1 percent.[1]

The context of wealth growth and inequality in the last decade situates our concern about racial inequality and the progress of American families, as indeed, the rich have gotten richer. The number of families with net worth of

$10 million or more in 2001 quadrupled since 1980. A *New York Times* article even bemoaned how the super rich are leaving the mere rich far behind.[2] These 338,400 hyper-rich families emerged as the biggest winners in the new global economy, as new technologies spurred by tax incentives evolved, as the stock market soared, and as top executives in the corporate world received astronomical pay.

In 1965, CEOs took home twenty-four times more in pay than what average workers earned. In 1980, CEO compensation was forty-two times the average American worker's pay. The gap in pay between average workers and large company CEOs surpassed 300-to-1 in 2003. In addition, in 2004, the heads of America's 500 biggest companies received a whopping 54 percent pay increase. Our point here is neither to paint CEOs as poster children for greed nor to argue that everybody should receive equal pay; rather, it is to underscore the growing magnitude of pay inequity and to understand it as a source of inequality. By comparison, in Japan a typical executive makes eleven times what a typical worker brings home and in Britain, twenty-two times.

The wealthy were the biggest beneficiaries of tax policy during President Bush's first term. In fact, the bulk of the 2001 tax cuts—53 percent—will go to the top 10 percent of taxpayers.[3] The tax cut share of the top 0.1 percent will amount to a 15 percent slice of the total value of the tax cut pie. Another reason that the wealthiest fare much better is that the tax cuts over the past decade have sharply lowered tax rates on income from investments, such as capital gains, interest, and dividends. While there are many reasons for the continuing wealth inequality trend, government policy has clearly abetted, encouraged, and privileged the property, capital, and income of America's wealthiest families.

Politicians' rhetoric aside, the tax treatment of income from labor compared with earnings from investment reveals the kernel of the kind of ownership society advocated by the present Bush administration and others.[4] Alan Greenspan continues to talk about needing to lower taxes on capital investments, and the Bush version of the ownership society rewards those already owning property and capital. We discuss the politics of asset policy and ownership themes more fully later in this chapter.

What Facts Have Changed?

In 1995 when *Black Wealth/White Wealth* was published, we presented data that was in many respects a new way of gauging the economic progress of black Americans vis-à-vis white Americans. Most commentators and analysts were familiar and comfortable with income comparisons that provided a window on whether there was growing or declining racial economic inequality. But the focus on wealth, "the net value of assets (e.g., ownership of stocks, money in the bank, real estate, business ownership, etc.) less debts" created a different gestalt or perspective on racial inequality.

This gestalt had two dimensions.[5] The first is the conceptual distinction between income and assets. While income represents the flow of resources earned in a particular period, say a week, month, or year, assets are a stock of resources that are saved or invested. Income is mainly used for day-to-day necessities, while assets are special monies not normally used for food or clothing but are rather a "surplus resource available for improving life chances, providing further opportunities, securing prestige, passing status along to one's family," and securing economic security for present and future generations.[6] The second dimension is the quantitative; to what extent is there parity between blacks and whites on assets? Do blacks have access to resources that they can use to plan for their future, to enable their children to obtain a quality education, to provide for the next generation's head start, and to secure their place in the political community? For these reasons, we focused on inequality in wealth as the sine qua non indicator of material well-being. Without sufficient assets, it is difficult to lay claim to economic security in American society.

The baseline indicator of racial wealth inequality is the black–white ratio of median net worth. To what degree are blacks approaching parity with whites in terms of net worth? The change in gestalt is amply demonstrated in comparisons of black–white median income ratios to black–white median net worth ratios. For example, the 1988 data reported on in *Black Wealth/White Wealth* showed that black families earned sixty-two cents for every dollar of median income that white families earned. However, when the comparisons shift to wealth, the figure showed a remarkably deeper and disturbing level of racial inequality. For every dollar of median net worth that whites controlled, African Americans controlled only eight cents![7] This markedly different indicator of inequality formed the basis of the analysis contained in *Black Wealth/White Wealth* as we attempted to describe its origins, its maintenance, and its continuing significance for the life chances of African American families and children.

How has this landmark indicator on racial inequality changed in the period since the publication of *Black Wealth/White Wealth*? Using the most recent data available, it appears, not unsurprisingly, that the level of racial wealth inequality has not changed but has shown a stubborn persistence that makes the data presented in 1995 more relevant than ever because the pattern we discerned suggests a firmly embedded racial stratification. The most optimistic analyses suggest that the black–white median net worth ratio is 0.10, that is, blacks have control of ten cents for every dollar of net worth that whites possess.[8] However, the most pessimistic estimate indicates that the ratio is closer to seven cents on the dollar.[9] This slim range demonstrates that the level of wealth inequality has not changed appreciably since the publication of *Black Wealth/White Wealth*.[10] However, the story is far more complex.

Using 1988 data, we tabulated the racial wealth gap at $60,980.[11] By 2002 the racial wealth gap increased to $82,663, meaning the wealth of the average African American family fell further behind whites by more than $20,000 over this period. Isolating the period and dynamics of the past decade a little more closely, the racial wealth gap grew by $14,316 between 1996 and 2002. In the decade since *Black Wealth/White Wealth*, then, white wealth grew and then leveled off; black wealth grew and then declined. As a result, the overall racial wealth gap ratio persists at a dime on the dollar, and the dollar amount of the racial wealth gap grew.

To gain a flavor for what has happened to African American wealth since 1998, we take the liberty to present four "composite cases" that characterize some of the circumstances that have contributed to the persistence of racial wealth inequality during this period. These "composites" are based on our extensive academic and policy experience in trying to understand the dynamics of wealth accumulation in the United States over the past ten years, and our work with many organizations around the country that has led to a deep familiarity with hundreds of families who have struggled to secure a solid asset base. None of these stories represent actual people, but their circumstances are those that many face, with the consequences being that black wealth has stagnated relative to white wealth, and that ten years after our initial publication of the baseline data on racial wealth inequality, there has been a gnawing persistence of the basic trends.

A Striving Black Middle Class

Cynthia and James Braddock are the epitome of the black middle class. Both are college graduates, have steady jobs (Cynthia as a public school teacher and James as a corporate middle manager in the human resources division of a Fortune 500 company). During the 1980s and 1990s they have saved steadily in their employer-sponsored 403(b) and 401(k) savings plans, converting part of it into a down payment on their first home. They provide their two children with fashionable clothes, extra tutoring, and social opportunities that enrich them both academically and culturally. Since the stock market bust of 1999 they have seen their savings eaten away at by diminishing stock returns and found their purchasing power eroded by paltry pay raises. Consequently, maintaining their standard of living is increasingly dependent on the five credit cards that they have, two of which have reached their maximum. Their net worth has increased thanks to the increasing value of their home, but the decline of their stock portfolio in their employment-sponsored savings program has not been replaced by higher earnings even though they make steady monthly contributions.

The Struggling Working Class

The lives of Kenneth and Barbara Jones characterize the struggling working class of black America. Married for ten years, they have managed in the last five years to both gain steady employment. Kenneth works for a local retail establishment that does not have a broad array of benefits programs. His wife Barbara is a teacher's aide who does have access to health care and an employer-sponsored savings program, which provides needed benefits for the whole family (one preschooler and one child in a local public elementary school). They have not been able to save much, but demonstrated a strong record of making their rent and utility payments on time that helped them qualify for an affordable mortgage sponsored by a major bank in their city. With no down payment, they were able to purchase a small home that costs about the same in terms of monthly costs as their rental unit. They depend on credit cards to make routine and emergency repairs and are thus in debt. However, with the value of their home increasing, they generally feel optimistic about their future and that of their children.

The Disenfranchised Black Elderly

Rosa Williams is a resident of an inner city community whose homes were among the first owned by African Americans in the mid-fifties in a formerly all-white neighborhood. She is representative of what is happening to too many African American elders who worked hard to pay off their homes and had hoped to live a life of dignity and respect in their final years in their own home. Instead, Mrs. Williams has lost her home as a consequence of a contract she entered into with a subprime lender who promised her a sufficient loan to not only make a major repair but to also have money left over that would serve as a cushion for other major expenses. Mrs. Williams thought that the loan terms were similar to charges at a conventional bank, and even though her only income derived from social security, she felt confident she could pay it back. However, she did not read the fine print that was written in complicated legal language that contained a balloon payment that required full payment of the loan after one year and restricted her ability to refinance. Thus, Mrs. Williams lost her home, her only major asset and shelter, and has had to move in with her daughter and three grandchildren. Stripped of her hard-earned equity, Mrs. Williams has lost what little wealth she has and must spend her golden years on the edge of economic insecurity.

The Legacy of TANF

Donna Smith, head of a household that includes three school-aged kids, joined the labor market for the first time because of the stringent requirements associated with Temporary Assistance For Needy Families. Working first in a temporary job, Donna landed a position as a housecleaner in a hotel where the wages do not lift her and her family out of poverty. In fact, Donna cannot make ends meet from paycheck to paycheck. Without a credit history and with only a recent employment record, Donna cannot obtain credit from conventional lenders or even major credit card suppliers. Her only recourse is to secure payday loans so that she can pay her electricity before her service is canceled or provide money for her daughter's field trip that the school requires. Consequently, she is falling further and further behind economically because the payday lender has already garnished her meager check, making it even more difficult to make ends meet.

Embedded in these composite stories are some of the contradictory facts and new dimensions of financial life in America that have affected the persistence of the black–white racial wealth gap. They include a strong economy of the 1990s that enabled greater savings, especially in employer-based savings programs, but which has petered out recently; a stock market bust that punished some of the newest entrants into the market most severely; increasing credit card debt; a growing trend of black home ownership complemented by growing subprime and predatory lending directed at minority communities; and growth in the working poor due to the influx of the TANF population into the labor market. This mix of factors weaves the mosaic underlying the story of the continuing racial wealth gap in the first decade of the twenty-first century.

The Story of the Persistence of the Racial Wealth Gap

Traditionally, economists assume that wealth accumulation is the consequence of a "combination of inheritance, earnings, and savings and is enhanced by prudent consumption and investment patterns over a person's life course."[12] How these individual variables interact with the human capital attributes of family members, their education, their occupation, and their ability to begin asset accumulation at an early stage in their life course (the earlier one begins to accumulate assets, the more wealth one can accrue) moves us forward in explaining how differential accumulation occurs. But these individual factors are not the whole story.

As *Black Wealth/White Wealth* convincingly demonstrated, wealth accumulation occurs in a context where these individual attributes unfold to produce varying levels of wealth for different families and social groupings. It has been the different "opportunity structure" for savings and investment that African Americans have faced when compared with whites that has helped to structure racial inequality in wealth holding.

We developed a sociology of wealth and racial inequality in *Black Wealth/White Wealth*, which situated the study of wealth among concerns with race, class, and social inequality. This theoretical framework elucidated the social context in which wealth generation occurs and demonstrated the unique and diverse social circumstances that blacks and whites face. Three concepts we developed provided a sociologically grounded approach to understand the racial wealth gap and highlighted how the opportunity structure disadvantages blacks and contributes to massive wealth inequalities between the races. The first concept, racialization of state policy, explores how state policy has impaired the ability of most black Americans to accumulate wealth from slavery throughout American history to contemporary institutional discrimination. The "economic detour" helps us understand the relatively low level of entrepreneurship among the small scale and segmentally niched businesses of black Americans, leading to an emphasis on consumer spending as the route to economic assimilation. The third concept—the sedimentation of racial inequality—explores how the cumulative effects of the past have seemingly cemented blacks to the bottom of America's economic hierarchy in regards to wealth.

These concepts do much to show how this differential opportunity structure developed and worked to produce black wealth disadvantages. It also builds a strong case that layering wealth deprivation generation after genera-

tion has been central in not only blacks' lack of wealth but also whites' privileged position in accumulating wealth. As we noted:

> What is often not acknowledged is that the accumulation of wealth for some
> whites is intimately tied to the poverty of wealth for most blacks. Just as
> blacks have had "cumulative disadvantages," whites have had "cumulative
> advantages." Practically every circumstance of bias and discrimination
> against blacks has produced a circumstance and opportunity of positive gain
> for whites.[13]

The past opportunity structure that denied blacks access or full participation in wealth-building activities serves as a powerful deterrent to current
black ambitions for wealth. Without an inheritance that is built on generations
of steady economic success, blacks, even when they have similar human capital and class position, lag far behind their white counterparts in their quest to
accumulate a healthy nest egg of assets. In *Black Wealth/White Wealth* we
examined those current institutional and structural constraints that African
Americans faced in the 1980s and early 1990s that curtailed and limited the
ability of many African Americans to build assets. One area we focused upon
was housing, the largest single element of most American's portfolio of assets,
and a major part of the wealth in most African American's asset portfolio. We
identified a number of institutional constraints ranging from differential access
to mortgages, higher costs of mortgages, and differential levels of equity accumulation in homes owing to persistent residential segregation.

We want to extend this mode of theorizing and analysis to the period of
the 1990s and into the first decade of the twenty-first century. We attempt to
formulate a compelling picture of why African Americans continue to lag so
far behind whites in asset holding. Here we focus on the social context of the
labor market, the stock and housing market, and growing debt.

The Rise and Decline of a Tight Labor Market and a Bull Stock Market

Black Wealth/White Wealth documented wealth data that reflected a period in
the American economy characterized by relatively high unemployment rates and
a stagnant economy. However, this period was followed by one of the largest and
longest economic expansions in the history of the United States. From its beginning in March 1991 to its ending in November 2001, the United States endured
a record expansion. Positive economic indicators that were in sharp contrast to

the previous period characterized this expansion. For example, family incomes went from stagnation during the 1979 to 1993 period, where they grew only 0.7 percent over the entire time frame to an increase of 17 percent, or more than $7,000 per family, from 1993 to 2000. In terms of job growth, during the 1992 to 2000 period, the nation created more jobs than at any similar period in American history: 22.6 million, 92 percent of which were in the private sector. Moreover, in contrast to the previous period, where 1.9 million manufacturing jobs were lost, the 1992 to 2000 period saw manufacturing job growth increase by 303,000. Finally, the unemployment rate fell by 42 percent, reaching below 5 percent from July 1997 through January 2001. The 4 percent unemployment rate in 2000—the lowest in over 30 years—stands in striking contrast to an average unemployment rate of 7.1 percent for the 1980 to 1992 period.[14]

For African Americans this was a period of tight labor markets that led to greater levels of labor force participation owing to the existence of greater demand for their participation in the economy. Employers made "extra efforts … to overcome the barriers created by skill and spatial mismatch" to reach out to African American workers to fill their growing labor needs.[15] Moreover, "employers may find discrimination more costly when the economy is strong and their usually preferred type of job candidate is fully employed elsewhere."[16] In the throes of a heated and tight labor market, *Business Week* proclaimed, "With the economy continuing to expand and unemployment at its lowest point in 30 years, companies are snapping up minorities, women, seniors, and any-one else willing to work for a day's pay."[17]

African Americans, however, did not wholly benefit from this extraordi-nary period in American history. Black joblessness continued to be a problem. The historical ratio of two-to-one black-to-white unemployment rates persisted with black men averaging 7.1 percent compared with 3 percent for white men, while black women averaged 6.8 compared with 3.2 percent for white women in the latter half of 1999.[18] Nevertheless, those African Americans who were employed during this period saw real wage gains that could be translated into savings, investments, and an increase in net worth.

Another aspect of the expansion of the economy during the 1990s was the rapid rise in the stock market. Fueled by technology stocks and the growth of key stocks like Microsoft, Sun, Yahoo, and other new stock offerings in the technology sector, the stock market started to attract investments not only from high-income and high-wealth individuals, but also from an increasing number of middle-class families and even working-class families. This invest-ment was facilitated by growing participation in employer-sponsored savings programs that enabled employees to make tax-deferred and/or matched contri-butions through payroll deductions. The ease of the transaction and the con-stant media and public interest in the high-flying stock market encouraged mass participation. The market rose steadily and rapidly. Beginning from a monthly average in 1992 in the low 400s, the Standard and Poor's 500 tripled in size by 1999.[19] If one were lucky enough to purchase Microsoft or Yahoo early then his or her gains would have been astronomical. For example, when Yahoo was first available as a public offering shares were sold for $1.24. By December 1999 Yahoo listed for $108.17.[20] It was the desire for these kinds of returns that fueled an overheated market and led to the description of "irratio-nal exuberance" concerning the frenzy for the "market."[21]

African Americans, while constrained by resources, also entered into this frenzy. The decade of the 1990s was the breakthrough era for African American involvement in the stock market. Facilitated by employer savings plans and, for the first time, sought after by stock and brokerage firms, African Americans invested readily into the market. In 1996 blacks had a median value of $4,626 invested in stocks and mutual funds. At the height of the market, that value had almost doubled to $8,669. During this period African American stock market investors had closed the black–white ratio of stock market value from twenty-eight cents on the dollar to forty cents on the dollar. However, the market's plunge after 1999 sent African American portfolio values down to a median average of $3,050. This brought the black–white ratio of stock market value back in line with the 1996 level, eroding all the gains that the bull market had bestowed.[22]

African Americans did better in 401(k) and thrift savings plans, which were more likely to be diversified holdings. In 1996 African American investors held a median average of $6,939 in these instruments. With the market surging and regular savings deposits facilitated by payroll deduc-tions, African Americans increased their value in savings or thrift plans to a median average of $10,166 in 2002. The comparison to whites is quite inter-esting in regard to thrift plans. Between 1996 and 2002 African Americans closed the black–white ratio slightly from 0.43 to 0.50. This is in striking contrast to the data on stock ownership.[23]

Home Ownership, New Mortgage and Credit Markets

Over the past several years more families than ever across the United States have been able to buy homes. Home ownership rates reached 69 percent in 2004, a historic high. The main reasons for the high level of home ownership include the new mortgage market, where capital is readily available to both families and economic sectors where home ownership was always part of the American Dream—but in dream only. With home ownership comes the opportunity to accumulate wealth because the value of homes appreciates over time. Indeed, approximately two-thirds of all the wealth of America's middle class families is not in stocks, bonds, investments, or savings accounts but in the form of home equity.

Home equity is the most important wealth component for average American families, and even though home ownership rates are lower, it is even more prominent in the wealth profiles of African American families. Although housing appreciation is very sensitive to many characteristics relating to a community's demographics and profile (which realtors euphemistically call "location, location, location"), overall home ownership has been a prime source of wealth accumulation for black families. For example, for the average black home owner, homes created $6,000 more wealth between 1996 and 2002.[24] However, fundamentally racialized dynamics create and distribute housing wealth unevenly. The Federal Reserve Board kept interest rates at historically low levels for much of this period, and this fueled both demand and hastened converting home equity wealth into cash.

Black Wealth/White Wealth demonstrated the color coding of home equity, and Shapiro's 2004 book, *The Hidden Cost of Being African American*, updates the data and extends our understanding of how residential segregation affects home equity. The typical home owned by white families increased in value by $28,000 more than homes owned by blacks. Persistent residential segregation, especially in cities where most blacks live, explains this equity difference as a compelling index of bias that costs blacks dearly. This data point corroborates other recent research demonstrating that rising housing wealth depends upon a community's demographic characteristics, especially racial composition. One study concludes that homes lost at least 16 percent of their value when located in neighborhoods that are more than 10 percent black. Thus, a "segregation tax" visits black home owners by depressing home values and reducing home equity in highly segregated neighborhoods.[25] Shapiro summarizes the case: "The only prudent conclusion from these studies is that residential segregation costs African American home owners enormous amounts of money by suppressing their home equity in comparison to that of white home owners. The inescapable corollary is that residential segregation benefits white home owners with greater home equity wealth accumulation."[26] Furthermore, most African American families rent housing and thus are not positioned to accumulate housing wealth, mainly because of affordability, credit, and access issues.

The term "affordable housing" has many meanings. We are concerned with increasing minority home ownership because of the use value of homes to owners and because home owners are more likely to become stakeholders in communities, schools, local politics, and civic engagement. Most pertinent to the racial wealth gap is that home equity is the largest component in the portfolio of the average American families. We limit this discussion to affordable home ownership, even though, in comprehensive and progressive housing policy, affordable housing includes a spectrum from renting to owning that supports asset accumulation.[27]

Affordable home ownership programs come in many varieties and from many sources, including federal and state programs, regional and local initiatives, churches, community organizations, foundations, and the private sector. They aim to bring home ownership opportunities to lower income families and communities previously precluded because of affordability, bad credit histories, or lack of knowledge and information. Premortgage education and counseling, agreements with lenders, and connecting potential home owners to responsive lenders are some of the methods used in home ownership programs. Mortgage terms that make mortgages more accessible to low- and moderate-income families are another critical component of these programs. Recommendations often include:

- Increased public and private financing, such as down payment assistance programs and purchase–rehabilitation programs
- High-quality and local home ownership training programs
- Better dissemination regarding home ownership opportunities
- Marketing to communities of color
- Consistent enforcement of fair housing laws
- Hiring and training staff people of color
- Financial literacy programs around housing, finance, mortgages, and credit

But, home ownership and the new opportunity to accumulate wealth also bring additional risks.

The home mortgage marketplace has evolved considerably since 1990, when mortgage packages were offered at a unitary price reflecting the terms of the loan, targeting prospective home owners who met stringent credit history rules and financial criteria. As housing wealth grew and the United States mortgage market became integrated into the global market system, mortgage products proliferated and thus has changed the way American families buy homes. Underwriting standards have become more relaxed, both as financial institutions ease rules to compete in this evolving market and as federal regulations and oversight has become less stringent.[28]

Minorities are making significant inroads into all segments of the housing market. Indeed, important components feeding the general trends of increasing rates of new home construction and home value appreciation include the demographic push from new immigrants, the accomplishments of second-generation immigrants, and the success of a segment of African American families. In 2004, home ownership reached historic highs as 69 percent of American families live in a home they own. In 1995, 42.2 percent of African American families owned homes, increasing to a historic high, 49.5 percent, in 2004. This 17.3 percent increase in African American home ownership is quite remarkable, indicating striving, accomplishment, and success. The black–white home ownership gap in 1995 stood at 28.5 percent and narrowed to 26.2 percent in 2004.[29] We might expect the home ownership gap to continue closing as black home ownership starts from a considerably lower base while the higher white rate may be close to exhausting the potential of those who want to become home owners.

In 1995, access to credit for minorities was a major issue. Financial institutions responded both to criticisms regarding credit discrimination and to the newly discovered buying capacity of minorities. Increasing numbers of African American and Hispanic families gained access to credit cards throughout the 1990s: 45 percent of African American and 43 percent of Hispanic families held credit cards in 1992 and by 2001 nearly 60 percent of African American and 53 percent of Hispanic families held credit cards.[30] The irony here is that as access to credit broadened under terms highly favorable to lenders, debt became rampant and millions of families became ensnared in a debt vice.

Credit card debt nearly tripled from $238 billion in 1989 to $692 billion in 2001.[31] These figures represent family reliance on financing consumption through debt, especially expensive credit in the form of credit cards and department store charge cards. During the 1990s, the average American family experienced a 53 percent increase in credit card debt—the average family's card debt rising from $2,697 to $4,126. Credit card debt among low-income families increased 184 percent. Even high-income families became more dependent on credit cards: There was 28 percent more debt in 2001 than in 1989. The main sources of credit card debt include spiraling health care costs, lower employer coverage of health insurance, and rising housing costs amid stagnating or declining wages after 2000 and increasingly unsteady employment for many. This suggests strongly that the increasing debt is not the result of frivolous or conspicuous spending or lack of budgetary discipline; instead, deferring payment to make ends meet is becoming the American way for many to finance daily life in the new economy.

Given that a period of rising income did not lift the African American standard of living, and given the context of overall rising family debt, an examination of the racial component of credit card debt furthers our understanding of the contemporary processes associated with the continuation of the economic detour and the further sedimentation of inequality. The average credit card debt of African Americans increased 22 percent between 1992 and 2001, when it reached an average of nearly $3,000.[32] Hispanic credit card debt mirrored blacks by rising 20 percent in the same period to $3,691. As we know, the average white credit card debt was higher, reaching $4,381 in 2001. One of the most salient facts involves the magnitude and depth of African American reliance on debt. Among those holding credit cards with balances, nearly one in five African Americans earning less than $50,000 spend at least 40 percent of their income paying debt service. In other words, in every 8-hour working day these families labor 3.2 hours to pay off consumer debt. Even though black families carry smaller monthly balances, a higher percentage of their financial resources goes toward servicing debt.

The median net worth of African American families at the end of 2002 was $5,988, essentially the same as it was in 1988.[33] Again, it is not as if nothing happened since we wrote *Black Wealth/White Wealth*; indeed, African American fortunes expanded with good times and contracted with recessions and the bursting of the stock market bubble. In the last decade, the high point of African American (and Hispanic) wealth accumulation was 1999, when it registered $8,774, just before the bursting of the stock market bubble in early 2000. Between 1999 and 2002, African American wealth declined from $8,774 to $5,988, wiping out more than a decade's worth of financial gains.

Median wealth and racial wealth gap data tell us about absolute wealth accumulation and the relative positioning of African American families. Another sense of the dynamics of the last ten years concerns the dispersion of assets among African American families. In 1996, 31.9 percent of African American families owned zero net worth or—worse still—had bottom lines that put them in the red. By 1999, this figure declined to 28.2 percent but deteriorated again after the stock market burst and the beginning of the recession, by increasing to 32.3 percent in 2002. This has left more African American families in absolute asset poverty than at the time of the book's initial publication.

New Dynamics of Markets and Institutions

As we have indicated, the decade between 1995 and 2006 really is marked off by two distinct periods: African American family wealth accumulates considerably and more families move into positive wealth positions until early 2000. From 2000 through 2005, however, the financial wealth of African American families made a U-turn, both losing actual wealth and increasing the number of families with zero or negative wealth once more. Throughout the entire period, home ownership and home equity continued to rise for all segments of American families, including African Americans. An important narrative, then, involves this great expansion of financial wealth, home ownership, and housing wealth; understanding what happened to this wealth; examining the opportunities this new wealth created, especially for financial institutions looking for new markets; and importantly, the impact of these developments and new dynamics on African Americans.

Housing Wealth and Its Uses

Households cashed out $407 billion worth of equity from homes in just three years, 2002 through 2004, in the refinancing boom that began in 2001. Although such data have not been collected for very long, American families were refinancing homes at record levels, three times higher than any other period.[34] Nearly half of all mortgage debt was refinanced between 2002 and

2003, averaging $27,000 in equity per home in the early stages of the refinancing wave.[35]

As mortgage interest rates fell to record low levels during the refinance boom, and as housing continued to appreciate and result in wealth accumulation, many Americans cashed out home equity to pay down debt and finance living expenses, trading off wealth to pay off past consumption and fund new purchases.

Refinancing at lower interest rates and hence lower monthly payments is certainly a good deal for families paying off mortgages because it leaves more money in the family budget for living expenses, discretionary purchases, or savings. We need to ask the important question of how families used this bonanza. Investing in human capital through continued education or career retooling, investing in other financial instruments, building a business, home improvements, and similar choices expand opportunities, improve living standards, and may launch further social mobility. On the other hand, paying down high-interest debt may slow down temporarily the debt-driven consumption treadmill but most likely does not improve the long-term standard of living or life chances of a family, and certainly does not improve the future wealth accumulation picture. Slightly over one-half used housing wealth to cover living expenses and to pay down store and credit cards. Another 25 percent used funds for consumer expenditures such as vehicle purchases and medical expenses. Thus it appears that a majority of households used these new home equity loans to convert credit card debt and current living expenses into long-term mortgage debt.

One result is that between 1973 and 2004, home owners' equity actually fell—from 68.3 percent to 55 percent so that Americans own less of their homes today than they did in the 1970s and early 1980s. And, it is worth remembering that home equity is by far the largest source of wealth for the vast majority of American families. The intersection of wealth and race illustrates the magnified importance of home equity for African Americans and Hispanics. Among whites, home equity represented 38.5 percent of their entire wealth portfolio in 2002. In sharp contrast, home equity accounted for 63 percent of wealth among African Americans and 61 percent for Hispanics.[36]

The Dark Side of Home Ownership

Subprime lending is targeted to prospective homebuyers with blemished credit histories or with high levels of debt who otherwise would not qualify for conventional mortgage loans. A legitimate niche for these kinds of loans brings home ownership within the grasp of millions of families. These loan products are essential in expanding home ownership rates. In return for these riskier investments, financial institutions charge borrowers higher interest rates, often requiring higher processing and closing fees, and often containing special loan conditions like prepayment penalties, balloon payments, and adjustable interest rates.

The subprime market expanded greatly in the last decade as part of new, aggressive marketing strategies among financial institutions hungrily eyeing rising home ownership and seeing promising new markets. Moreover, the mortgage finance system in the United States became well integrated into global capital markets, which offer an ever-growing array of financial products, including subprime loans. Subprime loan originations grew fifteen-fold, from $35 billion to $530 billion between 1994 and 2004. Reflecting the increasing importance of subprime loans to the financial industry, the subprime share of mortgage loans has seen a parallel meteoric rise from less than 4 percent in 1995 to representing about 17 percent of mortgage loans in 2004.[37]

Loan terms like prepayment penalties and balloon payments increase the risk of mortgage foreclosure in subprime home loans, even after controlling for the borrower's credit score, loan terms, and varying economic conditions.[38] One study from the Center for Community Capitalism demonstrates that subprime prepayment penalties and balloon payments place Americans at substantially greater risk of losing their homes.

A key finding is that subprime home loans with prepayment penalties with terms of three years or longer faced 20 percent greater odds of entering foreclosure than loans without prepayment penalties. Prepayment restrictions mean that home owners are stuck with loan terms, unable to refinance, to obtain lower rates, to weather financial difficulties, or to take advantage of lower interest rates. Another important finding shows that subprime home loans with balloon payments, where a single lump sum payment many times the regular payment amount is due at the end of the loan term, face 46 percent greater odds of entering foreclosure than loans without such a term. In addition, borrowers whose subprime loans include interest rates that fluctuate face

49 percent greater odds of entering foreclosure than borrowers with fixed rate subprime mortgages. Under these terms, home borrowers are more likely to lose their homes.

In the fourth quarter of 2003, 2.13 percent of all subprime loans across the country entered foreclosure, which was more than ten times higher than the rate for all prime loans. One in five of all first-lien subprime refinance loans originated in 1999 had entered foreclosure by December 2003.[39]

Delinquency (falling behind in mortgage payments) and losing one's home through foreclosure are hitting vulnerable neighborhoods hardest. Concentrated foreclosures can negatively affect the surrounding neighborhoods, threatening to undo community building and revitalization efforts achieved through decades of collaborative public–private partnerships, community organizing, and local policy efforts.

Los Angeles is a case in point.[40] In a short three-year period, 2001 to 2004, over 14,000 Los Angeles families lost their homes through foreclosure. The foreclosure rate is highest in the most vulnerable neighborhoods. In predominately minority neighborhoods (80 percent or more minority) of Los Angeles County the foreclosure rate is almost four times the rate that it is in neighborhoods where minorities are less than 20 percent of the population. In the City of Los Angeles, foreclosures occur nearly twelve times more often in predominately minority communities compared with areas that have fewer than 20 percent minorities.

About one in four of all homes in Los Angeles lost through foreclosures occur in neighborhoods where low-income minority families are concentrated. The impact has been devastating because 7.2 percent of all families paying mortgages lost their homes between 2001 and 2004. Los Angeles is not alone; data from Atlanta, Baltimore, Boston, Chicago, and others show that Los Angeles is part of the larger, national pattern.

A study examining pricing disparities in the mortgage market provides more context, placing the Los Angeles story in a broader pattern. Of all conventional loans to blacks, nearly 30 percent were subprime compared with only 10 percent for whites.[41] These ratios would be in closer alignment in lending markets operating with maximum efficiency and equity. Creditworthy criteria, like debt-to-income ratios, do not explain the greater propensity for African Americans to receive subprime loans. The report also discovered that subprime loans in minority communities increased with levels of racial segregation. This finding suggests an alarming new form of modern redlining that targets minority neighborhoods for subprime loans.

Using a testing methodology adapted from those that explored job discrimination, the National Community Reinvestment Coalition was able to explore how pricing disparities resulting from intensified subprime lending in minority areas occurred. Essentially, white and black testers with similar credit records and qualifications applied for preapproval for mortgages. Given similar scripts and profiles (with African Americans actually presenting better qualifications), the testing uncovered a 45 percent rate of disparate treatment based on race. The testing revealed practices that may have destructive effects on African American families and communities. These include: differences in interest rates quoted; differences in information about fees, rates, loan programs, and loan terms; and whites more often referred up to the lender's prime lending division. In *Black Wealth/White Wealth* we wrote that differences in loan rejection rates and interest rates did not result from discriminatory lending practices but from blacks bringing fewer financial assets to the mortgage table; as a result, they paid higher loan terms. Racial pricing disparities and the targeted spread of subprime lending to minority communities, however, now persuades us that minority America is experiencing a new form of redlining organized by race and geographic space.

With data like this, foreclosure, transparency, fair lending, and federal regulatory responsibility have become central to public policy debates. In particular, while the Los Angeles foreclosure story is not specific to subprime or predatory lending practices, it is safe to assume that it is a large part of the story.

Black Wealth/White Wealth demonstrated the power of policy, government, institutions, and history to order and maintain racial inequality. The previous sections show further the significance of financial institutions in granting access to credit and the terms of credit, and the increasing dependence on credit and debt. The basis for excluding African Americans from opportunities and creating different rules in the competition for success is no longer just who is a capable worker. Now we must add who is a worthy credit risk and on what terms. Job discrimination against individual blacks based on perceived characteristics is not the only major arena in the struggle against inequality; exclusion in terms of creditworthiness is as well.

Developments and Challenges of the Past Decade

The significant increase in housing wealth in the last decade also financed a consumption boom. That boom brought to our attention the relative underemphasis of consumption and its racialization in our original book. Moreover, the recent spate of cashing out home equity appears to be an essential component of personal consumption that drives the economy, accounting for a good chunk of economic growth in the United States. The amount of home equity cashed out increased tenfold from $13.9 billion in 1995 to $139.2 billion in 2004.[42] These cash-rich households accounted for a third of the growth in personal consumption in 2004.[43] In other words, housing wealth effects became an important player in economic growth over the past ten years, especially so since 2001, as cash from home owner wealth has led the economy out of the recession and kept spending levels high. Families without large amounts of housing wealth utilized easier access to credit to keep apace, and in the process faced the dangers of easy credit.

Fewer Ways Out: Changes in the Bankruptcy Law

As we have seen in the past decade, credit card companies have made credit easier, credit card debt and debt hardship has skyrocketed, and more American families are losing their homes through foreclosure. Personal bankruptcy filings broke the one-million mark in 1996 and reached a historic high in 2003 when 1.6 million people filed for personal bankruptcy. Prior to 2004, most individual bankruptcies were simple to file and the consumers did not need to repay all their debts. But they still suffered the consequence of badly damaged credit records, which greatly restricted future access to credit, home ownership, and entrepreneurship since bankruptcies remained on a person's financial history for up to ten years. The 2005 reform of bankruptcy, dubbed the "vampire bill" by one expert, favors financial institutions over consumers. This makes it harder for people to declare bankruptcy and allows financial institutions a better chance of recouping their credit along with mountains of interest and late fees.

Financial institutions and their lobbyists applied tremendous pressure, supporting and passing the new bankruptcy law that protects their loans in the face of record high credit card debt, debt hardship, and foreclosures. The new law closed the most frequently used legal option available to consumers overwhelmed by debt.

The bankruptcy code, even including the new revision, systematically favors debtors with wealth over those with income because it lets debtors—especially Chapter 13 debtors—retain some of their property but requires them to use only disposable income to repay debts. Specifically, to benefit the most from bankruptcy laws, the "ideal debtor" would be a married, employed home owner who is the beneficiary of a trust or has a large employer-provided retirement account; provides financial support only to legal dependents; and has little (or no) student loan, alimony, or child support debt. According to one recent law review article, "because statistical data suggest that white people are more likely to fit the Ideal Debtor profile, race matters in bankruptcy."[44]

The 2005 bankruptcy law was framed in the language of "irresponsible consumers" avoiding their responsibilities by declaring bankruptcy. Some saw this as an attempt to code the debate in racialized terms.[45] This racialized framing prevented other explanations of the rise of bankruptcies—like consumer bankruptcies resulting from traumatic or chronic health events—from framing the political debate and culture war over debt.

A 2005 study of bankruptcy filers concludes that medical causes trigger half of personal bankruptcies, essentially indicating that Americans are experiencing a wave of medical bankruptcies.[46] Among those whose illnesses triggered bankruptcy, out-of-pocket medical costs averaged $11,854. Most American families do not have $12,000 in bank accounts, stocks, or bonds to meet unexpected medical costs like these, especially considering that chronic or serious medical conditions also mean employment is severely curtailed or no longer possible. Thus, it is not too many trips to the mall for trendy sneakers but the cost of health care (and its increasingly private financing) and health status that explains most legal bankruptcies. Consumption, debt, and bankruptcy thus circle back to our understandings of the economic detour and racialization of state policy, which in turn link back to health disparities.

Black Consumers and the Urban Market

Our discussion of the "economic detour" stressed that blacks were the only group that came to America and found insurmountable barriers to establishing sustainable businesses. This has led to their being "forced into the role of the consumer."[47] At the eve of the twenty-first century, blacks have come to be identified in corporate America as one of the most important market niches for consumer goods. Euphemistically termed the "urban market," black communities and black youth are bombarded with and urged to consume a range of commodities that are designed to meet their perceived "cultural tastes" and "lifestyle." These goods range from fashionable clothes to the latest athletic shoes, from cigarettes and specialized alcoholic beverages to high-tech stereo and audio equipment. With a combined purchasing power of $372 billion in 2002, major retail and consumer services have found the "urban market" to be a motherlode of opportunity. As a consequence, African Americans are targeted through advertisements that are designed to reach them specifically, whether through television, radio, magazines, or billboards. For example, magazine advertisers spent over $300 million dollars in 2002 in the top twelve advertising categories (e.g., toiletries and cosmetics, apparel, auto, etc.) directly targeted toward African Americans. Their advertising dollars bring strong returns. For example:

- African Americans account for more than 30 percent of industry spending in the $4 billion hair market.
- Black consumers spend more on telephone services than any other consumer group. Their expenditures in this category totals $918 per capita annually, or 8.1 percent more than the average.
- According to a 2001 study by Cotton Incorporated, African American consumers will spend an average of $1,427 on clothing per year for themselves—$458 more than the average consumer.
- The average African American family spends 30 percent more on weekly groceries than the U.S. population at large.[48]

In *Black Wealth/White Wealth* we underplayed the "conspicuous consumption" thesis, pointing out that the African American savings rate was as high or higher than the white rate of savings, especially at higher class levels. However, it is clear that African Americans, at least on some consumer goods, especially those that are necessities (e.g., food and clothing), may be areas in which African Americans spend more owing to the direct impact of intense and directed advertising campaigns. On the face of it, this appears as incontrovertible evidence of conspicuous consumption.

But the evidence is not that this is conspicuous consumption, but rather it is the consequence of living in communities and cities where the cost of goods and services, especially for the poor, are higher. Data consistently show that the "poor pay more" for essential goods and services. The following are some examples from a recent study of Philadelphia.[49]

- Car purchases—Lower-income families can pay over $500 more for the same car bought by a higher-income household.
- Car loans—Poor buyers pay higher interest rates than the average buyer.
- Car insurance—For an inner city neighborhood, the poor pay $400 more for the same car and driver than middle-income car owners.
- Establishing utility service—Lower-income households pay a higher security deposit than other households.
- Gas prices—The typical inner-city family pays $300 more than those in the suburbs.

Moreover, low-income families have less access to mainstream financial institutions and thus are much more likely to need the services of a check casher, typically a storefront operation offering check-cashing services and payday loans. Unusually high interest rates and fees distinguish these alternative financial services, which more low-income families rely upon because low-income and minority communities are not where mainstream banks look for customers or locate branches. Reports from Philadelphia and North Carolina demonstrate that storefront payday services target poor communities.[50] In North Carolina, for example, African American communities have three times as many payday lending storefronts as white neighborhoods. This ratio increases as the proportion of blacks in a neighborhood increases. In North Carolina, the threefold disparity is related to race because the disparity remained even when income, home ownership rate, poverty level, unemployment, and other sociological variables were held constant.

Many low-income families live paycheck-to-paycheck. When a pothole in the road blows out a tire, a child needs to visit the emergency room for medical treatment, or the family budget simply comes up short of the next paycheck, emergency loans seem to offer a temporary fix. Short-term loans come with a high price, especially when they come from payday lenders. These cash advances or borrowing against the next paycheck invariably lead to further financial crisis. The Center for Responsible Lending reports that repeat borrowers account for 99 percent of payday loans and that the average payday borrower pays $800 to borrow $325, which includes all fees, interest, and charges.

Check-cashing services and predatory payday lending is part of the price that families pay for being poor and living in neighborhoods where low-income minorities are concentrated.

Given the overrepresentation of African Americans among the low-income population of urban central cities across the country, a significant part of their consumer dollars goes into a "poor tax" that comes about because of higher prices, limited information, and lack of access to high-quality, fairly valued goods and services. As well, weak regulation of lenders has facilitated "abuses" that take advantage of low-income households. As the authors of the Philadelphia study note: "Higher prices undermine the ability of low-income working families in Philadelphia to accumulate wealth, stalling the efforts underway to make the economy truly competitive."[51]

Even with these greater costs of goods and services, they may not approach the spending of whites. Data indicate that whites disproportionately spend on alcoholic beverages, reading materials, small appliances, and gifts.[52] While we may not be able to answer definitively to what extent these differences between blacks and whites contribute to the racial gap in wealth, it is clear that they do deprive African Americans of a source of discretionary spending that could go into asset building. But we still contend that there is little systematic data that would support a conspicuous consumption thesis. Nevertheless, the conspicuous consumption thesis is a popular canard that continues to "stigmatize" African Americans whether it comes from Bill Cosby and his comments on African Americans' preference for "expensive tennis shoes over Hooked on Phonics" or is embedded in the still-prevalent stereotypes of African Americans as "indulgent, impulsive, and wasteful."[53]

On the other side, however, is the role that the black middle class plays in producing demand for consumer products. It has long been known that one of the chief domains in which blacks have found success in corporate America is marketing.[54] Bringing their own insight from growing up black in America in combination with their training and talent, black marketing experts have been called upon to develop the ad campaigns that gain entrée and dominance in the underserved urban market. Thus, while black consumerism may drain the black lower and working class of discretionary dollars for asset building, it surely builds black wealth through the economic success that it brings to black corporate employees (and increasingly black CEOs and executives) whose reputation and value derives from their ability to tap the urban black market.

The developments discussed in the last section resulted from changes in African American wealth created by home ownership, how this wealth was used, credit hardship, and a burgeoning new African American urban consumption market. This extends our mode of theorizing into the areas of credit and consumption. The next section continues this theme by extending our conceptualizion of the racialization of state policy into the arena of the criminal justice system and incarceration. This analysis is important because prison time and records have direct negative impacts on job prospects, wealth accumulation opportunities, and citizenship.

The Racialization of State Policy: Incarceration

Over the past thirty years we have seen a sixfold increase in the U.S. penal population, leaving 1.3 million men in state and federal prisons by the end of the century. For African American men this has been a catastrophic tragedy, with 12 percent of black men in their twenties in prison or jail in 2002.[55] Compared with whites, incarceration rates for blacks are about eight times higher, and prison inmates usually have low levels of education, averaging less than 12 years of completed schooling. These high rates of incarceration are related in large part to changes in state crime control policy and policing procedures responsible for sweeping up large numbers of African American men into the criminal justice system.[56] This is especially the case in regard to the war on drugs. As the pioneering research of Marc Mauer demonstrates, the intensification of the criminalization of drug use has bloated the state and federal prison populations by increasing arrest rates, making the risk of imprisonment almost certain, and lengthening the jail term owing to mandatory sentencing.[57] As Wacquant argues, the racial disparity in the incarceration of African Americans and the growth of the penal system developed in tandem with the economic decline of the central city.[58] This has led to a "racialization of U.S. imprisonment" fed by a large "population of younger black men who either reject or are rejected by the deregulated low-wage labor market."[59]

Since most analyses of economic indicators used in this book and other reports exclude the incarcerated population, there is a strong likelihood that we are underestimating the gap between black and white wealth because we are not including a large segment of the black population who, if included, would most likely have low levels of wealth accumulation. In taking young prime-age working and school-age males out of the possibility of securing schooling or gaining a foothold in the labor market, the racialization of U.S. imprisonment ensures that this population will not be able to begin the process of wealth accumulation at an early age, increasing the racial wealth gap between them and their white counterparts. Given that their presence in prison creates a stigma that has a negative effect on labor market and economic outcomes during their postprison reentry, this group will be further disadvantaged in attempting to build wealth over their life course.

If this "racialization of imprisonment" continues, it will negatively affect the accumulation of wealth among African American households for generations into the future. As Petit and Western note, "imprisonment has become a common life event for recent birth cohorts of black noncollege men."[60] In fact, about 30 percent of this group had gone to prison by their mid-thirties. The group most at risk is the less educated (that is, those without a college education). Their lifetime risk of incarceration has doubled from 1979 to 1999. Analyzing the probability of a cohort of black men born between 1965 and 1969 on being in jail or the military, Petit and Western concluded, "For black men in their mid-thirties at the end of the 1990s, prison records were nearly twice as common as bachelor's degrees" and among the noncollege black men in this cohort "imprisonment was more than twice as common as military service."

Summary of Developments

Our review of important developments affecting racial inequality in the past decade yields some significant themes. As wealth accumulation among African American families began to expand, recession, declining stock prices, and processes of financial institutions converge to shrink, strip, and consume it. New home ownership and credit markets, in particular, arose in response to new wealth and wealth-creating opportunities in minority communities, and this poses new opportunities, challenges, and dangers. Amid these contractions, the bottom line is that the racial wealth gap worsened during the last decade. Thus, even though we could make an argument that African American achievements on the job and in schools were improving, an escalating racial wealth gap reversed these accomplishments. Increased incarceration rates have dampened African Americans' ability to compete and succeed—much less accumulate wealth—in America even further.

This sets the stage for chapter 9, which focuses on scholarly developments in wealth inequality, the public response to wealth and big-ticket tax policy, and asset-based public policies. The issues we highlight in the next chapter raise serious political challenges that must be confronted in the campaign for racial equality and justice. No doubt, the toughest challenge involves the age-old dilemma of how to simultaneously improve the well-being and mobility of millions of American families through asset-based social policy for the poor, regardless of race, while continuing to confront the deep structures of race in America.

The Emergence
of Asset-Based Policy

9

One of the signal contributions of *Black Wealth/White Wealth* was its call for a new policy direction in the attenuation of wealth inequality. The focus on wealth, we argued, opened up new vistas of opportunity for those interested in emancipatory social policy. We identified a three-pronged approach:

> First, we must directly address the historically generated as well as current institutional disadvantages that limit the ability for blacks, as a group, to accumulate wealth resources. Second, we must resolutely promote asset acquisition among those at the bottom of the social structure who have been locked out of the wealth accumulation process, be they black or white. Third, we must take aim at the massive concentration of wealth that is held by the richest Americans.[1]

What has happened in these three areas since our call? The answer is an intricate story of a disjuncture between what we know and what we can or are able to do. On the scholarly level we have seen an explosion of knowledge about the sources and consequences of wealth inequality. The body of evidence strongly supports the original research uncovered in *Black Wealth/White Wealth*, deepening and enriching it as well. However, on the policy front we have seen the agenda of asset-based social policy develop in ways that while encouraging have had to confront a massive effort that continues to concentrate wealth in American society in the hands of the few instead of the many.

This is a story that we tell from a unique perspective. After the publication of *Black Wealth/White Wealth* we became part of the cast of characters and institutions who were involved in social policy efforts to address asset inequalities. In part, because of the work on asset inequality, Melvin Oliver was appointed by the incoming president of the Ford Foundation, Susan Berresford, to become vice president of a reorganized U.S. and international grant-making unit charged with the Foundation's mission of "reducing poverty and injustice." Reflecting a new emphasis on assets, the program's central proposition was that:

> Durable improvements in the lives of poor people and communities are most likely to occur if the poor acquire and gain access to assets, restore or protect their assets, and control, deploy, or enhance the condition of their assets.

Under Oliver's leadership for eight years, the Asset Building and Community Development Program of the Ford Foundation invested over $1.4 *billion* dollars worldwide in support of grantees working to reduce poverty and injustice, many working directly from an asset-building perspective. Thomas Shapiro meanwhile continued research in the tradition of *Black Wealth/White Wealth,* publishing *The Hidden Cost of Being African American: How Wealth Perpetuates Inequality,* and being an active participant on research advisory committees to major asset-building demonstrations, an advisor on policy research advisory committees in the field, and working with community-based organizations on asset building for poor and minority communities. We therefore describe from the inside out some of the promises, dilemmas, tensions, and contradictions, as we see it, of asset-based social policy efforts of the last ten years or so.

We begin by reviewing the burgeoning scholarly work on wealth and racial inequality. This is a welcome development that has brought to the fore new data and bold conceptual and theoretical developments that move our understanding forward on this important topic. We then ask what has the translation of this work to policy wrought. We suggest that there has been a disjuncture between the work on the scholarship of wealth and public policy: Public policy is increasing, not decreasing, wealth inequality. We analyze public policies and discussions related to the estate tax, tax cuts, and social security, and demonstrate how they continue to intensify the racial and class divide in asset holding. We then review the developments in asset-based policy that are progressive and consistent with our understanding of how to attenuate racial wealth differences. We focus on individual asset building, institutional changes in the financial services sector, and social policies related to regional equity. While these policies are creative and based on solid research, it is too early to tell the scope of their impact. The next section focuses on the politics of asset-based social policy and addresses some of the knotty issues that have surfaced with their emergence. Finally, we end by addressing the difficult issue of how we create and implement policy that directly challenges the structures of inequity, thereby closing the racial wealth gap.

Wealth Studies in the Academy

The social scientific study of wealth has been slow in developing. Prior to the publication of *Black Wealth/White Wealth*, inconsistent attention was paid to wealth, particularly to the topic of race and wealth. Since then a consistent flow of studies have appeared and the focus on wealth, and particularly the racial context of wealth, seems well established. It is now a given in social science that any complete analysis of inequality or economic well-being must include wealth. Textbooks on American society, social stratification, race and ethnicity, and inequality all now regularly provide information on wealth and race.[2] Moreover, wealth has assumed status as an important explanatory variable in such outcomes as health, quality of schools, child development, and, of course, housing.[3] While *Black Wealth/White Wealth* helped contribute to this blossoming of work, other factors surely were more important, including the inclusion of wealth data in accessible longitudinal surveys widely used in the social scientific community. Also, popular interest in wealth grew in the 1990s, as "Lifestyles of the Rich or Famous" or on any of the many infomercials that promise that "you can become wealthy too" attest.[4]

Over the last decade, three important lines of academic work have appeared that have advanced our understanding of wealth and racial inequality. First, there was an explosion of empirically grounded research in the social sciences documenting trends in wealth inequality and race. Second, there has been a steady drumbeat of work in the field of law, particularly critical legal studies, which examines the racialized aspects of legal analysis in fields such as taxation, bankruptcy, and property. Finally, there is the theoretical work linking differences in wealth to the racial privilege that whites enjoy—what has popularly been called "white studies."

When *Black Wealth/White Wealth* was published, the major academic study on wealth was Michael Sherraden's path breaking *Assets and the Poor: A New American Welfare Policy*. This work informed a number of aspects of our work, including the conceptual difference between income and wealth, our understanding of the social welfare state, and several of our policy proposals on youth and individual development accounts. The empirically based scholarship is much deeper today. Following closely on the heels of *Black Wealth/White Wealth*, Dalton Conley's highly regarded *Being in the Black, Living in the Red* employed longitudinal data to assess how controlling for wealth could better explain black–white differentials on such important indicators as educational attainment and family structure. He uses these findings to suggest that the race–class conundrum can be transcended with a focus on a wealth-based measure of class. Other analysts have focused on the distribution of wealth inequities generally and by race. These include studies on the composition of racial assets and home ownership.[5] Lisa Keister has employed simulations using data from multiple data sets to estimate the impact of a host of factors on wealth inequality and wealth mobility.[6] These studies have achieved high levels of methodological rigor, include comprehensive data, and have uncovered a mass of information on the demographics and distribution of wealth holding in America.[7]

The second set of studies in the academy that have been thought provoking and have extended our understanding of racial wealth inequality have been, interestingly enough, in the field of legal studies. Both conceptual and theoretical, these studies attempt to understand how wealth inequality fits into the matrix of law and its application to various fields. Growing out of the field of critical legal studies, these works examine the ways in which law in a particular field has built into its neutral language concepts, principles, and assumptions that are racially tinged and that lead to disparate racial outcomes, such as racial wealth inequality.[8] For example, work on the tax code demonstrates that so-called racially neutral language and procedures in fact disadvantage African Americans.[9] This occurs in innumerable ways. Two examples will suffice. First, African Americans pay relatively more taxes because their monetary resources are concentrated in income as opposed to investments; wages are taxed at a greater rate than investments. Second, married black households usually have dual wage earners in which both have close to equal incomes, leading to a greater tax rate than a single wage earner in a married household where the spouse does not work or a married couple in which one worker's income is considerably higher than the other's income. The Internal Revenue Service code also taxes married workers who are the sole family wage earners at a lesser rate than single wage earners. This racial disparity in outcome is found in other legal statutes, namely, bankruptcy, as described earlier. This focus on how law's present day construction still creates disparate outcomes, especially in terms of racial differences in wealth, extends *Black Wealth/White Wealth*'s original focus on racialization.[10] Significantly, this focus also provides a compelling explanation of how so-called color blindness can still produce a discriminatory world that "persists even in the face of formal equality and even in the absence of current racial discrimination."[11]

The third scholarly area where the themes, issues, and ideas that propelled *Black Wealth/White Wealth* have expanded is the area of "white studies." A growing body of work explores the social construction of "whiteness" by uncovering the historical processes by which "white identity" fused with privilege in U.S. society, creating what historian George Lipsitz cites as a "possessive investment in whiteness."[12] Scholars in this tradition have been producing fascinating studies that demonstrate how various ethnic group identities were racialized—"how the Irish became white" or how Jews over time gained the privileges associated with whiteness, for example.[13] Key to this work is identifying both the symbolic and concrete privileges that extend to whiteness. One key privilege is access to wealth. This deepens the insights identified in *Black Wealth/White Wealth*, whereby whites gain advantages in the accumulation and inheritance of wealth. Many whites are born with advantages that come to families through profits made from housing secured in discriminatory markets, through the unequal educations allocated to children of different races, and through networks that channel employment opportunities to relatives and friends. Scholarship in the emerging field of white studies demonstrates how whites have come to develop a psychological and material stake in the current social and economic arrangements that continue to marginalize and stigmatize people of color.[14]

These scholarly developments appreciably deepened our understanding of race in America, especially the importance of financial wealth in structuring advantage and disadvantage, and the transmission of inequality; how neutral laws, policies, and tax expenditures contain embedded racial (and class) standing; and how financial resources provide the material scaffolding for white privilege. With these advances in our scholarly knowledge, one might expect some political translation into politics and policy arenas. With more interest in reporting issues of wealth inequality in the media, it seems the public is more aware of wealth issues than ever. Unfortunately, there has been little, if any, political translation. From our point of view, this political deficiency is particularly apparent and disappointing on some of the largest issues of this decade—policy debates around the repeal of the estate tax, tax cuts, and reforming Social Security.

Wealth Inequality and Public Understanding

Our understanding of the role of family wealth fits the original meaning of the two-headed Janus sculpture, where one head represents new beginnings and the other head represents vigilance. Accumulating family wealth is critical to social mobility and living standards in the United States and represents new beginnings; vigilance is necessary to balance the trend of great wealth inequality sedimenting into advantages for the few and disadvantage for the many. We think this captures the American political dilemma concerning wealth. On the one hand, most Americans want to become rich, think it might actually happen, and support policies that reward hard work, investment and risk, and creativity. On the other hand, we do not want the rules to change in the fifth inning of the game to favor the wealthy and diminish similar opportunities for all, nor do Americans believe advantages of wealth should overwhelm opportunity, merit, and achievement. The conservative appropriation of the "ownership society" recasts Janus to one face that hides the dangers of wealth inequality. In sociological terms, this approach overemphasizes mobility while denying stratification.

Estate Tax

Inheritance and the estate tax pose the most striking instance of this dilemma. In 2005, permanent repeal of the estate tax is at the center of the Bush administration's political and tax agenda. Advocacy groups battle to frame the estate tax either as a "death tax" or about fairness, and it is often difficult to read public opinion because advocacy groups frequently commission the polling data.[15] In any case, our review of the existing public opinion data indicates that many Americans think they will become rich one day and will have to pay estate taxes. Most Americans oppose an estate tax, but when given some straightforward information about the tax, and how few actually pay it, most Americans change their opinions from repealing the estate tax to supporting it with reforms.[16]

Very few Americans, in fact, pay the estate tax. Only if your estate is worth $17 million or more do you fit the profile of who the estate tax payer will be in 2009. One-and-a-half-million dollars are exempted in 2005; by 2009, the exemption raises to $3.5 million and the tax rate decreases. Kansas, a heartland state, is representative in the size and variety of estate tax filers. Of the 25,000 Kansas residents who died in 2003 when the estate tax exemption was $1 million, only 198 estates paid the estate tax. In other words, in 2003, 99.2 percent of the descendents of Kansans who died paid no estate tax. As exemptions escalate under the current law, only an estimated 58 estates a year in Kansas will be wealthy enough to pay the tax by 2009. Nationally, by 2009, less than 6,000 estates will pay the estate tax; thus, about 99.75 percent of the descendents of those who die will not face estate tax liabilities.[17]

The 2001 law lowers the estate tax in a step-by-step fashion, finally culminating in zeroing out the tax in 2010. If Congress takes no action, in 2011 the law reverts to the 2002 provisions (exemption back down to $1 million and the tax rate reverts to 56 percent). This Republican strategy seems meant to ensure that Congress will take action before 2011; otherwise, it will look like a tax hike. Indeed, the Bush repeal version is in play as we write in 2005. Because of the law's provision, the super-rich who die in 2010 will leave an untaxed bonanza to their heirs. Moreover, the Treasury will lose more than $30 billion in this one year alone. Our main concern is about the real and symbolic weather vane the estate tax represents—inheritance versus opportunity and achievement. Others, like Federal Reserve Board Chairman Alan Greenspan, are concerned about lost revenues and budget deficits, arguing against repeal of the estate tax unless there are equal spending offsets or increased revenues from other taxes.[18] Indeed, under the current law, and if the estate tax is repealed by 2010, nearly $1 trillion will be lost through 2021.[19] Still others are concerned about the negative affect on charitable giving because the current estate tax encourages charitable giving because it reduces the tax bite of large estates. Estimates suggest that charitable and tax-exempt institutions could lose $10 billion a year upon repeal.[20]

We are strong advocates of estate tax reform, the kind of reform with a "reasonable" exemption, say $2 million or some smaller figure, and protection for family businesses.[21] For us, a fundamental principle is at stake—the power of very wealthy individuals to assure succeeding generations economic success, material comfort, advantages, and power through unearned advantages, regardless of any achievements or contributions they may make. *The Hidden Cost of Being African American* stakes out this case: "In thinking about racial inequality in particular and inequality in general, it makes a great deal of sense to draw political and philosophical lines around questions of inheritance and meritocracy."[22] Repeal of the estate tax gives imprimatur to the sedimentation of inequality for African Americans and hence framing it as a civil rights issue is legitimate. It is clear that passing on to heirs unearned "great" wealth and advantages results in greater inequality and is not consistent with the ideals of the American people. Framing the estate tax this way refocuses the debate back to ideals and realities of equality and opportunity. Equal opportunity and a level playing field do not coexist with inherited status. Inheritance is the enemy of meritocracy, and perhaps democracy too.

Tax Cuts

Taking the estate tax in broader context of other tax cuts, we note that capital, corporations, and the wealthiest families won ideological and practical victories during the last decade. The context and rationales for the 2001 tax cuts demonstrate the extreme policy tilt enabling further wealth and income inequality. Unlike other presidents who proposed huge tax cuts for the wealthy, George W. Bush did little to balance lowered rates on earnings from capital and on the highest incomes with meaningful cuts for middle- or working-class families. Furthermore, the public and political arguments strongly reflected a philosophy concerned with rewarding wealth and financial investments instead of encouraging asset acquisition among middle-income and poor families. From an asset perspective, the rationales prefigure the conservative version of the ownership society, privileging in policy a small but powerful group of wealthy and top-income families. This vision contrasts with policies focusing on inclusion and spreading wealth accumulation.

Those opposed to the 2001 tax cuts focused on the fairness issue, pointing out implications for wealth inequality, as well as arguing that Bush was rewarding wealthy friends, backers, and corporate interests. Alternative proposals promoted by the opposition tinkered with the formula to target middle- and low-income families for larger proportions of the tax cut. The public discourse then focused on who was more deserving of tax cuts: Those who "earn" it, already pay huge tax bills, and should be allowed to keep more of their own money? Or those struggling to keep pace and the forgotten middle class?

The tax cuts were never justified as making life more comfortable for the wealthy. Instead, the Bush administration explained that they were just a component of a larger economic stimulus package that would have systemic effects. Small businesses created the most new jobs, so the argument was that tax cuts to business owners would stimulate job growth and hence drive the economy forward to new heights of growth and prosperity. More income, as the argument went, also might stimulate employment because the wealthy would use part of their tax breaks on new consumption. Many argued that tax cuts for the wealthy would not stimulate new jobs. Subsequent experience demonstrates that the tax cut effect stimulated no economic waves, leaving no ripples on the economy. In fact, total private employment was lower in January 2005 than in January 2001. The political dust has now settled on the last major round of income tax cuts, in 2001, and while debates concerning the effects of these cuts still swirl, the question of who benefited has a clear answer. Assets and capital trumped jobs and income. Earnings from investments, capital gains, interest, and dividends were subject to sharply reduced tax rates. Moreover, those with the highest incomes benefited the most. In fact, the top 10 percent of taxpayers garnered the bulk of the 2001 tax cuts—53 percent. And the wealthiest 0.1 percent received 15 percent of the total tax cut pie.

Social Security

Privatization of Social Security is the leading edge of the conservative "ownership society" agenda, and since this mode of privatization often is confused with asset policy, our discussion of Social Security attempts to clarify the crucial differences. First, we discuss and describe Social Security. Next, we examine the curious argument by privatization advocates about privatization being in the interests of African Americans.[23] Then we analyze some crucial differences between conservative and progressive narratives about asset policy and the ownership society.

Individuals pay Social Security taxes on earnings up to the maximum level, $90,000 in 2005. The highest earners have gotten substantially better off. They are the great beneficiaries of tax cuts in the last decade, and their growing share of earnings has been free of Social Security tax. Thus, because Social Security is essentially a working tax, collection of Social Security dollars has gotten more regressive over the years.

Most Americans associate Social Security only with old-age retirement, but Congress created it to do much more than that and it does. It is a "pay as you go" social insurance system financing retirees today with the contributions of current workers. Currently, retirees receive 70 percent of Social Security funds. This is the best-known part of Social Security. The less well-understood part includes the 15 percent that goes to disabled workers and the 15 percent that goes to surviving family members of deceased Social Security recipients. As we have seen already, the payroll tax is regressive; however, the benefits are progressive. Lower-wage workers are more likely to get disability benefits and their children are more likely to receive survivor's benefits. In fact, survivor's benefits helps to lift children out of poverty and pay for higher education.[24]

The strange argument that privatization will benefit African Americans originates from conservative and libertarian think tanks,[25] and it is built entirely around the argument that since blacks die younger, they receive a smaller share of retiree benefits. Thus, if blacks owned their own private accounts, they could pass them along to heirs when they die at an earlier age. This argument conveniently leaves aside the progressive benefits blacks receive because they are more likely to be disabled workers and their children are more likely to get survivor's benefits. Indeed, the age of the average African American Social Security beneficiary is younger than the average white beneficiary, which is explained by disability and children's survivor status. William Spriggs, an economist who has analyzed and written widely about blacks and Social Security, reports that blacks pay about 9 percent of payroll taxes and collect about 9 percent of the benefits.[26] Thus, the argument that Social Security disadvantages blacks is specious from the start.

Whites, in fact, live longer than African Americans. This is explained by higher death rates at young ages due to health care disparities and higher death rates of young black men. As morbid as the subject may be, death at early ages affects overall life-expectancy figures, but it is not very important for Social Security and privatization debates. Among workers who live long enough to reach retirement age, that is, those workers who have paid fully into the system, life expectancies do not differ much by racial groups, even among black and white men.

Finally, William Spriggs devastates the argument that African Americans have the most to gain from privatizing Social Security because black seniors are more reliant upon it than white seniors. Indeed, African Americans are more reliant on Social Security, with 40 percent of all African American seniors having Social Security as their sole source of income. Spriggs writes, "This is a result of discrimination in the labor market that limits the share of African Americans with jobs that offer pension benefits. Privatizing Social Security would not change labor market discrimination or its effects."[27] All of the plans under discussion predict a decline in Social Security benefits, which would be devastating for black families who rely so centrally upon them for their sustenance in old age. Because African Americans and Hispanics have substantially less wealth upon retirement than whites, they are far more dependent on Social Security. Converting the program into a system where their retirement income would be more dependent on investment markets would make black and Hispanic seniors even more vulnerable to poverty.

Given this analysis of Social Security and its connection to African American families, we can articulate some important principles. Since the current distribution of Social Security benefits appear progressive for blacks and other minorities, reform schemes changing or cutting back or delaying benefits threaten this progressivity. For instance, because blacks rely more on Social Security for retirement income, benefit cuts gravely imperil living standards of black retirees, survivors, and children. Social Security taxes are regressive for most Americans, and thus financing reforms that make this tax less regressive are welcome, especially removing the cap so that more income is taxed, not just incomes up to $90,000. Finally, from an asset perspective, we embrace accounts that add on to—not take away from—the current Social Security program. Assuming fiscal reform and solvency, we support the ability of workers to set aside additional percentages of their incomes into asset development accounts with no tax liability, especially if these accounts are matched.[28]

Connecting an asset perspective to current political issues like Social Security is not occurring as fast as we would like. This perspective introduces a sharp contrast with the conservative ownership theme, where the fundamental idea is to transform Social Security from a social insurance program protecting against the risks of disability, death of a spouse and parent, and old age to a private system where individuals take on greater risks in return for owning their benefits. For some, transferring Social Security to a private account is confused with the concept of an individual development account, but they are not the same. In fact, one can draw some sharp distinctions. The privatization of risk—President Bush's plan—neither generates new assets nor spreads them to asset-poor families. As we noted already, privatizing Social Security has regressive impacts for working Americans, especially minorities. Individual development accounts, on the other hand, put new financial resources in the hands of families with little or no assets. Privatizing Social Security, however, transfers risks of disability, dying too young, or living too long from a pool of millions of workers across several generations to individuals.

The Hidden Shift from Social Investment to Privatized Citizenship

Through steady erosion under Democratic and Republican administrations alike—a process that has only intensified since 2000—the civic infrastructure for the common good has deteriorated considerably. Our commitment to, and resources for, first-rate, democratic public education and high-quality health care are two of the main casualties, and the nation has suffered as a result. Declining social investment in education and health forces families to use private wealth to take up this slack. Those with little or no wealth fall further behind, incur debt, or drain mobility seed-money to stay in place. One main point is that withering investment in civic infrastructure places a greater burden on family financial wealth, transferring some cost of common goods from the public to families. Another major theme is that race and class educational inequalities and health disparities become exacerbated further by the hidden shift from social investment to privatized citizenship. To illustrate these dynamics, we examine health care disparities and family financial resources in the next section.

Racial disparities in health are commonly accepted facts. The Center for Disease Control reports that the risk factors, incidence, morbidity, and mortality rates for the top three causes and seven of the ten leading causes of death and injuries are greater among blacks than whites.[29] Our knowledge about health disparities—especially racial differences in health status, life expectancy, and morbidity—has grown tremendously in the past decade. Because of more reliable data and better studies, we know much more clearly today than ten years ago the extent to which African Americans die younger and have higher rates of life-threatening diseases like high blood pressure and prostate cancer. The mortality rate for blacks with diabetes is more than twice that for whites, heart disease carries a 40 percent higher mortality rate, and stroke carries an 80 percent higher mortality. Black women are three times more likely than white women to die during pregnancy, and twice as many black babies as white babies die in infancy.

Equitable access to quality health care, along with culturally appropriate public health initiatives and community support, is key to ameliorating the human ravages produced by the second-class health status of African American families. About one in five (19 percent) African Americans under the age of 65 do not have health insurance, which compares to 13 percent for whites. Among other things, this translates into lower vaccination rates and a considerably lower rate of women receiving prenatal care in the first trimester (75 versus 69 percent). About 20 percent of black Americans lack a usual source of health care compared with less than 16 percent of whites. Adding in residential segregation and the location of health care facilities, African Americans are twice as likely to rely on hospitals or clinics for their usual source of care as white Americans.

Health and family financial resources intersect at two critical junctures. More well-known is the connection between health insurance and coverage that come with decent incomes and jobs that carry health care benefits. Health and wealth intersect too. Whites spend about $700 more annually on health care services than African Americans. This private safety net of wealth better enables a family to meet unexpected medical costs, emergencies, and crises.[30] A recent study on elders' health problems and wealth depletion makes a significant contribution to our understanding in this area.[31] Health events for seniors contribute to wealth depletion with varying impact for racial and ethnic groups. In particular, African Americans are the most vulnerable to wealth depletion with the onset of new severe chronic health events. Of African American households experiencing a severe chronic condition, 14 percent deplete their wealth cache by 30 percent or more. This was twice the wealth depletion rate for whites. African Americans elders are less healthy and wealthy than white seniors. The impact of health on wealth depletion for African Americans is a significant and troubling issue for public policy.

America's underdeveloped social investment in health means that families compensate by depleting their private wealth. As health care costs have spiraled upward, employer-sponsored health plans are becoming stingier, with employers picking up less of the health insurance premiums, employees receiving fewer employer-sponsored benefits, and more businesses dropping health coverage altogether. This leads to a growing group of underinsured citizens who are forced to assume the financial burden of family health, illustrating the trend toward a shift from social investment in work benefits to private wealth. This is a sure sign of the society's drift toward privatized citizenship.

What have we learned from this review of developments? In this chapter, three sets of conclusions emerge from our analysis thus far. Contributions in the area of law, tax code, and policy, and in the area of understanding material, psychological, and ideological advantages of whites have advanced our understandings of wealth inequality and the racial wealth gap, and they strongly support a progressive social change agenda. The open question is how this scholarship affects the public discourse where the master narrative concerns opportunities for and infatuation with becoming rich and famous. From our point of view, the 2001 tax cut debate was a setback, the current status of the estate tax is not encouraging—although there are optimistic signs that this battle is no longer uncontested—and the Social Security debate shows more promise, but the outcome is still unsettled. The counternarrative focuses on how wealth inequality structures racial inequality by reversing gains in other areas. Furthermore, extreme and worsening levels of wealth inequality warp democracy and American ideals. The contradiction between advances in wealth scholarship and retreats on big-ticket policy ultimately is a political issue. Finally, in the last decade, financial assets have become even more critical for the well-being and success of American families as citizens bear greater risks because of weakening social investments. This is producing a privatized form of citizenship, best illustrated by our examination of wealth and health disparities.

Developments in Asset-Based Social Policy for the Poor

Asset-based social policy proposals have been directed at three areas. First, there have been significant developments in asset-based social policy that attempts to increase the wealth of poor and working-poor households through a "matched savings" strategy. Second, there has been an attempt to change the institutional context of the lending and banking system to provide access to mortgages and banking services for minorities and the "unbanked." Third, there has been a concern with increasing individual and community assets that have been undervalued and isolated. These urban-based communities have been the causalities of urban policies that have led to metropolitan fragmentation and social isolation from the growing economic sectors of the regional economy. Policies that reconnect these communities to the core of the region's economy increase the value of community assets, leading to the need for new policies to ensure that community residents have access to these assets for individual and community benefit.

Individual Asset-Based Social Policy for the Poor

One of the liveliest developments since the publication of *Black Wealth/White Wealth* has been the growth of and relative success of asset-based social policy for the poor. Under the intellectual guidance of Michael Sherraden and the policy leadership of the Corporation for Enterprise Development (CFED), the social policy innovations associated with asset building—matched savings accounts and children's savings accounts—have achieved a body of strong applied research results, real policy and popular interest, and considerable private and public funds to test and demonstrate whether these ideas can truly work.[32]

Individual asset-based social policy for the poor is premised on the fact that U.S. public policy has, for generations, been concerned with providing resources to help middle-class and well-to-do Americans build assets. Historically, Homestead Acts, land-grant colleges, Veteran's Administration benefits, the GI Bill of Rights, and mortgage interest deductions have greatly facilitated the building of America's middle class. Millions of individuals and families have taken advantage of these policies to plan for the future, buy homes, prepare for retirement, send their children to college, and weather unexpected financial storms. It is impossible to gauge the importance of or the expenditures on these programs if one examines only direct government spending. Christopher Howard's *The Hidden Welfare State* and *Hidden in Plain Sight* by CFED reveal the magnitude of governmental assistance for asset accumulation, growth, and preservation among those who already own assets. Through the tax code allowing individuals and families lower rates or to exclude taxable earnings, the taxpayers financed $335 billion worth of asset policies for the nonpoor in fiscal year 2003, most of which accrue to wealthy families.[33]

The biggest single ticket item is home ownership, totaling $111 billion a year, of which $70 billion is for mortgage interest deductions, $22 billion for property tax deductions, and $18 billion for capital gain exclusions on the sale of primary residences. Retirement account write-offs come next—$101 billion. Savings and investment tax code allowances, like reduced tax rates on long-term capital gains, add another $122 billion. A sprinkling of small business tax write-offs along with spending for rural housing and the like add another $2 billion.[34]

Federal spending programs targeted at people of modest or scarce means are dwarfed by tax expenditures that heavily favor Americans who already have significant assets. CFED calculated actual income distributions for tax benefits from the three largest tax expenditures—capital gains and dividend rates, the mortgage interest deduction, and home property tax deduction. It turns out that 34 percent of these tax savings go to the top 1 percent of taxpayers—those with incomes averaging over $1 million. By contrast, the bottom 60 percent of taxpayers receive less than 5 percent of the savings.[35]

Individual asset-based social policy tries to implement social policy that will direct more resources to poor individuals and families to help them build assets just as the government has subsidized the movement of the World War II generation into the middle class and home ownership and helped the well-off consolidate their wealth.[36] The major innovation developed to accomplish this has been various versions of what is called the Individual Development Account (IDA). Sherraden describes this social policy mechanism in an expansive way as

> ... a matched saving strategy [so] the poor can accumulate assets if they, like the middle and upper classes, have incentives and opportunities. IDAs are special savings accounts, started as early as birth, with savings matched for the poor, to be used for education, job training, home ownership, small business, or other development purposes. IDAs can have multiple sources of matching deposits, including governments, corporations, foundations, community groups, and individual donors.[37]

Asset-based social policy has been characterized by a focus on facilitating savings and the accumulation of financial assets for low-income families and the poor who usually fall outside of traditional asset-building opportunities.

Over the last fifteen years individual asset-based social policy has gained a foothold in policy discussions and in the policy-making process. Among the achievements are:

- Gaining the attention and support of a bipartisan group of legislators and policy advocates to introduce legislation and support policy that moves the ideas and programs forward.
- Implementation of a long-term demonstration of the efficacy of IDAs, the American Dream Demonstration (ADD) that definitively established the ability of the poor to save along with their use of and impact of savings on the beliefs and attitudes of savers.[38]
- The inclusion of IDAs as a state option in the federal welfare reform act (U.S. Congress 1996), which replaced AFDC with Temporary Assistance to Needy Families (TANF). This effectively excluded IDA funds from asset limits for all means-tested programs and permitted TANF funds to match savings in IDAs.
- Passage of *Assets for Independence* in 1998 with bipartisan support, and signed by the President, provided $125 million in federal funding for IDA demonstrations over five years; though in the first year the appropriation was only $10 million. The recent authorization was $25 million.
- Asset policies are up and running in all fifty states with over 25,000 account holders taking part in approximately 600 different programs.[39]
- Initiation of the SEED (Saving for Education, Entrepreneurship, and Downpayment) Policy, Practice, and Research Initiative, a multiyear, national initiative to test the efficacy of a national system of asset-building accounts for children and youth.[40]

While IDAs have come to dominate the asset-building social policy movement, increasingly policy analysts and practitioners are thinking about asset building over the life course. For example, Children's Savings Accounts enable youth to enter young adulthood with a sizeable asset that they can use for education or home ownership, IDAs help families hoping to pay for a home or their children's higher education, and retirement accounts enable seniors to have greater independence and control over their financial life in their twilight years.[41] All of these accounts would be universal yet progressive. Universality enables the program to create broad-scale social support that a poverty-focused program would have difficulty garnering. The progressivity of these programs would enable them to provide significantly more resources to the poor. For example, matches would be provided for contributions by low-income households. This, of course, would enable them to generate greater rates of savings and asset accumulation than those without matches.

Policies promoting asset acquisition among the poor have achieved amazing policy traction in a short period, with policies, programs, and tools that are quite developed, widely used, and fairly well evaluated. Ten years ago, we had little confidence that asset policy would blossom, develop an infrastructure, touch as many lives, and take hold to the extent that it did. What remain are significant issues of scale, funding, and political will. Nevertheless, this clearly represents a significant and hard-won victory for asset development policy, a place from which we can continue building.

Institutional Change: Access to the Banking System

Asset accumulation requires integration into and access to the formal credit and banking system. In the US the ability to function financially, purchase a home, and save for the future all require a connection to our banking system. Most Americans have such a connection. However, 22 percent of all low-income families—about 8.4 million families—lack the basic connection to the formal banking system, a checking account. This leads to a situation where the unbanked poor pay more for everyday financial services taken for granted by the banked and which subject them to abusive financial services practices. Michael Barr, in reviewing the situation for the unbanked poor, describes this cascade of consequences:

> These "unbanked" households and other "underbanked" low and moderate-income individuals face high costs, relative to their income, for basic financial services. For example, a worker earning $12,000 a year would pay approximately $250 annually just to cash payroll checks at a check cashing outlet. Low-income workers often turn to tax preparation services and costly refund loans to access their government tax refund check under the Earned Income Tax Credit (EITC) ... Low-income families often lack any regular means to save.... The unbanked are also largely cut off from mainstream sources of credit, whether for short-term consumer borrowing or home ownership, because, without a bank account, it is more difficult

and more costly to establish credit or qualify for a loan, particularly those without bank accounts.[42]

Moreover, another segment of the poor are "under-banked." That is, they may have an account in a depository institution, but they depend on alternative financial institutions and arrangements for their financial needs. These include such arrangements as check-cashing establishments and payday lenders (described in chapter 8).

Then there is the issue of access to mortgage markets and fair costs for loans. Increasingly, access to mortgage loans is predicated on a model of creditworthiness that increasingly disqualifies low- and moderate-income borrowers who have one or more of the following: credit blemishes on their record, no relationship with formal credit and banking institutions, or who are in arrears because of a medical emergency. On top of this, access to mortgage markets continues to be racially structured, so that blacks and Hispanics are disproportionately denied mortgages despite their creditworthiness. This has led to greater reliance on the subprime mortgage market and thus a greater exposure for predatory lending practices (see chapter 8).

This isolation from the mainstream of the financial system has dire consequences for the ability of this group to accumulate wealth. Their cost in aggregate for being consigned to high-cost and high-interests financial services is astounding. Using the best data available in 2001, Eric Stein of the Center for Responsible Lending estimated that U.S. borrowers lose $9.1 billion annually to predatory lending practices. These practices refer to "equity stripping" (financed credit insurance, exorbitant up-front fees, and subprime prepayment penalties), which cost borrowers $6.2 billion and excess interest charges of $2.9 billion. These figures do not even refer to losses borrowers have endured from foreclosures.[43] The cost of predatory payday lending fees is equally exploitative. The Center for Responsible Lending conservatively estimated a cost of $3.4 billion annually extracted from borrowers caught in a debt trap of repeated transactions. At the time, over nine of ten payday loans went to borrowers who were taking out five or more payday loans per year. Indeed, two-thirds of borrowers get five or more payday loans per year, and about 5 million borrowers have been caught in this "debt trap" each year.[44]

The agenda for social policy in this area has revolved around three strategies: institutional changes through policy reform, the development of new products, and regulatory reform. The following example features all three of these strategies, demonstrating how asset-based policy could foster increasing access to and integration in the formal banking system.

Access to Home Mortgages:
The Self-Help-Fannie Mae Partnership

Ever since the struggles of local communities that culminated in the Community Reinvestment Act (CRA) in 1977, there has been a strong concern with access to home mortgages in inner-city, rural, and disadvantaged communities. Now there is a federal government requirement that banks invest in their local communities. While this law has triggered some $400 billion in bank loan pledges in its first twenty years—with most of the capital dedicated to projects in poor, inner-city neighborhoods—this issue has continued to be a struggle for the advocacy community. It has forced them to mount significant efforts to preserve fair lending in poor neighborhoods some twenty-five years later. CRA's geographically based rules and enforcement provisions may no longer fit the realities of the financial services market. Widespread consolidation in the financial services industry and the globalization of many financial institutions have rendered neighborhood banking a relic of the past. This has made it much harder for community organizations to develop partnerships with banks that go beyond the minimum required by CRA guidelines.[45]

A creative response has been attempts to secure institutional change in the way that banks provide mortgages by leveraging the resources of the largest player in the process, the secondary market. A central problem limiting a bank's efforts to do more lending to low-income buyers is the fact that they are usually unable to bundle these loans and sell them to the secondary market, to institutions like Fannie Mae and Freddie Mac. Once sold, new funds are freed up to reinvest in more mortgages. Without the ability to sell these loans to the secondary market, banks close down their affordable lending programs once they meet government-imposed limits.

Self Help, a progressive community-development finance institution led by the visionary Martin Eakes, had tried to convince Fannie Mae, the U.S. government-chartered and largest secondary market player, to relax its stringent criteria and to purchase loans that were characterized by nontraditional flexible underwriting guidelines; higher loan-to-value ratios, higher debt burden limits, little or no cash reserves, low credit scores, and alternative evidence of creditworthiness. Self Help had been buying loans of this type from banks in North Carolina with near zero losses for years. Fannie Mae, sensing that its new market was the minority community, wanted to experiment but was wary to do so since their models of repayment predicted that they would lose considerable dollars. Thus, they would only experiment if they could cover the losses that their models predicted would occur.

Approaching the Ford Foundation for an unprecedented $50 million dollar grant to insure the losses that Fannie Mae might experience, Eakes made the convincing argument that if "this demonstrates that the kind of borrowers that they could serve would include more African Americans, immigrants and families headed by women and that they would have losses similar to their total portfolio" then the advocacy community could "hold their foot to the fire" and change the way loans are provided nationally.[46] The Ford Foundation agreed and provided the grant with an equally ambitious study of the borrowers and a matched sample of non-home owners to uncover both the financial and social impacts of home ownership.

The goals of the program—termed the Community Advantage Program (CAP)—were to provide $2 billion dollars of home loans to borrowers and to learn from their experience whether these so-called high-risk and less creditworthy buyers could succeed in home ownership. The ultimate goal was "to encourage mainstream lenders, secondary market institutions, and housing policymakers to incorporate loan products that feature more flexible underwriting into their core lending business, federal regulations, and national housing policies."[47]

The results of CAP have been rather eye-opening, and consequently Self Help and Fannie Mae have continued their partnership. Because of the initial success of the program, they now anticipate that instead of providing $2 billion in home loans, they will provide loans of up to $4 billion. The demographics of who is in the CAP loan portfolio differs in important ways from the traditional Fannie Mae or Freddie Mac distribution: CAP's portfolio has more African American borrowers (27 percent to 3 percent), more female-headed households (41 percent to 16 percent), and more low-income borrowers with less than 60 percent of the area's median income (49 percent to 10 percent for Fannie Mae and 7.5 percent for Freddie Mac). Moreover, one-quarter of the borrowers had credit scores less than the industry cutoff of 620. These distributions demonstrate that conventional lenders, by removing some of the most onerous aspects of their application process, can reach deeper into the disadvantaged and minority population to provide mortgages.[48]

While Fannie Mae's expectations were that losses would be considerable, they have not been borne out. Instead, losses have been quite consistent with their regular loan portfolio. However, what has been different is the delinquencies. Not surprisingly, without large financial surpluses of wealth and with jobs that are likely unstable, 9.37 percent of the CAP loan portfolio have a thirty-day or more delinquency in paying their monthly mortgage. This is over four times the rate for conventional loans, but about a third less than the FHA rate. What is surprising, however, is that the higher delinquencies do not seem to convert into very high default rates. These borrowers appear to be highly committed to home ownership and do whatever is necessary to keep their homes.

As to the borrowers, they have experienced strong growth in equity and increases in wealth. Stegman and his colleagues summarize the results thusly

> ... the vast majority of CAP families realized substantial gains in paper wealth as a result of their transition from renting to owning ... Our analysis also found that families with spotty credit records, or no established credit history at all, accrued significant gains in gross wealth, which underscores the importance of preparing more of these families to gain a foothold in the homeownership market.[49]

Data on African American housing equity appreciation was particularly instructive. While blacks had impressive gains, they were about 10 percent less than whites. Even when blacks get homes, the high costs of segregation saps their ability to share fully in the equity returns that are enjoyed by whites.

The results of this demonstration were beginning to have an impact at Fannie Mae. However, right when the institution was starting to make these major changes, critics citing a concern with lax financial oversight and controls managed to pursue and purge Franklin Raines, the president and a major supporter of these efforts.[50] It is too early to tell if the legacy of his work will continue to inform institutional change at the world's largest secondary mortgage corporation. With the strong data from the Community Advantage experience, there is no reason for Fannie Mae and others in the secondary market to pull back from their commitment to affordable home ownership; it is both good business and good public policy.

Regional Equity and Asset Building

Black Wealth/White Wealth described how federal policies put in place during the New Deal and extending through the 1960s encouraged the growth of the American suburb and precipitated the decline of the central city. This has led to a situation where those living in the suburbs are increasingly more prosperous and have access to the best schools, hospitals, and social services. Those living in the city, however, attend worse schools and receive both poor-quality health care and deficient social services. Not coincidentally, whites are more likely to inhabit the suburbs while minorities are more likely to inhabit the cities (particularly inner cities). Thus it is becoming increasingly clear that opportunity has been racialized in American society and enshrined more and more into geography. Given this divide, however, it is also becoming evident that city and suburb are inextricably linked in a regionwide economic and social web, connected to one another in innumerable ways. The more this division between the haves and have-nots increases, the less competitive and the more unsustainable American metropolitan areas will become in the future.[51]

This has led to the development of efforts to create regional equity as a strategy to harness the potential of American metropolitan communities to become economically competitive, and socially and environmentally sustainable.[52] The leading edge of this movement explicitly sees regional equity as "... giving children and families of all races and classes the best possible environment in which to live. Advancing regional equity thus involves reducing social and economic disparities among individuals, social groups, neighborhoods, and local jurisdictions within a metropolitan area." Specifically,

> Reducing inequities within regions means providing economic opportunity and secure, living-wage jobs for all residents. It involves building healthy, mixed income neighborhoods with sufficient affordable housing distributed throughout the region. It means fostering strong civic engagement and responsive institutions to ensure that all residents have a voice in the major decisions that affect their lives. It means providing low-income residents with the opportunity to build assets and become beneficiaries of reinvestment and positive change in their communities. Finally, regional equity involves greater cooperation to promote a broader tax base and to have a more fair distribution of resources for quality schools and other public services.[53]

Only by thinking and acting regionally will these disparities be challenged successfully. As john powell, one of the key architects of the regional equity perspective, puts it:

> We cannot solve unemployment disparities, the affordable housing crisis, and racially disparate school achievement levels, among other concerns, unless we act from a regional viewpoint. A single community, even a single munici-pality, faces enormous obstacles to linking low income workers of color in the city with jobs emerging in the metropolitan periphery. A single com-munity organization or advocacy group can be frustrated trying to improve schools in a high poverty, racially segregated district when "racially neutral" policies privilege schools in affluent, majority White districts. The commu-nity's work is on target, but the dynamics of inequality are region-sized.[54]

The regional equity perspective is growing, and community economic devel-opment policymakers, community organizations, and scholars employ this perspective regularly. A broad range of policy proscriptions and mechanisms have been proposed, practically all of them designed to increase the opportu-nities afforded people in the inner city. Many of them are focused on *creating value* for undervalued assets in inner-city communities; *retaining the value* of assets in inner cities that are in danger of declining; and ensuring that the poor and disadvantaged can *take advantage of rising values* in the inner city. This goes to the heart of some of the racial disparities we found in how the homes of blacks appreciate compared with those of whites, and the differential equity accumulation noted among CAP participants described above.

powell has described a just regional equity result as resulting in a region where

> ... resources of all varieties would not favor the suburban periphery where Whites predominate. Instead, resources and development would be distrib-uted fairly throughout the region. Each municipality would have adequate revenue to provide public services, an adequate supply of affordable housing, homes that can appreciate in value without restraint from forces like segrega-tion, high-performing schools not marked by disproportionately high levels of student need, effective transit infrastructure, and economic development. If resources and opportunities were fairly distributed and racial discrimina-tion did not limit genuine access to them for people of color, a metropolitan region would be more racially just. In turn, racial disparities in life chances and outcomes would be diminished.[55]

What kinds of policies would create this dynamic and how do they relate to the accumulation of wealth? Part of the answer lies in the debilitating impact of racial segregation. Since the publication of *Black Wealth/White Wealth* only modest declines have occurred in racial segregation.[56] Inner-city black neigh-borhoods continue to suffer from segregation, isolation from jobs, and poor city services and schools. Regional policy that directly attacks these issues would increase the value of homes in these communities, making access to better jobs and greater incomes available, and improve the quality of schools. Several areas are ripe for this kind of intervention: transportation, regional housing policy, and educational policy. From this perspective, there are actions that need to be taken at the regional or national level as well as local actions.

For example, transportation funds have been directed at providing transit routes for suburban residents to commute to jobs in the central city. Reverse commutes to the suburbs would enable low-income central city workers to connect with job-rich suburban industries and retail establishments, improving job access. On the national level this has translated to support for important provisions for a "new transportation charter" that would provide "... more funding for access to jobs, public transit, system preservation, and programs that explicitly promote coordination between transportation and land use, including incentives for affordable housing close to transit."[57] For the local community, building inner-city economic, social, and cultural development around transit centers would revitalize economic activity in these communities. For example, the West Garfield Park community in Chicago struggled to have a transit stop that was designated to be closed to become a transit center. Utilizing the cultural resource of the Garfield Park Conservancy as an anchor, the community coordinated economic activity around the transit center, building affordable housing adjacent to the area, and as a result, they have seen a 10 percent increase in ridership. This has led to increased property values in the community and a larger customer base for retail outlets. Also, the transit center has connected workers to jobs in the suburban community.[58]

A regional housing policy that increased the overall supply of affordable housing and distributed it through the region would do much to help sustain inner-city neighborhoods as viable housing markets. A policy proposal that has shown some success is "inclusionary zoning" wherein by regulation, communities are required to build a percentage of housing units in new residential developments for low- and moderate-income households. These restrictions to developers are balanced by benefits such as zoning variances, development rights, and other permits. With about twenty-five years of experience in inclusionary zoning, we know that it can foster mixed-income households. Inclusionary zoning combined with other types of housing policies ensures that enough low- and moderate-income housing is built and that it is sited in a way that does not increase the concentration of poverty.

As Thomas Shapiro has documented in *The Hidden Costs of Being African American*, there is an intimate connection between housing, schools, and wealth. For whites, housing choices are often conscious expressions of their concern for the educational opportunities that living in a certain neighborhood provides. Those choices combine to maintain racially segregated communities in which white wealth increases and black wealth, as we have seen, stagnates. Any attempt to change the wealth distribution must deal with this deadly connection. Regional equity advocates start with the premise that unequal funding is at the heart of the imbalance between central city and suburban schools. Policies that break down racially isolated schools, that enable equal funding across regions or districts, and small schools that are anchored in neighborhoods could go a long way in addressing these issues. Promoting school desegregation has become fraught with legal limitations and social anxieties. But john powell describes an effort in Chattanooga, Tennessee that has a regional perspective.

> [In] Chattanooga ... local communities, developers, and city planners are building two new schools downtown that will educate nearby residents (predominantly low-income and students of color) and set aside seats for the children of downtown employees (tending to be more middle income and White students). This approach considers the regional employment market and matches it with a regional educational approach targeted to produce integration.

Coupled with revenue and investment strategies that equalize per student funding and create attractive and fully functioning neighborhood schools, one could turn around the advantages that derive purely from living in an all-white community and spread educational opportunity and achievement across the urban landscape.

Asset-based social policy is developing along a number of dimensions, as this review demonstrates. On the individual level, bold asset-based policies are being promoted through such mechanisms as IDAs and children's development accounts. On the institutional level, efforts are being made to change the financial services sector to better integrate low-income borrowers and provide services and products that match their needs and particular circumstances. Advocates of regional equity attempt to address the imbalance between city and suburb that has persistently devalued the assets of African Americans. Taken together these are powerful policy tools that can collectively produce tangible results.

Assets and Leveraging Change

While much of our discussion concerns financial wealth, something easy to put a number to, our ultimate concern is that families use this resource or tool for their betterment in whatever way they choose. Thus, counting is important but we are deeply interested in the qualitative ways lives change as situations improve. Furthermore, we are keenly interested in how communities change as families acquire assets; how their lives improve, and they become more invested citizens. In brief, we are interested in "the wealth effect": how improving wealth profiles change individuals, families, and communities. The notion of a stakeholder society, something very American with roots in the political philosophy of Thomas Paine and Thomas Jefferson, provides a theoretical frame for this discussion.[59]

The concept of a stakeholder society holds much promise because it animates a different kind of society with individuals having a stake or investment in all aspects of society. Research clearly indicates that families building financial assets experience more marital stability, move less, and see their children perform better in school (as measured by fewer behavioral problems, better grades and test scores, and higher college attendance) when compared with families of similar socioeconomic status but without assets. Families building assets participate more in community organizations like PTAs, vote more, and are engaged in community and civic issues. Rates of spousal and child abuse are lower in families that accumulate assets.[60] Although we should be cautious about the small number of studies, it is clear that building assets does far more than simply add money to bank accounts.

An important core sociological insight is that attitudes, behavior, and outlooks change as social conditions change. The positive family, school, civic engagement, and psychological changes associated with wealth accumulation occur because of changing circumstances and outlooks that accompany brighter futures. Assets are, as Michael Sherraden notes, "hope in concrete form."[61] Behaviors change in the context of other, positive life-changes. One concern is that asset policy is yet another attempt to change the behavior of the poor without fundamentally changing their conditions, that is, a new version of blaming the poor that demands middle-class values without middle-class status. Asset policy focuses on enabling families to acquire and control key financial resources so that they can leave the threat and reality of poverty behind and become more self-reliant, independent, and stable. Unlike conservative, victim-blaming, and even some liberal policy ventures, if successful, asset policy changes conditions and behavior simultaneously.

We are optimistic that families that accumulate assets and use them for social mobility also will be invested in other equity-based reforms. For example, as families become more invested in their communities, as home owners, stakeholders, and citizens, they will begin pressuring for improved civic services such as better schools, libraries, playgrounds, and open spaces; police and fire protection; and other public services. As families begin expecting more from their communities and participate in community organizations to bring about these changes, they become powerful actors for social change. Public officials, businesses, and corporations are more responsive to home owners, engaged citizens, consumers, and organized communities.[62]

One key here is that asset development programs in the demonstration, testing, and initial policy phases occur in the context of community organizations whose missions typically are built around improving the lives of low-income and minority families. Although our data here is anecdotal, both of us have attended many conferences or given presentations before audiences full of program participants and graduates who clearly consider their striving to secure success as incomplete. Their social activism spills into other critical areas like improving schools, community services, creating stable diverse communities, fighting practices that lead to foreclosures and redlining, and more. And, we can relate powerful stories of small-scale economic and community-development programs that change people's lives and become community builders. It's the builder-entrepreneur with seed money from North Shore Bank in Chicago who fixes up dilapidated properties, turns a profit, and then sells these affordable homes to local residents. That person stays in the community as a prosperous model, providing good craft and construction jobs to others, trains them to become entrepreneurs someday, and continues to turn urban decay into thriving communities, a new kind of community builder. It's also the program that created a small laundry business, B.I.G., in the Columbia Heights neighborhood of Washington, D.C., producing a small investment that leveraged social change. Small shareholders have turned around the pattern of stealing from the coin-operated machines, and now the community takes pride in a resource they own and control, and which provides crucial services they need.[63]

Our contention is that new stakeholders become more attentive to their family's future and look to improve the civic infrastructure that promotes well-being and social mobility. Our bet, for example, is that the new group of first-time home owners who obtained opportunities through new lending programs or IDAs will not pull the ladder up behind themselves and hoard these opportunities. Rather, they struggle with monthly mortgage payments, credit card bills, a harsher economy, the threats of bankruptcy and foreclosure, inferior schools and other community services, and thus their mobility is still very much a work in progress. Finally, if large groups of families successfully accomplish mobility and join the home-owning middle class, these programs may have leveraged "social reform on the cheap,"[64] where social policy with a limited investment may be able to change larger social dynamics in urban America.

The Politics of Asset Policy

Asset development policy emerged from the academy, foundations, civil society, and community organizations. The Center for Social Development at Washington University, St. Louis, started in 1994 under the direction of Michael Sherraden, has pioneered asset policy and plays a crucial leadership role. CFED, founded by Bob Friedman, is an exemplar of new emerging civil society (or "third sector") organization with a significant role in policy development. It is a nonprofit, nonpartisan organization working to expand economic opportunity that combines think-tank innovation with practitioner insight to identify promising ideas, test and refine them in communities, and craft policies to help good ideas reach scale. The entry of the Ford Foundation into the asset field provided significant resources, leadership, intellectual support, and visibility that helped move these ideas from a cottage industry to national policy. Finally, community organizations like the Community Action Project in Tulsa County (CAPTC) bridged the intellectual ideas to local communities and families. This organization helps thousands of people in the Tulsa community gain greater financial security and control over their lives. Founded in the heady days of President Johnson's War on Poverty, asset development policy provided a focus and new coherence to the work and experience of organizations like CAPTC.[65]

Building support for local, state, and federal policy, then, focused on bringing a set of ideas and programs to the attention of policy makers, politicians, thought leaders, and organizations, which is a top-down strategy to influence elites and opinion makers. This approach was coupled with projects and programs to demonstrate commonsense and core ideas—i.e., poor people would save under conditions of institutional support and encouragement, and they would use their new assets to improve their lives. Thus, grassroots organizations became both partners and constituents of asset policy, and these organizations mediated the participation of individuals. In a sense, the asset field grew from the top down and incorporated existing community organizations. Growing in this way meant there was no large base of poor families to push, guide, and shape this movement directly; instead, the movement needed to be responsive to the on-the-ground programmatic experience of community organizations, to funders, and to national politics.

Developments in asset policy have run far ahead of knowledge building. It is one of those instances where careful methodological rigor, national demonstration projects, studious evaluation of the field, and well-thought-out policy rationales seemed superfluous because on-the-ground events outpaced the careful building of the empirical and intellectual asset case. This is another way of saying practice led theory. Not all policy development follows a logical sequence of demonstration, testing, evaluation, and then putting the case before policy makers. In a sense, a perfect storm converged to lift programs off the ground and provide funding. Welfare reform was swirling around, which left a policy vacuum in its wake as people began searching for an alternative to welfare. The strong commonsense appeal of asset development policy, along with powerful testimony of program participants talking about how an IDA program changed their lives, also pushed asset policy forward. Finally, community organizations and traditional antipoverty agencies understood immediately how this new approach fit the needs of their clientele, how it corresponded with new directions in their missions, and how it matched their own organizational capacities. Within a few short years, more than half of the states had viable asset development programs up and running.

Where few existed prior to 1994, as we write today, asset development policy guides the work of dozens of centers, institutes, and policy advocacy organizations inside and outside the academy. Approximately six hundred programs in all fifty states deliver IDAs, establishing a network of federal, state, and community organizations deeply invested in asset development social policy. In addition, many national and local civil rights, women's, labor, and disability organizations have asset divisions or personnel responsible for issues in the assets domain. New policy organizations such as Demos, New American Foundation, The Center for American Progress, the Institute on Assets and Social Policy, and dozens more have become central players in the asset policy movement. One point here is not so much the numbers or listings, but how asset policy moved from something nobody heard of or knew anything about in 1995 to being a main player and topic of conversation at the policy table today. Another important point is that we are witnessing an institutionalization of core asset-policy ideas and programs so that developments no longer need to rely on the participation of a few key social entrepreneurs. That is, from a Weberian perspective, there is a routinization of charisma. In addition, a growing number of foundations and private funders support this work, providing a sustainable base for research, programs, demonstrations, and policy development and implementation.

Asset-based legislation has been introduced with assiduous bipartisan sponsorship and support, producing unlikely allies and bedfellows, such as senators Santorum (R-PA) and Corzine (D-NJ) and congressmen Ford (D-TN) and English (R-PA). Liberals and conservatives "buy into" asset-based social policy from different perspectives. Conservatives promote the value-changing aspects of saving, deferring consumption, and future-orientation while liberals endorse the poverty reduction, open opportunity, and mobility features. Indeed, asset policy is seen as a bold, new idea not easily pigeonholed because of its commonsense, broad appeal. This surprising coalition has been able to pass several important pieces of legislation; however, while important for demonstration and infrastructure-building purposes, the programs still are piecemeal and funded at a level that taps only a small fraction of the need. In our assessment, critical issues of universality, scalability, program design, and, ultimately, the need for substantial public funding will prove decisive in determining the political direction, support, and future of individual development accounts specifically and asset policy more broadly.

Are Financial Assets All You Need?

Asset-based social policy takes its lead from what it terms the power of assets; its ability to leverage change in behaviors that are positive and that radiate to other areas of the family, community, and society. The basic definition of an asset comes from the conceptual distinction between "assets" and "income." But as several others point out, there are many kinds of assets. For example, education is one of the most important assets needed to be successful in modern societies. An asset is defined as:

> A stock ... that can be acquired, developed, improved and transferred across generations. A stock endures; it is not entirely consumed. It generates flows or consumption, as well as additional stock.[66]

Once this asset is in place, it has a stocklike quality; it can be drawn upon, built upon, and it can be passed on to the next generation. It also creates positive changes in behavior, and these changes have impacts on other dimensions of the individual and community. Both financial and educational assets can gain practically unanimous agreements from all sectors and analysts, but there are a range of other assets that are more equivocally thought of as assets. These include social, natural, and human assets.[67]

The significant question is how these assets interact, and whether and under what circumstances there is any ordering in the importance of these assets for the well-being of individuals, families, and communities. The succinct answer is that every person, family, and community needs a "bundle" of assets to be fully effective. However, each asset or bundle is activated differently under diverse circumstances. Under authoritarian regimes, for example, social and human capital may be the most vulnerable because they threaten the status quo. Without the ability to use social and human assets, financial capital may be less important. In parts of the world that depend on their natural resource environments for livelihoods, the natural resource assets may be dominant. In U.S. society, we argue, financial assets are often the most important in assuring the cultivation of other assets and in opening up the political spaces to make the "bundle" more effective. One example may demonstrate this effect.

In 1932 Rexford Tugwell, one of President Roosevelt's "Brain Trusters," embarked upon a brave experiment. Noting the large number of bankruptcies that had beset the large plantations of the South at the onset of the Depression, Tugwell came up with the brilliant idea to redistribute this land as a foundation for the creation of a small farm-holding class among this population, reserving several sites for African American shareholding and tenant farmers.[68] Tugwell and his idealistic bureaucrats put this idea in place in several Southern counties.

As a social scientist, Tugwell even planned in advance for regular evaluations to see how this experiment would work. The last evaluation was not entirely optimistic about either land retention or improvements in income, health, and overall well-being among all families who worked their own land for the first time. Congressional hostility reached a crescendo in 1943, and the program elevating sharecroppers and tenants into landowner status ended abruptly.

Fast-forward to Mississippi during the civil rights movement in 1963, when the Freedom Rides were underway. Northern university students, black and white, flooded Mississippi to challenge the denial of voting rights to the black population. The world watched in familiar horror as the Freedom Riders were beaten and jailed. Early voter registration efforts were stymied by intimidation, violence, and threats of losing social assistance benefits. A delegation of black farmers from Holmes County approached the neighboring Greenwood, Mississippi Student Nonviolent Coordinating Committee volunteers because they wanted to register to vote. This was a group of landowning, independent, self-reliant farmers from Tugwell's experiment of thirty years earlier. They were ready to spearhead civil rights and challenge the Southern caste system. Federal policy had helped transform a group of landless black tenants in the 1930s into a permanent landed middle class that emerged as the backbone of the civil rights movement in the rural South.[69]

While the formal evaluations did not demonstrate much immediate positive change for these families, this event shows that the independence that these landholders had from the white plutocracy, thanks to Tugwell's experiment, gave them the independence to challenge their power. Without these financial assets, they could not have played the exceptional role that they did in one of the most important political transformations this country has ever experienced. In comparison to black tenant farmers in the same county, black landowning farmers subscribed to and read more newspapers and magazines, were more engaged in civic organizations, more active in supporting civil rights activities and other political activity, earned higher incomes, and owned more assets. Furthermore, more children of landowning farmers in Holmes County completed high school, and considerably more became managers, professionals, and other middle-class occupations.[70] These positive changes seem to foreshadow perfectly current studies on the wealth, or stakeholding, effect.

Our point is that financial assets in the context of the United States are essential in animating the development and use of social, natural, and human capital. We would argue that there is a strong case to be made that financial assets are a necessary but not sufficient factor for the development and use of other assets and rights. As such, we argue that the current focus on asset-based social policy built around financial assets is a necessary complement to those political and social developments associated with social, human, cultural, and natural assets.

To raise financial asset building to this prominence for poverty and injustice reduction leads to some inherent tensions with other approaches and perspectives on poverty reduction. Below we outline some of these tensions.

How can asset-based social policy impact the very poor? Asset-based policy is premised on the proposition that the poor will be able to leverage few resources into more resources either through savings or investments in housing and education. What of the poor who do not have the resources to get on the asset accumulation train (e.g., the homeless)? How can asset-based policy impact this group?

How can the process of building assets be accelerated? So far, asset-based policy has not been able to achieve rapid asset accumulation for poor or working class families. This slow process that takes more time, and sometimes squeezes "valuable" resources out of household budgets that could go for other necessities.

What are the best ways to support low-income people in managing and protecting the assets they build? Once the poor start to accumulate assets, they need supports that will help them preserve and protect those assets. Financial education that helps the poor manage and protect their assets becomes necessary.[71]

Where does asset building fit in the larger framework of community and economic development? One keen analyst put it this way:

> The assets theory is an explanation of why people are poor ... Yet when we talk to people, they say it explains something, but not everything. The thing is to look at how to connect building assets to other things. How to create linkages to community organizing, to institutional development, to promoting educational opportunities.[72]

Thus far, asset-based social policy, while growing from a larger theoretical perspective, has a rather narrow band of social policies that

don't seem to integrate well with other social change and social policies usually addressed at poverty reduction.

*If the asset-based social policy agenda is fully funded, there will be a
dwindling base of resources for traditional social services to the poor.*
A growing tension between traditional social service deliverers (e.g.,
affordable rental housing, children and youth services, elder care, etc.)
and the proponents of asset-based social policy are the scarce resources
for social service and poverty reduction efforts in the federal and state
budgets. Asset-based policy appears as a voracious newcomer whose
"novelty" and "appetite" for large resources threatens to decimate the
budget outlays now set aside for social and human services.

These are all intrinsic tensions in asset-based policy. Some of them will
be answered over time. For example, we know that asset-based policy is
not a strategy for the most disadvantaged, but many poor families, as the
IDA demonstration shows, will be able to take advantage of this policy. The
dynamics of incorporating asset building in community and economic development is a story of praxis; as practitioners take up the challenge of asset
building, they have come to value its contributions and to make a place for
it in the broader panoply of strategies that they use. Finally, the issue of
resources is one that is endemic to poverty reduction; there is always not
enough money to do what is needed to be done. But the assets approach does
open up opportunities for us to expand the resources available for poverty
reduction by making the "hidden welfare state" a site of contention for funding asset-building programs.

Confronting the Past: The Reparations Conversation

With legal prohibitions increasingly closing options to address race-specific
policy, the agenda of the reparations movement is one of the few arenas in
which the complex and highly controversial issues of America's racial legacy
can be discussed. The reparations conversation has changed considerably since
we wrote *Black Wealth/White Wealth*. Frankly, we were ambivalent about the
politics of reparations. Without consciously intending to do so, our book clearly
builds a brief for the reparations case. Since then, the reparations movement
is shifting from thinking about individual payments to building a social infrastructure that would support a strong base of economic and social support for

the African American community. This transformation moves the debate away from those who are the descendents of slaves and slaveholders to community and infrastructure legacies, such as inferior schools and second-class health care. From our travels, experiences, and many presentations across the United States in the last decade, we understand the saliency of the reparation conversation as, invariably, it comes up during discussions, conferences, and presentations. Our brief intervention here is twofold: examining its justification and thinking about what an asset perspective adds to this conversation.

The legacy of race lies at the core of *Black Wealth/White Wealth*. This legacy is not simply an important historical experience but one that still lives in its profound and structuring consequences, as well as in continuing contemporary institutional discrimination. For us, the legacy concerns both the past and the present and how the past continues to frame contemporary racial inequality. Reparations provide the political space to reclaim memory and narrative about race in America. Otherwise, discussions about the legacy of race do not occur other than in the context of some current event or crisis, and circumstances of the moment become the lens of discussion. A basic problem results, as explanations focusing on immediate events and individual behavior compete with ones prioritizing the history and context that structure an event or outcome.

The effect of history and experience on the present is the explicit conceptual frame of reparations. This shifts the grounds of the conversation so that African American memory and narrative can be reclaimed. Among other things, the primary contribution of African Americans in creating America's great wealth, how they were denied systematically from sharing the bounty of resources they created, and the prosperity they helped to build and sustain, are the essential elements of this memory and narrative.[73]

We would like to see this process formalized and broadened to wider segments of America. All over the world, societies are facing up to their past injustices.[74] We endorse a process similar to what South Africa did with its Truth and Reconciliation Commission. Such an effort would pull together top scholars in history, sociology, anthropology, political science, urban planning, social policy, and other disciplines to gather the best evidence on the legacy of race in America and to assess its impact. Open to all citizens and holding hearings in all parts of the country, the commission would evaluate the evidence and publish its findings.

Policies to address America's racial legacy would be part of a political process based on the commission's report. This would provide the country an opportunity to address positively its past or to continue denying it. For us, developing and reclaiming the narrative is more important than specific policy remedies, although asset and community-based strategies logically seem to flow from this history, or at least it seems so for us.

To Improve Lives and Challenge Structures

We began this epilogue by drawing a composite of four black families describing their current economic situation and identifying the strategies and processes of asset accumulation they have used to create an asset nest egg. These four families demonstrate many of the themes discussed in the epilogue.

The "Striving Black Middle Class" family, the Braddocks, demonstrate the importance of home ownership for asset accumulation. Their home is the bedrock of their wealth. Moreover, their ability to expand their assets is facilitated by their access to and involvement in their employer-sponsored savings plan, which enables them to contribute through payroll deduction pretax income. Their ability to have a positive asset base is clearly a consequence of their structural position in the economy whereby they are able to take advantage of a government-supported savings policy that enabled them to save for a down payment, gain access to the housing market, and have a savings plan. At the same time, their debt is steadily increasing because their access to credit cards seems unlimited.

The struggling working class representatives, the Joneses, are prime examples of how affordable mortgages provided to those with less-than-stellar credit histories can lead to the development of real equity. But this equity is vulnerable because they are living close to the edge, dependent on credit card debt, and unable to accumulate savings because of low wages. Moreover, the amount of home equity for this family is threatened by racial segregation that limits their returns compared with working-class white families who usually buy homes in suburban settings. Rosa Williams, the elderly representative in this group, has felt the sting of predatory lending, losing her home and having to move in with her daughter and grandchildren. With her "equity stripped" from her, she becomes a dependent of another household who now finds it difficult to move ahead in terms of savings. Finally, the single mother and former TANF recipient, Donna Smith, illustrates the lives of so many black families that cannot get on the asset accumulation train. Working for poverty-level wages, she is unable to maintain her family at a minimum standard of living without access to "payday" loans, which forces her into a cyclical "debt trap."

Each of these families must confront the implications of an increasingly privatized form of citizenship. As the social safety net is ripped away, each of these families must come to terms with a socioeconomic environment where their access to good education and health care is increasingly a function of their wealth. For the black middle class, this may mean that their wealth will be used to provide private education for their children or depleted during old age for health needs. Or they may be preyed upon by unscrupulous lenders, end up losing their equity, and be forced into dependency. Storefront payday services thrive in low-income communities only because mainstream financial services are absent or intentionally restrictive. Working-class and working-poor African Americans face a daunting effort to maintain living standards in communities that cost more for basic services, which leads to credit card reliance and a payday lending debt that puts them in perpetual debt servitude. And given changes in the bankruptcy laws, there seems to be few ways out of this harrowing conundrum.

The strategies that we have identified are ones that can improve the lives of millions of families like these. These policies provide for mechanisms that enable them to save to accumulate the kind of assets that can help them to "get ahead": funds for education, home ownership, and small business development. Children's savings accounts can provide their children nest eggs that can help them make the crucial investments they need to increase their educational financial assets. Access to the credit and mortgage system in ways that are fair and transparent is a necessary precondition of asset building in the twenty-first century. The poor and working class cannot become the perpetual victims of payday lenders who operate a debt peonage system no less rapacious than the one that followed the end of the Civil War. Regulatory reform of this nefarious system is a must if we are to bring financial services to this crucial group. Likewise, predatory lending targeted to minorities and the elderly must be attacked and made illegal, with sufficient penalties to deter the largest and most powerful financial interests engaged in this activity. The mortgage markets need to realize that they are missing out on significant business opportunity by discriminating against African American and other minorities on the basis of so-called "objective credit scores." These scores are not great indicators of individual families' abilities and desire to make their payments on their home. The steering of minority homebuyers to the subprime lending market adds significant costs to their home purchases that are not necessary. Issues of disparate loan pricing, mortgage loan portfolios, subprime and predatory lending, how definitions of creditworthiness tend to be the new basis for exclusion, and the racialized implications of credit scoring bring to light the ways in which supposedly neutral rules of credit systematically disadvantage the wealth accumulation abilities of minorities and the poor.

We have identified a trend of withering social investment where the cost of common goods is transferred increasingly to individuals and families. In areas such as health care, education, safety and security, and others, an asset perspective is wholly supportive of building opportunities for the common good, not only so that opportunities and human development reach high, equitable levels, but also so that the responsibilities and costs of government are not parceled out to families and deplete key family resources. A painful example is the devastation that occurred during Hurricane Katrina where the lack of social investment in public infrastructure combined with low levels of asset development on the part of the mostly African American poor (e.g., the lack of private vehicles) created a volatile and deadly mix. A related challenge of asset-based policy is to prevent its limited successes from becoming another justification for diminishing social infrastructure investments in areas like public education and health care, placing greater burden on families. Simply put, as families begin to accumulate important assets for their future mobility, costs of providing for the public good should not be privatized. With the success of children's savings accounts, for example, federal and state financial commitments to higher education should not be transferred to young adults who are accumulating assets for the first time.

Before concluding, it is sobering to remember the integral connection between the broadest context of racial inequality and the structures of opportunity and wealth generation. Residential segregation is the lynchpin of race relations in America. Most important for our story is the way that residential segregation structures the "segregation tax" producing far less housing wealth in African American communities and the way in which substandard, inferior schools are located predominately in neighborhoods where minorities and low-income families are concentrated. The fundamental relationship between residential segregation and housing wealth is an essential new challenge we and others have been raising. We need regional equity to make the geographic isolation a thing of the past. This isolation dampens the economic opportunity of inner-city residents, leads to unequal schools, and diminishes the equity returns of black home owners.

While asset-based social policy clearly has the potential to improve the lives of real families, the fundamental question is: Can it simultaneously challenge the deeply embedded structures that order advantage and disadvantage? In our experiences, the proponents and advocates of asset-based policy have done a remarkable job in advancing these ideas to center stage in the policy arena. We have no doubts that there will be successes and setbacks. For these policies and ideas to evolve further, there must be an expansion of ownership of these ideas to broader and larger constituencies. The narrow range of policy groups, foundations, and civil society organizations must be complemented with the constituencies of African American, minority, and low-income communities. In addition, policy advocacy must be coupled with movements challenging the structures and institutions that disadvantage the wealth-accumulating ability of minority and low-income groups. Building a coalition that can move forward on these issues and on complementary fronts must also include organizations and constituencies organized around issues that worsen wealth inequality, like the estate tax, regressive tax cuts, and Social Security privatization.

If we are correct that racial wealth inequality is the hidden fault line of American democracy, then what is necessary is no less than a new civil rights movement for the twenty-first century that focuses on economic inclusion and closing the racial wealth gap.

Appendix A

Table A4.1 Wealth by Age

Age of Household Head	Median Income	Median Net Worth	Median Net Financial Assets
<36	$25,503	$5,995	$0
36–49	32,740	41,310	4,200
50–64	28,015	75,000	16,078
>64	11,813	69,072	17,499

Table A4.2 Parents' Occupation and Wealth

Parents' Occupation	Net Worth	Net Financial Assets
Upper-white-collar	$45,975	$8,230
Lower-white-collar	46,950	7,659
Upper-blue-collar	45,338	5,800
Lower-blue-collar	29,300	1,239

Note: Self-employed workers are included in the upper-white-collar-category

Table A4.3 Wealth and Education

Education of Household Head	Median Income	Median Net Worth	Median Net Financial Assets
Elementary	$11,328	$24,358	$500
Some high school	15,637	21,635	582
High school degree	23,318	33,000	2,180
Some college	26,853	29,000	3,300
College degree	37,145	62,972	16,000
Postgraduate	40,287	78,999	22,310

Table A4.4 Wealth and Occupation

Householder's Occupation	Median Income	Median Net Worth	Median Net Financial Assets
Upper-white-collar	$39,136	$59,975	$12,710
Lower-white-collar	26,100	20,768	1,500
Upper-blue-collar	29,890	27,751	985
Lower-blue-collar	21,212	10,144	0
Self-employed	28,300	93,276	36,824

Table A4.5 Wealth and Labor Market Experience

Years in Labor Market	Median Income	Median Net Worth	Median Net Financial Assets	N
All ages				
1 to 4	$22,100	$3,950	$0	1207
5 to 8	27,551	15,000	700	1402
9 to 13	30,847	27,783	1,952	1223
more than 13	29,270	70,449	13,850	1007
35 or younger				
1 to 4	20,940	2,350	0	807
5 to 8	27,740	8,825	200	775
9 to 13	30,480	12,950	474	578
more than 13	32,509	29,606	1,964	100
36 to 49				
1 to 4	24,580	10,225	138	227
5 to 8	28,048	23,101	1,000	435
9 to 13	34,691	40,000	5,500	441
more than 13	35,505	51,500	8,340	359
50 to 64				
1 to 4	21,932	50,600	1,800	119
5 to 8	25,402	49,852	7,800	184
9 to 13	22,935	60,112	7,512	197
more than 13	24,893	92,900	28,880	497

Table A4.6 Resources of the Regions

	Income	Net Worth	Net Financial Assets
Northwest	$25,988	$51,123	$5,749
West	26,202	32,950	3,613
Midwest	24,188	37,461	5,500
South	21,659	28,604	1,758

Table A5.1 Wealth by Income Groups and Race

	Poverty Income	Moderate Income	Middle Income	High Income
		Net Worth		
Whites				
Mean	$48,276	$49,165	$77,782	$168,592
Median	2,173	12,868	38,699	119,151
Blacks				
Mean	7,585	18,733	34,380	81,085
Median	0	2,100	13,061	61,390
Median ratio	-	0.16	0.33	0.52
		Net Financial Assets		
Whites				
Mean	$28,683	$21,567	$34,052	$85,508
Median	0	500	5,500	31,706
Blacks				
Mean	184	2,741	10,606	28,310
Median	0	0	138	7,200
Median ratio	-	-	0.03	0.23

Table A5.2 Education and Wealth by Race

	Income	Income Ratio	Net Worth	Net Worth Ratio	Median NFA	NFA Ratio
			Whites' Education[a]			
Elementary	$7,001		$24,943		$1,899	
Some high school	11,554		23,410		1,100	
High school degree	17,328		32,711		3,287	
Some college	27,594		38,989		5,500	
College degree	35,068		66,665		17,300	
Postgraduate	40,569		79,573		23,200	
			Blacks' Education[a]			
Elementary	$6,942	0.99	$2,500	0.10	$0	-
Some high school	8,724	0.76	430	0.02	0	-
High school degree	11,534	0.67	1,199	0.04	0	-
Some college	21,076	0.76	5,714	0.15	0	-
College degree	28,080	0.80	15,175	0.23	5	0.001
Postgraduate	31,340	0.77	17,874	0.23	78	0.003

[a] Educational attainment of most educated in household

Table A5.3 The Wealth Rewards from Education

Returns[a]	White	Increase	Black	Increase
		Income		
Some high school	$4,533	65%	$1,782	26%
High school degree	5,774	50	2,810	32
Some college	10,266	59	9,542	83
College degree	7,474	27	7,004	33
Postgraduate	5,501	16	3,260	12
		Net Worth		
Some high school	-		-	
High school degree	$9,301	40%	$769	179%
Some college	6,278	19	4,515	377
College degree	27,676	71	9,461	166
Postgraduate	12,908	19	2,699	178
		Net Financial Assets		
Some high school	-		-	
High school degree	$2,187	199%	$0	
Some college	2,213	67	0	
College degree	4,800	87	5	
Postgraduate	5,900	34	73	

[a] Gain in median from median of prior educational level

Table A5.4 Age and Wealth by Race

	Age Household Head			
	<36	36 to 49	50 to 64	>64
		Income		
White	$27,412	$34,984	$29,538	$12,172
Black	15,277	19,700	19,816	9,792
Ratio	0.56	0.56	0.67	0.76
		Net Worth		
White	8,320	50,950	88,356	77,020
Black	500	4,800	18,039	15,774
Ratio	0.06	0.09	0.09	0.20
		Median Net Financial Assets		
White	150	7,199	25,120	22,902
Black	0	0	0	0
Ratio	-	-	-	-
		Mean Net Financial Assets		
White	11,791	44,195	72,188	71,510
Black	535	6,446	9,730	6,640
Ratio	0.05	0.15	0.14	0.09

Table A5.5 Labor Market Experience and Wealth by Race

Years of Experience	Income	Net Worth	Net Financial Assets
	Whites		
1 to 4	$23,146	$4,700	$0
5 to 8	28,342	16,159	1,050
9 to 13	32,436	31,079	3,400
>13	30,198	75,786	19,088
	Blacks		
1 to 4	$13,586	$374	$0
5 to 8	17,880	1,875	0
9 to 13	15,545	899	0
>13	18,328	17,686	0

Note: Labor market experience was only asked of those aged 18 to 64 who had worked two or more consecutive weeks in the past ten years.

Table A5.6 Number of Earners and Wealth by Race

Number of Earners	Income	Net Worth	Net Financial Assets
	Whites		
0	$7,754	$27,636	$884
1	22,660	18,600	1,800
2	34,960	34,528	4,300
3	44,205	74,018	15,510
4 or more	57,940	96,530	15,086
	Blacks		
0	$4,594	$0	$0
1	14,210	1,288	0
2	26,303	6,422	0
3	35,434	18,575	69
4 or more	44,265	30,769	0

Table A5.7 Family, Gender, Marriage, and Wealth by Race

	Income	Net Worth	Net Financial Assets
Family Type			
Married Couples			
White	$32,400	$65,024	$11,500
Black	25,848	17,437	0
Married with Children			
White	33,143	33,143	2,000
Black	23,021	23,021	0
Single Household			
White	15,599	20,083	2,400
Black	11,200	800	0
Single with Children			
White	17,336	4,010	0
Black	9,322	0	0
Gender			
Male Heads			
White	21,342	13,900	2,100
Black	13,637	1,200	0
Female Heads			
White	13,202	23,530	2,549
Black	10,245	500	0
Marital Status			
Never Married			
White	22,150	6,575	760
Black	12,008	0	0
Separated			
White	18,659	3,900	0
Black	11,016	400	0
Divorced			
White	18,474	14,342	700
Black	13,465	1,373	0
Widowed			
White	9,031	60,000	15,587
Black	8,816	12,029	0

Table A5.8 Family, Gender, Status, Labor Market Participation, and Wealth by Race

	Income	Net Worth	Net Financial Assets
Whites			
Couples			
Man works	$30,704	$61,324	$8,800
Woman works	21,704	17,328	10,218
Both work	40,865	56,046	8,612
Neither works	15,006	100,800	33,600
Single Heads			
Man works	27,277	12,000	1,774
Man not working	9,140	27,865	4,000
Woman works	22,336	12,655	730
Woman not working	7,188	38,944	5,749
Blacks			
Couples			
Man works	19,575	11,864	0
Woman works	*	*	*
Both work	34,700	17,375	0
Neither works	11,780	24,301	80
Single Heads			
Man works	18,525	1,549	0
Man not working	5,427	800	0
Woman works	17,594	2,152	0
Woman not working	6,154	2,152	0

* Fewer than 10 cases

Table A5.9 Children and Wealth by Race

No. of Children	Income	Net Worth	Net Financial Assets
Whites			
1	$31,078	$31,029	$2,075
2	31,974	30,308	1,557
3	30,151	24,116	605
4	24,640	10,787	0
5 or more	35,354	32,022	1,474
Blacks			
1	$18,729	$3,610	0
2	19,109	681	0
3	12,286	1,100	0
4	10,620	1,800	0
5 or more	12,062	700	0

Table A6.1 Correlation Matrix for Regression Analysis of Income and Wealth

	NW[a]	NFA[b]	Black	South	Grade Completed	Age	Age Squared	Work	Upper-White-Collar	No. of Workers	Male	Children	Widow
Household Income	0.3644	.2535	-0.1658	-0.1174	0.3063	0.1000	0.0675	0.0882	0.2581	0.4968	0.1130	0.0261	-0.1030
NW		--	-0.1310	-0.0793	0.1408	0.2467	0.2428	0.1894	0.2051	0.1051	0.0101	-0.0726	0.0075
NFA			-0.0926	-0.0433	0.1163	0.1609	0.1613	0.1243	0.1742	0.0511	0.0024	-0.0760	-0.0025
Black				0.1222	-0.0996	-0.0309	-0.0303	-0.0766	-0.1002	-0.0891	-0.0844	0.0763	0.0578
South					-0.0746	0.0161	0.0159	0.0191	-0.0280	-0.0464	0.0143	0.0037	0.0281
Grade Completed						-0.1534	-0.1697	-0.1384	0.4062	0.0436	0.0152	-0.0184	-0.0709
Age							0.9906	0.7725	0.0817	-0.0131	-0.0145	-0.2164	0.2160
Age Squared								0.7666	0.0609	-0.0407	-0.0180	-0.2544	0.2264
Work Experience									0.0607	0.0270	0.0545	-0.1573	0.1435
Upper-White-Collar										0.0773	0.0668	-0.0023	-0.0370
No. of Workers											0.0584	0.0692	-0.1122
Male												0.0519	-0.0854
Children													-0.0647

[a] Net worth
[b] Net financial assets

Table A6.2 Decomposition of Racial Differences in Wealth and Income of the Total Sample

	Black Equations		White Equations	
Net Worth				
(1) Evaluated at black means	$25,629	29.7%	$51,271	59.5%
(2) Evaluated at white means	43,086	50.0	86,229	100.0
(3) Unadjusted differential	60,602	70.3	60,602	70.3
(4) Explained (2) − (1)	17,459	20.2	34,958	40.5
(% of unadjusted)		28.8		57.7
(5) Unexplained (3) − (4)	43,143	50.0	25,644	29.7
(% of unadjusted)		71.2		42.3
Net Financial Assets				
(1) Evaluated at black means	$7,145	17.4%	$20,394	49.8%
(2) Evaluated at white means	15,180	37.0	40,974	100.0
(3) Unadjusted differential	33,829	82.6	33,829	82.6
(4) Explained (2) − (1)	8,035	19.6	20,580	50.2
(% of unadjusted)		23.8		60.8
(5) Unexplained (3) − (4)	25,794	63.0	13,249	32.3
(% of unadjusted)		76.2		39.2
Income				
(1) Evaluated at black means	$22,895	66.2%	$27,997	80.9%
(2) Evaluated at white means	28,717	83.0	34,586	100.0
(3) Unadjusted differential	11,691	33.8	11,691	33.8
(4) Explained (2) − (1)	5,822	16.8	6,589	19.1
(% of unadjusted)		49.8		56.4
(5) Unexplained (3) − (4)	5,869	17.0	5,102	14.8
(% of unadjusted)		50.2		43.6

Table A6.3 Decomposition of Racial Differences in Wealth and Income Married Households

	Black Equations		White Equations	
Net Worth				
(1) Evaluated at black means	$38,121	37.9%	$68,758	68.4%
(2) Evaluated at white means	54,197	53.9	100,491	100.0
(3) Unadjusted differential	62,370	62.1	62,370	62.1
(4) Explained (2) − (1)	16,076	16.0	31,733	31.6
(% of unadjusted)		25.8		50.9
(5) Unexplained (3) − (4)	46,294	46.1	30,637	30.5
(% of unadjusted)		74.2		49.1
Net Financial Assets				
(1) Evaluated at black means	$11,949	25.3%	$27,959	59.1%
(2) Evaluated at white means	20,128	42.6	47,288	100.0
(3) Unadjusted differential	35,339	74.7	35,339	74.7
(4) Explained (2) − (1)	8,179	17.3	19,329	40.9
(% of unadjusted)		23.1		54.7
(5) Unexplained (3) − (4)	27,160	57.4	16,010	33.9
(% of unadjusted)		76.9		45.3
Income				
(1) Evaluated at black means	$30,839	79.0%	$35,936	92.0%
(2) Evaluated at white means	34,155	87.5	39,056	100.0
(3) Unadjusted differential	8,217	21.0	8,217	21.0
(4) Explained (2) − (1)	3,316	8.5	3,120	8.0
(% of unadjusted)		40.4		38.0
(5) Unexplained (3) − (4)	4,901	12.5	5,097	13.1
(% of unadjusted)		59.6		62.0

Table A6.4 Decomposition of Racial Differences in Wealth and Income
Single Households

	Black Equations		White Equations	
Net Worth				
(1) Evaluated at black means	$17,762	30.2%	$39,364	66.9%
(2) Evaluated at white means	26,591	45.2	58,856	100.0
(3) Unadjusted differential	41,094	69.8	41,094	69.8
(4) Explained (2) − (1)	8,829	15.0	19,492	33.1
(% of unadjusted)		21.5		47.4
(5) Unexplained (3) − (4)	32,265	54.8	21,602	36.7
(% of unadjusted)		78.5		52.6
Net Financial Assets				
(1) Evaluated at black means	$4,120	14.3%	$16,697	57.9%
(2) Evaluated at white means	8,177	28.3	28,858	100.0
(3) Unadjusted differential	24,738	85.7	24,738	85.7
(4) Explained (2) − (1)	4,057	14.1	12,161	42.1
(% of unadjusted)		16.4		49.2
(5) Unexplained (3) − (4)	20,681	71.7	12,577	43.6
(% of unadjusted)		83.6		50.8
Income				
(1) Evaluated at black means	$17,894	68.8%	$21,106	81.2%
(2) Evaluated at white means	21,583	83.0	26,007	100.0
(3) Unadjusted differential	8,113	31.2	8,113	31.2
(4) Explained (2) − (1)	3,689	14.2	4,901	18.8
(% of unadjusted)		45.5		60.4
(5) Unexplained (3) − (4)	4,424	17.0	3,212	12.4
(% of unadjusted)		54.5		39.6

Table A6.5 Factors Related to Mortgage Rate Differences

	White	Black	Rate Difference
Income			
<$11,500	9.3%	9.4%	0.1
$11,500–25,000	9.3	9.9	0.6
$25,000–50,000	9.1	9.5	0.4
$50,000–100,000	8.9	9.5	0.6
> $100,000	9.1	—	—
Year of purchase			
1984–1988	9.5	9.9	0.4
1979–1983	9.8	10.2	0.4
1969–1978	8.4	9.2	0.8
1959–1968	7.8	9.1	1.3
< 1958	9.0	9.8	0.8
Age			
< 30	9.5	10.5	1.0
31–40	9.4	9.9	0.5
41–50	9.0	9.6	0.6
51–60	8.7	9.3	0.6
61–70	8.5	9.0	0.5
> 70	8.8	9.8	0.1

Table A6.6 Regression Predicting Mortgage Interest Rate

Variable	Standardized Estimate
Race (Black = 1)	0.0818***
South	0.0327*
Year	-0.2830***
Household income	0.662***
Age	-0.0334*
Size of first mortgage	0.0154
Rate	
FHA-VA	0.0969***
R^2	.11
N	3,799

*p,0.05   **p<0.01   ***p<0.001

Table A6.7 Regression Predicting Housing Appreciation

Variable	Standardized Estimate
Race (Black = 1)	-0.0898***
Inflation	0.2350***
Year	0.1950***
Hypersegregation	-0.2190***
Mortgage rate	0.0863***
R^2	.19
N	3,799

*p,0.05 **p<0.01 ***p<0.001

Appendix B

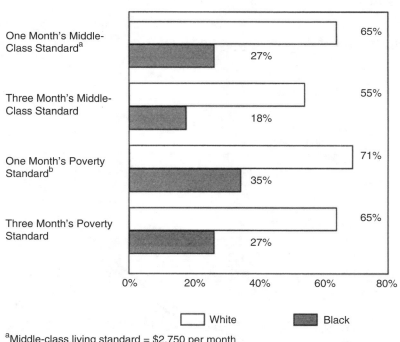

Figure B5.1 Living on the Edge: How Far Will Wealth Reserves Stretch?

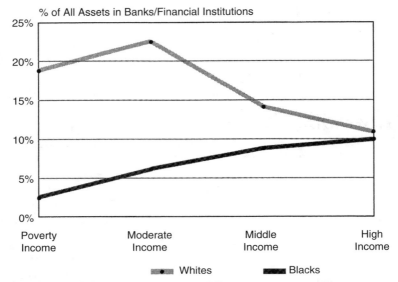

Figure B5.2 Savings by Income and Race

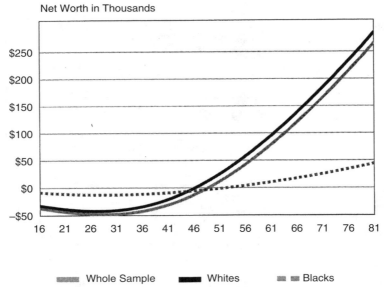

Figure B6.1 Partial Effect of Age on Net Worth

Percent Not Explained by Controlling for Differences between Similar White and Black Households

Figure B6.2 The Costs of Being Black for Married Households

Percent Not Explained by Controlling for Differences between Similar White and Black Households

Figure B6.3 The Costs of Being Black for Single-Headed Households

Notes

Introduction

1. The nation's wealthiest 400. For the *Forbes* magazine profile see Senecker 1993.
2. Robert Nozick quoted in Ravo 1990.
3. On the persistence of racial segregation in housing see Farley and Frey 1994 and Massey and Denton 1993.

Chapter 1

1. This is a modified version of the argument advanced by Wilson's *The Declining Significance of Race* in 1978. Much of the literature on race in American society since then has been an attempt to address Wilson's question via empirical test and theoretical argument. The proponents of the class argument concentrate on how race is less important than class and impersonal forces like economic restructuring (see, e.g., Kasarda 1990; Smith and Welch 1989; Wilson 1987); opponents quickly respond that race has endured in significance (Oliver 1980; Willie 1979) and in some cases become more important, especially for the black middle class (Feagin and Sikes 1994; Landry 1987). Others have attempted to map out the ways in which race and class interact to produce racial inequality (Franklin 1991; Fainstein 1993).
2. The quote on "the accumulation of disadvantages ..." is from Wilson 1987, 120.

3. The quote on the "basis of real democracy ..." is from Myrdal 1944, 223.
4. For the percentage of white applicants for Southern Homestead Land Act see Lanza 1990.
5. The quote on "the freedman's badge of color ..." is from Lanza 1990, 87.
6. "'No, ' he said emphatically ..." The quote is from Myrdal 1944, 226-27.
7. "When the avenues of wealth opened" is from John Rock's Address to the Boston Antislavery Society, March 5, 1858.
8. For discussions of the suburbanization of America see Feagin and Parker 1990; Jackson 1985; Lipsitz 1995; and Squires 1994.
9. On the constrainment of black American's residential opportunities see Jackson 1985.
10. For quotations from *Crabgrass Frontier* on the discriminatory impact of HOLC standards see Jackson 1985, 196.
11. "We had been paying ..." The quote is from Jackson 1985, 206.
12. The quote on "real estate subject to covenants" is from Jackson 1985, 208. See also Bell 1992b, 691–94.
13. On FHA "redlining" see Lipsitz 1995.
14. Levittown's exclusion of blacks. The quote is from Jackson 1985, 241.
15. On banking discrimination and redlining in Atlanta see Dedman 1988.
16. On lending bias in the nation's capital see Brenner and Spayd 1993.
17. On "reverse redlining" see Zuckoff 1993.
18. For the study of high-interest loans in Boston see *Boston Globe* 1991a.
19. On "social inequality" see Weber 1946.
20. For discussions of the improvements in blacks' social status between the 1960s and the 1980s see Hacker 1992; Jaynes and Williams 1989; and Wilson 1987.
21. For figures on black elected officials see *Black Elected Officials* from the Joint Center for Political Studies 1993.
22. The quote on African American political powers is from Yetman 1991, 394.
23. For information on the trends in education for blacks see Carnoy 1994; Jaynes and Williams 1989; and Yetman 1991.
24. On black-white differentials on social and medical well-being see Carnoy 1994; Hacker 1992; Jaynes and Williams 1989; Thio 1992; and Wilson 1987.
25. For the quote on "the status of black America today ..." see Jaynes and Williams 1989, 4.
26. On black middle-income earners see Wilson 1987.
27. On black-to-white ratio of net financial assets see Oliver and Shapiro 1989.
28. For the quote on Americans' deteriorating living standards see Harrison and Bluestone 1988, 137.
29. On the adverse effects for blacks of slow job growth and deindustrialization see Danziger and Gottschalk 1993 and Hill and Negrey 1989.
30. On the changing quality of life for middle-class families see Levy 1987 and Schor 1991.

31. On it took 21 percent of the average wage of a 30-year old male see Levy and Michel 1986.
32. For by 1990 the average home consumed nearly one-half see Oliver and Shapiro 1992.
33. For the kinds of adjustments made by young families in order to purchase a home see Levy and Michel 1986.
34. On economic conditions during the 1990s see Danziger and Gottschalk 1993; Harrison and Bluestone 1988; and Levy and Michel 1991.
35. For the quote on "caste and class restraints …" see Phillips 1990, 19.
36. Four percent of the richest men … see Dye 1979, 200.
37. For discussion of inherited wealth and financial success see Kessler and Masson 1988, Wolff 1987a, and Kotlikoff and Summers 1981.
38. On the distinction between wealth and income see Wolff 1995.
39. For information on wealth data see Turner and Starnes 1976. Soltow 1989 discusses the comparative value of older and more recent data on wealth in the United States
40. For the quote on "income inequality in the United States …" see Kerbo 1983, 32.

Chapter 2

1. For discussions of black-white inequality see Farley 1984; Farley and Allen 1987; Jaynes and Williams 1989; and West 1994. The notion of "two nations" comes from Hacker 1992.
2. The quote on "the most disadvantaged …" comes from Wilson 1987, 8.
3. The notion of the "structural linchpin of American racial inequality" comes from Bobo 1989, 307.
4. For discussions of race and racism see Omi and Winant 1986.
5. "Ownership …" The quote is from Franklin 1991, xviii.
6. For discussions of class as a factor in racial inequality see Baran and Sweezy 1966 and Cox 1948.
7. For discussion of black-white class solidarity see Hill 1977 and Jacobson 1968.
8. On structural changes in employment see Johnson and Oliver 1992; Kasarda 1988; and Wilson 1987.
9. On negative racial attitudes and employment see Kirschenman and Neckerman 1991.
10. On slavery's effect on black savings habits see Butler 1991; Light 1972; and Myrdal 1944.
11. For the quote on "three-quarters of America's colonial families" see Anderson 1994, 123.
12. On black homesteaders in California see Beasley 1919.
13. On the exclusion of blacks from New Deal legislation see Quadagno 1994, 20–24.
14. The quote on black earnings and social security taxes comes from Quadagno 1994, 161, and the one on black women's taxes subsidizing "the benefits of white housewives" comes from ibid, 162.

15. For the quote on Boyle Heights see Lipsitz 1995.
16. For the quote on "legal restrictions …" see Thomas 1992, 140.
17. "White households will begin …" The quote is from Mieszkowski and Syron 1979, 35.
18. "In sum …" The quote is from Franklin 1991, 126.
19. On community decline see Skogan 1990.
20. On the nature of the AFDC program see Rank 1994 and Stack 1974.
21. Figures on black and Hispanic AFDC recipients come from Sherraden 1991, 63.
22. "The assets test …" The quote comes from Sherraden 1991, 64.
23. For the relation between "means tested" and "non-means tested" social insurance programs see Katz 1986, 247.
24. For the 1989 capital gains income figures see Barlett and Steele 1992.
25. On blacks and the tax benefits accruing to home ownership see Jackman and Jackman 1980; Ong and Grigsby 1988; and Horton and Thomas 1993.
26. On blacks' so-called self-employment failings in relation to Japanese and Jewish ethics see Light 1972 and 1980.
27. For a discussion of racial stereotypes in self-employment see Butler 1991, 1–78.
28. The central notion of blacks' unparalleled levels of hardship with respect to self-employment cannot be developed within the confines of this discussion. Several works state the case well. See Part 1 in Blauner 1972 for a theoretical discussion; Du Bois 1935 for a monumental discussion of Reconstruction; Eric Foner 1988 and C. Van Woodward 1955 for trenchant analyses of Jim Crow; and Baron 1971, Bloch 1969, and Bonacich 1976 for penetrating studies of the integration of blacks into the industrial order.
29. On the deficit model of black business failure see Frazier 1957 and Light 1972.
30. For the quote on nonblack ethnics' ability to "enter the open market …" see Butler 1991, 71.
31. For a discussion of Japanese business success outside the Japanese community see Bonacich and Modell 1980.
32. "It is true throughout history …" The quote is from Butler 1991, 72.
33. "This [exclusion from the market] is not his preference …" The quote is from Stuart 1940, xxiii.
34. The quote on "centuries of unrequited toil …" can also be found in Stuart 1940, xxiii.
35. "Seeking a way …" The quote is from Stuart 1940, xxxi.
36. For the various occupations and businesses of blacks in Philadelphia in 1838 see Butler 1991, 38.
37. On the business ventures of free blacks during Reconstruction see Harris 1936, 9.
38. On Cincinnati as the "center of enterprise …" see Butler 1991, 42.
39. On nineteenth-century black instruments of capital formation and business development see Butler 1991, 41–48.

40. "Between 1867 and 1917 ..." The quote is from Butler 1991, 147.
41. "Restricted patronage does not permit ..." The quote is from Pierce 1947, 31.
42. On the blacks' business enclave in Durham, North Carolina, see Butler 1991, 180.
43. "There was grumbling ..." The quote is from Prather 1984, 179. The quote on the impact of "the massacres" is from ibid., 183.
44. For information on the Greenwood district in Tulsa see Butler 1991, 206–21.
45. "Every increase in the price of oil ..." The quote is from Butler 1991, 221.
46. "What happened in Tulsa ..." The quote is from Butler 1991, 209.
47. On schooling in the South during Reconstruction see Jaynes 1986 and Lieberson 1980. On blacks in the smokestack industries see Bloch 1969 and Bonacich 1976.
48. On the connection between white wealth and black poverty see Blauner 1972; Lipsitz 1995; and Thurow 1975.
49. On housing values during the 1970s see Adams 1988 and Stutz and Kartman 1982.
50. On the upcoming transfer of housing wealth to the postwar generation of whites see Levy and Michel 1991.

Chapter 3

1. On field surveys of wealth concentrations see Ericksen 1988.
   The 1983 SCF sample included 3, 824 households and, "to increase the representation of the wealthy in the survey," 438 high-income families drawn from tax files (see Avery et al. 1986). SCF is a stratified sample, which oversamples the rich. The SCF survey design is particularly valuable in investigating the general distribution and concentration of wealth, because it oversamples wealthy households and therefore captures large wealth holdings better than SIPP.
2. SIPP respondents are drawn from the resident population of the United States excluding persons living in institutions and military barracks. SIPP was a multipanel survey that introduced a new sample at the beginning of four successive calendar years starting in 1984. SIPP was also a longitudinal survey in which each sampled household was reinterviewed at four month intervals for a total of seven interviews, or "waves." The selection of households used in the survey was based on sample selection methods similar to those used for the Current Population Survey (see U.S. Bureau of the Census 1990). The initial 1984 SIPP panel surveyed more than 20, 000 households. After weeding out households that could not be reinterviewed or for which SIPP estimated data, we were left with 11,257 households.
3. Pension funds. There is some disagreement among scholars as to whether or not social security, private pensions, and defined contribution programs constitute wealth. For a discussion ofthese issues see Levy and Michel 1991, 119–23. Even though these pensions clearly provide a measure of

economic security for their holders, for our purposes it is important to note that private and public pensions are not transferable to heirs.

4. On very wealthy subjects' underrepresentation in wealth surveys see Avery et al. 1986.

5. SIPP's provision of social and economic data over time. We organize our SIPP data set to accommodate access to a year's information on relevant topics. One computer file combined household data from waves 2, 3, and 4. We were thus able to link crucial material from topical modules that contained more than cursory information on parental background, work and education histories, and assets to basic core demographic and social data.

6. On family pooling of resources see Oliver 1988 and Stack 1974.

7. "Household head" and "householder." For the definitions of these terms see U.S. Bureau of the Census 1990, 3–1.

8. Definitional and conceptual questions about wealth. See Henretta and Campbell 1978; Lampman 1962; Projector and Weiss 1966; and Wolff 1991.

9. Most people do not sell their homes ... Home equity loans, which allow families to draw on what is otherwise not a liquid asset, theoretically permit residential equity to be used to purchase various kinds of life chances. Yet although these loans may provide needed assets, they also create new debts, which not only deplete existing wealth but also inhibit a family's ability to generate new wealth or to build on existing wealth. The pitfalls of these loans have been highly publicized; they confirm our contention that equity in homes is a special form of wealth that must be considered separately from other, more liquid assets.

10. The standard theory of wealth inequality. See Kuznets 1953; Lampman 1962; and Williamson and Lindert 1980.

11. "Seems to have undergone a permanent reduction." The quote is from Williamson and Lindert 1980, 63.

12. An "unprecedented jump ..." The quote is from Nasar 1992.

13. For the quote on "the upper-wealth classes" see Wolff 1995, 36.

14. On the 1994 Census Bureau update see U.S. Bureau of the Census 1994.

15. On upper-class consumer spending during the Reagan era see Ratcliff and Maurer 1995.

16. This money is "enormously consequential ..." The quote is from Millman 1991, 3.

Chapter 4

1. Ten percent of America's families ... Survey of Consumer Finance (SCF) data cited in chapter 3 suggest considerably greater wealth concentrations than SIPP. On this point we place greater confidence in SCF's reliability for the reasons cited in the previous chapter. However, we recount the SIPP data on wealth concentration to provide consistent comparisons with income inequality.

2. Median household income. As a point of comparison, the Census Bureau lists 1987 median household income as $25, 986. This indicates SIPP's close approximation of the American population. In addition, it suggests either that SIPP slightly undersampled the better-off households or oversampled low-income households. In contrast to the SCF surveys SIPP, then, understates inequality.

3. The poverty level. The 1988 poverty line for a family of four was $11, 611, or about $968 per month.

4. "Our central ..." The quote is from Bellah et al. 1985, 119.

5. In the mid-to-late 1980s $25, 000 to $50, 000 can be considered a reasonable range indicating middle-income families. This is not to say, however, that a family earning $55, 000 was then among America's upper class or elite.

6. Middle-class living standards. Using the white-collar category to represent the middle class (which yields the largest middle class), the typical American middle-class family income is roughly $33, 000 a year. Hence one month's median income for the middle class equals $2, 750.

7. On savings rate rises with income see Morley 1984.

8. Those sixty-five and over. While seniors" income is on average close to the official poverty line, one should remember that this official figure is for a family of four. Seniors most likely live alone or in small households and thus on average, in terms of income, live above the poverty line.

9. The life-cycle model of wealth accumulation. See Atkinson 1980; Brittain 1978; Modigliani and Brumberg 1954.

10. "Being in the right place ..." The quote is from Levy and Michel 1991, 56.

11. On gender equality in economic matters see Millman 1991.

12. On parental wealth and the financial well-being of the next generation see Kessler and Masson 1988 and Thurow 1975. Survey data on this topic appears in Projector and Weiss 1966, 148.

13. Different occupational groups. SIPP's extensive section on occupation and work history recorded occupation for all household workers. Using the 1980 Census of Population Occupation Classification System, we classified all managerial and professional specialty occupations and technical occupations as upper-white-collar. Lower-white-collar occupations included all sales, administrative support, and clerical positions. Upper-blue-collar includes protective service occupations, farm operators and managers, and precision production, craft, and repair occupations. Lower-blue-collar includes private household occupations, service occupations, agricultural, forestry, logging and fishing workers, and operators, fabricators, and laborers. The self-employed classification includes people owning all or part of their own businesses.

14. On industrial segmentation see Beck, Horan, and Tolbert 1978, and Taylor, Gwartney-Gibbs, and Farley 1986.

15. Work stability is determined by the number of weeks within the past nine months during which a household's most experienced worker did not have employment (high stability——four or less weeks without a paying job;

moderate stability—five to thirty-four weeks; low stability-thirty-five or more weeks). Ideally we would have wanted a measure that established a worker's employment history throughout his or her career since wealth is based in great part on accumulation over the life course. Thus this measure only documents recent work instability. The data exclude those over sixty-five years of age. On first examination of these data we were struck by the number of people with very high incomes and/or very high sums of wealth who were labeled as having highly disrupted work histories. An analysis of who this group was led us to reconsider their placement in this category. Among those we recoded from high stability to low stability were widows with above-poverty-level incomes, those between fifty-five and sixty-five years old, and all those with incomes above the sample median ($23, 958). They appeared to have wealth based more on inheritance and accumulated savings than on stable work histories.

16. Our analysis of earnings inequity. The sectoral classification we used for core and periphery industries is taken from Beck, Horan, and Tolbert 1978. We created the government sector classification by aggregating out all state, federal, and local government employees, including letter carriers and postal clerks, firefighters, police, elementary and secondary teachers, and social workers. Sector designation is identified for a household's most experienced worker.

17. For a discussion of cross-sectional measures of wealth acquisition see Steckel and Krishnan 1992.

Chapter 5

1. "The wealth of blacks and whites …" The quote is from O'Hare 1983, 27.
2. On definitions of the black middle class see Landry 1987.
3. SIPP data from 1984. See Oliver and Shapiro 1989.
4. Full-time workers are those who have worked thirty-five or more hours a week during the past month.
5. The fragility of black middle-class living standards. See Levy and Michel 1991, and Wilson 1987.
6. $8 to $19. Several factors accounting for this range have already been discussed or will be discussed in fuller detail later in this chapter. First, the use of differing wealth definitions (see chapter 2) yields dissimilar results. Second, some studies report means and others use medians as summary statistics. As with income data, wealth means, because of their sensitivity to extreme values, reveal greater inequality. Third, the studies we cite report wealth statistics from different years, databases, or subsamples.
7. For discussions of racial differences in wealth see Birnbaum and Weston 1974; Blau and Graham 1990; Oliver and Shapiro 1989; Smith 1975; Sobol 1979; Soltow 1972; and Terrell 1971.
8. On young black families in 1976 held only about 18 percent of the wealth see Blau and Graham 1990.
9. Mean net worth is used in our asset comparison because it is the statistic most often used in previous studies on racial wealth differences.

10. "Income difference ..." The quote is from Blau and Graham 1990, 321.
11. "A large portion of the black population ..." The quote is from Terrell 1971, 370.
12. On wealth concentration in the black community see Jaynes and Williams 1989.
13. On similar wealth distributions in the white and black populations see Bradford 1987.
14. On the differing asset holdings of blacks and whites see Blau and Graham 1990; Bradford 1987; Lundsten and Black 1978; O'Hare 1983; Terrell 1971; and Tidwell 1987.
15. On blacks and conspicuous consumption see Frazier 1957; and Landry 1987.
16. The so-called comparative savings rate. Most measures of savings, like the one used here, examine interest-bearing accounts at banks and financial institutions. In so doing, they exclude many investment instruments, such as real property, business investments, stocks, bonds, mutual funds, and mortgages. The "savings rate" then distinguishes between very low-risk and steady savings and higher-risk and higher-earning financial investments. As such, "savings" is not the most reliable indicator of what families save versus what they spend.
17. For studies of the savings rates of blacks and whites see Alexis 1971; Friedman 1957; Galenson 1972; Hamermesh 1982; and Swinton cited in Robinson 1993.
18. On housing values during the 1970s see O'Hare 1983.
19. On home equity and overall black assets see Birnbaum and Weston 1974; Brimmer 1988; Henretta 1979; Landry 1987; Long and Caudill 1992; and Parcel 1982.
20. Black home-ownership rates. See Long and Caudill 1992. As reported by Long and Caudill, the U.S. Bureau of the Census reported a 0.64 black-white home-ownership ratio for 1988, confirming SIPP's accuracy.
21. The impact of remunerable human capital characteristics on earnings. See Taylor, Gwartney-Gibbs, and Farley 1986.
22. "Various social institutions ..." The quote is from Taylor, Gwartney-Gibbs, and Farley 1986, 110.
23. On blacks' net job loss during 1990–91 see Sharpe 1993.
24. A household earner is someone who works for a wage, not necessarily one who works full-time.
25. Inequality stratified by race. Some might object that these broad categorical data present a misleading impression, because white-collar blacks are concentrated in lower-status sectors within each category. The methodical and extensive disparities, nonetheless, clearly overwhelm whatever distortion may be contained in utilizing such broad occupational categories.
26. The "truncated Afro-American middleman." The quote is from Butler 1991, 234, as are the two Butler quotes that follow.
27. On woman-headed households in the black community see Levy 1987.
28. Single-parent households are largely female-headed, at the rate of 90 percent among blacks and 80 percent among whites. The resource circum-

stances of male- or female-headed single-parent households matter little. The only remarkable exception occurs in the total net worth males possess, which amounts to about $1, 000 more.

Chapter 6

1. The "eliminating all the disadvantages of blacks" quote is from Blau and Graham 1990, 322.
2. A set of variables. Upon exploration, several variables, like sector and work stability, were dropped from the model because their statistical importance proved to be contingent on other factors already included in the model.
3. Table 6.1 The correlation matrix for the regression analyses reported in table 6.1 is in the Apendix (see table A6.1).
4. The variable for net worth (NW) and net financial assets (NFA) contain a large number of 0 observations (no wealth) and are highly skewed to lower values. In order to assess how measurement would affect the results we ran the regressions using a number of different measurements of the dependent variables. So as not to exclude those with 0 values, we substituted the value of 1 for each occurrence of 0 in the data set. From there we ran two versions of the regressions. The first regression analysis used logged values of NW and NFA. The second version did not log the observations. We found that the results were virtually identical. To enhance interpretability we used the latter values so that we could represent the unit change in dollars, making the interpretation straightforward. These unreported analyses are available from the authors.
5. The importance of each variable ... Standardized coefficients that allow us to determine which variable is most important are not presented so as not to confuse the reader. However, when we indicate in the text that one variable is more important than another, it refers to our examination of the standardized coefficients.
6. A $27, 075 disadvantage. It is worth noting the change in sign for males in all of the regression equations. Where income is concerned, being a male has a positive impact. But for net worth and net financial assets being male is a negative. This statistical anomaly is created by the interaction between maleness and the number of workers in a household. In fact the zero-order correlation between measures of wealth and male householder is almost zero.
7. Figure 6.1. The regression analyses on which these results are based are presented in the Appendix (see tables A6.2 through A6.4).
8. "Past studies ..." The quote is from Blau and Graham 1990, 332.
9. The "neighborhood's problem with crime ..." The quote is from Acuna 1989. On pride in home ownership in white and black neighborhoods see Lehman 1991.
10. "It is hidden." The quote is from Brenner and Spayd 1993.
11. On one Boston bank's minority lending record see Zuckoff 1992.

12. The quotes on "greater debt burdens ..." and "black and Hispanic mortgage applicants ..." are from Munnell et al. 1993, 2.

13. On the mortgage-denial rate for minority applicants see Bradbury, Case, and Dunham 1989.

14. "Whites seem to enjoy ..." The quote is from Munnell et al. 1993, 3.

15. The quote on "affirmative action" is from Cose 1993, 191.

16. The quotes on banking regulators and rules are from Brenner and Spayd 1993.

17. On Shawmut's 1993 takeover bid in New Hampshire see Blanton 1993.

18. "The Fed is sending ..." The quote is from Greenhouse 1993.

19. Table A6.6. Along with race, the equation used in table A6.6 includes a number of control factors that might reasonably be expected to cause differences in mortgage rates: year home was purchased, South, household income, purchaser's age, size of first mortgage, and whether the home was bought with VA or FHA guarantees. The age of the home owner and the size of the first mortgage are not significant contributors to variations in interest rates.

20. "It's purely a matter of economics." The quote is from Lehman 1990.

21. On low-end loans and minorities see Squires 1994.

22. On tiered interest rates and low-end mortgages see Smith 1992.

23. The quote on "segregated [loan] patterns" is from Franklin 1991, 124.

24. To calculate the black mortgage penalty we multiplied the median black mortgage ($35,000) by the interest rate differential (0.54 percent) to yield a $3,951 extra cost for each current black mortgage holder. To calculate the cost to all blacks with home mortgages, we multiplied $3,951 by the number of black homeowners (4.48 million) by the percent of black homeowners with mortgages (59 percent).

25. The "price of being black." We estimate the median black mortgage for the next twenty-five years at $72, 000. This figure represents the post-1986 median black mortgage and surely understates what the median mortgage will be over the next twenty-five years. Nonetheless, we multiplied this figure by the mortgage rate difference (0.54 percent). which yields $8, 130, then by current number of blacks with home mortgages (2.65 million, hopefully another conservative assumption), which produces $21.5 billion.

26. One report found... See Long and Caudill 1992.

27. The quote on "housing in black neighborhoods" is from Franklin 1991, 125.

28. Purchase price. Although SIPP contains detailed data on housing costs, inexplicably it did not ask a direct question on purchase price. Amount of first mortgage is thus used in place of purchase price. First mortgages usually constitute 85 to 95 percent of purchase price, the buyer's down payment making up the rest. The reliability of using first mortgages as a proxy for purchase price depends on there being a minimal racial difference in the proportion of a house's purchase price covered by the mortgage. For example. using mortgage amount as a proxy would not be reliable if blacks systematically made larger proportionate down pay-

ments than whites. Given what we already know about parental economic well-being, inheritance, and parental gift-giving behavior, we confidently believe that, if anything, whites pay a higher percentage of purchase price in down payment than blacks. If this is the case, then, the proxy understates racial differences in housing appreciation.

29. Mean value. The mean statistic is more appropriate here because it is more sensitive to extreme values. Medians would place an artificial cap on "average" housing appreciation.

30. The racial net worth difference. The mean total net worth for white homeowners with mortgages is $118, 625 and for blacks it is $54, 975, resulting in a $63, 650 difference.

31. Regression analysis. Along with race, the regression considered a number of likely control variables, such as regions with high housing inflation (the Northeast and West), year the home was bought, the amount of the first mortgage, and whether the home was located in a hypersegregated city. A list of twenty-six hypersegregated cities was taken from Massey and Denton 1988. All these factors are significant contributors in determining housing appreciation, as indicated by results displayed in table A6.7.

32. Several studies. See Johnson and Oliver 1992; and Kasarda 1988, 1990.

33. $58 Billion. This figure is arrived at by multiplying the $21, 917 difference in housing appreciation by 2.65 million blacks with mortgages.

34. 177, 501 applications. See Federal Reserve Bulletin 1992.

35. Table 6.4. If the parent's occupational code was not available, then the occupational code of the spouse's parent was used instead.

36. Our occupational-mobility results stand in stark contrast to Hauser and Featherman's (1977) exhaustive findings. The differences may be due in part to the use of different samples, our inclusion of both men and women, and our substitution of any parent's occupation for that of the father.

Chapter 7

1. Quote on no prejudice in the Yankee see Rock 1858.

2. David Dinkins. The quote is from Cose 1993, 28.

3. Middle-class blacks "tell of mistreatment ..." The quote is from Feagin and Sikes 1994, 15.

4. "The secret point of money ..." The quote is from Didion's 1967 essay "7000 Romaine, Los Angeles" reprinted in Didion 1968, 71.

5. On restrictive covenants see Zarembka 1990, 101–2. On the Fair Housing Act see ibid., 106.

6. Our emphasis on asset acquisition is not meant to discount the need for income and employment policy. On the contrary, we believe that it is imperative to institute policies that encourage full employment at wages consistent with a decent standard of living. In fact, many of our proposals assume that people have some kind of income. However, to dwell on the intricacies of this area would divert our attention from the unique implications of our argument. There are several important proposals already

under discussion that merit serious consideration (see Carnoy 1994; Ellwood 1988; Weir 1992; Wilson 1987).

7. "Asset accumulation ..." The quote is from Sherraden 1991, 294.

8. "Only after a business plan ..." The quote is from Sherraden 1991, 256–57.

9. The Congressional Joint Taxation Committee. See Dreier and Atlas 1994.

10. "Different dollar bills ..." The quote is from Barlett and Steele 1994, 29.

11. "Better still ..." The quotes are from Barlett and Steele 1994, 335.

12. Low-income and minority neighborhoods. Our focus is on the role of financial institutions in providing mortgages. However, an equally important aspect of the low wealth accumulation of black households has been persistent residential segregation. Massey and Denton (1993, 186–216) have provided a blueprint for policy in this area that we need not rehash here. Their proposals, if implemented, would be an important complement to the ones we suggest regarding lending discrimination.

13. "Fair lending ..." The quote is from Federal Reserve Bank of Boston 1993.

14. "Fleet did nothing ..." The quote is from Ryan and Wilke 1994, A5.

15. "Lingering negative effects ..." The quote is from U.S. House of Representatives 1993.

16. The quote on "the costs of federal policies and programs" is from Edsall and Edsall 1991, 11.

17. "The negative intertwining ..." The quote is from Carnoy 1994, 225–26.

18. On efforts to "promote entrepreneurship among [black] community residents" in Los Angeles see Jackson, Johnson, and Farrell 1994.

19. Self-help books. See Anderson 1994 and Fraser 1994.

20. If "one lost ..." The quote is from Morrison 1987, 110.

Chapter 8

1. Wolff, 2004.

2. Johnson, 2005.

3. Johnson, 2005.

4. The vision of an ownership society is one developed by libertarian conservatives and co-opts much of the language used by proponents of asset-based social policy. They too focus on the social impact of asset ownership: "Just as homeownership creates responsible homeowners, widespread ownership of other assets creates responsible citizens. People who are owners feel more dignity, more pride, and more confidence. They have a stronger stake, not just in their own property, but in their community and their society; People can also profit by improving themselves, of course, through education and the development of good habits, as long as they are allowed to reap the profits that come from such improvement," and "Another benefit of private property ownership, not so clearly economic, is that it diffuses power ... The institution of private property gives many individuals a place to call their own, a place where they are safe

from depredation by others and by the state." (See Boaz, 2005.) However, this vision is distinct from the vision of an inclusive perspective on asset building. There is no commitment to progressive benefits for the poor and disadvantaged but rather a commitment to purely market and regulatory reforms that eschew direct benefits and subsidies to the poor that enable them to accumulate assets. The conservative ownership society is premised on assets as a substitute, not a complement to the social safety net. As such, the policies that it implicitly and explicitly supports tend to widen rather than lessen wealth inequality.

Bush's ownership society promotes a program that turns away from well-established, successful strategies of broadening ownership, placing a far greater burden of risk on individuals. We think it is not coincidental that the conservative–libertarian ownership society push comes at a time when social investments are being reduced and risks shifted from public to private. For example, health insurance and pension coverage are shifting from government and employers onto individuals (see Brown et al.).

5. Oliver and Shapiro, p. 30
6. Oliver and Shapiro, p. 32.
7. Oliver and Shapiro, pp. 85–86.
8. Shapiro, 2004a.
9. Kochhar.
10. Federation of Consumer Services data yield a more narrowed ratio. These data are inconsistent with virtually all other data measuring wealth inequality. We are not confident with its methodology or operational definitions of wealth. See Consumer Federation of America and BET.com, 2003.
11. We adjusted the 1988 figure originally reported in the book to reflect 2002 dollars.
12. Oliver and Shapiro, p. 36.
13. Oliver and Shapiro, p. 51.
14. The National Bureau of Economic Research's Business Cycle Committee keeps track of business expansions and recessions; see http://www.nber.org/cycles/recessions.html. For a general overview of the Clinton expansion's impact on the poor, see Blank and Ellwood.
15. Bradbury, p. 14, and Holzer, Raphael, and Stoll.
16. Bradbury, p. 14.
17. Bradbury, p. 15.
18. Bradbury, p. 4.
19. Shiller. Also see http://www.irrationalexuberance.com/index.htm for historical data on the stock market.
20. See quarterly stock prices for Yahoo at http://finance.yahoo.com/q/hp?s=YHOO&a=03&b=12&c=1996&d=07&e=14&f=2005&g=m&z=66&y=66.
21. The origin of the descriptor "irrational exuberance" is found in a speech by Federal Reserve Board Chairman Alan Greenspan, 1996.
22. These data are from a survey of high-income blacks (yearly incomes of $50, 000 or more) sponsored by Ariel Mutual Funds/Charles Schwab & Co., Inc. This very valuable survey examines the financial behavior, asset

value, and composition of this group of African Americans. See Black Investor Survey.

23. Black Investor Survey.
24. Kochhar, p. 18.
25. Rusk.
26. Shapiro, 2004a.
27. Affordable home ownership is conceptualized as home ownership that costs no more than 30 percent of housing costs for a family of four at 80 percent of the region's median income.
28. The exemplar for "easing" regulatory oversight and financial institution accountability was the repeal of the Glass-Steagall Act of 1933. This act was designed to protect the public from collusion between commercial banks, insurance companies, and brokerage firms, which contributed to the stock market crash of 1929. The Financial Services Modernization Act of 1999 does away with restrictions on the integration of banking, insurance, and stock trading, which has encouraged a rash of mergers leading to greater concentration in the financial sector. As a result, banks were looking for new markets and were anxious to provide new products. As part of the 1999 Act, regular oversight opportunities provided to community organizations through the Community Reinvestment Act were relaxed considerably. Consequently, the frequency of CRA examinations was limited. See Berton and Futterman.
29. Joint Center for Housing Studies, 2005.
30. Silva and Epstein.
31. Draut and Silva.
32. Silva and Epstein.
33. This section uses SIPP data from 2002 as reported in the Pew Hispanic Center report.
34. Joint Center for Housing Studies, 2004.
35. Silva.
36. These are based on distribution of mean worth, so the figure for whites, in particular, because of the skewed distribution, looks low and vastly understates the importance of home equity in the wealth portfolios of middle-class white families (Kochhar).
37. Joint Center for Housing Studies, 2005.
38. Quercia, Stegman, and Davis.
39. Quercia, Stegman, and Davis.
40. Duda and Apgar.
41. National Community Reinvestment Coalition; Adams.
42. Joint Center for Housing Studies, 2005.
43. Joint Center for Housing Studies, 2005.
44. Dickerson.
45. Crockett.
46. Himmelstein et al.
47. Stuart.
48. Cited in African American Market Profile. Magazine Publishers of America, http://www.magazine.org/content/files/market_profile_black.pdf.

49. The Brookings Institution.
50. The Brookings Institution; Center for Responsible Lending, 2005a; 2005b.
51. The Brookings Institution, pp. 5–6.
52. Joint Center Data Bank.
53. Crockett; Dyson.
54. Sharon Collins.
55. Harison and Karberg.
56. Blumstein and Beck.
57. Mauer.
58. Wacquant 2000, 2001
59. Wacquant 2001, pp. 83–84.
60. Petit and Western.

Chapter 9

1. Oliver and Shapiro, p. 177.
2. See Grusky; Ferguson; Shapiro, 2004b; Giddens, Dunier, and Applebaum.
3. Kim and Lee; Holme; Shanks.
4. Prior to the mid-1980s, there was little reliable information on wealth and liabilities of normal American families. Since then, several excellent, nationally representative surveys began collecting and reporting wealth data. These include the Panel Study on Income Dynamics, the Survey on Income and Program Participation, and the Health and Retirement Survey.
5. Chiteji and Stafford; Segal and Sullivan.
6. Keister.
7. The work of Edward Wolff anchors much of the wealth inequality field, especially see his *Top Heavy*. Many scholars have made important contributions to understanding racial wealth inequality. This includes the work of Alontji, Doraszelski, and Segal; Kerwin and Hurst; Scholz and Levine; and Hao. The work of Mariko Chang also has been important.
8. Moran and Whitford; and Harris.
9. Moran and Whitford.
10. A conceptualization on wealth as an essential component of class refocuses the analytic discussion to family and property relations and how wealth is accumulated by and inherited through families. Family and history thus regain prime stature in discussions about class. Patricia Hill Collins.
11. Banks.
12. Lipsitz.
13. Roediger, 2000; 2005; Ignatiev; Brodkin.
14. See Doan and Bonilla-Silva.
15. Birney and Shapiro.
16. Greenberg Quinlan Rosner Research conducted the survey for OMB Watch. See http://www.ombwatch.org site for data.

17. http://www.faireconomy.org/Maine/index.html
18. Testimony given July 21 before the Senate Committee on Banking, Housing, and Urban Affairs.
19. OMB Watch.
20. http://www.ombwatch.org/estatetax/pdf/Estate_Tax_Principles_Final_03.pdf.
21. A recent Congressional Budget Office report effectively lays to rest the myth that the estate tax poses a significant threat to America's farms and small businesses by levying too large a tax on families who cannot afford to pay it. This has been a main claim made by anti–estate tax proponents, including President Bush. The report finds that very few farms are affected by the estate tax with 2005 exemption levels (and thus even fewer would be affected by exemption levels through 2009). In fact, if the current exemption level of $1.5 million had been in place in 2000, only three hundred farms would have owed any estate tax. Raising the exemption to $3.5 million, the 2009 level, drops the number of farms affected to sixty-five. Furthermore, those very few farms have sufficient liquid financial resources to pay the estate tax. See "Effects of the Estate Tax on Farms and Small Businesses," July, 2005. http://www.cbo.gov/ftpdocs/65xx/doc6512/07-06-EstateTax.pdf.
22. Shapiro 2004a, p. 196.
23. See Cato Institute Web site. Many of these arguments were picked up by the Bush administration.
24. Survivors' benefits lifted one million children out of poverty and helped another one million avoid extreme poverty (living below half the poverty line). See Spriggs 2005b.
25. Again, see the Cato Institute Web site.
26. See his work on the Economic Policy Institute and Dollars and Sense Web sites.
27. Spriggs, 2005a.
28. This idea is developed in an op-ed by Stoesz, Sherraden, and Shapiro found on the PolicyAmerica.org Web site.
29. Center for Disease Control.
30. Kim and Lee.
31. Kim and Lee.
32. For more, see the Web sites for the Center for Social Development (http://gwbweb.wustl.edu/csd/) and for CFED (http://www.cfed.org/).
    This work is especially important because it directly addresses an emerging new understanding of poverty from the work of Rank. If welfare policy only targets those currently below the official poverty line, it focuses on about one in eight Americans, but it neglects the nearly six in ten Americans who will experience at least one year of poverty while they are adults. The economic fragility of those who will experience poverty would be improved vastly by building an asset safety net.
33. Center for Enterprise Development; Howard.
34. Center for Enterprise Development.
35. Center for Enterprise Development.
36. Shanks.

37. Sherraden 2000.
38. The main research and evaluation reports include: Sherraden et al.; Schreiner, Clancy, and Sherraden; and Abt Associates.
   From the outset of the national demonstration project, the key questions included how Individual Development programs could be implemented; whether the poor could save in IDA programs; how much the programs cost; how savings and accumulation occurred in IDAs; and assessing the outcomes of IDA programs and impacts on participants. Perhaps the foremost finding is that the poor save in structured savings programs and welcome the opportunity to do so. The programs provided a structured savings opportunity that included a strong set of incentives, time-intensive input from program personnel, financial literacy, and support. Participant psychological and cognitive changes were particularly notable.
39. Karen Edwards, Center for Social Development, August, 2005, Personal communication.
40. For a description of this program see the Seed Policy & Practice Initiative at http://www.cfed.org/focus.m?parentid=31&siteid=288&id=289.
41. Clinton proposed Universal Savings Accounts in his 1999 State of the Union Address. He proposed a form of a retirement account based on an IDA model and was influenced directly by preliminary results from the American Dream Demonstration project.
42. Barr.
43. Stein.
44. Erns, Farris, and King.
45. Joint Center for Housing Studies of Harvard University.
46. Eake's quotes come from conversations with Oliver at the time he approached the Ford Foundation for this then unprecedented grant (circa 1996).
47. Stegman, p. 349.
48. Stegman, pp. 360–362.
49. Stegman, Quercia, and Davis.
50. As an African American, Raines was a very strong supporter of closing the racial wealth gap and saw homeownership as a prime strategy. See Raines.
51. Pastor et al.
52. The policy work on regional equity is spearheaded by PolicyLink, http://www.policylink.org/, led by Angela Glover Blackwell, and the Brookings Institution Metropolitan Policy Program, http://www.brookings.edu/metro/, headed by Bruce Katz.
53. PolicyLink.
54. john powell.
55. john powell.
56. As John Logan says: "Residential segregation among blacks and whites remains high in cities and in suburbs around the country. There were some signs of progress in the 1980s, with a five-point drop in the segregation index (from 73.8 to 68.8). The change continued at a slower rate in the 1990s (a decline of just under four points). The good news is that these small changes are cumulating over time. The source of concern is that at this pace it may take forty more years for black-white segregation to come down even to the current level of Hispanic-white segregation." (See Logan.)
57. PolicyLink, p. 10.
58. PolicyLink, p. 11.

59. See Alstott and Ackerman.
60. For a superb summary, see Scanlon and Page-Adams.
61. Sherraden, 1991.
62. The other side of this argument is that the economic stake of home ownership creates a fundamental conservative set of politics where protecting
home and property values invariably dominates over other issues. The
basis of this argument is twofold. First, societies with high home-ownership rates have less well-developed welfare states. One reason for this may
be that home ownership negates the necessity for high levels of housing
subsidies and old-age assistance. Second, societies with high home-ownership rates tend to have stronger right-wing political parties. The thinking
here is that home ownership enshrines individual rights rooted in private
property over social investment for the common good. The correlation
between home ownership and lower welfare-state investment and right-
wing parties is established empirically, but the direction of causality and
possible intervening explanatory mechanisms still need much exploration.
It is undoubtedly true that ownership of capital corresponds to supporting
the status quo, less support for social assistance, and hence a better likelihood of support for right-wing parties. However, owning a home does not
transform a family into the propertied class in modern America, nor does
it mean that stakeholders become part of the status quo and become more
interested in protecting what they have against social change. Finally, the
home ownership-creates-conservatives argument needs specification and
contextualization. It may contain some resonance for upper-middle-class
home owners, but first-time home ownership means something very different for a struggling low-income family. See Castles; Korpi and Palme;
and Conley.
63. Stegman, Quercia, and Davis, p. 6.
64. Phrase is from Salamon.
65. We list these organizations because of the prominent role they played in
the development of asset policy. Many, many others could be named if our
job was to give proper credit. Our purpose here, however, is to give the
reader an understanding of how an idea grew into national prominence, so
we apologize to all the great people and the organizations they represent
who have contributed so much to this growing social movement but who
we have not named.
66. The Ford Foundation, 2003, p. 9.
67. The Ford Foundation's Asset Building and Community Development
Program worked on building social, financial, natural, and human assets.
They defined social assets as "the social capital and civic culture of a
place that can break down the isolation of the poor, strengthen the relationships that provide security and support, and encourage community
investment, including philanthropic capital, in institutions and individuals;" natural assets as "Natural resources, such as forests, wildlife, land,
and livestock that can provide communities with sustainable livelihoods
and cultural value; and environmental services, such as a forest's role in
the cleansing, recycling, and renewal of the air and water that sustain life;"

and human assets as "human assets, such as the marketable skills that allow low-income people to obtain and retain employment that pays living wages; and comprehensive reproductive health, which affects people's capacity to work, overcome poverty, and lead satisfying lives." These were clearly definitions that encompassed their areas of work, but in greater and lesser form that adapt to the definition of an asset as "A stock of financial, human, natural or social resources that can be acquired, developed, improved and transferred across generations. A stock endures; it is not entirely consumed. It generates flows or consumption, as well as additional stock." Ford Foundation, p. 9.

68. Gilbert and O'Connor.

69. Salamon.

70. However, even this experiment described by Salamon was marred by racially disparate treatment. Examining two New Deal settlements, only twelve miles apart in North Carolina that were reserved for poor "whites" and poor "blacks," Thomas W. Mitchell found that from the beginning, federal authorities made decisions that systematically favored the white settlement of Roanoke Farms over the black settlement of Tillery.

"Preliminary analysis of our data shows that the original settler families on the Roanoke Farms section were allotted 9322 acres in the aggregate, and the original settler families on the Tillery Farms sections were allotted 6754 acres. Further, the average acreage of the farmstead for the original settlers on the Roanoke Farms section was 86.69 acres, and the average acreage of the farmstead for the original settlers on the Tillery Farms section was 66.89 acres. In term of sales prices, the average price per acre for the original farmsteads on the Roanoke Farms section was $40.17 per acres; the average price per acre for the original farmsteads on the Tillery Farms section was $50.28 per acres, 25% more per acre than the prices paid by the original Roanoke Farms settlers. In each instance as can be seen, the white farm families were advantaged. Today there are significant differences in the current racial compositions of the property. Whites still own almost all of the property on the former white section of the New Deal project; in contrast, there has been significant black land loss on the Tillery Farms section." (Mitchell)

These initial advantages were compounded by the favorable access to capital from the Agricultural Extensions Services and the Department of Agriculture that led to the ability of white farmers to improve and maintain their farms as profitable ventures. The black farmers, in contrast, were denied loans and support from these same agencies, and not surprisingly, have not been able to keep their farms alive, nor invested in their homesteads. This discriminatory treatment was documented and confirmed in the now infamous case, Pigford v. Glickman, 1998.

71. Los Angeles Neighborhood Housing Services used to focus primarily on affordable home ownership but with foreclosures rising in their communities, their focus now provides a helping hand to local homeowners by offering financial counseling, affordable loans for refinancing, foreclosure

prevention and home repair, construction management services, remediation of environmental hazards, and neighborhood preservation strategies.

72. Comments from a participant interviewed for an assessment of the Ford Foundation's Asset Building and Community Development Program.

73. Robinson.

74. Hayner.

References

Abrams, Charles. 1955. *Forbidden Neighbors: A Study of Prejudice in Housing*. New York: Harper.

Acuna, Armando. 1989. "Home Savings Named in Redlining Suit." *Los Angeles Times,* 1 January: Metro sec., 3, (San Diego County edition).

Adams, John. 1988. "Growth of U.S. Cities and Recent Trends in Urban Real Estate Values." In *Cities and Their Vital Systems,* ed., J. H. Ausubel and R. Herman. Washington, DC: National Academy Press. 108–45.

Alexis, Marcus. 1971. "Some Negro-White Differences in Consumption." In *The Black Consumer,* ed., George Joyce and Norman A. P. Govoni, New York: Random House. 257–74.

Anderson, Claud. 1994. *Black Labor, White Wealth: The Search for Power and Economic Justice*. Edgewood, MD: Duncan and Duncan.

Atkinson, A. T., ed. 1980. *Wealth, Income, and Inequality*. 2d edition. New York: Oxford University Press.

Avery, Robert B., Gregory E. Elliehausen, Glenn B. Canner, and Thomas A. Gustafson. 1984. "Survey of Consumer Finances, 1983." *Federal Reserve Bulletin,* 70:679–92.

Avery, Robert B., Gregory E. Elliehausen, Glenn B. Canner, Thomas A. Gustafson, and Julie Springert. 1986. "Financial Characteristics of High-Income Families." *Federal Reserve Bulletin* 72:163–77.

Baldwin, James. 1985a. "The Harlem Ghetto." In Baldwin 1985b. 1–11.

———. 1985b. *The Price of The Ticket*. New York: St. Martin's/Marek.

———. 1985c. "A Talk to Teachers." In Baldwin 1985b. 325–32.

Baran, Paul A., and Paul M. Sweezy. 1966. *Monopoly Capital*. New York: Monthly Review Press.

Barlett, Donald L., and James B. Steele. 1992. *America: What Went Wrong?* Kansas City: Andrews and McMeel.

————, 1994. *America: Who Really Pays the Taxes?* New York: Touchstone.

Baron, Harold M. 1971. "The Demand for Black Labor: Historical Notes on the Political Economy of Racism." *Radical America,* vol. 5, no 2:1–46.

Barth, Ernest, and Donald Noel. 1972. "Conceptual Frameworks for the Analysis of Race Relations: An Evaluation." *Social Forces* 50:333–48.

Beasley, Delilah. 1919. *Negro Trail Blazers of California.* Los Angeles: Times Mirror Print and Binding House.

Beck, E. M, P. Horan, and C. Tolbert. 1978. "Stratification in a Dual Economy: A Sectoral Model of Earnings Determination." *American Sociological Review,* 43:704–20.

Becker, Gary S. 1964. *Human Capital.* New York: National Bureau of Economic Research.

Bell, Derrick. 1992a. *Faces at the Bottom of the Well.* New York: Basic Books.

————, 1992b. *Race, Racism, and American Law.* 3d. ed. Boston: Little Brown.

Bellah, Robert N., Richard Madsen, William Sullivan, Ann Swidler, and Steven M. Tipton. 1985. *Habits of the Heart.* New York: Harper and Row.

Birnbaum, Howard, and Rafael Weston. 1974. "Home Ownership and the Wealth Position of Black and White Americans." *Review of Income and Wealth,* March, 103–18.

Blanton, Kimberly. 1993. "Fed Blocks Shawmut's Bid to Gain N.H. Bank." *Boston Globe.* 16 November, sec. 1, 1.

Blau, Francine D., and John W. Graham. 1990. "Black-White Differences in Wealth and Asset Composition." *Quarterly Journal of Economics,* May, 321–39.

Blau, Peter M., and Otis Dudley Duncan. 1967. *The American Occupational Structure.* New York: Wiley.

Blauner, Bob. 1972. *Racial Oppression in America.* New York: Harper.

Bloch, Herman David. 1969. *The Circle of Discrimination: An Economic and Social Study of the Black Man in New York.* New York: New York University Press.

Bluestone, Barry, and Bennett Harrison. 1982. *The Deindustrialization of America.* New York: Basic Books.

Bobo, Lawrence. 1989. "Keeping the Linchpin in Place: Testing the Multiple Sources of Opposition to Residential Integration." *Revue Internationale de Psychologie Sociale* 2:306–23.

Bonacich, Edna. 1976. "Advanced Capitalism and Black-White Relations in the United States: A Split Labor Market Interpretation." *American Sociological Review* 37: 547–59.

Bonacich, Edna, and John Modell. 1980. *The Economic Basis of Ethnic Solidarity: Small Business in the Japanese American Community.* Berkeley: University of California Press.

Boston Globe. 1991a. "Risk Perception Burdens Minorities." 28 May, 21.

————. 1991b. "Fed Finds a Racial Gulf in Mortgages." 22 October, sec. 1, 5.

Boxill, Bernard. 1984. *Blacks and Social Justice*. Totowa, NJ: Rowman and Allanheld.

Bradbury, Katharine L., Karl I. E. Case, and Constance R. Dunham. 1989. "Geographic Patterns of Mortgage Lending in Boston, 1982–87." *New England Economic Review,* September/October, 3–30.

Bradford, William, D. 1987. "Wealth, Assets, and Income of Black Households." Paper prepared for the Committee on the Status of Black Americans, National Research Council, Washington, DC.

Braun, Denny. 1991. *The Rich Get Richer: The Rise of Income Inequality in the United States and the World*. Chicago: Nelson-Hall.

Brenner, Joel, and Liz Spayd. 1993. "Separate and Unequal: Racial Discrimination in Area Home Lending." *Washington Post*. 6–8 June. A1.

Brimmer, Andrew F. 1988. "Income, Wealth, and Investment Behavior in the Black Community." *American Economic Review Papers and Proceedings,* 15 May, 1–5.

Brittain, John A. 1978. *Inheritance and the Inequality of Material Wealth*. Washington, DC: Brookings Institution.

Browne, Robert. 1974. "Wealth Distribution and Its Impact on Minorities." *Review of Black Political Economy* 4:27–38.

Buchele, Robert. 1981. "Sex Discrimination and Labour Market Segmentation." In Frank Wilkinson *The Dynamics of Labour Market Segmentation*. London: Academic Press. 211–27.

Butler, John Sibley. 1991. *Entrepreneurship and Self-Help among Black Americans: A Reconsideration of Race and Economics*. Albany, NY: State University of New York Press.

Carnoy, Martin. 1994. *Faded Dreams: The Politics and Economics of Race in America*. Cambridge: Cambridge University Press.

Clignet, Remi. 1992. *Death, Deeds, and Descendants: Inheritance in Modern America*. New York: Aldine de Gruyter.

Corcoran, Mary E., and Greg J. Duncan. 1979. "Work History, Labor Force Attachment, and Earning Differences between the Races and Sexes." *Journal of Human Resources*. 14:3–20.

Cose, Ellis. 1993. *The Rage of a Privileged Class*. New York: HarperCollins.

Cox, Oliver C., 1948. *Caste, Race, and Class*. New York: Modern Reader Paperback.

Dahrendorf, Ralf. 1979. *Life Chances: Approaches to Social and Political Theory*. Chicago: University of Chicago Press.

Danziger, Sheldon, and Peter Gottschalk, ed. 1993. *Uneven Tides: Rising Inequality in America*. New York: Russel Sage Foundation.

Darity, William A., Jr. "The Human Capital Approach to Black-White Earnings Inequality: Some Unsettled Questions." *Journal of Human Resources* 17:72–93.

Dedman, Bill. 1988. "The Color of Money." *Atlanta Journal and Constitution*. May, 15–19.

Didion, Joan. 1968. *Slouching towards Bethlehem*. New York: Dell.

Dorn, Edwin. 1979. *Rules and Racial Equality*. New Haven: Yale University Press.

Dreier, Peter, and John Atlas. 1994. "Tax Break for the Rich: Reforming the Mansion Subsidy." *Nation,* 258, no. 17:592–95.

Du Bois, W. E. B. 1935. *Black Reconstruction in America*. New York: Harcourt, Brace.

―――. 1953. *The Souls of Black Folk*. New York: Fawcett.

Duncan, Greg J., and Martha S. Hill. 1985. "Conceptions of Longitudinal Households: Fertile and Futile." *Journal of Economic and Social Measurements* 13:361–76.

Duncan, Otis Dudley. 1968. "Inheritance of Poverty or Inheritance of Race." In *On Understanding Poverty,* ed., Daniel P. Moynihan. New York: Basic Books. 85–109.

Dye, Thomas R. 1979. *Who's Running America?* Englewood Cliffs, NJ: Prentice-Hall.

Edsall, Thomas Byrne, and Mary Edsall. 1991. *Chain Reaction*. New York: Norton.

Edwards, Audrey, and Craig K. Polite. 1992. *Children of the Dream*. New York: Doubleday.

Ericksen, Eugene P. 1988. "Estimating the Concentration of Wealth in America." *Public Opinion Quarterly* 52:243–53.

Ellwood, David. 1988. *Poor Support*. New York: Basic Books.

Fainstein, Norman I. 1993. "Race, Class, and Segregation." *International Journal of Urban and Regional Research,* 17:384–03.

Farley, Reynolds. 1984. *Blacks and Whites: Narrowing the Gap?* Cambridge, MA: Harvard University Press.

Farley, Reynolds, and Walter R. Allen. 1987. *The Color Line and the Quality of American Life*. New York: Russell Sage Foundation.

Farley, Reynolds, and William H. Frey. 1994. "Changes in the Segregation of Whites from Blacks During the 1980s: Small Steps Toward a More Integrated Society." *American Sociologial Review* 59: 23–45.

Feagin, Joe R., and Robert Parker. 1990. *Building American Cities: The Urban Real Estate Game*. Englewood Cliffs, NJ: Prentice Hall.

Feagin, Joe R., and Hernan Vera. 1994. *White Racism*. New York: Routledge.

Feagin, Joe R., and Melvin P. Sikes. 1994. *Living with Racism: The Black Middle-Class Experience*. Boston: Beacon Press.

Federal Reserve Bank of Boston. 1993. *Closing the Gap*. Brochure published by the Federal Reserve Bank of Boston.

Federal Reserve Bulletin 1992. "Expanded HMDA Data on Residential Lending: One Year Later." *Federal Reserve Bulletin* 78, 11.

Foner, Eric. 1988. *Reconstruction: America's Unfinished Revolution*. New York: Harper.

Franklin, Raymond S. 1991. *Shadows of Race and Class*. Minneapolis: University of Minnesota Press.

Fraser, George C. 1994. *Success Runs in Our Race: The Complete Guide to Networking in the African American Community*. New York: William Morrow.

Frazier, Edward F. 1957. *Black Bourgeoisie*. Glencoe, IL: Free Press.

Friedman, Milton. 1957. *A Theory of the Consumption Function*. Princeton: Princeton University Press.

Galenson, Marjorie. 1972. "Do Blacks Save More?" *American Economic Review,* 62 (March): 211–16.

Gilbert, Neil, and Barbara Gilbert. 1989. *The Enabling State: Modern Welfare Capitalism in America*. Oxford: Oxford University Press.

Glastris, Paul, Robert Black, Lynn Adkins, Bill Ahrens, Charles Flowers, Anne Moncreiff-Arrarte, Ken Brown, and Stephanie Capparell. 1990. "The New Way to Get Rich." *U.S. News and World Report* 108, no. 18 (7 May): 26–32.

Greenhouse, Steven. 1993. "Fed Stops Bank Merger, Citing Bias in Lending." *New York Times,* 17 November, sec. D, 2.

Hacker, Andrew. 1992. *Two Nations: Black and White, Separate, Hostile, Unequal*. New York: Scribner's.

Hamermesh, Daniel S. 1982. "Social Insurance and Consumption." *American Economic Review,* 72. (March): 101–13.

Harris, Abram L. 1936. *The Negro as Capitalist*. College Park, MD: McGrath.

Harrison, Bennett, and Barry Bluestone. 1988. *The Great U-Turn: Corporate Restructuring and the Polarizing of America*. New York: Basic Books.

Hauser, Robert, and David Featherman. 1977. *The Process of Stratification*. New York: Academic Press.

Henretta, John C. 1979. "Race Differences in Middle Class Lifestyles: The Role of Home Ownership." *Social Science Research* 8:63–78.

Henretta, John C., and Richard T. Campbell. 1978. "Net Worth as an Aspect of Status." *American Journal of Sociology,* 83:1204–23.

Hill, Herbert. 1977. *Black Labor and the American Legal System: Race, Work, and the Law*. Madison: University of Wisconsin Press.

Hill, Richard Child, and Cynthia Negry. 1989. "Deindustrialization and Racial Minorities in the Great Lakes Region, USA." In *The Reshaping of America: Social Consequences of the Changing Economy,* ed. D. Stanley Eitzen and Maxine Baca Zinn. Englewood Cliffs, NJ: Prentice-Hall. 168–78.

Hill, Robert B. 1978. *The Illusion of Black Progress*. Washington, DC: National Urban League.

Hirschman, Charles, and Morrison G. Wong. 1984. "Socioeconomic Gains of Asian Americans, Blacks, and Hispanics: 1960–1976." *American Journal of Sociology* 90: 584–607.

Horton, Hayward Derrick, and Melvin E. Thomas. 1993. "Race, Class, and Family Structure: Differences in Housing Values for Black and White Homeowners." Unpublished ms.

Jackman, Mary R., and Robert W. Jackman. 1980. "Racial Inequalities in Home Ownership," *Social Forces* 58: 1221–33.

Jackson, Kenneth T. 1985. *Crabgrass Frontier: The Suburbanization of the United States*. New York: Oxford University Press.

Jackson, Maria-Rosario, James H. Johnson, Jr., and Walter C. Farrell, Jr. 1994. "After the Smoke Has Cleared: An Analysis of Selected Responses to the Los Angeles Civil Unrest of 1992." *Contention,* 3, no. 3. (Spring). 3–22.

Jacobson, Julius, ed. 1968. *The Negro and the American Labor Movement.* New York: Anchor.

Jaynes, Gerald D., 1986. *Branches without Roots: Genesis of the Black Working Class in the American South, 1862–1882.* New York: Oxford University Press.

Jaynes, Gerald D., and Robin M. Williams, eds. 1989. *A Common Destiny: Blacks and American Society.* Washington, DC: National Academy Press.

Johnson, James H., and Melvin L. Oliver. 1992. "Structural Changes in the U.S. Economy and Black Male Joblessness: A Reassessment." In *Urban Labor Markets and Job Opportunity,* ed. George Peterson and Wayne Vroman. Washington, DC: Urban Institute Press. 113–47.

Joint Center for Political Studies. 1993. *Black Elected Officials.* Washington, DC: Joint Center for Political and Economic Studies Press.

Kasarda, John D. 1988. "Jobs, Migration, and Emerging Urban Mismatches." In *Urban Change and Poverty,* ed. M. G. H. McGeary and L. E. Lynn, Jr. Washington, DC: National Academy Press. 148–98.

———. 1990. "Structural Factors Affecting the Location and Timing of Underclass Growth." *Urban Geography* 11, no. 3:234–64.

Katz, Michael. 1986. *In the Shadow of the Poor House: A Social History of Welfare in America.* New York: Basic Books.

Kerbo, Harold R. 1983. *Social Stratification and Inequality: Class Conflict in the United States.* New York: McGraw-Hill.

Kessler, Denis, and Andre Masson, eds. 1988. *Modeling the Accumulation and Distribution of Wealth.* Oxford: Clarendon Press.

Kirschenmann, Joleen, and Katherine Neckerman. 1991. "'We'd Love to Hire Them But': The Meaning of Race for Employers." In *The Urban Underclass,* ed. Christopher Jencks and Paul Peterson. Washington, DC: Brookings Institution. 203–32.

Kotlikoff, Laurence, and Lawrence Summers. 1981. "The Role of Intergenerational Transfers in Aggregate Capital Accumulation." *Journal of Political Economy* 89: 706–32.

Kuznets, Simon. 1953. *Economic Change.* New York: W.W. Norton.

Lampman, Robert J. 1962. *The Share of Top Wealth-Holders in National Wealth.* Princeton, NJ: Princeton University Press.

Landry, Bart. 1987. *The New Black Middle Class.* Berkeley: University of California Press.

Lanza, Michael L. 1990. *Agrarianism and Reconstruction Politics: The Southern Homestead Act.* Baton Rouge: Louisiana State University Press.

Lehman, H. Jane. 1990. "Low End Loans Cost More: Critics." *Chicago Tribune,* 17 June, 1D.

————. 1991. "Is Secondary Mortgage Market Showing Bias?" *Chicago Tribune,* 17 March, 2L.

Levy, Frank S. 1987. *Dollars and Dreams: The Changing American Income Distribution.* New York: W.W. Norton.

————. 1988. "Preface to the Paperback Edition." *Dollars and Dreams: The Changing American Income Distribution.* New York: Norton.

Levy, Frank S., and Richard Michel. 1986. "An Economic Bust for the Baby Boom." *Challenge,* March/April, 33–39.

————. 1991. *The Economic Future of American Families: Income and Wealth Trends.* Washington, DC: Urban Institute Press.

Lieberson, Stanley. 1980. *A Piece of Pie.* Berkeley: University of California Press.

Light, Ivan. 1972. *Ethnic Enterprise in America.* Berkeley: University of California Press.

————. 1980. "Asian Enterprise in America: Chinese, Japanese, and Koreans in Small Business." In *Self-Help in Urban America: Patterns of Minority Economic Development,* ed. Scott Cummings. New York: Kennikat Press. 33–57.

Lipset, Seymour Martin, and Reinhard Bendix. 1959. *Social Mobility in Industrial Society.* Berkeley: University of California Press. Fall.

Lipsitz, George. 1995. "The Possessive Investment in Whiteness: The 'White' Problem in American Studies." *American Quarterly.* Fall.

Long, James E., and Steven B. Caudill. 1992. "Racial Differences in Homeownership and Housing Wealth, 1970–1986." *Economic Inquiry* 30 (January) 83–100.

Los Angeles Times. 1989. "Blacks Rejected More Often than Whites for Home Loans, Survey Shows." 23 January, Business sec., 2.

Lundsten, Lorman L., and Harold Black. 1978. "The Impact of Race and Other Variables on the Composition and Value of Individual Portfolios." *Review of Black Political Economy* 8:360–67.

Malkiel, Burton G., and Judith A. Malkiel. 1973. "Male-Female Pay Differentials in Professional Employment." *American Economic Review* 63:693–705.

Marx, Karl, and Fredrich Engels. 1947. *The German Ideology.* New York: International Publishers.

Massey, Douglas S., and Nancy A. Denton. 1988. "Suburbanization and Segregation in U.S. Metropolitan Areas." *American Journal of Sociology* 94: 592–626.

————. 1993. *American Apartheid: Segregation and the Making of the Underclass.* Cambridge: Harvard University Press.

Mayer, Susan, and Christopher Jencks. 1989. "Poverty and the Distribution of Material Hardship." *Journal of Human Resources* 24, no. 1: 88–114.

McMillen, David B., and Roger A. Herriot. 1985. "Toward a Longitudinal Definition of Households." In *Survey of Income and Program Participation and Related Longitudinal Surveys: 1984,* comp. Daniel Kasprzyk and Delma Frankel. Washington, DC: U.S. Bureau of the Census. 49–54.

Mieszkowski, Peter, and Richard F. Syron. 1979. "Economic Explanation for Housing Segregation." *New England Economic Review,* November–December, 33–34.

Miller, S. M., and Pamela Roby. 1970. *The Future of Inequality.* New York: Basic Books.

Millman, Marcia. 1991. *Warm Hearts and Cold Cash: The Intimate Dynamics of Family and Money.* New York: Free Press.

Mink, Gwendolyn. 1990. "The Lady and the Tramp: Gender, Race, and the Origins of the American Welfare State." In *Women, the State, and Welfare,* ed. Linda Gordon. Madison: University of Wisconsin Press. 92–122.

Mirowsky, John, and Catherine E. Ross. 1989. *Social Causes of Psychological Distress.* New York: Aldine de Gruyter.

Modigliani, Franco, and Richard Bromberg. 1954. "Utility Analysis and the Consumption Function: An Interpretation of Cross-Section Data." In *Post Keynesian Economics,* ed. Kenneth K. Kurihara. New Brunswick, NJ: Rutgers University Press. 388–436.

Morley. S. A. 1984. *Macroeconomics.* New York: Dryden Press.

Munnell, Alicia H., Lynn E. Browne, James McEneaney, and Geoffrey M.B. Tootel. 1993. "Mortgage Lending in Boston: Interpreting HMDA Data." Boston: Federal Reserve Bank of Boston.

Myrdal, Gunnar. 1944. *An American Dilemma;* New York: Harper.

Nasar. Sylvia. 1992. "Fed Gives New Evidence of 80's Gains by Richest," *New York Times,* 21 April, A1, 17.

O'Hare. William P. 1983. *Wealth and Economic Status: A Perspective on Racial Inequality.* Washington, DC: Joint Center for Political Studies.

Oliver, Melvin L. 1980. "The Enduring Significance of Race." *Journal of Ethnic Studies,* 7, no. 4:79–91.

———. 1988. "The Urban Black Community as Network: Toward a Social Network Perspective." *Sociological Quarterly* 29: 623–45.

Oliver, Melvin L., and Thomas M. Shapiro. 1989. "Race and Wealth." *Review of Black Political Economy* 17: 5–25.

———. 1990. "Wealth of a Nation: At Least One-Third of Households Are Asset Poor." *American Journal of Economics and Sociology,* 49: 129–51.

———. 1991. "Poverty. Wealth, and the Underclass: An Economic Resource Perspective." UCLA Center for the Study of Urban Poverty. *Occasional Working Paper Series* 2, no. 4.

———. 1992. "The Structure of Inequality in American Society." UCLA Center for the Study of Urban Poverty. *Occasional Working Paper Series* 3, no. 3.

Omi, Michael, and Howard Winant, 1986. *Racial Formation in the United States: From the 1960s to the 1980s.* New York: Routledge.

O'Neill. J. 1984. "Earnings Differentials: Empirical Evidence and Causes." In *Sex Discrimination and Equal Opportunity: The Labor Market and Employment Policy,* ed. Gunther Schmiel and Renate Weitzel. New York: St Martin's Press. 69–91.

Ong. Paul, and Eugene Grigsby III. 1988. "Race and Life Cycle Effects on Home Ownership in Los Angeles, 1970 to 1980," *Urban Affairs Quarterly* 23: 601–15.

Osberg, Lars. 1984. *Economic Inequality in the United States.* New York: Sharpe.

Osthaus, Carl. 1976. *Freedmen, Philanthropy, and Fraud: A History of the Freedman's Savings Bank.* Urbana: University of Chicago Press.

Oubre, Claude. 1978. *Forty Acres and a Mule: The Freedmen's Bureau and Black Land Ownership.* Baton Rouge: Louisiana State University Press.

Parcel, Toby L. 1982. "Wealth Accumulation of Black and White Men: The Case of Housing Equity." *Social Problems* 30: 199–211.

Phillips, Kevin. 1990. *The Politics of Rich and Poor.* New York: HarperCollins.

Pierce, Joseph A. 1947. *Negro Business and Business Education.* New York: Harper.

Prather, H. Leon. 1984. *We Have Taken a City.* Rutherford, NJ: Farleigh Dickinson University Press.

Projector, Dorothy, and Gertrude Weiss. 1966. *Survey of Financial Characteristics of Consumers.* Federal Reserve Technical Paper. Washington, DC: Government Printing Office.

Quadagno, Jill. 1994. *The Color of Welfare.* New York: Oxford University Press.

Radner, Daniel B. 1988. *The Wealth of the Aged and Nonaged, 1984.* Survey of Income and Program Participation Working Paper, no. 8807. Washington, DC: U.S. Department of Commerce.

Rank, Mark R. 1994. *Living on the Edge: The Realities of Welfare in America.* New York: Columbia University Press.

Ratcliff, Richard E., and Susan Maurer. 1995. "Savings and the Decline of Entrepreneurship: In *Research in Politics and Society,* vol. 5, ed. Richard E. Ratcliff, Melvin L. Oliver, and Thomas M. Shapiro. Greenwich, CT: JAI Press. 99–126.

Ravo, Nick. 1990. "A Windfall Nears in Inheritances from the Richest Generation." *New York Times,* 22 July E4.

Robinson, Lori S. 1993. "Economist: Inequities of the Past Block Progress." *Emerge,* October, 18–20.

Rock, John S. 1858. "Address to Boston Antislavery Society, March 5." *Antislavery Collection.* Rare Book Division, Boston Public Library.

Ruggles, Patricia, and Robertson Williams. 1989. "Longitudinal Measures of Poverty: Accounting for Income and Assets Over Time." *Review of Income and Wealth* 35 no. 3: 225–43.

Ryan, Suzanne Alexander, and John R. Wilke. 1994. "Banking on Publicity, Mr. Marks Got Fleet to Lend Billions." *Wall Street Journal,* 11 February: A1, 5.

Schor, Juliet B. 1991. *The Overworked American: The Unexpected Decline of Leisure.* New York: Basic Books.

See, Katherine O'Sullivan, and William J. Wilson. 1988. "Race and Ethnicity." In *Handbook of Sociology,* ed. Neil J. Smelser. Newbury Park, CA: Sage. 223–42.

Senecker, Harold. 1993. "The *Forbes* 400: The Richest People in America." *Forbes,* 18 October, 110–13.

Sharpe, Rochelle. 1993. "In Latest Recession, Only Blacks Suffered Net Employment Loss." *Wall Street Journal,* 14 September, A1.

Sherraden. Michael. 1991. *Assets and the Poor: A New American Welfare Policy.* New York: Sharpe.

Simmel. Georg. 1990. The *Philosophy of Money.* London: Routledge.

Skogan, Wesley G. 1990. *Disorder and Decline: Crime and the Spiral of Decay in American Neighborhoods.* New York: Free Press.

Smith, Ann Kates. 1990. "Why the Inheritance Boom Is for Real." *U.S. News and World Report,* 108. no. 18 (7 May): 33–34.

Smith, James D. 1987. "Recent Trends in the Distribution of Wealth: Data, Research Problems, and Prospects." In *International Comparisons of the Distribution of Household Wealth,* ed. Edward N. Wolff. New York: Oxford University Press. 72–90.

———. 1975. *The Personal Distribution of Income and Wealth.* New York: Columbia University Press.

Smith, James, and Finis Welch. 1989. "Black Economic Progress after Myrdal." *Journal of Economic Literature* 27: 519–64.

Smith, Shanna L. 1992. "Looking Honestly at Fair Housing Compliance" (Part I). *ABA Bank Compliance,* Autumn: 32–36.

Sobol, Marion Gross. 1979. "Factors Influencing Private Capital Accumulation on the 'Eve of Retirement.'" *Review of Economics and Statistics,* 61, no. 4: 585–93.

Soltow, Lee. 1972. "A Century of Personal Wealth Accumulation." *The Economics of Black Americans,* ed. Harold G. Vatter and Thomas Palm. New York: Harcourt.

———. 1975. *Men and Wealth in the United States 1850–1870.* New Haven and London: Yale University Press.

———. 1989. *Distribution of Wealth and Income in the United States in 1798.* Pittsburgh: University of Pittsburgh Press.

Sowell, Thomas. 1981. *Ethnic America: A History.* New York: Basic Books.

Squires, Gregory D. 1994. *Capital and Communities in Black and White.* Albany: State University of New York Press.

Stacey, Judith. 1994. "The New Family Values Crusaders." *Nation,* 259, no. 4: 119–22.

Stack. Carol. 1974. *All Our Kin.* New York: Harper.

Steckel, Richard H., and Jayanthi Krishnan. 1992. "Wealth Mobility in America: A Long View from the National Longitudinal Survey." *National Bureau of Economic Research Working Paper,* no. 4137. Cambridge, MA: National Bureau of Economic Research.

Stuart, Merah S. 1940. *An Economic Detour: A History of Insurance in the Lives of American Negroes.* New York: Wendell Malliett.

Stutz, Fred, and A. E. Kartman. 1982. "Housing Affordability and Spatial Price Variation in the United States." *Economic Geography* 58: 221–35.

Tawney, R. H. 1952. *Equality.* London: Allen and Unwin.

Taylor, Patricia A., Patricia A. Gwartney-Gibbs, and Reynolds Farley. 1986. "Changes in the Structure of Earnings Inequality by Race, Sex, and Industrial Sector, 1960–1980." In *Research in Social Stratification and Mobility,* vol. 5, ed. Robert V. Robinson. Greenwich, CT: JAI Press. 105–138.

Terrell, Henry S. 1971. "Wealth Accumulation of Black and White Families: The Empirical Evidence." *Journal of Finance* 26: 363-77.

Thio, Alex. 1992. *Sociology: An Introduction.* 3rd ed. New York: Harper.

Thomas, Richard Walter. 1992. *Life for Us is What We Make It: Building Black Community in Detroit, 1915-1945.* Bloomington: Indiana University Press.

Thurow, Lester C. 1975. *Generating Inequality: Mechanisms of Distribution in the U.S. Economy.* New York: Basic Books.

Tidwell, Billy J. 1987. *Beyond the Margin: Toward Economic Well-Being for Black Americans.* Washington, DC: National Urban League.

Titmuss, Richard. 1962. *Income Distribution and Social Change.* London: Allen and Unwin.

Tocqueville, Alexis de [1835]. 1954. *Democracy in America,* ed. Phillips Bradley. New York: Vintage Books.

Treiman, Donald J., and Heidi I. Hartmann, eds. 1981. *Women, Work, and Wages: Equal Pay for Jobs of Equal Value.* Washington, DC: National Academy Press.

Turner, Jonathan H., and Charles E. Starnes. 1976. *Inequality: Privilege and Poverty in America.* Santa Monica, CA: Goodyear Publishing.

U.S. Bureau of the Census. 1986. "Money Income of Households, Families and Persons in the United States: 1984." *Current Population Reports,* series P–60, no. 151. Washington, DC: Government Printing Office.

———. 1987. *Survey of Income and Program Participation User's Guide.* Washington, DC: U.S. Department of Commerce.

———. 1989. *Statistical Abstract of the United States: 1989.* Washington, DC: Government Printing Office.

———. 1990. *Survey of Income and Program Participation (SIPP), 1987 Panel, Wave 2 Rectangular Microdata File Technical Documentation.* Washington, DC: Bureau of the Census.

———. 1991. "Money Income of Households. Families, and Persons in the United States, 1990." *Current Population Reports,* series P-60, no. 174. Washington. DC: Government Printing Office.

———. 1994. "Median Net Worth of Households Dropped 12 Percent." Press Release. Public Information Office, January, 26.

U.S. Council of Economic Advisors. 1992. *Economic Report to the President.* Washington, DC: Government Printing Office.

U.S. House of Representatives. 1993. H.R. 40. 103d Congress, 1st session. 5 January.

Wall Street Journal. 1994. "Toward Quota Loans?" 26 September: A14.

Walt, Vivienne. 1989. "Chase Move Is Disputed." *Newsday,* 3 July: 8.

Weber, Max. 1946. "Class, Status, and Party." In *From Max Weber: Essays in Sociology,* ed. C. Wright Mills and Hans H. Gerth. New York: Oxford University Press. 180–95.

―――. 1958. The *Protestant Ethic and the Spirit of Capitalism.* New York: Scribner's.

Weir, Margaret. 1992. *Politics and Jobs: The Boundaries of Employment Policy in the United States.* Princeton, NJ: Princeton University Press.

Weisbrod B. A., and W. L. Hansen. 1968. "An Income-Net Worth Approach to Measuring Economic Welfare." *American Economic Review* 58: 1315–29.

Wells, Rob. 1993. "Fleet Unit's Lending Practices under Fire in Georgia." *Chicago Tribune,* 10 January: M1.

West, Cornel. 1994. *Race Matters.* New York: Vintage.

Williams, Robin M., Jr. 1975. "Race and Ethnic Relations." In *Annual Review of Sociology,* vol. 1, ed. Alex Inkles. Palo Alto, CA: Annual Reviews. 125–64.

Williamson, Jeffrey G., and Peter H. Lindert. 1980. *American Inequality: A Macroeconomic History.* New York: Academic Press.

Willie, Charles Vert, ed. 1979. *The Class-Caste Controversy.* Bayside, NY: General Hill.

Wilson, Kenneth L., and Alejandro Portes. 1980. "Immigrant Enclaves: An Analysis of the Labor Market Experiences of Cubans in Miami." *American Journal of Sociology,* 86: 295–319.

Wilson, William J. 1978. *The Declining Significance of Race.* Chicago: University of Chicago Press.

―――. 1987. *The Truly Disadvantaged.* Chicago: University of Chicago Press.

Wolff, Edward N. 1987a. "Estimates of Household Wealth Inequality in the U.S., 1962–1983." *Review of Income and Wealth* 35, no. 1: 231–42.

―――. 1987b. *Growth, Accumulation, and Unproductive Activity.* Cambridge: Cambridge University Press.

―――. 1990. "Wealth Holdings and Poverty Status in the U.S." *Review of Income and Wealth,* 36, 2: 143–65.

―――. 1991. "The Distribution of Household Wealth: Methodological Issues, Time Trends, and Cross Sectional Comparisons." In *Economic Inequality and Poverty: International Perspectives,* ed. Lars Osberg. Armonk, NY: M.E. Sharpe. 33–68.

―――. 1995. "The Rich Get Increasingly Richer: Latest Data on Household Wealth During the 1980s." In *Research in Politics and Society,* vol. 5., ed. Richard E. Ratcliff, Melvin L. Oliver, and Thomas M. Shapiro. Greenwich, CT: JAI Press. 33–68.

Woodward, C. Van. 1955. *The Strange Career of Jim Crow.* New York: Oxford University Press.

Woolf, Virginia. 1929. *A Room of One's Own.* New York: Harcourt.

Yetman, Norman R., ed. 1991. *Majority and Minority: The Dynamics of Race and Ethnicity in American Life.* 5th ed. Boston: Allyn and Bacon.

Zarembka, Arlene. 1990. *The Urban Housing Crisis.* New York: Greenwood Press.

Zelizer, Viviana A. 1989. "The Social Meaning of Money: 'Special Monies.'" *American Journal of Sociology* 95: 342–77.

Zuckoff, Mitchell. 1992. "Mortgage Gap Still Exists for Minorities." *Boston Globe,* 27 September: Metro sec., 1.

———. 1993. "Senator Says Feb. 17 Hearing to Look at 'Reverse Redlining.'" *Boston Globe,* 28 January, Economy sec., 37.

References to Epilogue, Chapter 8, and Chapter 9

Abt Associates. 2004. Evaluation of the American Dream Demonstration: final evaluation report. Cambridge, MA: Abt Associates.

Adams, Stella, Executive Director North Carolina Fair Housing Center, Inc. Testimony before the Committee on House Financial Services Subcommittee on Housing and Community Opportunity Subcommittee on Financial Institutions and Consumer Credit, May 24, 2005.

Alontji, Joseph, Ulrich Doraszelski, and Lewis Segal. 2000. "Black/White Differences in Wealth." *Federal Reserve Bank of Chicago. Economics Perspectives* 24 (38–50).

Alstott, Anne, and Bruce A. Ackerman. 2000. *The Stakeholder Society.* New Haven: Yale University Press.

Banks, R. Richard. 1996. "'Nondiscriminatory' Perpetuation of Racial Subordination." *Boston University Law Review* 76: 668–701.

Barr, Michael S. 2004. "Banking the Poor." *Yale Journal on Regulation* 21 (Winter 2004): 121–237.

Berton, Brad, and Susan Futterman. 2003. "Community Groups see Continuing Chill on CRA, Affordable Housing Finance." http://www.housingfinance.com/ahf/articles/2002/02OctCommunityLending/BET.com.

Birney, Mayling, and Ian Shapiro. 2005. "The Political Uses of Public Opinion: Lessons from the Estate Tax Repeal. Paper prepared for Capitalism, Socialism, and Democracy: A Conference Honoring Professor John Roemer on his 60th Birthday.

Black Investor Survey. "Saving and Investing Among Higher Income African-American and White Americans," July 2005. www.arielmutualfunds.com/forms/2004-survey/2004%20AAIS%20FULL%20EXTERNAL.ppt.

Blank, Rebecca, and David T. Ellwood. 2002. "The Clinton Legacy for America's Poor." In *American Economic Policy in the 1990s*, Jeffrey A. Frankel and Peter R. Orszag. Cambridge, MA: MIT Press.

Blumstein, Alfred, and Allen J. Beck. 1993. "Racial Disproportionality in the U.S. Prison Population Revisited." *University of Colorado Law Review* 64: 743–60.

Boaz, David. 2005. *Defining the Ownership Society*. Cato Institute. http://www.cato.org/special/ownership_society/boaz.html.

Bradbury, Katharine L. 2000. "Rising Tide in the Labor Market: To What Degree do Expansions Benefit the Disadvantaged?" *New England Economic Review* 4 (May/June): 3–33.

Brodkin, Karen. 1999. *How Jews Became White Folks and What That Says About Race in America*. New Brunswick, NJ and London: Rutgers University Press.

Brown, Larry, Robert Kuttner, and Thomas Shapiro. 2005. *Building a Real Ownership Society*. New York: The Century Foundation Press.

Castles, Francis. 1998. "The Really Big Trade-Off: Home Ownership and the Welfare State in the New World and the Old." *Acta Politica* 33:5–19.

Center for Disease Control. 2005. "Health Disparities Experienced by Black or African Americans — United States." *MMWR* January 14, 2005, 54 (01): 1–3.

Center for Enterprise Development. 2004. *Hidden in Plain Sight*. Washington, DC: CFED.

Center for Responsible Lending. 2005a. "Race Matters: The Concentration of Payday Lenders in African American Neighborhoods." http://www.responsiblelending.org/news_headlines/032205release.cfm.

——— 2005b. "Predatory Payday Lending Traps Borrowers." http://www.responsiblelending.org/payday/index.cfm.

Chang, Mariko. 2003. Shortchanged: Gender Differences in the Process of Wealth Attainment. Presentation at the Annual Meeting of the American Sociological Association.

Chiteji, Ngina S., and Frank P. Stafford. 1999. "Portfolio Choices of Parents and their Children as Young Adults: Asset Accumulation by African-American Families." *American Economic Review* 89 (2): 377–80.

Collins, Patricia Hill. 1997. "African American Women and Economic Justice: A Preliminary Analysis of Wealth, Family, and African American Social Class." *University of Cincinnati Law Review* Vol 65 (Spring, 1997): 825-52.

Collins, Sharon M. 1996. *Black Corporate Executives: The Making and Breaking of a Black Middle Class*. Philadelphia: Temple University Press.

Congressional Budget Office. Effects of the Federal Estate Tax on Farms and Small Businesses, July, 2005. http://www.cbo.gov/ftpdocs/65xx/doc6512/07–06-EstateTax.pdf

Conley, Dalton. 1999. *Being Black, Living in the Red*. Berkeley: University of California Press.

—————. 2000. "Home Ownership, Poverty and the Welfare State." www.sscnet.ucla.edu/soc/groups/ccsa/conley.pdf.

Consumer Federation of America. 2003. "More African-Americans Save and Begin To Close Wealth Gap." http://www.consumerfed.org/102903blackamsaves.pdf.

Crockett, David. 2005. "Credit, Conspicuous Consumption and Crisis." http://blackcommentator.com/132/132_guest_blacks_credit.html.

Dickerson, A Michele. 2005. "Race Matters in Bankruptcy." *Washington and Lee Law Review* 64: 1726–76.

Doan, Ashley, and Eduardo Bonilla-Silva, eds. 2003. *White Out: The Continuing Significance of Racism*. New York: Routledge.

Draut, Tamara, and Javier Silva. 2003. *Borrowing To Make Ends Meet: The Growth of Credit Card Debt in the 90s*. New York: Demos.

Duda, Mark. and William Apgar, 2004. Mortgage Foreclosure Trends in Los Angeles: Patterns and Policy Issues. A report prepared for the Los Angeles Neighborhood Housing Services.

Dyson, Michael. 2005. *Is Bill Cosby Right?: Or Has the Black Middle Class Lost its Mind?* New York: Basic Civitas.

Erns, Keith, John Farris, and Uriah King. 2004. Quantifying the Economic Cost of Predatory Payday Lending: A Report from the Center for Responsible Lending. February 24, 2004.

Ferguson, Susan J., ed. 1998. *Mapping the Social Landscape: Readings in Sociology*, 2nd ed. Mountain View, CA: Mayfield Publishing.

Ford Foundation. 2003. "Asset Building for Social Change: Pathways to Large-Scale Impact, Asset Building and Community Development Program." New York: The Ford Foundation. http://www.fordfound.org/publications/recent_articles/docs/asset_pathways.pdf

—————. 2004. "Building Assets to Reduce Poverty and Injustice." New York: Ford Foundation http://www.fordfound.org/publications/recent_articles/docs/assets_bw.pdf.

Giddens, Anthony, Mitchell Dunier, and Richard P. Applebaum. *Introduction to Sociology*, 4th ed. New York: Norton.

Gilbert, Jess, and Alice O'Connor. 1996. Leaving the Land Behind: Struggles for Land Reform in U.S. Federal Policy, 1933–1965. Land Tenure Center, University of Wisconsin-Madison. http://www.ies.wisc.edu/ltc/ltc156.html.

Gordon, Nembhard, Jessica and Ngina Chiteji, eds. 2006. Forthcoming. *Wealth Accumulation and Communities of Color in the United States: Current Issues*. Ann Arbor: University of Michigan Press.

Greenspan. Alan. 1996. The Challenge of Central Banking in a Democratic Society. Address to the American Enterprise Institute at the Washington Hilton Hotel, December 5, 1996.

Grusky, David B., ed. 2001. *Social Stratification: Class, Race, and Gender in Sociological Perspectives*, 2nd ed. Boulder, CO: Westview Press.

Hao, Lingxin. 2004. "Wealth of Immigrant and Native Born Americans." *International Migration Review* 38: 518–46.

Harison, Paige M., and Jennifer Karberg. 2002. "Prison and Jail Inmates at Midyear 2002." *Bureau of Justice Statistics Bulletin*, NCJ 198877. Washington DC: U.S. Department of Justice.

Harris, Cheryl. 1993. "Whiteness as Property." *Harvard Law Review* 106 (June): 1709–91.

Harvard University Joint Center for Housing Studies. The 25th Anniversary of the Community Reinvestment Act: Access to Capital in an Evolving Financial Services System. Cambride, MA: Joint Center for Housing Studies.

Hayner, Priscilla B. 2002. *Unspeakable Truths: Facing the Challenge of Truth Commission*. New York: Taylor & Francis.

Himmelstein, David U., Elizabeth Warren, Deborah Thorne, and Steffie Woolhandler. 2005. "MarketWatch: Illness and Injury as Contributors to Bankruptcy." *Health Affairs* 10 (February 2, 2005).

Holme, Jennifer Jellison. 2002. "Buying Homes, Buying Schools: School Choice and the Social Construction of School Quality." *Harvard Educational Review* 72 (2): 177–205.

Holzer, Harry J., Steven Raphael, and Michael A. Stoll. 2003. "Employers in the Boom: How Did the Hiring of Unskilled Workers Change During the 1990s?" http://www.urban.org/UploadedPDF/410780_BoomPaper.pdf.

Howard, Christopher. 1997. *The Hidden Welfare State*. Princeton, NJ: Princeton University Press.

Ignatiev, Noel. 1996. *How the Irish Became White*. New York: Routledge.

Johnson, David Cay. 2005. "Richest are Leaving Even the Rich Far Behind." *New York Times*, June 5.

Joint Center Data Bank. August 5, 2003. http://www.jointcenter.org/DB/factsheet/customer_expenditures.htm.

Joint Center for Housing Studies of Harvard University. 2004. The State of the Nation's Housing. Cambridge, MA.

———. 2005. State of the Nation's Housing, 2005. Cambridge, MA.

Keister, Lisa. 2005. *Wealth in America and Getting Rich*. New York: Cambridge University Press.

Kerwin, Charles, and Erik Hurst. 2002. "The Transition to Home-Ownership and the Black-White Wealth Gap." *Review of Economics and Statistics* 84 (2): 281–97.

Kim, Hyungsoo, and Jinkook Lee. 2005. "Unequal Effects of Elders' Health Problems on Wealth Depletion Across Race and Ethnicity." *The Journal of Consumer Affairs* 39 (1): 148–72.

Kochhar, Rakesh, 2004. *The Wealth of Hispanic Households: 1996 to 2002*. Washington, DC: Pew Hispanic Center.

Korpi, Walter, and Joakim Palme. 1998. "The Paradox of Redistribution and Strategies of Equality: Welfare State Institutions, Inequality, and Poverty in the Western Countries." *American Sociological Review* 63: 661–87.

Lipsitz, George. 1998. *Possessive Investment in Whiteness*. Philadelphia: Temple University Press.

Logan, John. 2001. "Ethnic Diversity Grows, Neighborhood Integration Lags Behind." Albany, NY: The Lewis Mumford Center, State University of New York.

Magazine Publishers of America. 2004. African American Market Profiles. http://www.magazine.org/content/files/market_profile_black.pdf.

Mauer, Marc. 1999. *Race to Incarcerate*. New York: The New Press.

McCulloch, Heather. 2001. *Sharing the Wealth: Resident Ownership Mechanisms*. Oakland, CA: PolicyLink.

Mitchell, Thomas W. 2005. "Destabilizing the Normalization of Rural Black Land Loss: A Critical Role for Legal Empiricism." *Wisconsin Law Review* 2005 (2): 607–8.

Moran, Beverly, and William Whitford. 1996. "A Black Critique of the Internal Revenue Code." *Wisconsin Law Review* 4: 751–820.

National Community Reinvestment Coalition. 2005. Preapprovals and Pricing Disparities in the Mortgage Marketplace, June 2005. http://ncrc.org/pressandpubs/press_releases/documents/Preapproval_Report_June05.pdf

Oliver, Melvin L., and Thomas M. Shapiro. 1995. *Black Wealth/White Wealth: A New Perspective on Racial Inequality*. New York and London: Routledge.

OMB Watch 6 (15), July 25, 2005.

Pastor, Manuel, Jr., Peter Dreier, J. Eugene Grigsby, III, and Mart Lopez Garza. 2000. *Regions That Work: How Cities and Suburbs Can Grow Together*. Minneapolis: University of Minnesota Press.

Petit, Becky, and Bruce Western. 2004. "Mass Imprisonment and the Life Course: Race and Class Inequality in U.S. Incarceration." *American Sociological Review* 6 (April): 151–69.

PolicyLink. 2002. Promoting Regional Equity: A Framing Paper. Paper presented at Promoting Regional Equity: A National Summit On Equitable Development, Social Justice, and Smart Growth, November 17–19.LosAngeles,California.http://www.policylink.org/Research/RegionalEquity/.

powell, john. 2002. Racism and Metropolitan Dynamics: The Civil Rights Challenge of the 21st Century. A briefing paper prepared for the Ford Foundation. Minneapolis, MN: The Institute on Race & Poverty.

Quercia, Roberto G., Michael A. Stegman, and Walter R. Davis. 2005. "The Impact of Predatory Loan Terms on Subprime Foreclosures." Center for Community Capitalism. http://www.kenan-flagler.unc.edu/assets/documents/foreclosurepaper.pdf.

Raines, Franklin D. 2002. Harnessing the Mystery of Capital: Closing the Wealth Gap. Remarks at Howard University, Charter Day Convocation, March 8, 2002.

Rank, Mark. 2005. *One Nation, Underprivileged*. New York: Oxford University Press.

Robinson, Randall. 2001. *The Debt: What White America Owes Blacks*. New York: Plume.

Roediger, David R. 2005. *Working Toward Whiteness: How America's Immigrants Become White. The Strange Journey From Ellis Island to the Suburbs.* New York: Basic Books.

———. 2000. *The Wages of Whiteness: Race and the Making of the American Working Class.* New York: Verso.

Rusk, David. 2001. *The 'Segregation Tax': The Cost of Racial Segregation to Black Homeowners.* Washington, DC: Brookings Institution Center on Urban and Metropolitan Policy.

Salamon, Lester M. 1979. "The Time Dimension in Policy Evaluation: The Case of the New Deal Land-Reform Experiments." *Public Policy* 27 (2, Spring): 129–83.

Scanlon, Edward, and Deborah Page-Adams. 2001. "Effects of Asset Holding on Neighborhoods, Families, and Children: A Review of Research." In *Building Assets: A Report on the Asset-Development and IDA Field*, ed. Ray Boshara. Washington, DC: Corporation for Economic Development.

Scholz, John Karl, and Kara Levine. 2004. "U.S. Black-White Wealth Inequality: A Survey." In *Social Inequality*, ed. Kathryn Neckerman. New York: Russell Sage Foundation.

Schreiner, Mark, Margaret Clancy, and Michael Sherraden. 2002. Saving Performance in the American Dream Demonstration: A National Demonstration of Individual Development Accounts. A research report. St. Louis: Washington University, Center for Social Development.

Segal, Lewis M., and Daniel G. Sullivan. 1998. "Trends in Homeownership: Race, Demographics, and Income." *Economic Perspectives. Reserve Bank of Chicago*, issue QIIO: 53–72.

Shanks, Trina Williams. 2004. The Impacts of Household Wealth on Child Development. Working Paper. Center for Social Development, George Warren Brown School of Social Work, Washington University.

———. 2005. "The Homestead Act: A Major Asset-Building Policy in American History." In *Inclusion in the American Dream: Assets, Poverty, and Public Policy,* ed. Michael Sherraden. New York: Oxford University Press.

Shapiro, Thomas M. 2004a. *The Hidden Cost of Being African American: How Wealth Perpetuates Inequality.* New York: Oxford University Press.

——— ed. 2004b. *Great Divides: Readings in Social Inequality in the United States.* Boston: McGraw Hill.

Sherraden, Michael. 1991. *Assets and the Poor: A New American Welfare Policy.* New York: Sharpe.

———. 2000. "From Research to Policy: Lessons from Individual Development Accounts." *Journal of Consumer Affairs* 32 (2): 159–81.

Sherraden, Michael, Amanda McBride, Elizabeth Johnson, Stacie Hanson, Fred Ssewamala, and Trina Shanks. 2005. Saving in Low Income Households: Evidence from Interviews with Participants in the American Dream Demonstration. Research report. St. Louis: Washington University, Center for Social Development.

Shiller, Robert J. 2005. *Irrational Exuberance.* Princeton, NJ: Princeton University Press.

Silva, Javier. 2005. *A House of Cards: Financing the American Dream.* New York: Demos.

Silva, Javier, and Rebecca Epstein. 2005. *Costly Credit: African Americans and Latinos in Debt.* New York: Demos.

Spriggs, William E. 2005a. "African Americans and Social Security." http://www.dollarsandsense.org/1104spriggs.html.

———. 2005b. "Busting the Social Security Myths." *The Black Commentator* February 18, 2005.

Stegman, Michael. 2002. "Performance of Community Reinvestment Loans: Implications for Secondary Market Purchases." In *Low Income Homeownership: Examining the Unexamined Goal,* ed. Nicolas P. Retsinas and Eric S. Belsky. Washington, DC: The Brookings Institution Press.

Stegman, Michael A., Roberto G. Quercia, and Walter R. Davis. "Sharing the Wealth Through Homeownership: A Preliminary Exploration of the Price Appreciation Experiences of Low- and Moderate-Income Families Who Bought Homes Under the Community Advantage Secondary Market Loan Program," July 21, 2004, Revised September 2, 2004, Revised July 8, 2005, p 18. http://www.kenan-flagler.unc.edu/assets/documents/ccc-sharethewealth.pdf.

Stein, Eric. 2001. Quantifying the Cost of Predatory Lending: A Report From the Center for Responsible Lending. October 30, 2001.

Stoesz, David, Michael Sherraden, and Thomas Shapiro. 2005. "Sensible Reform of Social Security." http://PolicyAmerica.org.

Stuart, Merah. 1940. *An Economic Detour: A History of Insurance in the Lives of American Negroes.* New York: Wendell Malliett.

The Brookings Institution. 2005. *The Price is Wrong: Getting the Market Right for Working Families in Philadelphia.* The Brookings Institution Metropolitan Policy Program.

Wacquant, Loic. 2000. "The New 'Peculiar Institution': On the Prison as Surrogate Ghetto." *Theoretical Criminology* 4: 377–89.

———. 2001. "Deadly Symbiosis: When Ghetto and Prison Meet and Mesh." In *Mass Imprisonment: Social Causes and Consequences,* ed. David Garland. London: Sage.

Wolff, Edward N. 2000. *Top Heavy.* New York: New Press.

———. 2004. "Changes in Household Wealth in the 1980s and 1990s." In the U.S. Economics Working Paper Archive, Number 47. Annandale-on-Hudson, NY: The Levy Economics Institute.

Index